Human Skills

Wiley Series on
Studies in Human Performance

Series Editor

Dennis H. Holding

*University of Louisville,
Kentucky, USA*

Further titles in preparation

Human Skills

Edited by

Dennis H. Holding

*University of Louisville,
Kentucky, USA*

JOHN WILEY & SONS
Chichester · New York · Brisbane · Toronto

British Library Cataloguing in Publication Data:
Human skills — (Wiley series on studies in human performance).
  1. Ability
  I. Holding, Dennis Harry
  153.9   BF431   80-49977

  ISBN 0 471 27838 6

Phototypeset by Dobbie Typesetting Service, Plymouth, Devon, England.
Printed in the United States of America.

Preface

Research on human performance has made considerable progress during the past forty years, reaching a respectable depth of analysis in several areas while at the same time becoming broader in scope. As a result, there have emerged a number of theoretical ideas which impinge on the general development of experimental psychology and, moreover, a great deal of knowledge has been obtained in ways which encourage direct, practical application. The series of Studies in Human Performance, beginning with this volume, is intended to explain these ideas and their applications in adequate detail.

Approximately half of the books in the series are monographs while the remainder, like the present text, are edited volumes. Although writing a monograph is often regarded as the more difficult assignment, producing an edited volume presents something of a challenge. On one hand, it provides an opportunity to bring to bear a concentration of expertise which is otherwise unattainable; on the other hand, the multiplicity of contributors carries with it a risk that the overall result may be disorganized or, literally, incoherent. In the Human Performance series, every effort has been made to counter the disadvantages attendant on using the edited format, while preserving the advantages of drawing upon special knowledge. The chapters have been commissioned in accordance with an integrated plan for each volume, draft versions of each chapter have been circulated among the contributors in order to ensure cohesion, and editorial control has extended to the level of difficulty as well as to the format of each text.

The result of these preparations should be a series of books which combine readability with high standards of scholarship. The aim has been to supply a good deal of content, but within an expository framework which emphasizes explanation rather than mere reporting. Thus, although each volume contains sufficient material for the needs of graduate students, or advanced undergraduates, in experimental psychology, the books should provide readily accessible information for applied psychologists in many areas. In addition, it is hoped that the books will be useful to practitioners in ergonomics, to persons with interdisciplinary interests in production and industrial engineering, in physical education and in exercise physiology, and to psychologists in other fields.

The analysis of human skills is of central importance to an understanding of the wider area of human performance. Partly for this very reason, the subject of skills is fraught with more theoretical problems than many other topics in human performance; in fact, many of the more applied issues have been quite appropriately reserved for inclusion in the companion volume on *'Training for Performance'*. A further difficulty encountered in dealing with skills is that the relevant research has in many cases reached a stage where some facility with mathematical notation is required for thorough understanding. The policy adopted here has been to grasp the nettle by introducing mathematical concepts when necessary, but always in the context of an explanation. Where the use of a mathematical formula has been unavoidable, the simplest form of expression has always been chosen. We believe that the result is compatible with our overall objective, that each book should be within the grasp of any educated person who has the motivation to study its subject-matter.

Dennis H. Holding
Louisville, 1980

The Contributors

W. D. ALAN BEGGS   Senior Lecturer, Department of Psychology, University of Nottingham, *England*.

M. HAMMERTON   Professor, Department of Psychology, University of Newcastle upon Tyne, *England*.

DENNIS H. HOLDING   Professor, Department of Psychology (Research Professor, Performance Research Laboratory), University of Louisville, Kentucky, *USA*.

C. IAN HOWARTH   Professor, Department of Psychology, University of Nottingham, *England*.

MARCEL KINSBOURNE   Professor, Departments of Paediatrics and Psychology, University of Toronto, Ontario, *Canada*.

GERALD J. LAABS   Research Psychologist, US Navy R & D Center, San Diego, California, *USA*.

NEVILLE MORAY   Professor, Department of Psychology, University of Stirling, *Scotland*.

KARL M. NEWELL   Associate Professor, Institute for Child Behavior and Development, University of Illinois at Urbana-Champaign, *USA*.

PATRICK M. A. RABBITT   Senior Lecturer, Department of Experimental Psychology (Fellow, Queen's College), University of Oxford, *England*.

CLARK A. SHINGLEDECKER   Senior Scientist, Systems Research Laboratory, Dayton, Ohio, *USA*.

ROGER W. SIMMONS   Assistant Professor, Department of Physical Education, San Diego University, California, *USA*.

JEFFERY J. SUMMERS   Lecturer, Department of Psychology, University of Melbourne, Victoria, *Australia*.

Contents

Preface   v

1. Skills Research . . . . *Dennis H. Holding*   1
   Background   1
   Kinds of skill   3
   Basic research issues   5
   Reaction time and anticipation   7
   Processing and storage 11
   Summary 12

2. Feedback and the Control of Skilled Behaviour . . . . *Neville Moray* 15
   Definition of feedback and closed-loop control 16
   Tracking tasks and control theory 19
   Applications to human and animal skills 27
   Prediction, strategies, and skill 32
   Problems of measurement 37
   Summary 39

3. Motor Programs . . . . *Jeffery J. Summers* 41
   Motor program control 42
   Role of feedback 48
   The schema concept 52
   Current view of motor control 58
   Implications for skill learning 62
   Summary 64

4. Single-channel Theory . . . . *Marcel Kinsbourne* 65
   Limited-capacity models 66
   Effort 72
   Task similarity and interference 73
   Developmental aspects 77
   The brain as a functional unit 79
   Capacity limitations and consciousness 87
   Summary 88

5. Discrete Movements .... *C. Ian Howarth and W. D. Alan Beggs*   91
   Historical   92
   Information theory   95
   Control theory 101
   A new look at choice reactions............................... 110
   Intersensory localization.................................... 111
   Other factors degrading sensory judgements 113
   Strategies in the control of movement........................ 114
   Summary 116

6. Motor Memory .... *Gerald J. Laabs and Roger W. Simmons* 119
   Movement reproduction paradigm 120
   Bias in reproduction 123
   Recall memory... 130
   Theoretical formulations 140
   Recognition memory.. 142
   Comparison with verbal short-term memory 147
   Summary 151

7. Sequential Reactions .... *Patrick M. A. Rabbitt* 153
   Limitations of static models................................. 154
   A 'tracking' model for maintaining speed and accuracy........... 161
   Management of temporal control 168
   Summary 174

8. Tracking.....................................*M. Hammerton* 177
   Types of track 178
   Optimal controls and displays 184
   Measurement of tracking performance......................... 190
   Models of tracking behaviour 191
   Transfer of training... 195
   Tracking and channel capacity............................... 198
   Status and future of tracking studies......................... 199
   Summary 200

9. Skill Learning.................................*Karl M. Newell* 203
   Information and skill learning 204
   Conditions of practice....................................... 216
   Generalization of skill....................................... 220
   Summary 225

10. Handicap and Human Skill ....*Clark A. Shingledecker* 227
   Chronic handicaps... 227

Motor impairment.. 229
Sensory impairment 237
Mobility skills 247
Summary 255

11. Final Survey...............................*Dennis H. Holding* 257
Salient issues 257
The breakdown of skills 261
Probable trends 267
Summary 268

References and Author Index................................... 269

Subject Index 301

Chapter 1

Skills Research

Dennis H. Holding

Research on skills might reasonably cover the entire range of human activities. Riding a bicycle, for example, or playing a guitar, are clearly examples of skills; but so too, in a sense, are achievements like solving a crossword puzzle or delivering a political speech. The bicycle and guitar activities differ somewhat, but both are important as instances of perceptual-motor skill. Their skill component derives in a major way from the bodily actions which compose them. This is what distinguishes the skills covered by this book, setting them apart from the more restrictedly cognitive kinds of performance which puzzles and speeches demand.

It is true, for instance, that learning to read is often considered to be acquiring a skill, or that it is natural to talk in differences in skill at chess; in fact, Bartlett (1958) has gone so far as to argue that thinking itself is a human skill. However, extending the idea of skill in this way introduces quite different research issues, explanatory concepts, and kinds of methodology. Hence, we are legitimately concerned with the kinds of issues raised by studying tasks from sports and athletics, like playing football, sailing boats, or throwing the discus; from the armed services, like piloting aircraft or gun-laying; from business and industry, like key-punching or lathe operation; or from everyday activities, like opening cans or washing dishes. These kinds of perceptual-motor performance define a research area with historical continuity and some degree of theoretical coherence.

BACKGROUND

The study of skills began quite early in the history of experimental psychology, perhaps with Bryan and Harter's (1897) work on Morse code communication or with Woodworth's (1899) analysis of the characteristics of repetitive, timed movements. After this period, however, research activity was sparse until the Second World War. There had been a number of early finger-maze studies, some industrial studies of time, motion, and fatigue, Thorndike's (1927) demonstration of the effect of knowledge of results on line-drawing, and a sprinkling of relevant papers in the late 1930s; but the real impetus for skills research came from wartime demands for high-speed and high-precision performance.

Tracking skill, which requires the accurate following of a target or course (see Chapter 8), is involved in critical tasks like flying, driving, or aiming. Thus, although many studies of single movements were made, the tracking task became the major skills exemplar. The analysis of tracking entailed the use of formulations from control engineering, which soon led to the first description of the skilled performer as a 'closed-loop' system (Craik, 1947); this approach represents human functioning in the manner of a servo-mechanism with corrective feedback. This kind of engineering analogy has most recently been enriched by contributions from modern control theory, as discussed in Chapter 2. Further postwar liaisons with engineering led to the growth of applied human factors studies (cf. Fitts, 1951) and, in a different direction, to the adoption of mathematical information theory into psychology (Hick, 1952).

Studies of reaction time attained new importance in the context of information theory and its psychological applications. The finding that reaction times in close succession would interact, coupled with the idea that human servo-action was intermittent, yielded the conception of the human operator as a limited-capacity information channel (see Chapter 4). Together with converging developments concerning the selection of information in perception, these views soon led to more explicit, analytic attempts to trace the flow of information through various processing stages (Broadbent, 1958). Coupled with the flow diagram techniques derived from computer programming, the resulting information-processing approach rapidly migrated into what has become cognitive psychology, later to be reimported into the skills area.

The 1960s were relatively quiescent, perhaps to be characterized as a period of consolidation and are well represented by the Bilodeau and Bilodeau (1969) survey; however, the 1970s have seen a resurgence of motor skills activity, prompted in part by the interests of physical education and kinaesiology. The newer interests, in process-oriented analyses, have centred on the problem of how motor behaviour is controlled and organized. Discrete movement tasks, of the kind described in Chapter 5, have supplanted the tracking task as the preferred experimental setting; a parallel development has brought sequential, keyboard tasks into prominence (see Chapter 7). Tasks of these kinds lend themselves to studies of the human programming of motor sequences (Chapter 3) and to studies of the way in which motor memory is organized (Chapter 6). All of these issues are discussed in the book, together with the development of knowledge concerning skill acquisition (Chapter 9); for a fuller treatment of training issues the companion volume in this series (Annett, in preparation) should be consulted. Finally, the special insights afforded by the study of handicaps are shown in Chapter 10 to lead to practical contributions.

KINDS OF SKILL

A brief, historical outline, such as is presented in the preceding section, must obviously gloss over a number of distinctions concerning the kinds of skill which have been studied. Although we began by excluding verbal and intellectual skills from consideration, the question remains whether we can make useful distinctions within the central core of perceptual-motor skills. Many classifications have been proposed, mainly on commonsense grounds, but there is a good deal of overlap between them, and rather obscure technical backing for most.

For example, we may order tasks along a continuum from those with mainly perceptual demands, like radar watch-keeping, to those with mainly motor demands like weight-lifting. This distinction seems to overlap with Poulton's (1957a) division into 'open' skills, which require a good deal of interaction with external stimuli, as against 'closed' skills which may be run off without reference to the environment. The terminology is unfortunate since 'closed' skills are virtually 'open-loop' in feedback terms, and vice versa, but the distinction points up a real difference. In fact, we may compare the 'open-closed' distinction in turn with the older dichotomy between skill and habit, since it is only the closed skill which readily becomes habitual.

A different kind of distinction, which we can perhaps consider orthogonal to the group above, begins with the obvious continuum between simple and complex. Open, perceptual, skilful skills can be either simple or complex, as can closed, motor, habitual skills. These differences in complexity, in practice, often run parallel to the difference between gross and fine skills, although the correspondence is far from perfect. Gross skills are those which involve whole-body movement and, barring competition gymnastics, are often less complex than fine skills which require manual dexterity. Finally, tasks of discrete movement, and their sequential counterparts, may be contrasted with tasks of continuous movement. This distinction is not as clear cut as might first appear, since most discrete tasks involve segments of continuously graded responses rather than simple muscle-twitches, but the dichotomy does allow us to distinguish between pushing a button and steering a car. Again, the first is usually simple and the second more complex, so that for many purposes all three distinctions may be treated together.

It seems, then, that we have arrived at an intuitive two-factor classification of skilled tasks or, at least, an analysis in terms of two broad groups of factors. If such a result were to coincide with the outcome of statistical analysis of human abilities, the skills area might be simply partitioned. Unfortunately, those factor analyses of performance abilities which are available tell a much more complex story. In Fleishman's (1958) work, 31 different tasks were performed by over 200 airmen; the tasks included the pursuit rotor, rudder control, dial setting, and other apparatus tasks, measuring a wide range of different skills. Correlations between these tasks yielded as many as ten different factors, of which seven had some general importance. The most prominent factors were spatial response association, fine control sensitivity, speed of reaction, arm movement speed, arm–hand steadiness, limb coordination, and rate control; in addition, there were factors confined to particular experimental tasks. Later work has revealed many other factors such as manual dexterity, which is separate from finger dexterity and from wrist–finger speed; and whole-body factors like trunk strength and gross body equilibrium (Fleishman, 1966). In all, some eighteen factors have been clearly identified and a number of others undoubtedly exist. Furthermore, the relative importance of these factors changes as a function of the degree of practice an individual has had; one important difference, for example, is that visual abilities give way to kinaesthetic abilities as greater skill is acquired.

This situation is enlightening for research purposes, but is impossible to work with as an expository scheme. In order to provide a framework for discussion, therefore, Figure 1 presents a rough classification of a few representative skilled tasks based on the distinctions discussed above. These distinctions are those most commonly made, and are employed throughout the book. It is obviously an unsophisticated scheme which could be made more accurate, with some loss of intelligibility, by adding further dimensions or by separating out the existing ones. Note that the classification is by type of task rather than by ability factors, although it would make sense to assume that widely separated tasks in Figure 1 would carry quite different loadings on motor ability factors.

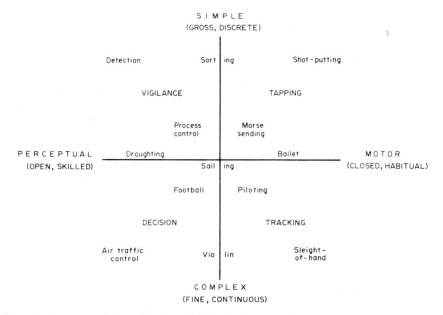

Figure 1. A suggested classification of skilled tasks. Further distinctions are made in the text.

With a little thought, and some tolerance for ambiguity, one may easily locate other skills on this surface. Choice reaction tasks, for instance, are relatively simple and about equally perceptual or motor, and are thus placed somewhere above the sorting tasks on the centre axis. For tasks like lathe operation, their placement must vary according to whether the job is simple and repetitive or has special, complex requirements. Certain skills disclose the problem of oversimplifying the major dimensions of the figure. Thus, operating a sewing machine clearly contains a tracking component, which should locate the task below the horizontal axis, but is relatively simple, locating it above the axis. Such minor inconsistencies serve to confirm that the figure is intended only for preliminary orientation. In general, consideration of Figure 1 shows that the interests of this book tend to graduate towards the right-hand and bottom quadrants. The problems of vigilance in particular, in the top left quadrant, raise a number of separate issues which are dealt with in another volume of the series (Warm, in press).

By and large, the discrete tasks in the upper right-hand quadrant have been represented by a literature separate from the body of work in the lower, tracking quadrant. They are represented by different chapters for convenience although, as the historical review implied, discrete task experiments are beginning to modify the theories originally generated by the study of continuous tasks. Many theoretical problems of skill are common to both areas of research; in fact, the major problems of how motor skills are organized cut across most classifications.

In what follows, we shall neglect questions of individual differences, being primarily concerned with describing average or standard human performance. It would be unfair to leave the impression that human skills are uniform, since variations in ability are well documented. Noble (1978) has summarized a very large amount of data concerning the effects of age, race and sex in human skills, while the Osborne, Noble, and Weyl (1978) text puts these issues into a wider perspective. However, the kinds of research question which arise in comparing individual are largely not those whose investigation is relevant here.

BASIC RESEARCH ISSUES

Some of the principal issues concern feedback, programming, and timing. Consider first the performance of a man who has learned to track the excursions of a pointer moving sinusoidally at the fairly fast rate of one cycle per second. If we obscure the display, or simply have him shut his eyes for a period of 5 seconds, a substantial number of times he will be able to continue tracking as accurately as before (Poulton, 1957b). The errors which begin to accumulate, it should be noted, are principally those of timing; his response cycle lags, or more probably leads, out of phase with the target course. However, once the display information is restored, for the part of a second which is long enough for velocity judgements to become reliable, a rapid correction can be made.

This segment of skilled behaviour illustrates a number of performance features. First, the operator obviously could not continue to track in the absence of input from the display unless his performance were maintained by an appropriate motor control *program*. Such a program must contain anticipatory, predictor components which, in this case, derive more from extrapolating the prior course of the target than from utilizing direct preview of the course. Next, when his performance drifted away from its original level of accuracy, its return to synchrony was dependent upon restoring the visual display, which presented information on the target course and the feedback from his control movements. In fact, *feedback* from the operator's own motor input, which we might render as knowledge of the results of his own actions, is needed at the very least to 'trim' the values at which his motor program operates. Earlier in learning, before any appreciable skill had been acquired, the need for corrective feedback would undoubtedly have been much greater. As implied by the work on abilities, in most tasks the early stages of skill tend to rely heavily upon visual feedback, with kinaesthetic cues from the joints, tendons, and muscles assuming greater importance as skill develops to the point where the learner can 'do it blindfold'.

Any precise, adjustive movement may be regulated by feedback in two different ways. In the form of terminal knowledge of results, occurring at the end of a movement, the feedback information is used to guide the formulation of the next response; it thus tends to be retained and to have a durable effect on skill learning. It is also true that the guidance of a response can be achieved directly; Smyth (1978) has recently confirmed an earlier finding (Holding and Macrae, 1964) that training by repeated movements to a mechanical stop may provide as effective a learning experience as knowledge of results. However, terminal feedback cues are not only sufficient for learning, but are by far the most commonly employed. The other way in which feedback functions has less effect on learning. In its more immediate form, known as concurrent feedback, the information guides the course of ongoing movements, always provided that these are controlled rather than merely ballistic.

This second function is best illustrated by another example. Consider now the performance of a man making a 3-inch movement with a stylus, aimed to finish exactly on a fixed target. He is operating under 'mixed' instructions, to move as quickly as possible, given that the target must be accurately hit. The shapes of two such movements, plotted against time, are shown in Figure 2. The first movement, carried out with eyes open, consists of (a) a brief initial acceleration, (b) a stretch at constant velocity, and (c) a long deceleration phase. The second movement, which is somewhat less accurate, represents a blindfold attempt. The movement begins in the same way, throughout phases (a) and (b), but the deceleration phase (c) is severely curtailed. The average component movement times, taken from unpublished data on eight subjects, are quite instructive. With eyes open, time (a) is 0.14, (b) is 0.59, and (c) is

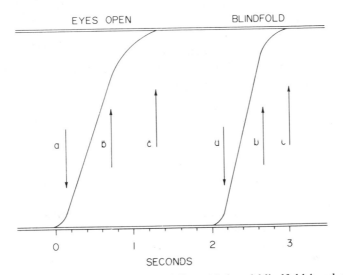

Figure 2. The average time course of visually guided and blindfold hand movements over a fixed distance, based on unpublishesd recordings. The interval (a) represents initial acceleration; (b) is the constant velocity phase; (c) is the deceleration phase.

0.58 second; almost half the time is spent in slowing down. With eyes closed, time (a) is similar, at 0.16, (b) is again similar, at 0.51, but the deceleration time (c) drops to 0.33 second.

The difference in deceleration times is statistically, and practically, significant; the experiment suggests two conclusions. First, the blindfold movement must be the result of a pre-existing program. Second, when visual feedback is available it is used to guide the stylus more accurately, if more slowly, to the target. In fact, the exponential shape of the deceleration curve strongly suggests a servo device homing on to a target by successively reducing the mismatch between the current and the target positions. Like the tracking example, the discrete movement case suggests that both response programming and feedback mechanisms have a part to play in directing skills.

REACTION TIME AND ANTICIPATION

If a person always waited until the appropriate display cue occurred before initiating a response program, his actions would be mistimed or late. A delay might not matter in a simple line-drawing movement, but would be crucial in any continuous or sequential task. The delay comes about because a fixed reaction time must elapse between stimulus and response. A typical reaction time will include several tens of milliseconds while the neural signal is conveyed from the sense organ to the brain, perhaps a hundred or so milliseconds for computation in the brain, and tens more milliseconds for the outgoing signal down the motor nerve. There is then a final delay while the neural action potential is translated into muscular contraction; recent studies (cf. Hanson and Lofthus, 1978; Stull and Kearney, 1978) have made use of this phenomenon, fractionating out the last component in order to distinguish between nervous and muscular fatigue. Together, all these delay intervals will total something approaching 200 milliseconds for a simple reaction time following a warning signal.

An enormous amount is known about reaction times, such that a bibliography of 1000 references would be easy to compile. A good, selective account of the application of reaction time studies to skills research is given by Welford (1968). Without attempting to encapsulate all this information, it is worth pointing out that the presence of a warning signal makes a big difference; the response to an unexpected stimulus will normally take at least twice, and perhaps up to ten times, as long as the forewarned version. The duration of the foreperiod matters, as does the distribution of the foreperiods when many tests are given. Reaction times also depend upon the sense modality which conveys the stimulus cue, the part of the body used for response, and of course the age, sex, and state of arousal or fatigue of the subject.

The reaction time to a highly probable stimulus is much faster than the reaction time to an improbable one; although a complication (Gottsdanker and Kent, 1978) is that low-probability stimuli embedded in blocks of high-probability trials seem to benefit from the subject's general preparedness. When the person has to prepare for a choice reaction, with one from among several possible stimuli to be presented, the probability of any one stimulus occurring is reduced according to the number of possible alternatives. Hence, it is not surprising that reaction times may be plotted as rising in proportion to the amount of information presented, since mathematically defined information is the inverse of probability (as explained in Chapter 5). What happens, roughly, is that an equal increment is added to the reaction time whenever the number of alternatives doubles. However, the slope of the increase may be flattened or even abolished by extensive practice or by the special kind of compatibility which occurs when the stimuli are signalled by the response keys touching the subject's fingers. Obviously, choice reaction times will particularly affect skills at the perceptual end of the continuum while tracking skills, located in Figure 1 towards the motor end, seems to correlate best with simple reaction times (Loveless and Holding, 1959).

One formulation which fits much of the choice data is Hick's (1952) law to the effect that choice reaction time is equal to $K \log (n + 1)$; here, n represents the number of alternatives, and K is a constant which, when n is 1, will equal the simple reaction time. This formula shows the increase in reaction time from, say, a two-light choice to a four-light choice, as equal to a further increase from four to eight lights, in accordance with information theory. More recently, Smith (1977) has proposed modifying the equation to read K log $(n\ C/E\ +\ 1)$; the new variable E is introduced to take into account the strength of the stimulus (reacting to a faint light will take longer than reacting to a bright one). The variable C is important since it draws attention to a feature of reaction times which we have not so far considered: their dependence upon requirements for speed or for accuracy. When the task conditions, or the subject's strategy, emphasize speed, the value of C will be small and the reaction time fast; with a set for accuracy, C will be larger and the reaction time correspondingly slower.

The fact that people may decide to opt for speed or for accuracy, thus modifying their reaction times or movement response times, has attracted a good deal of research in recent years. Fitts (1966), for example, showed that monetary pay-offs for speed or accuracy will influence choice reaction times, a set for accuracy inducing a skewed distribution of longer times. Later work has concentrated on the factors affecting individual speed–accuracy trade-off functions, with accuracy as the dependent variable plotted against constrained changes in reaction time. In tasks which permit a trade-off, the subject may achieve greater accuracy by the expenditure of more time. The exact form of the function will depend upon the measure of accuracy used, as well as upon extraneous factors. Fortunately, Pew (1969) finds that taking accuracy as $a\ +\ b$ log (prob. correct responses/prob. errors) makes the relationship with reaction time approximately linear (a and b are merely the intercept and slope constants). The ways in which reaction times may be manipulated have been discussed by Wickelgren (1977): issuing instructions; offering pay-offs; setting deadlines; setting lower and upper time limits; synchronizing responses to a second cue. The partitioning of naturally occurring reaction times, without constraints, seems to be the least satisfactory method.

The natural variation of elapsed time may not always reveal a speed–accuracy trade-off. However, in the case of response times for graduated movements, it will usually be found that slower responding yields higher accuracy (cf. Siddall, Holding, and Draper, 1957). A fairly clear example of the orthodox relationship between speed and accuracy is shown in Figure 3. The mean error and time scores are taken from the study on blindfold line-drawing, reported earlier in connection with the deceleration phase of discrete movements. It can be seen that a straight line produces a good fit to the data, with errors decreasing as the time taken lengthens. While the relationship will take this form for many tasks there are, obviously, some skills like dart-throwing, or even bicycle-riding, which provide reversals of the relationship such that slow responding leads to increased error.

There are also exceptions in reaction times, which in most cases are found in tasks based upon judgements. Holding and Dennis (1957), for instance, found that shorter times were associated with the correct responses rather than with

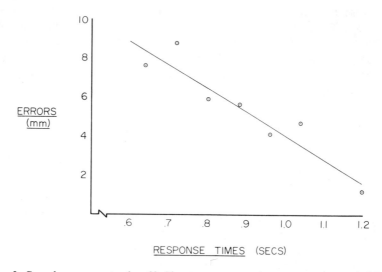

Figure 3. Speed–accuracy trade-off. Shorter response times are accompanied by larger errors.

the errors made in a sound localization task. Presumably the subjects made errors when they were uncertain, and the uncertainty made for delays in responding. Similar effects are to be expected in many cases where tasks may be varied in difficulty, since it is quite likely that a difficult version will provoke both long reaction times and many errors.

In general, measuring the time elapsing before a response gives a comparatively gross indication of the underlying processes. We may expect a long reaction time sometimes to result from useful processing activity, and thus to accompany accuracy, or else simply to reflect bafflement. Again, a short reaction time may occur because little processing is needed, or because the subject has abandoned any attempt at accuracy in favour of guessing. Thus, speed–accuracy functions will only yield reliable predictions in certain tightly-controlled situations, although the ability to make and to modify the trade-off will usually form part of the development of a skill.

Whether fast or slow, the existence of a reaction time of any length is a recurring obstacle to a skilled activity, as the smooth performance of a skill is disrupted whenever a response does not occur on time. Thus, achieving proficiency requires that the task cues must be predicted in advance in order to offset the delay in responding which would otherwise occur. For this reason, the most important single feature of highly skilled performance is the development of anticipation. Clearly, the most predictable skilled tasks are those which will yield best learning and performance. In one form, predict-ability may come about as a result of direct preview of forthcoming cues, as when portions of a tracking course are visible in advance; this has been termed 'receptor anticipation' (Poulton, 1957b).

Predictability in the form of 'perceptual anticipation' may come about as a result of practice with recurring features of a task, as Noble and Trumbo (1967) confirmed in several tracking studies. In one of these, varying the number of repeating, and therefore predictable, elements of a step-tracking course produced differences which remained throughout nine days of practice and a three-month retention interval. It can also be shown that individual skill development accompanies an increasing capacity for anticipation. Pew and Rupp (1971) tested children aged ten to sixteen, who showed consistent age differences, in two measures of tracking ability. Their 'system gain' scores, which imply responsiveness to error feedback, increased with age; more importantly, the older children showed smaller 'effective time delays', having successfully learned to discount their reaction time lags by making use of anticipation.

As an example from discrete movements, there is the classic demonstration by Leonard (1953) of the effects of advance information in a serial reaction task. In the standard form of the task, the subject moved a lever to one of the outer corners of the apparatus in response to the appropriate signal light. With provision for anticipation, the signal for the next destination was lit while the subject was still returning the lever to its starting point; this procedure led to fast and almost automatic performance. It is clear that such advance cues would permit the early initiation of an appropriate motor program for the control of timing and of spatial movement characteristics. Welford (1968) suggests that the automaticity of performance which advance cues produce results from their pre-emption of the attention normally directed at feedback cues, although it seems sufficient to assume that the programming by past experience of simple movements renders feedback unnecessary.

PROCESSING AND STORAGE

The preceding sections convey something of the background to research issues considered in the ensuing chapters. In addition, there are many problems concerning the internal processing of skills information. Cues from the task and from feedback must be integrated with stored experience, while the demands of decision-making, the planning and executing of response sequences, all form an additional information-handling load. If we view processing by the human brain as routing information through a single channel of limited capacity, as we might when observing that a person cannot satisfactorily execute two complex skills at once, questions will arise concerning the stage at which the limitation occurs.

It might be that the limitation of capacity is not one of processing, but of memory, or of response selection. The evidence suggests a fairly complex task for future research. McLeod (1977), for instance, has recently shown that two different manual responses will interfere, but that different response modalities, such as manual and vocal, seem to permit 'multiprocessing' to proceed without interference.

In appropriate circumstances, when the person is overloaded, performance on a secondary task will often suffer in comparison with a main task. This effect has been used in the assessment of various stresses, to reveal impairments which are not apparent in the scores for the main task. However, there are other occasions when two tasks may be performed together without loss of efficiency. Since Allport, Antonis, and Reynolds' (1972) demonstration that simultaneous attention to auditory and visual tasks is quite feasible, further questions have emerged concerning the processing, or time-sharing, of several streams of information in parallel. Yet another set of research questions address the possibility (Kahneman, 1973) that it is the mental effort required by attention, rather than the computing capacity of the brain, which sets a limit on processing. It will be seen in Chapter 4 that Kinsbourne suggests, as an alternative, that interference between dual tasks depends on the functional distance separating brain representation of the tasks.

At a different level of analysis, we have also to consider storage mechanisms and capacities. If motor programs are to be built up from the experience of past movements, the understanding of skills obviously demands a knowledge of the characteristics of motor memory. This area, too, has a long history beginning with Bowditch and Southard (1880), who compared memory for target positions located by vision or by touch. This kind of work has seen energetic revival in the present decade.

The questions have arisen whether motor and verbal memories are alike, or in what ways they differ, what kinds of movement information are retained and how they are coded for storage and retrieval. There are questions of movement recall and of movement recognition, and questions of short-term and long-term motor memory. The kinds of theory which have emerged include models which concern motor memory in its own right, and models of motor storage viewed as an integral feature of the control mechanisms for skilled movement.

It will be found that many of the foregoing issues recur throughout the text, not only in the chapters explicitly directed to them, but also in the treatments of discrete, sequential, and tracking skills. An appreciation of the issues posed by feedback and programming mechanisms, reaction times and anticipation, processing and storage seems fundamental to the understanding of skilled behaviour.

SUMMARY

This chapter attempts to describe the kinds of perceptual-motor skill appropriate to the book, and to introduce in a preliminary way some of the more important theoretical and research issues. The development of the subject is outlined, from its beginnings in the last century, through the wartime expansion, and to its present state of vigour. Distinctions are made between different types of skilled task according to the degree to which they are open, skilled, or perceptual, or are simple, gross or discrete. The factorial analysis of human abilities shows that skills depend upon a very large number of different factors. Basic research issues first focus upon the concepts of feedback, and of motor control programs, both of which are illustrated in discrete and continuous tasks. Next are the problems of timing, the lags in performance entailed by reaction and response times, whose effects must be circumvented by the development of anticipation. Finally, the issues of information processing and storage are introduced, as topics which claim increasing attention in the study of human performance.

Chapter 2

Feedback and the Control of Skilled Behaviour

Neville Moray

Almost from the beginning of modern research on the nature of perceptual-motor skills it has been assumed that feedback must play a central role in their control. The term 'feedback' has, however also been used in an extended sense in many areas of psychology. This has been particularly so when it has been desired to emphasize the role of information, rather than reinforcement, in determining behaviour (Bilodeau, 1966; Bilodeau and Bilodeau, 1969; Annett, 1969). In this chapter we shall be concerned almost entirely with the strict sense of the word, since only then can the properties of feedback be described in a quantitative, exact, and analytic way. Feedback in this sense is part of control theory.

For more than thirty years now the closed-loop negative feedback system, (CLNF), has served as the basic model for human skill, and many psychology textbooks imply that negative feedback is sufficient to guarantee the correction of errors. Such is not the case. Feedback theory indeed is certainly not an adequate general model for perceptual-motor skills, but is none the less often a good working approximation, and conceptually is a necessary starting point for their understanding. Like information theory and the theory of signal detection, feedback theory has its roots in engineering, in particular in that branch of mechanical engineering known as control theory. When used as a model of the human operator CLNFs are normative. We can specify the ideal performance which cannot be exceeded by any CLNF system, and use that as a standard against which to measure human performance. In fact, as we shall see, humans as often exceed their theoretical limits as do they fall short of them. We shall be concerned in this chapter to outline the normative properties of CLNFs, to show why they are 'skilled', and to outline where they fail as models of human skill.

DEFINITION OF FEEDBACK AND CLOSED-LOOP CONTROL

A system is said to contain a *feedback loop* when the output of that system interacts with its input in such a way as to modify the subsequent activity of the system as it continues to generate an output. The actual output (driving 1.5 metres from the kerb), of the system is compared with the *desired output* (which may also be called the input for reasons which will become clear later). If there is a discrepancy between them (we really want to be 1.0 metres from the kerb) the sign and magnitude of that discrepancy is used to modify the output so as to reduce the discrepancy. The desired output functions as a goal which the system tries to attain, a criterion towards the satisfaction of which the system strives. The system as a whole embodies teleology and is essentially orientated towards the future rather than towards a past stimulus. We shall return to this point later in analysing the conceptual implications of feedback theory in contrast to S–R theory.

The simplest and most common form of comparison of output with input is subtraction. The actual output is appropriately scaled and subtracted from the desired output. If the result is non-zero there is said to be an *error signal* –0.5 metres in our example). Since the output is returned and compared to the input there is *feedback*, and since the comparator performs a subtraction, we say there is *negative feedback*. In all realizable systems there will be some undesirable *disturbance* or *noise* which may enter the system at one or more points and cause discrepancies between the actual and desired outputs (bumps in the road, or wind turbulence). In some cases a disturbance may be injected deliberately into the system to test its functioning, and the disturbance is then called a *forcing function*. Since information flows from input to output and back to the input through the comparator, such systems are called closed-loop systems. A diagram of such a CLNF system is shown in Figure 4.

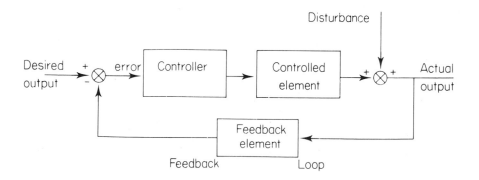

Figure 4. Closed-loop negative feedback system.

The conceptual implications of CLNF systems are very different from what is usually called S–R theory. The latter does not in any strict sense involve feedback, and is an *open-loop* theory. In an S–R formulation the system receives an input. It is a specific, identifiable input calling for a particular, specified response. Providing that the system produces the particular response associated with the particular stimulus which has just occurred, all is correct. Otherwise an error has occurred and the response is wrong (see Figure 5).

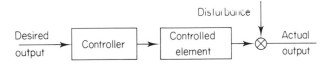

Figure 5. Open-loop S–R system.

By contrast a CLNF system might almost be said neither to have a well-defined stimulus nor a well-defined response. Rather, such systems have a *goal* towards which they strive. In many skills it is conceivable that the same response never occurs on successive trials and yet the skill is successfully exercised. It is probably the case that in normal driving over a particular route in traffic the same steering, acceleration, and braking movements never occur in anything like identical situations. But providing that the goal is approached, that the mismatch between actual and desired output is reduced, it is a matter of complete unimportance what actual behaviour occurs. The truly skilled operator, one may say, is characterized by an almost completely open-ended repertoire of behaviour which despite unforeseen disturbances will drive the system to its goal. The contrast with S–R theory could hardly be greater.

Because of this it is tempting to follow the literature cited earlier into a discussion of many situations in which the results of earlier behaviour are 'fed back' to the human subject in an experiment. Even reinforcement can be regarded in this way, as can the results of school examinations, the test phases of TOTE circuits (Miller, Galanter, and Pribram, 1960), and all kinds of 'knowledge of results' (Holding, 1965). In the books cited earlier by Bilodeau and by Annett the term 'feedback' is even used in discussing verbal learning experiments. But all such uses are analogical extensions of the strict theory of feedback, and as is so often the case with analogies, the precision of the original meaning is lost. Certainly in none of the above cases can the classical use in any way predict performance. As another example, compare the use of terms 'force' and 'tension' in psychology with their use in physics where they originated. In psychology they are almost primitive concepts which are undefined, while in physics force is strictly defined in terms of the acceleration which is imparted to a mass. The precision of the original use is lost in psychology.

Since control theory is intended to be a normative model let us consider the inherent properties of systems with negative feedback in a closed loop. There are four main properties which make such systems attractive as models for skilled performance. These are orientation towards a goal, automatic error correction, an ability to describe explicitly the properties of any equipment used, and the fact that the systems show behaviour which is dynamic in time.

We have already pointed out that CLNF systems are goal orientated rather than stimulus orientated. The second point is the one which has most commonly been invoked. Providing that a CLNF system is correctly designed it will compensate for any disturbances to which it is subjected, producing smooth, stable performance, a characteristic of human skills. Error compensation is not, however, an inherent property of CLNF systems; the presence of negative feedback of itself does not guarantee that it will occur, a fact often overlooked in psychological discussions of skills. The reason for failures under certain conditions will be discussed below. Negative feedback can, on occasion, actually increase error and cause instability. (It has been suggested that certain neurological disorders such as Parkinson's disease may be cases of this.)

The third characteristic is that control theory is particularly well suited for taking quantitative account of equipment used by the skilled operator, and that this remains true even when that equipment is as complex as an aircraft or a petrochemical plant. Such cannot be said of other types of theory.

For example, we think of reaction time as a property of behaviour, a property of the human being. But in fact it is a property of the human being in the context of the equipment with which we measure it. In laboratory tests we take care to see that there is little or no mechanical inertia, friction, etc. in the response keys. But in everyday situations we can never assume that similar conditions will obtain. Rather, the physical properties of the tools and equipment used may directly influence the measurable latency of response, which is properly speaking a *performance* measure — a measure of the man-machine system as a whole — rather than a *behaviour* measure — a measure of the human himself in isolation from equipment. If this were not in general true then the acquisition and exercise of skills would be much simpler than is the case. A violinist would not mind which instrument he played on, a skier would be indifferent to which skis he used, and vehicle-handling characteristics would not interact with driving skills. In most psychological theories there is no direct and quantitative way of incorporating the properties of the *controlled element* or *physical plant*. Control theory, as we shall see, can do so easily by means of the concept of the transfer function. Throughout this chapter we shall retain the distinction between the behaviour and the performance which we measure. The former is the movements of the human, for example the movements of his hands, arms, head, and feet when driving an automobile. The latter is the observable movements or changes in the whole man–machine system, for example the velocity, direction, and accelerations of the vehicle.

The last feature which is attractive in control theory as applied to CLNF systems is that is deals with dynamic processes. Such processes are those where inputs and disturbances are functions of time and mathematically should properly be described by sets of differential equations where the variables are functions of time. Many psychological theories deal with discrete 'stimuli' which have fixed descriptions (values) which do not change as time passes. But it is of course characteristic of everyday life that the relation between the human operator and the environment is dynamic, constantly changing. If we want a theory of skills which is at all applicable to everyday life, where most skills are exercised, it must be capable of dealing with dynamic rather than with static inputs. Almost all interesting skills require this. We would not call the tennis player who played exactly the same stroke every time he received a serve to his forehand a skilled player; we would call him a loser. The mathematics of control theory is ideally suited to predict not merely time-averaged performance where everything about the situation is held constant. Rather it is designed to predict moment-to-moment outputs of complex systems in real time in dynamic environments; precisely what our intuition tells us is required of a theory of skills.

There are, however, at least two very obvious properties which humans possess which are not present in classical control theory, namely learning and prediction, and we shall see that considerable simplifying assumptions will have to be made to apply the classical theory. More modern control theory can to some extent deal with these problems, but we shall begin by considering in some detail the properties of the classical systems of which the properties still form the hard core of CLNF control theory.

TRACKING TASKS AND CONTROL THEORY

As a paradigm for skill we shall use the laboratory *compensatory tracking task*. The task is both well suited for describing CLNF properties and also has face validity as a model of everyday tasks such as vehicular control, sports of many kinds, and the control of movements. For more detailed treatment, and introductions to the mathematical methods, the reader should consult Toates (1975), or Milsum (1966). For detailed reviews of tracking Pew (1974a), or Poulton (1974) will be found to give extensive coverage, although the latter is sometimes idiosyncratic and uses notation which is non-standard. A discussion of the relation of tracking skills to other areas of psychology with an emphasis on applications and the measurement of workload will be found in Moray (1979). Finally, a most fascinating and provocative treatment of the whole question of skill and control may be found in Kelley (1968), which should be read by anyone interested in the topic, as well as Chapter 8, by Hammerton, in this volume.

The compensatory tracking task is similar in essence to the task of driving a car over bumpy or icy roads, flying an aircraft in turbulent air, or steering a sailboat in rough seas. In each case the controlled element is subjected to random, limited bandwidth disturbances, for the effect of which the human controller is required to compensate. In the laboratory we may present a small reference circle on an oscilloscope screen together with a moving spot of light. The operator is required to keep the spot within the circle. The maintaining of the position of the spot within the circle is the desired output. White Gaussian noise of limited low-frequency bandwidth is used to disturb the position of the spot, and the operator moves a joystick to counter the effect of this disturbance. We may assume for simplicity that the spot moves only in one dimension, say left and right. The error signal is then the distance of the spot from the (centre of) the criterion circle. The noise is the forcing function (see Figure 6). It is perhaps worth noting that in all tracking experiments we are

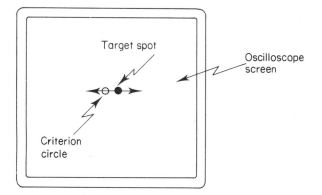

Figure 6. Compensatory tracking task.

talking of frequencies of less than about 2Hz (approximately 12 radians per second). With one or two rate exceptions voluntary compensatory movements cannot be made at frequencies higher than this, although preprogrammed motor sequences can be faster. The limitation appears to be in the central information-processing abilities of the nervous system, since the bandwidth is the same regardless of the power–weight ratio of the limb used. Higher frequencies do appear in the human operator output, but these are mainly due to twitches, muscle tremor, etc.

If the human operator takes no action in such a task the time history of the movements of the spot would look similar to the trace shown in Figure 7, which also shows the probability distribution of the forcing function.

Let us now construct a flow diagram of the way in which information and control interact in a CLNF system. In Figure 8 the components or elements of

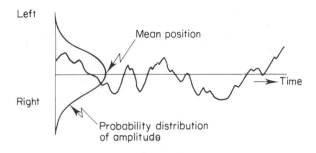

Figure 7. Movements of target driven by random Gaussian noise.

the system are shown, together with the various signals which are circulating round the loop. Thus *x(t)* is the desired output, *e(t)* the error signal, *m(t)* the human operator's behaviour, *z(t)* the output from the joystick, *d(t)* the forcing function, *y(t)* the actual output or performance of the system, and *w(t)* the feedback signal, all shown as functions of time and measured at time *t*. The figure brings out the way in which control theory can make explicit reference to the properties of the thing controlled, as well as to the properties of the human operator, so that in a specific application the theory predicts the performance of the entire system, not merely the behaviour of the human. The element called *human neuromuscular system* transforms the sensory input (the error signal) into behaviour. The latter may pass unchanged through the joystick, or it may be amplified, delayed, etc. to produce *z(t)*. In a similar way we may represent the transformation performed on the signals by each element as the signals circulate in the loop. All the components, not merely the human, determine the system's overall performance; and it is performance, rather than behaviour, that concerns us in most everyday skills.

In Figure 8b the properties of the components are rendered explicitly as mathematical operators *H(s)* (for the properties of the human operator); *F(s)* (for the properties of the controlled element); and *G(s)* (for the properties of the feedback loop). We can think of these properties as being in each case the operation which the element performs on its input to produce its output, which it then passes to the rest of the system. To calculate the output we multiply the input by the operator, as for example

$$m(s) \;=\; e(s) \bullet H(s)$$

Note that the variables and operators are no longer, however, functions of time, but functions of a variable *s*. This is conventional notation to indicate that before performing the calculation all the variables and operators have been transformed from the time domain into the domain of *Laplace transform variables*.

Although there is no room in this chapter to discuss Laplace methods in

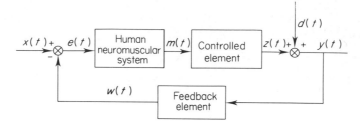

Figure 8a. Signals in the control loop.

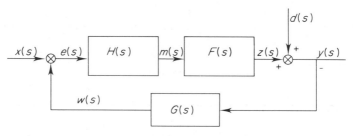

Figure 8b. The control loop in Laplace form.

detail, at least a few introductory remarks are required for readers completely unfamiliar with the methods. Toates (1975) provides a simple but extensive introduction to the topic, requiring only the simplest mathematics of the reader. In essence Laplace transforms perform a service to the user similar to that provided in arithmetic by logarithms. It is, for example, very tedious and difficult to compute the fifth root of an arbitrary number by ordinary arithmetic. But it becomes very simple if we first transform the number from the 'arithmetical domain' into the 'logarithmic domain' by looking up its logarithm. We can then simply divide the logarithm of the number by 5.0, and then return to the 'arithmetic domain' by using tables again to look up the antilogarithm of the result of our division. Similarly, the calculations required for control theory can be simplified by transforming the functions and operations from the time domain into the domain of Laplace variables, performing the calculations in that domain, and returning to the time domain when they are complete. The necessity arises because we are concerned with functions of time when analysing dynamic skills, and the appropriate way to describe such functions is by means of differential and integral equations of time. These are very difficult to handle, especially when a component, for example, both integrates its input and delays the output, or when the inputs are discontinuous functions of time such as a unit step, which is zero before time t_0, and 1.0 thereafter, with an infinite rate of change at the discontinuity. The representation of functions and operations in the Laplace domain is very simple, and the calculations reduce to simple algebra rather than calculus. Standard notation requires us to use lower-case letters for variables, *v(s)*, and upper-case letters for the operations performed by elements in the CLNF system, *V(s)*. Tables of transforms appear in many books of applied mathematics. Occasionally when talking about inputs which are composed of (mixtures of) pure sine waves the notation *v(jω)* will appear instead of *v(s)*.

To apply control theory to the loop containing the human operator requires, as mentioned earlier, that we make certain assumptions which are known to be unwarranted. We assume that all components in the loop are linear, that memory consists only of a simple time delay, and that there is no learning or prediction. This cannot be valid, since man has sensory thresholds, remembers inputs symbolically, learns, and predicts. But the theory none the less provides a working point of departure for more advanced theories. (In the writer's opinion psychology would do well to ask less often whether a theory is true, and instead concentrate on the range over which it can be applied. After all, that is even how physics behaves, and no one would ever go skating or skiing if they believed that the theory that water is a liquid were true, nor be able to slake their thirst if they believed it false. Theories which are known to have a range of applicability even though in general incorrect are extremely useful. Sanders (in Moray, 1979) has recently made this point with respect to theories of attention and human information processing in general.) Accepting the assumptions for the moment, let us examine some of the relationships between variables in a CLNF system. This will let us see how information is transformed as it flows round the loop.

Table 1. Relationships round the loop

I	II	
$m(s) = e(s) \bullet H(s)$	$H(s) = m(s)/e(s)$	(1)
$z(s) = m(s) \bullet F(s)$	$F(s) = z(s)/m(s)$	(2)
$w(s) = y(s) \bullet G(s)$	$G(s) = w(s)/y(s)$	(3)
$y(s) = z(s) + d(s)$		(4)
$e(s) = x(s) - w(s)$		(5)

More detailed relationships can obviously be derived from the equations given in Table 1. For example, since *e(s)* is a function of *w(s)*, and the latter of *y(s)*, from equations (3), (4), and (5) in Table 1 we can derive

$$e(s) = x(s) - (z(s) + d(s)) \bullet G(s) \qquad (6)$$

and so on. Note also the difference between columns I and II. While we can compute the output of an element in the loop if we know its properties and its input, we can also use the Laplace transforms of its input and output to deduce its properties if we do not know the latter but can observe the former. The ratio of the output to the input, both being in the Laplace transform domain, is called the *transfer function* of the element involved, and is a model of its properties. We can thus hope to use control theory to give us a strong quantitative model of the human operator as an element in the control loop if we can measure his input and output in situations where the properties of the rest of the CLNF system is known, and we provide inputs with known properties, enabling us to solve for *H(s)* in the loop equations.

For now it is sufficient to note that if we continue the process set out in Table 1 we will eventually arrive at the following:

$$y(s) \;=\; \frac{H(s){\bullet}G(s){\bullet}F(s)}{1 + (H(s){\bullet}F(s){\bullet}G(s))} {\bullet}x(s) + \frac{1}{1 + (H(s){\bullet}F(s){\bullet}G(s))} {\bullet}d(s)$$
$$(7)$$

Let us simplify the above by assuming the case where the joystick merely gives a faithful copy of its input; that is it behaves as an amplifier with a gain of 1.0. Its transfer function in Laplace form is then 1.0, and it can be dropped from equation (7) to yield the simpler form:

$$y(s) \;=\; \frac{H(s){\bullet}G(s)}{1 + (H(s){\bullet}G(s))} {\bullet}x(s) + \frac{1}{1 + (H(s){\bullet}G(s))} {\bullet}d(s)$$
$$(8)$$

Although this may seem at first somewhat complicated, it is actually very simple. The first term merely describes how passing round the loop alters the input, *x(s)*. The second merely does the same for the disturbance, *d(s)*. Hence, their sum describes the overall output of the system as a function of its properties, its input, and its disturbance. The algebra is actually very simple.

We are now able to see how negative feedback can act so powerfully to compensate for disturbance, and so provide skilled performance. Consider Figure 9, which shows the Laplace transform version of an 'open-loop' system, more commonly called an S–R system.

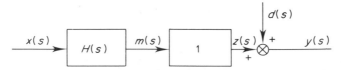

Figure 9. Open loop in Laplace form.

The open loop has a transfer function

$$y(s) = H(s) \bullet x(s) + d(s) \tag{9}$$

Hence, if the disturbance is great it will be a dominant feature of the output which is observed. Moreover, if the disturbance is not constant but is dynamic it will be of no avail to the human operator to be told how well he did a moment ago, ('knowledge of results'), and to modify his behaviour accordingly, since the disturbance will by that time have a different value, which might even be such as to require the very response which has just failed to produce desirable performance. Error correction by knowledge of results or reinforcement cannot be sufficient for skilled control in an open-loop system.

The closed-loop system with negative feedback, on the other hand, can do much to reduce the error, if properly designed; although it cannot, in real systems, eliminate error completely. What we can aim for is to maximize the effects of input, and minimize the effects of disturbance on the system performance. How to do this can be seen from equation (8), on the previous page. If we keep the value of $G(s)$ small, and the value of $H(s)$ large, and in particular if $G(s)$ is approximately equal to unity, then the first term in the equation becomes nearly equal to $1.0 \bullet x(s)$, and the second term can be made as small as we wish. For example, if we set $H(s) = 100$, and $G(s) = 1.0$, then

$$y(s) = (100/101) \bullet x(s) + (1/100) \bullet d(s) \tag{10}$$

and the effect of the disturbance is very heavily suppressed. Even if both $H(s)$ and $G(s)$ are equal to 1.0 the effect of the disturbance will be halved.

We see therefore that the existence of CLNF is a very powerful factor in reducing the effect of disturbances, even when the disturbance is dynamic and random. It should be noted that disturbances may be caused by external factors such as wind turbulence or a bumpy road, or may be due to postural tremor, loss of balance, etc. which arise within the organism. Systems with negative feedback, whether mechanical, electrical, or biological, will always tend to eliminate error and move towards their desired goal. If we are able to choose the forward loop gain and feedback loop gain appropriately, we can guarantee in many cases that the system will tend to be stable and show little error. The system will appear skilful.

Notice that CLNF is not being offered as a candidate for what happens inside the human operator at this point, but as a description of a skilful man-machine system, with a human being as part of the control loop. All we have shown so far is that if the human operator received an error signal continuously and *possessed the appropriate transfer function in the light of the transfer functions of the other elements in the loop*, then negative feedback theory would be a good model for the performance of the system as a whole.

Whether or not there are CLNF systems in the human nervous system itself is a separate question. In certain skills such as ballet dancing and gymnastics the behaviour of the system which controls posture shows that CLNF systems do in fact exist in the nervous system, and the appropriate theory can then be used as a model for behaviour as well as performance.

We can now turn to consider why, if negative feedback appears to be so powerful in compensating for error, CLNF systems are none the less defective as controllers in general, and models of human skill in particular. Far from always guaranteeing good performance there are certain situations in which large error and gross instability may arise. That such systems can never totally abolish error for more than a few moments at a time is obvious from the fact that error is used to correct error, and therefore some error must become apparent before control actions can be taken. It can be formally proven that only a system with a model of the disturbance and predictive power can become error free (Kickert, Bertrand, and Praagman, 1978).

Let us assume for the moment that the human operator's transfer function is fixed. That is, if we alter the properties of the controlled element, $F(s)$, or of the feedback loop, $G(s)$, the human will not change his transfer function to compensate, but will merely continue to function with the same $H(s)$ to the best of his ability. (We shall see later that the human operator has in fact a variety of transfer functions at his disposal, and can choose appropriate values with considerable skill to 'equalize' for the properties of the other components in the loop.) What may be the consequences?

In the first place, the controlled element may now have a function which simply cannot be controlled by the existing human operator transfer function. If the value of $H(s)$ required to compensate for the values of $F(s)$ and $G(s)$ in equation (7) cannot be provided by the nervous system, then the system will not adequately control disturbance or even achieve the desired goal in the absence of disturbance.

Humans cannot detect very small errors because of the limited acuity of the sensory systems. As the target begins to leave the criterion region there will therefore be a minimum error which will occur before the human operator detects it. Error of this magnitude will almost always be present. The sensitivity of the human operator can be increased by amplifying the error before displaying it, so making the error more apparent. But this can have undesirable effects. If the error is amplified excessively the slight random movements due to muscle tremor and other physiological signals will become apparent. The operator will not be able to distinguish between these and the 'real' disturbance, and will try to compensate for them, thus introducing further error, which would have been absent had he not tried to correct for error which only reaches noticeable proportions due to amplification. So too high a gain can cause instability, due to the human operator trying to compensate for his own motor noise. In fact, with very high gain, no externally generated forcing function is needed: the operator's internal noise alone is sufficient to provide a continuous random error signal.

A most important factor in causing error and instability is transmission delay in the feedback path. This is most easily seen where the forcing function is a periodic square wave. Suppose that the delay is exactly half the periodicity of the wave. Then the error signal will be a trough at the moment when the disturbance has changed to a peak, and a peak when it is a trough. The operator will produce a correction of the same magnitude but opposite in sign to the error signal. Usually this will mean that a trough is produced to compensate for a peak, and vice versa. But in the situation where the delay is half the period a peak will be generated and added to a peak, a trough to a trough, the error will rapidly increase, and the system will become unstable. Obviously this degree of instability will happen only when the forcing function frequency and the delay in the feedback loop are very precisely related. But equally obviously any delay will mean that error cannot be compensated, since the response will be appropriate to a state of affairs that actually obtained earlier, rather than one obtaining presently. Many transfer functions produce not delays, but phase shifts, which are in a certain sense equivalent to delays. When such transfer functions are present, the operator must compensate for them in some way, or error and instability may result. In particular, many transfer functions show amplification and phase lags which are functions of frequency, attenuating and lagging higher frequency components. Stability is impossible if the gain is greater than unity at that point in the spectrum where the phase lag is 180° or more. When that situation arises, negative feedback is no help in controlling error.

The attenuation of high-frequency signals shown by certain transfer functions is another source of error in CLNF systems. Strictly speaking, this means that no system, whether closed loop or open loop will be able to transmit high-frequency signals faithfully if it contains an element with such a transfer function. In addition, in some systems there may be mechanical inertia which means that not enough power is available to control high-frequency signals.

Thus, despite the great virtue of CLNF systems as controllers, they cannot in all circumstances guarantee the elimination of error and the achieving of the desired output (goal), irrespective of the nature of the components which combine with the human operator to form a skilled system. On the other hand, when they do fail, the way in which they fail may provide considerable insight into the nature of the components which make up the particular CLNF system, including the opportunity to model the human operator.

APPLICATIONS TO HUMAN AND ANIMAL SKILLS

It is generally agreed that the earliest writer to make the analogy between the human operator and a servo-control mechanism in discussion of skill was

Craik (1947), who developed ideas very similar to those of Wiener (1948) apparently independently in the 1940s. Craik's analysis both drew attention to the analogy and also pointed out some of its weaknesses: in particular he noted the important role which must be accorded to prediction in human behaviour, Craik noted that when tracking a step function the output contains overshooting followed by compensation in a way which would be shown by a CLNF system which sampled the error only intermittently, and suggested a sampling periodicity of about two samples per second. He thought that following each sample a response was emitted 'ballistically' (open loop) and then about 500 milliseconds later its effect was observed, and a correction response made if required. The existence of this periodicity has been questioned by subsequent workers, and its existence must be regarded as doubtful. Although several studies have found such a periodicity, there have been several which have used rather powerful mathematical analysis techniques and have found no trace of it in the power spectrum of the output. It is not clear under what conditions it appears and under what conditions not. But a hint may come from a simulation study by Bekey (personal communication) who found that if the periodicity of a sampled data system contained as little as 15 per cent variation in the frequency, power spectral analyses would not detect it. It is possible that the periodicity found by Craik appears only when the experimental situation causes rather stable sampling rates. Where aperiodic sampling occurs, it cannot be detected. And several workers have suggested reasons why sampling should, in order to produce optimal behaviour, be aperiodic (Sheridan, 1970; Senders, 1964; Moray, 1976).

Many areas of psychology show examples of behaviour and performance which are controlled by negative feedback. As Ashby (1957) has shown, all homeostatic systems require it, and the analysis of the mechanisms of feeding and drinking has made extensive use of control theory models (Toates, 1975). One of the most elegant examples is the control of posture and muscle tone, involving the gamma-fibre motoneurones and the receptors which sense muscle length and tension. The feedback loop operates both to maintain length and tension at the desired values, and also includes a means of tuning the sensitivity of the loop to keep error-detecting mechanisms sensitive.

Perhaps the most elegant examples of feedback control of the behaviour of whole organisms is found in the predatory behaviour of bats (Griffin, 1958). Insectivorous bats use a sampled data compensatory negative feedback system to capture their prey. The ultrasonic pulses which the bat emits produce echoes which the bat uses to compute the required change in its flight to compensate for movements of its prey. The pulses are not emitted at constant intervals, but as the bat approaches its prey and there is less time to make corrections the pulse rate rises, so as to reduce the sampling interval and increase the rate of corrections. Thus the error in the flight path is reduced and the need for very gross changes of direction, which would be aerodynamically difficult, is minimized. It is of interest that certain species of noctuid moths on which the bats prey have evolved a nervous system and pattern of behaviour which appears designed to minimize the effectiveness of feedback control by the predator. Certain cells are tuned to the frequency of the bats' signals, and when these cells are stimulated the moth at once turns away from the bat, reducing its echo-producing area to a minimum. If the bat continues to approach, the rate of firing of these bat detectors rises and eventually saturates. At that moment the behaviour of the moth appears to be random. It may loop, dive, fall, swerve, etc. in ways which are apparently out of control, and are highly unpredictable. Since this occurs at very close range, it forces the bat to abandon any anticipatory movements and to rely entirely on error correction, and a random pattern of disturbance is the best strategy, since the loop delay may make it impossible for the bat to make such tight turns as the smaller moth which has less inertia.

Another interesting example, showing the importance of phase relations in control, is the battle between mongoose and cobra. Each animal approaches the other slowly until the mongoose is just within the striking distance of the snake. The snake strikes, and at the first sign of movement the mongoose withdraws. As the snake remains extended at full length on the ground for a short moment the mongoose attacks and the snake withdraws. This pattern is repeated in a closed-loop pattern in which the two animals are linked. The mongoose, however, gradually changes the timing of its movements, beginning to lead the snake in phase. Its inward movement begins earlier and earlier in the cycle, until a moment arrives when it is moving back toward the snake almost while the snake is itself striking. The result is that the former is fully extended at the moment that the mongoose's inward rush finishes and the latter can seize the snake's head before it can begin its withdrawal. It appears that the ability of the mongoose to change its phase relation with respect to the snake's behaviour without the snake making a comparable change accounts for the success of the mongoose as a predator.

Finally let us return to studies of perceptual-motor skills in humans. The effects of delayed feedback have been examined by a number of workers in several sense modalities. Smith (1962; 1966) in his work on cybernetic models of learning used closed circuit television and online computers to introduce delays into the visual pathway. The subject was required to trace a pattern without seeing his hand directly. Instead either his own or a substitute hand was shown on the video screen after a delay of up to several seconds. As would be predicted from CLNF theory, performance deteriorated as a function of the delay. Similarly, the quality of speech deteriorates badly if the speaker is prevented from hearing his own voice, or hears it after a delay (Lee, 1950; 1951). The auditory loop, however, shows some properties which are not found in the 'classical' feedback loop. In the latter, performance deteriorates progressively as greater delay is introduced (except for periodic signals, where delays of exact multiples of the signal periodicity will show no deterioration). But in delayed auditory feedback the worse disruption occurs with delays, at normal speech rates, of around 350 milliseconds. With longer delays there is some improvement. The exact reason for this is not fully understood, but it is linked to the duration of phonemes and syllables, to the fact that the speech wave is not a continuous signal but made up of discrete signals linked in a chain; and it appears that it is necessary to hear each signal in order for its termination and the initiation of later signals to be properly controlled. It is interesting that while delayed auditory feedback tends to produce very marked stuttering in normal speakers, in those who stutter the defect can often be at least temporarily suppressed by masking or delaying feedback, which would be expected if 'pathological' feedback signals existed and were being suppressed by the experimental manipulation of feedback. Many normal speakers can overcome the effects of the delay if they can go open loop (and just talk without caring what it sounds like) or if they can concentrate on what the speech feels like. That is, they can change from relying on the auditory channel for feedback to reliance on the kinaesthetic loop, which is always present but probably seldom used consciously as a source of information for control. Deutsch and Clarkson (1959); and Clarkson and Deutsch (1978) have studied the role of feedback in the control of vibrato in singing, and although there is some dispute as to the identity of the controlled variable (Rostron, 1976) the findings in general fit well with a CLNF model, albeit one with an unusually short delay round the loop compared with most perceptual motor skills.

The fact that speakers seem to have some choice as to which feedback loop they will use to control speech suggests that in many tasks multiple loops may be involved in control, and that some of them may be redundant. In general, it seems that where visual feedback is available it will be used. Dissociation between redundant loops is dramatically shown in an experiment by Annett (1969). Operators had to learn to move a joystick through a specified angle, and to aid them a light moved up and down on an oscilloscope screen as they moved the lever. When performance had reached a high level of accuracy the light was removed, and despite the fact that kinaesthetic feedback had been present throughout training there was very little transfer to the new situation.

Further evidence for the role of feedback control comes from experiments in which the nature of the loop has been changed. Since the error is computed by subtracting feedback from input, then were we to reverse the sign of the feedback we would expect highly unstable performance, since the feedback would now be positive. Such a rearrangement can be done either with a closed-circuit system such as that used by Smith (1962; 1966) or by means of goggles containing mirrors or Dove prisms (see Figure 10). If the world is inverted left–right or up–down by such means, the human's behaviour becomes markedly disorientated. Slight displacements in position become greatly amplified, and

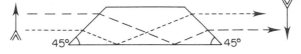

Figure 10. Ray paths in a Dove Prism.

control is lost. A mistake in direction of movement is amplified, not reduced, as one would expect with positive feedback. The effect is often noticed by people who see themselves on closed-circuit TV. Accustomed to seeing only by their own mirror images, movements to the right and left are extremely difficult to control when watching oneself the 'right way round' for the first time.

But while the initial behaviour in such situations is exactly what one would expect from a CLNF system which had been reversed, such experiments also reveal another way in which humans differ from classical CLNF systems, for within minutes compensation for the new transfer function begins. Given extensive practice a man can even learn to ride a bicycle in traffic wearing left-right inverting glasses (Kohler, 1962), a most remarkable achievement. And some subjects even report that with up-down inversion the world begins to *look* the right way up, in addition to movements becoming coordinated again. Such adaptation is not available to classical systems which have fixed transfer functions or, if a selection, do not have ways of discovering which to use. It is also of interest, and probably of considerably more importance than has been realized for our understanding of the nervous system's information-processing mechanisms, that while rearrangements of the *perceptual* response to reversal of feedback may take many days or weeks, a change in the *controlled element* such as reversing the required direction of movement is compensated in a few seconds, often without the operator even noticing that anything untoward has happened (Young, 1969).

The human's ability to compensate for changes in the properties of elements in the loop is very remarkable. The operator can also choose at what level to exercise control in systems where feedback loops are hierarchically nested and can choose transfer functions in a rational and adaptive way. As we saw earlier we cannot hope, in a classical CLNF system, to reduce error to zero because of delays round the loop; and of course with a human operator in a man–machine system there must of necessity be such delays, because of the reaction time. In the most frequently applied models of the human operator transfer function there is always a time delay included, which is the continuous signal equivalent for the reaction time in discrete signals. This implies that even if he matched a signal which he was tracking exactly in amplitude and frequency, time-on-target would be almost negligible, since he would lag behind the track, making a perfect copy about 0.2 second later. Yet it is often observed that with periodic signals this lag reduces to zero, and that the operator may actually lead the signal rather than lag it (Pew, Duffendach, and Fensch, 1967) (see Figure 11).

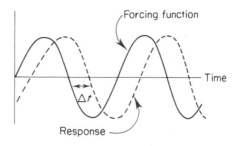

Figure 11. Perfect tracking of sine wave except for delay Δt.

PREDICTION, STRATEGIES, AND SKILL

Such behaviour suggests that the human operator does not merely compensate or copy the movements of targets, acting as a passive transmission channel, but that he builds an internal model of the properties of the input, and can use that model to generate the required output ahead of the occurrence of the input in such a way as to compensate for the reaction time or transmission delay. The S–R model is thus seen to be even less appropriate for skills, since the operator is now working in an R–S mode, generating a response which provides him (later) with an appropriate stimulus (the reduction of the error to zero or matching the position of a target). He may do this quite unawares, since as Pew (1974a) has shown, the performance on a segment of track which repeatedly occurs in an otherwise random track will gradually improve, even though performance on the rest of the track does not, and the operator does not realize that part of the track repeats.

The importance of such predictive behaviour is a main theme of the stimulating book by Kelley (1968) which was mentioned earlier (a book which deserves to be much better known by psychologists than it is). Kelley argues forcefully that the whole aim of control and all behaviour associated with it is not to compensate for the present state of affairs, for present or past error, but is directed towards control of the future state of the system.

Prediction by definition implies open loop performance, and we saw earlier that open-loop systems are poor controllers. How then can we say that the skilled but not the novice operator goes open loop? The critical point in explaining this is that it is safe to go open loop when one is certain what is about to happen, and can therefore respond in advance. And to respond in advance is to predict, which in turn implies the possession of a temporal and spatial model of the environment in which the skill is being exercised. McRuer and Krendel (1974) have argued for such a picture of skill acquisition, calling it the 'Successive Organization of Perception' model. At the start of practice the

the operator is a CLNF system, lagging the error and compensating. But while performng in the compensatory mode he begins to learn the statistics both of the input and of the effects created by his response, and begins to pursue the target rather than compensating for its motion. Finally the operator comes to have a full set of 'programs' which can be run off at suitable moments open loop when the motions of the target allow the operator to predict what is about to happen, with only occasional reversions to CLNF when gross maladjustments cause the error to rise (see Figure 12). Moray (1976) has suggested that it

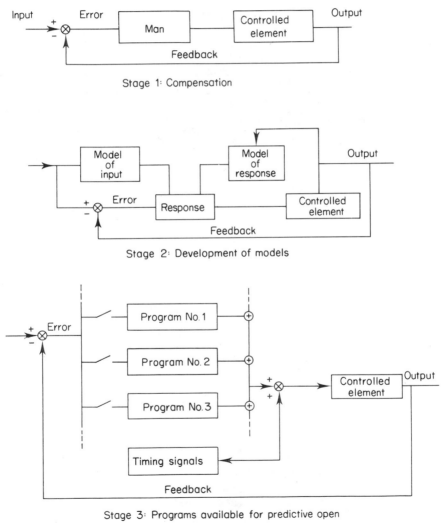

Stage 1: Compensation

Stage 2: Development of models

Stage 3: Programs available for predictive open loop response

Figure 12. Development of skilled behaviour. After McRuer and Krendel, 1974.

is this ability to go open loop, and therefore save the processing required to act as a transmitter, which makes the human operator's channel capacity appear to be infinite in highly practised operators.

The ability to form models of the environment and to incorporate them in the control loop gives the human operator his characteristic adaptability, and is another way in which he differs from classical CLNF linear systems. The richness of the information available to him and the way in which the information can be incorporated has been well summarized by Young (1969) (see Figure 13).

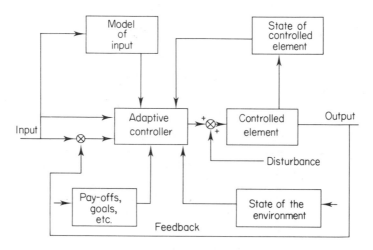

Figure 13. Sources of information for the human viewed as adaptive controller with the ability to form models. After Young (1969).

The only problem about the concept of the 'internal model', a concept which is coming into increasing vogue among those working with complex man–machine systems such as vehicles and process control systems, is that it is rather vague, and opens the door to the ability to explain any observed behaviour by appealing to the fact that the operator has the wrong model. Since the models cannot be observed directly, this is a temptation, and it is desirable to have some way of operationalizing the concept of model. One way is to identify the notion of a model with the notion of a transfer function, and make the strong requirement that the operator must be able to pick an appropriate function 'at will' to compensate for changes in other elements in the loop. If he can exactly 'equalize' changes in the controlled element transfer function by choosing an appropriate transfer function of his own, this would be one sense in which a precise meaning could be given to the idea of an 'internal model'. In fact, it seems that humans can indeed do this, as Table 2 shows.

Table 2. Human operator transfer functions as a function of controlled element transfer functions (after McRuer and Krendel, 1974).

Controlled element transfer function	Human transfer function		Combined transfer function
K_p	• $K_h e^{-\tau s}/s$	=	$K_c e^{-\tau s}/s$
k_p/s	• $K_h e^{-\tau s}$	=	$K_c e^{-\tau s}/s$
K_p/s^2	• $K_h s\, e^{-\tau s}$	=	$K_c e^{-\tau s}/s$
$K_p/s(s+a)$	• $K_h(s+a)e^{-\tau s}$	=	$K_c e^{-\tau s}/s$

K_p = controlled element gain, K_h = human operator gain, K_c = gain of combination; $e^{-\tau s}$ represents a delay, $1/s$ an integration.

The choice of an appropriate model for a situation is of course itself a kind of skill, but a cognitive, rather than a perceptual-motor skill. It is equivalent to changing the parameters of a system rather than changing the value of a variable within the system. It might perhaps be possible to think of such an ability as the property of a higher order control system which detects the failure of a loop at a lower level to compensate for the existing state of affairs, and therefore alters the properties of the loop, rather than altering the output of the controlled element. As such it cannot be regarded as a classical CLNF system, even though it tends to eliminate error.

(The reader will note a certain disagreement between this chapter and Hammerton's highly critical attitude to human operator transfer function models in Chapter 8. My attitude can be summarized as follows. Although Hammerton is right to draw attention to the assumptions of linearity, its large number of parameters, etc., the fact remains that as an heuristic, both for understanding the human and for practical design of man-machine systems, the approach is known to be valuable, even if not true. See the remarks earlier in the chapter about boundary conditions for theories.)

This makes a convenient point at which to refer to some modern developments in control theory, specifically those concerned with optimal control theory. The classical system is in one sense rather passive, since all it does is to pass signals round the loop, with (usually) no non-linear processing in the feedback path, and certainly no extensive computation on the signals in that path. However, in optimal control theory such is no longer the case (Gelb, 1974). Instead the feedback loop contains two computational elements, a Kalman filter and an optimal controller. The first of these extracts statistical parameters of the states of all the variables in the system, and keeps a running estimate of those statistics. From them an estimate (prediction) can be made of the immediate future state of the variables, and this information is made available to the optimal controller. This in turn uses the prediction to generate control actions designed to achieve the specified outcome of control in an optimal manner. Where the desired criterion is one that is computationally tractable, such as the minimization of mean-squared error, very precise control can be achieved. Remarkable similarity can often be observed between optimal control systems and human operators (Veldhuyzen and Stassen, 1976).

The Kalman filter is an internal model, and the system which possesses it learns. But notice that learning is not asymptotic but dynamic. What is learnt is not a particlar response at which the system becomes better and better. Rather the system constantly changes its model on the basis of recent information, discounting learning progressively as the time at which it occurred moves into the distant past. The success of such systems might make us change the way in which we regard humans and other animals when learning. Asymptotic learning is not advantageous in a dynamic environment, and any learning theory which does not emphasize the continuous unlearning and relearning and new learning which takes place in organisms which are in a dynamic relation with their environment is unlikely to be very realistic as a model for 'real life' learning. The success of optimal control lies in the fact that it includes a predictive model in the CLNF pathways. A flow chart of such a system and an example of its performance are shown in Figures 14 and 15.

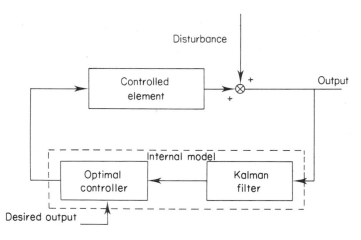

Figure 14. Optimal control theory loop.

The properties of optimal control systems have recently been the subject of a special tutorial issue of the journal *Human Factors* (1976, 1977).

Such systems are a long way from the simple negative feedback system with which we began this discussion. But even so, despite the greater sophistication of the modern theory the fundamental use of feedback to reduce error is the same. Indeed it *must* be the case that CLNF systems of one kind or another are

Course by human helmsman

Course by model

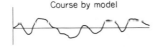

Helm movements of human

Helm movements of model

Figure 15. Examples of behaviour by human and optimal controller. From Veldhuyzen and Stassen (1976).

valid as models for skilled operators who are elements in a man–machine system control environment. Any system faced with a dynamic input and subject to random disturbances and which is required to minimize error *must* use negative feedback. The only real question is what kind of CLNF best fits the properties of the human operator as an element of the loop.

PROBLEMS OF MEASUREMENT

We may leave this chapter with a brief look at a fundamental but very difficult problem (it is discussed in more detail by Hammerton in Chapter 8). How should one measure the performance of such a system? Early workers who used equipment such as pursuit rotors used time-on-target as the measure. But, for many reasons, this is a singularly bad one. Nowadays it is common to use mean-squared error or integrated absolute error. Poulton (1974) discusses the question at length. The problem is most readily seen if we redraw Figure 11 using a random signal rather than a sine wave (Figure 16).

Obviously time-on-target is useless, since the output is almost a perfect copy of the input except that it is delayed in time. Similarly, mean-squared error or integrated error will not do justice to the performance. Shannon information transmission (see Chapter 5) will disregard the delay and assess the extent that the input can be reconstructed from the output. Cross-correlation can estimate

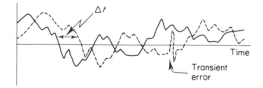

Figure 16. Almost perfect tracking of random forcing function with delay.

both the similarity of the input to the output and also estimate the delay, and Bode plot analysis will show what frequencies are present in the output and their phase and gain relations to those in the input. But all this last group require very long samples if they are to be statistically good estimates, and such long-term averaging will then conceal transients of quite large magnitude such as the one shown about two-thirds of the way along Figure 16. Those measures which reveal transients are not good at representing overall performance, and vice versa. At present there is no general advice that can be given, and perhaps the investigator would be advised to choose whatever measure seems most likely to reveal the features of the performance which are most relevant to his interest, rather than feeling that there is any one best measure. Probably the most comprehensive manual on methods of analysis is that by Sheridan and Ferrell (1974).

Until recently it would have been fair to conclude such a chapter as this by pointing out the great practical importance of feedback control for the understanding of man–machine systems. But it must now be said that the situation is changing. Almost all of the situations in which man was the controller of complex systems, such as aircraft, ship steering, process control, and power station control have now been automated to some extent. This is bound to be even more true in the next ten years with the advent and use of microprocessors. Man's task will be predominantly a monitor, and not a controller, and feedback theory of skill in such applied settings will become less relevant for normal functioning. It may, however, become even more important in understanding how man is to intervene when things go wrong; when he must take over in emergencies the control of a system which he has not been controlling, and where, because of the rarity of the intervention required, he will not be well practised, nor have a good internal model. Another field in which CLNF theory will remain of great importance is in the design of prosthetics (see Chapter 10). And overall, it will remain true that to regard man as a user of skills rather than as a learner of responses will remain the more fruitful attitude. As Wiener (1948), the founder of cybernetics, stated long ago: 'The central nervous system no longer appears as a self-contained organ, receiving inputs from the senses and discharging into the muscles. On the contrary, some of its most characteristic activities are explicable only as circular processes, emerging from the nervous systems into the muscles and re-entering the nervous system through the sense organs.'

As a basic description of human action that statement still remains true.

SUMMARY

The term 'feedback' is used very widely in psychology in a loose and qualitative way. Originally it had a precise, quantitative meaning in control theory, and if the control of continuous skilled movements is to be understood quantitatively it is necessary to use the original quantitative theory of feedback systems.

Studying man as a closed-loop negative feedback system emphasizes the poverty of S–R descriptions of human behaviour and instead emphasizes the purposive, goal-seeking character of that behaviour.

For many skills classical control theory can give a rather complete account of the nature and limitation of human skilled performance. Where it fails improvements are possible using optimal control theory. Furthermore, the nature of the failure of quantitative models draws attention to the way in which skill acquisition is related to the acquisition by the human operator of internal models of the environment and their use for prediction.

Examples of behaviour controlled by feedback in the strict sense are widespread in animal behaviour, although in general the difficulties of measurement have seldom been explicitly faced by psychologists in using feedback theory to describe them.

ACKNOWLEDGEMENTS

This chapter was written during sabbatical leave, while the author was at the Massachusetts Institute of Technology, partly supported by grants N00014-77-C-0256 and IST78-06749. My thanks are due to Professor T. Sheridan for making the visit possible.

Human Skills
Edited by D. Holding
©1981 John Wiley & Sons Ltd.

Chapter 3

Motor Programs

Jeffery J. Summers

Skilled performance often requires the organization of highly refined patterns of movements in relation to some specific goal. The role of the learner in such skills is to first combine the appropriate movements into the correct sequence or order. Once this has been achieved the correct temporal structuring or patterning of the movements must be acquired. Each submovement must be placed into the appropriate temporal structure and occur at the appropriate moment in time in relation to the other submovements making up the skill.

In the initial stages of skill learning performance is characterized by slow, jerky movements because of the continuous necessity to use feedback. The unskilled person will make a movement, visually observe the consequences of that movement, make another movement, re-evaluate the results, and so on. With practice, however, the sequencing and timing of movements seem to shift from direct visual control to an internal form of control. As a result performance appears to be rapid and coordinated.

Identifying the mechanisms by which the central nervous system produces a coordinated sequence of movements is clearly an important factor in understanding skilled performance. Historically, two major theoretical positions have been adopted to explain the control of highly practised movements. The first, a closed-loop system, emphasizes the role of sensory feedback in movements, as discussed in Chapter 2. The other stresses open-loop control and argues that the sequence of movements becomes stored in memory and can be executed without constant reference to feedback. An early closed-loop form of learning theory suggested that as practice progresses control of a series of movements passes from visual to kinaesthetic control. By means of an associative or conditioning process the kinaesthetic feedback from one segment of a movement series was thought to elicit a succeeding movement. Under such a scheme afferent impulses from the various joint, cutaneous, and stretch receptors in a moving limb are necessary for the execution of sequences of movements.

The most recent detailed application of closed-loop notions to the realm of motor behaviour has been made by Adams (1971, 1976). He proposes that at the base of all motor performance is a comparison between a memory of movement (perceptual trace) and kinaesthetic feedback from an ongoing response, with any resulting error signal serving as the stimulus for subsequent corrective movement. The perceptual trace is formed from the past experience with feedback from earlier responses and comes to represent the sensory consequences of the limb being correctly moved.

In contrast, open-loop theories of motor control stress the sequencing and timing aspects of skills, which they regard as being governed by central motor programs. Practice on a skill results in the acquisition, by the higher centres of the central nervous system, of a neuromotor program that contains all the information necessary for movement patterning. Thus there is 'a set of muscle commands that are structured before a movement sequence begins' (Keele, 1968, p.387). Furthermore, once the program is initiated the movement sequence is smoothly and precisely executed without requiring peripheral feedback from prior movements to elicit succeeding movements. This view does not deny the presence of feedback in almost all movements, but suggests that such feedback is usually redundant, since the motor program already contains the information necessary for movement execution.

The major difference between the two theories, therefore, is in the role of feedback in the control of skilled performance. In closed-loop theory peripheral feedback is essential to performance, while such feedback is not necessary in open-loop control.

Clearly, for motor program control to be a tenable alternative to closed-loop control it is necessary to show that (a) movement can occur in the absence of feedback, (b) that for some movements, even though feedback is present it is not used, and (c) that movements can be structured prior to the onset of movement rather than as the movement progresses. Let us now turn to a brief consideration of the evidence relating to the three criteria of programmed control.

MOTOR PROGRAM CONTROL

Movement in the absence of feedback

The motor program concept can be considered to have its empirical origins in the work of Lashley (1917), with a patient deprived of sensation as a result of a gunshot wound to the spinal cord. The patient was capable of reproducing active movements in the absence of kinaesthetic feedback from the affected limb. This finding led Lashley to propose that such movement was controlled centrally as there was no peripheral information to guide the movement.

Further evidence in support of open-loop control comes from studies that surgically eliminated kinaesthetic feedback in animals. These studies have shown that movements can be maintained following feedback removal. For example, Wilson (1961) severed the nerves that return feedback from wingbeats in the locust. Although the rate of beating slowed, the beat pattern was largely maintained, suggesting the existence of a motor program controlling wing movements. Similar data have been reported by Nottebohm (1970) with bird songs and by Fentress (1973) with grooming behaviours in mice.

However, the motor programs evident in locusts, birds, and mice are probably innate and do not provide evidence that learned acts can be programmed. Perhaps the strongest support for the existence of motor programs comes from experiments that surgically removed all kinaesthetic feedback from the limbs of monkeys. Early studies using this deafferentation technique reported lasting and severe impairment in voluntary movement (Mott and Sherrington, 1895; Twitchell, 1954). However, more recent work by Taub and his colleagues (see Taub, Heitmann, and Barro, 1977 for a review) has revealed that following post-operative recovery monkeys exhibit the ability to make use of the affected extremities for a wide variety of purposes. For example, the animals can use the limbs effectively for walking and climbing even when blindfolded (Taub and Berman, 1968). Furthermore, normal feedback is not required for the development of the sequence of movements involved in walking. Infant monkeys learned to walk despite blinding and deafferentation shortly after birth (Taub, Perrella, and Barro, 1973).

There are a number of problems with interpreting the deafferentation studies as convincing evidence of the existence of motor programs. Bossom and Ommaya (1968) have criticized the surgical techniques used in such studies, and suggest the possibility that some afferent fibres might have remained intact. Another issue that has been raised by Bossom (1974) relates to the loss of elegance in movement control following deafferentation. Although monkeys are able to produce coordinated sequences of movements relatively quickly after the operation, such movements are never quite 'normal'. Movements generally appear clumsy with a reduction in fine control and precise movement, particularly of the fingers. It may be, therefore, that skills involving gross rhythmic movements, such as walking, can be controlled without feedback, while skills involving fine manipulative movements are more dependent on feedback (Keele and Summers, 1976).

In spite of the above reservations in accepting the deafferentation work as providing strong support for the motor program concept, these studies do provide convincing evidence that skilled movements are possible without kinaesthetic feedback.

The investigation of movement control in humans without feedback is very difficult because of problems in manipulating kinaesthetic feedback without causing permanent neural damage. One potentially useful technique is the application of a pressure cuff on the upper arm to block sensory information from that part of the arm below the cuff. Laszlo (1966, 1967) claimed that with the cuff there is a loss of kinaesthetic sensation prior to any motor loss. Performance on both simple (e.g. finger tapping) and complex tasks (e.g. writing letters) was shown to be disrupted by this procedure (see Glencross, 1977, for a review). Unfortunately, three recent studies (Kelso and Stelmach, 1974; Kelso, Wallace, Stelmach, and Weitz, 1975; Glencross and Oldfield, 1975) have shown extensive efferent impairment accompanying the loss of kinaesthetic sensation. Consequently, the performance decrements following the cuff application may not be solely due to the loss of feedback.

Another potential source of information regarding the effects of kinaesthetic loss in humans comes from people who have had the sensory nerve fibres entering the spinal cord cut to reduce pain or relieve spasticity. Unfortunately, there are few studies reporting the consequences of such an operation for movement. Phillips (1969) reported a study by Foerster in which subjects with deafferentation of arms and hands were able to move them as directed, even without vision. However, as with monkeys there was a reduction in fine control of the fingers.

The general conclusion that can be made from the literature on deafferentation is that at least some simple movements can be made in the absence of peripheral feedback. There is more evidence for motor program control of gross limb movements and highly practised sequential skills than for skills involving fine motor control.

Feedback redundancy

Proponents of motor program control argue that feedback processing is too slow to account for the high rate of movement shown in some skilled performance, such as piano playing (Lashley, 1951), typing (Shaffer, 1976, 1978) and speech production (Lenneberg, 1967). In many skills the interval between successive movements is often less than 100msec, yet the time to react to kinaesthetic feedback has been shown to be apparently 100msec or greater (see Glencross, 1977, for a review). Thus, because of the speed of such movements, response-produced feedback would be out of phase with the ongoing movement. Some support for this argument comes from a series of experiments conducted by Glencross (1973, 1974, 1975). Electromyography and motion photography were used in a detailed analysis of a repetitive speed skill, hand cranking. The results suggested that as the speed of cranking was increased, at least one cycle (and possibly two or three cycles) of movements was controlled by motor program.

Similar conclusions have been drawn in studies using discrete movements that are very fast or 'ballistic'. For example, Schmidt and Russell (1972) investigated the relationships between the movement time (MT) of a response and the degree of preprogramming developed. It was shown in a discrete timing task that regardless of movement velocity, the shorter the MT the greater the programming, as indicated by an index of preprogramming (Schmidt, 1972), based on the correlation between the starting time and the time of finishing a response. If a movement is totally programmed (i.e. unmodifiable by feedback) then the two measures should be highly correlated. As the feedback involvement in the movement increases the correlation should decrease. Movements which took 150sec or less to make were completely preprogrammed while responses taking longer than 0.750sec involved much less preprogramming and more use of feedback (see also Roy and Marteniuk, 1974).

The study of eye movements provides further evidence of open-loop control. The most common form of eye movement is called the 'saccade', which is a rapid and abrupt jump made by the eye as it moves from one fixation to another. Such saccadic movements take between 10 and 70msec to complete, depending on the amplitude. The duration of the saccade suggests that the individual movements cannot be monitored by sensory feedback, although successive movements are directed towards externally cued targets (see Festinger and Canon, 1965, for a review).

Some reservations must be made, however, regarding the assumption that kinaesthetic processing times are too slow to account for the control of fast or ballistic movements. Recently, Evarts and Tanji (1974) reported that monkeys can make use of kinaesthetic feedback in about 40 or 50msec to correct a learned arm movement. The monkeys were taught to move a handle back to a correct position after it had been mechanically displaced and kinaesthetic processing time was measured by recording the electrical discharge from the muscles.

Clearly, the issue of changes in feedback use that occur with learning is where closed-loop and open-loop formulations are most sharply divided. Adams (1971, 1976) predicts an increased role of feedback as a function of practice, whereas open-loop theory sees learning as involving a decrease in the use of feedback with practice, as control shifts to a motor program.

The research evidence showing shifts from feedback control to motor program control is rather meagre, but one study does suggest that such a process occurs. Pew (1966) used a continuous tracking task in which subjects attempted to keep a dot, which moved across a screen, centred on a line. The subject could control the continually moving dot by pressing one of two keys with his index fingers. Pressing one key accelerated the dot to the left; pressing the other accelerated the dot to the right. Thus, centring the dot required alternate tapping of the two keys. Early in practice, the subjects used visual feedback to guide their performance in that they observed the consequences of each tap before making another tap. This closed-loop control resulted in slow, jerky performance. After several weeks of practice, however, it appeared that some subjects were developing a motor program. These subjects exhibited a very rapid and regular pattern of responding in which there was a gradual drift of the dot from the target and then a single correction to bring it back on target (see Figure 17, Subject A). The movement series did not appear to be under visual control but visual feedback was used periodically to effect a correction. Other subjects seemed to incorporate a correction strategy into their organization. When the dot began to drift off target the pattern of responding was modified so that one button was held down slightly longer than the other for a series of responses, causing the dot to slowly move back towards the centre. In this case feedback was used to modify the motor program controlling the ongoing sequence of responses (see Figure 17, Subject B).

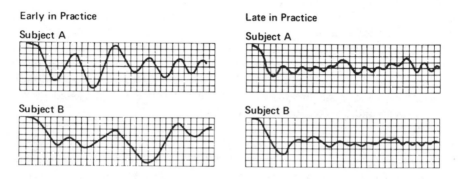

Early in Practice   Late in Practice

Subject A   Subject A

Subject B   Subject B

Figure 17. Position of a dot about a centre position as controlled by two different subjects early and late in practice. The vertical axis indicates dot position and the horizontal axis indicates time. Source: Modified from Pew (1966, p.768). © 1966 by the American Psychological Association. Reprinted by permission of the author and the American Psychological Association.

Schmidt and McCabe (1976) showed a similar reduction in the use of feedback in a discrete timing task. Subjects watched a 0.01 sec timer and attempted to knock over a barrier at the moment the clock reached 2.0 sec. The degree of feedback involvement was measured by the index of preprogramming (Schmidt, 1972) computed for each of five days of practice. The index showed a linear increase with practice, suggesting decreased use of feedback to correct the movement while in progress and increased reliance upon motor program control.

Preprogramming of responses

So far I have concentrated on evidence supporting the notion that feedback is not necessary for control of some types of movements. A different approach to the assessment of programmed control focuses on the idea of organizing the motor command sequence prior to the onset of the movement, and considers the possibility that such organization may take measurable time. The time required for programming has been investigated in experiments which measure reaction time prior to the beginning of the response as a function of the nature of the response to be made. Changes in reaction time as a function of response parameters are interpreted as reflecting changes in the time required to generate the appropriate motor program. It is argued that the relationship between reaction time and response parameters should be restricted to movements that are programmed in advance and would not be observed for feedback-controlled movements. Consistent with this suggestion is the finding by Klapp (1975) that choice reaction time increased with the required accuracy of short, visually aimed movements directed towards a target. This result was restricted to short, and apparently programmed, movements, with no effect for longer feedback-dependent movements.

One of the predictions from the preprogramming concept is that there should be a longer reaction latency for a complicated movement than for a simpler movement since a more comprehensive program would be required for the complex response. A number of studies have reported increases in reaction time with increases in movement complexity. Programming time has been shown to increase with the physical length of movements, the temporal duration of movements, the number of movements required, and the complexity of the timing requirements for the components of a movement (see Kerr, 1978a; Klapp, 1978 for a review). For example, the time to initiate the first word in a pre-cued string of words to be pronounced (i.e. Monday, or Monday–Tuesday, or Monday–Tuesday–Wednesday) increases with the number of words to be uttered (Sternberg, Monsell, Knoll, and Wright, 1978).

There are a number of problems in this area, such as in the use of simple or choice reaction time paradigms, and the extent to which the external task parameters usually manipulated (i.e. movement extent, direction) are the same as those used by the central nervous system in organizing a movement (Kerr, 1978; Marteniuk and Mackenzie, in press). However, the studies do lend some support to the concept of preprogramming inherent in motor program theory. Klapp (1976) postulated that programming time may reflect the conversion of abstract representations of responses in long-term memory into some other form, a form which can control the muscles. In particular, recent evidence (Klapp and Greim, 1979; Rosenbaum, in press) suggests that the organization of the timing aspect of a response is the critical determinant of initiation time.

Reflexes as motor program subroutines

Proponents of the concept of a motor program often appeal to triggered-off motor sequences in lower animals which imply a non-adaptive rigid structure to the resultant program. Although a 'built-in' automatic series of movements is rarely observed in man, Easton (1972, 1978) suggests that such stereotyped fragments of motion do exist in the form of inherent reflex patterns. The existence of such reflex patterns in normal human motor movements has been shown by a number of investigators (i.e. Fukuda, 1961; Hellebrandt, Houtz, Partridge, and Walters, 1956). For example, the tonic neck and labyrinthine reflexes have been identified in a number of activities including soccer, baseball, and judo (Fukuda, 1961). Furthermore, there is now good evidence that locomotion, at least in cats and dogs, is controlled at the spinal cord level with little if any influence from higher centres (see Grillner, 1975; Shik and Orlovski, 1976; Stein, 1978 for details). Easton (1972, 1978) suggests that reflex patterns serve as subroutines of motor programs and provide the building blocks from which voluntary movements may be constructed. Recent studies (see Hayes and Marteniuk, 1976 for a review) have clearly shown that reflexes are capable of being chained into complex movement patterns, modified according to the 'intent' of the subject, and capable of being appropriately conditioned. To produce a sequence of movements the central nervous system connects sets of neurons into 'coordinative structures' which when activated result in a patterned movement (Easton, 1978).

In this section I have reviewed some of the evidence supporting the notion that movement may occur as the result of centrally stored neural commands which are 'structured before the movement begins and allows the entire movement to be carried out uninfluenced by peripheral feedback' (Keele, 1968, p.387). The main conclusion that can be drawn from this review is that at least some skills appear to be under motor program control. This does not mean, however, that in such skills feedback is not present. In fact, recent theories of movement control (i.e. Glencross, 1977; Keele and Summers, 1976) have emphasized the interaction between program and feedback in skill development and maintenance. Let us now turn, therefore, to a discussion of the role of feedback in motor program theory.

ROLE OF FEEDBACK

Keele (1973) has outlined four functions of feedback in motor program theory: (a) feedback provides information relevant to the initial conditions; (b) feedback is used as a program monitor; (c) feedback is used to make fine adjustments; and (d) feedback is used in the development of motor programs.

Initial conditions

Prior to movement execution information is needed regarding the position of the body and limbs in space and the state of the environment. Visual and auditory information will allow an individual to organize an appropriate motor program to meet the existing environmental conditions. Kinaesthetic feedback will provide information regarding any large adjustments in body orientation needed to facilitate the execution of the intended movement. Easton (1978), however, has argued that minor adjustments of the body musculature (i.e. to maintain balance during the forthcoming movement) are preprogrammed and are not the direct result of kinaesthetic feedback produced by the standing posture (see section on spinal tuning).

Program monitor

It has previously been argued that practice on a skill results in the development of a motor program, which allows performance to become relatively automatic requiring minimal conscious attention. Highly skilled performers, however, probably use both motor programs and feedback to control and correct their movements. Although most of the skill would be under program control, it is likely that visual and kinaesthetic feedback is used continually to monitor the movement. As long as any discrepancy between the motor program and the actual position of the limbs (as determined by feedback) is within certain tolerance limits then performance continues under program control. However, if the comparison between the motor program and feedback informs the person that relatively gross errors are being made then program modification is necessary. This form of control, in which feedback is used periodically to correct gross errors in performance, is similar to that adopted by some subjects in Pew's (1966) study discussed previously. Another example can be seen in the situation in which a person trips while walking. Normally, walking would be carried out under motor program control. However, when a person unexpectedly trips then a discrepancy arises between the neural commands to place the foot in a certain position and the kinaesthetic feedback, indicating that the foot is in another position. To avoid falling the person must consciously attend to his movements and make a rapid correction to the motor program.

The comparison process between the program and feedback is seen to involve the notion of corollary discharge or efference copy (Von Holst, 1954). It is postulated that when movement commands are sent out to the muscles, the commands are accompanied by other kinds of information that prepares the system for the intended motor act or for the receipt of sensory information (Kelso, 1977b; Schmidt, 1976a). Thus, before the movement begins the expected sensory consequences (i.e. kinaesthetic, visual, and auditory) are generated and fed forward to be compared with the incoming response-produced feedback in order to detect any error in the movement. This comparison process will not only inform the individual whether the movement chosen was executed correctly but will also provide information as to the effectiveness of the selected movement in achieving the desired goal. For example, a tennis player may execute a smash shot perfectly, but the ball lands way out of court. The generation of expected sensory consequences may also be necessary to inform the individual that the actual feedback produced is the result of executing a motor program (active movement), rather than a result of the limbs being moved by an external source (passive movement).

Feedback and fine motor control

When the environment in which a skill is performed is very stable or predictable, it is likely that the skill can be largely maintained by motor program. Poulton (1957b) has termed such skills as 'closed skills', for example, gymnastics, bowling, and golf. In many human skills, however, the conditions under which the skill is performed are continually changing and the skill itself may be imperfectly executed so that error constantly arises. These are termed 'open skills' and would include such sports activities as basketball, tennis, and soccer. In these activities feedback is essential for monitoring the movement to ensure that performance is progressing as planned and for updating or changing programs as required (Pew, 1974a).

We have previously discussed how feedback may be used periodically to correct gross errors in responding. However, it has been suggested (Gibbs, 1970) that an organism can deal with small but unexpected changes in the environment without reverting to this slow and inefficient closed-loop mode of control. In addition to the feedback loop from the limbs to the brain, there is a reflexive feedback loop between stretch receptors embedded in the muscles (muscle spindles) and the main muscles. This lower level of control is a very rapid (about 50 msec), subconscious and automatic process. Its function is to correct small, unexpected discrepancies between intended movement and actual movement. Recent theories of motor control (i.e. Granit, 1975) propose that the motor program not only sends commands to the main muscles causing them to contract or relax, but also sends a 'copy' of each command to the receptor muscles in the muscles spindles. Through the servo-action of the muscle spindles, the activity between the main muscles and muscle spindles is coordinated, so that small, unexpected errors in the movement pattern are rapidly detected and corrected via spindle-initiated feedback loops (see Keele and Summers, 1976 for a detailed discussion of this mechanism).

The human thus appears to have at least two levels at which movement can be controlled. At the highest level are voluntary decisions based on a comparison in the brain between feedback from the actual movement and the expected feedback from the intended movement. This system is used to detect gross errors in performance or as Schmidt (1976a) has defined them 'errors in response selection'. Such errors arise when something in the environment informs the individual that the movement selected was inappropriate. For example, the tennis player may have swung the racket too early to contact the ball correctly. The correction of these large errors involve the long feedback loops from the various sensory receptors to the brain and are limited by reaction times of about 100 to 260 msec. As a result the intended movement is often carried out as planned, even though the feedback might indicate that it is going to be incorrect. To correct an error of this type would usually require the individual to change the goal of the movement such as swinging the racket in a different place.

At the same time a lower level of control is operating involving spinal level feedback mechanisms. This system acts to smooth out movement by correcting small, unexpected disturbances to the intended movement that occur in the time interval between successive motor commands from the higher level of control. These errors in response execution (Schmidt, 1976a) can be detected and corrected very quickly in contrast to the long delays required to change the goal of the movement.

This view of motor control suggests that feedback is essential for all types of movement. Although the motor program may generate all the necessary information required by the main muscles and muscle spindles to achieve a certain goal, feedback is involved in successfully attaining that goal. However, if the goal of a movement needs to be changed, the original motor program must continue to run for at least one reaction time before it can be changed to achieve the new goal. Meanwhile, the lower level control mechanism will ensure that the original program will be carried out as planned. This concept has led Schmidt (1976a, p.59) to redefine the motor program as a set of prestructured motor commands that 'when activated, result in movement oriented toward a given goal, with these movements being unaffected by peripheral feedback indicating that the goal should be changed'.

Motor program acquisition

Keele (1973) and Keele and Summers (1976) have argued that feedback is essential for the development of a motor program. The initial stage in the learning of a motor skill is seen as involving the development in the learner of a template or model of how the feedback should appear if the skill is performed correctly. At the beginning of the learning process the individual will probably use an external model to guide performance. For example, watching another person perform the desired skill would provide an external model against which the feedback from the learner's own movements can be compared. Eventually, however, it is likely that a permanent representation of the model becomes stored in memory. Evidence for the existence of such internal models has come from studies on the development of bird song (see Keele and Summers, 1976 for a review). A series of movements is then produced by a motor program via motor commands to the muscles. The kinaesthetic and exteroceptive feedback (i.e. vision and audition) arising from these movements is matched to the template (the expected sensory consequences) and any resultant error leads to a modification of the motor program. In time the motor program will produce an appropriate spatial–temporal pattern of movements, and with further practice on the skill the program will become stabilized. The process of motor program development is illustrated in Figure 18. Once the motor program has been established performance can be maintained by a close interaction between program and feedback in the manner previously described.

This model of skill learning is similar in many respects to closed-loop accounts of skill development (Adams, 1971). In closed-loop theory, feedback is also compared to a template of expected feedback established during training and any discrepancies between current feedback and the template are the basis for corrections.

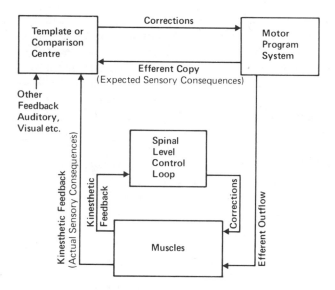

Figure 18. A model of skill learning and a mechanism for the detection and correction of errors. Source: Modified from Keele and Summers (1976, p.122). Reprinted by permission of Academic Press Inc.

THE SCHEMA CONCEPT

There are two inherent problems with both the traditional open-loop and closed-loop theories of movement control. The first is concerned with the amount of material that must be stored by the central nervous system. Basic to the operation of both programmed and closed-loop control modes is the assumption that stored in memory is some representation of past successful responses. For open-loop control the representation is of the motor commands needed to produce a certain movement. Thus, for every response a subject makes, there must be a separate motor program that controls it. In closed-loop theory the representation is of the feedback information which has arisen from successful responses which provide a reference of correctness against which current feedback must be compared. Again this implies that there must be a reference of correctness for every movement we wish to make, leading to a storage problem.

A further problem for any model of perceptual-motor performance is to account for the tremendous flexibility evident in human skill. Human skills are seldom performed in exactly the same way twice. A movement can be small or large, such as signing your name on paper or on a blackboard; there may also be differences in speed, exact sequencing, orientation, etc. Even the same movements performed under identical environmental conditions have been shown by cinematographic analysis to result in slightly different movement patterns (Higgins and Spaeth, 1972). It is apparent that skilled individuals could not achieve the tremendous number of different movements required in a complex game just through the use of a finite store of fixed motor programs or references of correctness. Under either scheme it would be impossible for an individual to produce movements that have never been performed previously. Furthermore, it is difficult to see how a motor program or reference of correctness is acquired in the first place since no situation ever repeats itself.

Recent theories of movement control (Pew, 1974a; Schmidt, 1975a, 1976a) have attempted to deal with the problem of skill variation by proposing a schema-like process operating in motor program representation. The schema memory is seen as containing the general characteristics about a movement that then must be organized to meet the specific environmental demands and the goal required by the performer. A movement sequence is therefore represented rather generally, perhaps in terms of spatial patterns which are applicable to a large range of specific movements with respect to a particular goal. If, for example, a tennis player wishes to make a forehand stroke, a particular movement pattern (called a schema instance) will be selected from the generalized schema for movements of this type. The movement pattern chosen will depend on the environmental conditions (i.e. the position of the ball, wind conditions, etc.) and the goal of the movement (i.e. where to place the ball). Once the schema instance has been selected from the schema the next stage is the translation of the stored program into a temporal string of motor commands. Depending on the context of the particular situation, various movement parameters specifying such elements as the speed of the movement, the forces involved and so on are applied to the program to generate a particular sequence of movement. Finally, this string of motor commands activates the appropriate muscles to produce a spatial–temporal pattern of movement. A further consequence of the selection of the schema instance is that a set of expected feedback consequences (the template) that should arise if the skill is performed correctly is also generated. A comparison between the intended movement (the template) and the actual movement (feedback) allows for closed-loop control of movement. Schmidt has further elaborated the concept of a schema in motor control and suggests how the movement parameters (response specifications) and expected sensory consequences are generated (see Schmidt, 1975a, 1976a for details).

There are many advantages of the schema theory over traditional open-loop and closed-loop models. There is no necessity for a separate motor program or reference of correctness to be stored for each movement that a person makes. By applying various response specifications to a generalized motor program a large number of movements can be generated from this abstract representation. In this way the tremendous flexibility evident in human skills can be achieved. Furthermore, the model emphasises the interaction between program and feedback in the control of movement.

There is, however, little strong experimental evidence for the existence of generalized motor programs. Pew (1974b) reports a study in which subjects were required to track a target that moved smoothly across a screen wtih an arm-controlled target follower. A trial lasted 1 min, in which the first and last 20 sec differed on each trial, but the middle segment was always the same. As a function of practice, performance on all three segments improved. However, the performance advantage of the middle segment gradually increased in comparison with performance on the first and last segments. After subjects had practised the task for eleven days, a block of trials was run in which the repeated segment was exactly inverted. Whenever the subject had to move to the right before, now he had to move to the left and vice versa. Under this condition subjects performed significantly better on the inverted repeated segment than the average of the beginning and ending segments, but significantly worse than they were performing on the preceding trials with the repeated segment. If subjects had been learning a very specific sequence of motor commands for the repeated sequence, then one might expect that reversing the signal would make performance on that segment worse than on the random segments. Rather, subjects seemed to have acquired more abstract information about the sequence of movements that appeared to generalize, at least to some extent, to corresponding patterns symmetrically reversed.

In another study Armstrong (1970b) used various forms of concurrent feedback to teach a subject to execute a particular irregular movement pattern from memory. It was found that all concurrent feedback groups performed better than a control group receiving only terminal feedback during practice. However, the experimental groups did not perform significantly better than the control in the test conditions involving the reproduction of the movement pattern from memory. Pew (1974b) argues that these results suggest that whatever was learned about such movement patterns depends on a more global picture of the movement pattern than was provided by concurrent feedback techniques. Finally, Glencross (1975) investigated the effects of changes in task conditions on the serial organization in a repetitive speed skill, hand-cranking.

Changes were made in the load or resistance to cranking, the distance of movement, and direction of cranking. The results suggested that there existed one basic motor program to control the skill and that minor changes in the task could be accommodated by using the same program. Only large changes in the task, such as changes in direction of cranking, seemed to require the organization of a completely new program. Furthermore, Rosenbaum (1977) has presented evidence suggesting that the same motor program is used to control a skill (hand-cranking) when performed by either the left or right hand.

The concept of a motor schema poses a number of questions regarding the exact properties of a movement that are stored. For example, what properties are intrinsic to a particular generalized motor program and what properties are only dimensional parameters that are free to vary from one execution to another? Research into these questions is only beginning; however, some attempts have been made and they will be reviewed in the next section.

Memory structure of movements

The schema is some form of stored representation of an individual's past experience that allows for the generation of unique sequences of motor commands. Russell (1976) has argued that information regarding the desired location of the body and limbs in space is the only specific information about a movement that is stored in memory. An individual uses feedback information regarding the current spatial location of the body and limbs to generate a set of motor commands to achieve the desired spatial location. Movement information from vision, audition, and kinaesthetic sources regarding the position of the individual in space are transformed and placed in a 'space coordinate' system (Lashley, 1951) — reference systems which allow us to remember our location with reference to other locations. Thus, in a complex skill such as the forehand stroke in tennis, there is a position in space relative to the player's body at which the racket must contact the ball if the ball is to go in the desired direction. There are, however, a number of similar positions the arm must pass through before the point of contact with the ball, for example, the end of the backswing and the point at which the elbow must wait for the hand to accelerate past it so the racket will contact the ball. The role of the motor system in such skills, therefore, is to reduct the discrepancy between the current locations of the body component and the next series of desired spatial locations.

The strongest support for the notion that spatial location is the basis of movement production and control comes from a series of experiments by Bizzi (1974) and colleagues (Bizzi, Deu, Morasso, and Polit, 1978; Bizzi, Polit, and Morasso, 1976; Bizzi and Polit, 1979). Well-trained monkeys made head and arm movements to briefly illuminated visual targets. Some of the movements were unexpectedly impeded by the application of a load to the head or arm. In both types of movement the load produced an undershooting of the target. However, if the load was released at that point the movements were corrected to attain the intended terminal location. This phenomenon was also obtained with deafferented monkeys. A second way of disrupting the movements was investigated in the arm-positioning experiments. Just prior to movement initiation the arm was unexpectedly displaced from its starting position in a direction either closer to or away from the target location. Despite the displacement both normal and deafferented monkeys were able to achieve the intended terminal location of the movement.

The importance of the final position of a movement has also been shown for human subjects in studies of motor short-term memory, which are discussed more fully in Chapter 5. It has been suggested (Laabs, 1973) that there are two general cues that can be used in the reproduction of a movement. One cue a subject may store is the final position of the limb (location) and can use this cue by moving the limb to the reference location when later reproduction is attempted. Likewise, the extent of a movement (distance) can be stored and used as a cue for reproduction. In general, studies that have attempted to differentiate these two cues have shown that reproduction of the end-location of a movement is more accurate than reproduction of the movement extent (i.e. Keele and Ells, 1972; Marteniuk and Roy, 1972; Stelmach, Kelso, and Wallace, 1975). These findings suggest that location is codifiable in memory. Other studies have further indicated that spatial location is accessible in memory independently of the movement(s) associated with its storage. Subjects are capable of accurately reproducing the end location of a movement even when the extent or direction of the reproduction movement differs from that of the original criterion movement (i.e. Marteniuk and Roy, 1972; Laabs, 1973; Russell, 1976). Furthermore, the reduction of sensory cues, by the application of a pressure cuff to the wrist, has been shown to severely impair distance reproduction while leaving location reproduction unaffected (Kelso, 1977b; Stelmach, 1977). Accurate recall in the location condition was obtained, even though subjects were unable to perceive the starting position of the reproduction movement.

The above studies provide strong evidence that spatial location can provide the necessary information for movement production. Bizzi and his colleagues have suggested that final location is an equilibrium point (i.e. a particular length–tension relationship) between agonist and antagonist muscles involved in the movement. Once the motor program has specified a particular equilibrium point the inherent mechanical properties of the moving limb will ensure that the correct final position is reached regardless of external perturbations to the movement (see section on spinal tuning).

A number of attempts have been made to identify other properties of a movement sequence that are intrinsic to a particular generalized program and those aspects that are specified just prior to movement initiation. Marteniuk and Mackenzie (in press) have concluded from a review of the literature in the neurosciences that the abstract plan of action or schema contains information about the goal of the performer and the environmental consequences. In addition, the schema contains a spatial map which includes representations of such things as 'the effecting limbs, the direction of movement, and the terminal location of the intended movement' (p.16). There is also good evidence that information regarding the relative timing between the sub-movements making up a skill is part of the generalized motor program. For example, Summers (1975) used a sequential finger-tapping task in an attempt to capture in abstract form the sequential property of many skills. Subjects were trained to execute a particular sequence of nine key-presses containing an inherent timing structure specifying the interval between one response and the next. By the end of a long training session subjects were able to reproduce both the correct sequence and time pattern entirely from memory. Subjects were then told to execute the motor sequence as rapidly as possible while keeping errors to a minimum — timing was no longer important.

It was argued that if the relative timing of movements is stored as part of the generalized motor program, then increasing the rate at which a skill is performed should result in the speeding up of the skill as a whole. In this case the temporal relationships among the various movements should remain approximately constant. On the other hand, if timing is one of the movement parameters input to the program, then it should be possible to change not only the overall execution speed but also the timing of the various submovements involved. The results showed that under speed instructions the entire sequence was speeded up, but performance was still strongly influenced by the learned timing pattern. This was particularly true for subjects who had learned a sequence involving a rhythmic timing structure. Apparently, then, relative timing is an integral part of motor program representation, whereas the overall execution speed of a skill is a parameter that is input to the program at the time of movement initiation. This conclusion has been further supported in studies by Summers (1977a) and Shapiro (1977).

A particularly powerful demonstration that sequencing and timing are inherent properties of a motor program was made by Conrad and Brooks (1974). Monkeys were trained to make rapid elbow flexions and extensions between mechanical stops. Following training the stops were unexpectedly moved closer together, by shortening the flexions or extensions or both, with the effects shown in Figure 19. Physiological measures showed that the monkeys continued to exert muscular force for the usual length of time by pressing the handle against the stops when they were encountered. In this way the rhythm of flexions and extensions was the same as that originally learned.

The specification of timing seems to play a special role in programming which is not shared by other components of a movement sequence, such as the

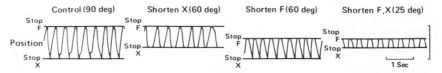

Figure 19. Movements made after unexpected changes of movement range. In the second, third, and fourth tracings the mechanical stops for extension (X), flexion (F), and both, were moved towards the centre. Calibrations for position: 90°. Tracings representative of 877, 214, 306, and 392 movements so measured. Source: Conrad and Brooks (1974, p.796). © 1974 by the American Physiological Society. Reprinted by permission of the first author and the American Physiological Society).

spatial and muscular aspects. For example, recent evidence suggests that two movements of different durations can neither be programmed together nor executed together, a limitation which does not apply to other aspects of a movement (Klapp and Greim, 1979).

CURRENT VIEW OF MOTOR CONTROL

The preceding sections have discussed the various ways in which movements can be controlled. It is clear that the present evidence does not provide convincing support for either a totally closed-loop or open-loop system. Rather, it appears that the control of skilled movements involves the integration of both feedback and motor program processes.

The current view of motor control regards the motor system as being organized in a hierarchical manner. At the highest level is the motor schema; control then proceeds through a series of control loops, each one of which becomes more concrete and simple in function. However, movements are not seen as being generated simply by streams of motor commands passing from the brain to the muscles. Rather, movement organization and execution involves multiple feedback and feedforward interactions at various levels of the central nervous system concurrently (Brooks, 1978).

Let us consider the basic sequence of operations involved in producing a motor response (i.e. throwing a ball). The individual starts with the desired outcome (goal) of the movement, such as 'throw the ball overarm very hard to person X'. Information will be provided from the various sensory receptors regarding the positions of the limbs and body in relation to the target and the state of the environment. A particular generalized motor program is then selected from the motor schema to achieve the desired goal and environmental demands. Next a set of response specifications are generated and input to the generalized program to produce the desired movement. These movement parameters specify such things as the effector unit (i.e. synergistic groups of muscles), the sequencing and phasing of these structures, and details of force intensity and timing of force required by each of these structures (Marteniuk and Mackenzie, in press). At the same time the expected sensory consequences of the movement are generated. When these processes have been completed the motor program is initiated and a particular spatial–temporal pattern of movement is produced.

As the movement is executed sensory receptors in the body provide information about the ongoing movement. This feedback information is fed back to the brain to be compared with the expected sensory consequences, and any discrepancy between the anticipated and actual status represents an error in the movement. At the same time a lower-level, closed-loop control is operating to make rapid adjustments to small, unexpected disturbances to the intended movement.

Spinal tuning

The way in which the abstract central representation of a movement is translated into the appropriate muscular movement has been the topic of much discussion. One mechanism involving the coordinated activity of the muscle spindles and the main muscles has been previously described (see pp.50-51). Another mechanism that has recently been proposed involves the concept of 'preparatory set' or tuning (see Easton, 1978 and Turvey, 1977 for a detailed discussion of tuning). It is postulated that the higher levels of the motor system are concerned only with the general aspects of a movement (i.e. the effector units and their coordination) and are not involved in specifying the micro details of movement execution. Rather, the fine structuring of a movement is left to control centres in the spinal cord. However, in order for the movement to be carried out as planned the higher centres can prepare (bias) the lower centres for the anticipated movement. This biasing of spinal level mechanisms for a particular movement is termed 'tuning'. Tuning can therefore 'be regarded as preparation of motor centres to act towards the intentions of the higher centre once the trigger for movement is supplied' (Marteniuk and Mackenzie, in press, p.12). The higher centres adjust the behaviour of selected lower-level coordinate structures by specifying movement parameters, such as the specific length–tension relationship between agonist and antagonistic muscles reflecting the terminal location of the movement (Turvey, 1977). In addition, various supraspinal reflexes can be selectively facilitated to assist in rapid correction of anticipated external loads or disturbances to the movement (Hayes, 1978). Once their preparatory adjustments have been established the lower motor centres can execute the movement rather autonomously. This is essentially a feedforward mechanism in that compensation for any external perturbation in the movement is due to the intrinsic mechanical properties of the muscle tissue. Bizzi and colleagues have suggested that the ability of monkeys to attain the terminal location of head and arm movements despite external disturbances was due to the operation of such a mechanism (see pp.55-56). Furthermore, a number of investigators (i.e. Hayes, 1978; Requin, Bonnet, and Semjen, 1977) have found changes in excitability of the spinal motor-neuron pool during the time between a warning signal and a stimulus indicating the subject should respond (reaction signal (RS)). Requin, Bonnet, and Semjen (1977) have outlined three possible levels in the motor organization in which the preparatory adjustments triggered by a warning signal (WS) could occur (see Figure 20).

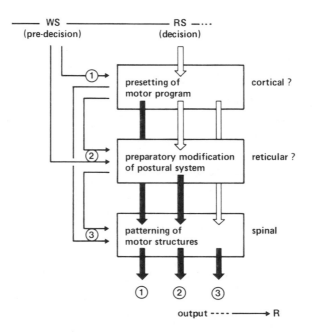

Figure 20. Schematization of the three possible levels in the motor organization in which the preparatory adjustments triggered by the WS could intervene. The diagram indicates the likely nervous pathways (on the left) and structures (on the right) involved. In each hypothetical mechanism, the vertical arrow corresponding to the execution stage of the response is changed from white to black as soon as preparatory adjustments are effective in modulating the motor program. Source: Modified from Requin, Bonnet, and Semjen (1977 p.168). Reprinted by permission of Lawrence Erlbaum Associates Inc.

The information given by the WS could be primarily used in presetting the motor program at the highest level of organization. This presetting may involve the selection of a particular generalized motor program from the schema and the specification of the general movement parameters. Next, an intermediary level of reticular formations is proposed which may be concerned with preparatory modifications of the postural system. For example, an adjustment in body posture may be necessary in order to be compatible with the biomechanical requirements of the selected movement. Finally, spinal level mechanisms can be biased in anticipation of the forthcoming movement.

It is probable that both spinal tuning and the closed-loop system involving the muscle spindles operate during movement execution. For example, spinal tuning may be effective in overcoming certain types of external disturbance to the intended movement, while the muscle spindle system may be used to compensate for other forms of disturbance.

Interim Summary

The current view of a hierarchical motor organization makes it difficult to identify any part of the total control system as a motor program in the traditional sense. As a result various writers have defined a motor program in different ways, ranging from such general statements as 'motor programs are communications in the central nervous system that are based on past experience and that can generate postural adjustments and movements' (Brooks, 1978, p.1) to the concept that motor programs are descending force signals from the motor cortex (Evarts, 1968). Other writers have chosen a particular level in the motor hierarchy, such as the abstract plan of action, as a motor program (Bernstein, 1967; Miller, Galanter, and Pribram, 1960) or have abandoned the concept completely (Marteniuk and Mackenzie, in press). Alternatively, one could argue that the recently identified spinal level control mechanisms come closest to the original concept of a motor program. However, as Hayes (1978) has pointed out the movement-specific pattern of spinal tuning is always necessary prior to movement initiation, indicating a central 'model' of the intended movement.

It is perhaps best to view a motor program simply as the central representation of the sequential structure of a skill (Keele and Summers, 1976). The representation is seen as being abstract in nature, similar to the concept of the motor schema (Pew, 1974a; Schmidt, 1975a, 1976a). The important aspect of the program is that it allows the organism to organize, through a sequence of operations, a series of movements in advance of movement execution. Furthermore, these movements can be carried out without requiring feedback from one movement to elicit a succeeding movement. Feedback, however, is constantly being monitored during program operation and is used to update and modify well-learned movement patterns.

Clearly, in the execution of any perceptual-motor skill, the ultimate way in which a skill is performed would be to have it almost completely programmed so that very little conscious attention is required. In general, the greater the ability of the central nervous system to 'predictively determine' a motor response, the less is the need for peripheral feedback. For example, Brooks and associates (see Brooks, 1978, for a review) have examined two movement strategies exhibited by monkeys when performing tasks involving moving a handle into learned target zones. When the target zones were wide the monkeys used fast continuous movements which could be made without tactual, visual, or auditory feedback. Furthermore, these movements were unaffected by unexpected withdrawal of target cues or by their unexpected insertion in unusual parts of the trajectory. To narrow targets the monkeys often made discontinuous exploratory-type movements using peripheral feedback to place the handle inside the target zones. These movements were greatly affected when target cues were omitted. Similar strategies have been observed in studies of motor short-term memory in humans. Kelso (1977b) has shown that when voluntary movements are made in which the subject is allowed to plan and execute a desired movement (preselected) kinaesthetic feedback is not absolutely necessary for accurate reproduction. In contrast, constrained exploratory movements (movement to an experimenter-defined stop) demand closed-loop control.

It seems likely, therefore, that closed skills involving the execution of relatively long sequences of movements in a static environment can be almost completely programmed in advance with a minimum of feedback involvement. In contrast, the performance of skills demanding high accuracy or where the environment is constantly changing involve both program and feedback control. In such skills an individual may make short programmed movements followed by an evaluation of response-produced feedback. It is possible that the central representation of such skills contain instructions for sensing and responding to feedback at particular points in the movement sequence (Sternberg *et al.*, 1978).

The maximum length of a motor program is difficult to estimate. Once the program has been organized it must be possible to hold the programmed representation until the onset of movement. This suggests that there exists a temporary storage of motor commands for programmed responses. Klapp (1976) has suggested that one of the processes of short-term memory may be the retention of motor programs prior to their release as an overt response. If this view is accepted then the capacity limitations of the short-term memory system may define the maximum length of a programmed response.

IMPLICATIONS FOR SKILL LEARNING

It has been argued that at the base of all skilled performance is the ability to generate an appropriate sequence of motor commands from a generalized source of movement information, the motor schema. The initial problem facing the learner, however, is the establishment of a template or model of how the feedback should appear if the skill is performed correctly. The acquisition of the skill is then accomplished by a matching process in which the feedback from the movements generated by the subject are compared to the template. The system that generates movements (the motor program) and the system that evaluates feedback (the template and comparison centre) are seen as separable units. Once the motor program has been established feedback can be eliminated and the program can produce the learned movement in open-loop fashion.

One implication of this formulation is that 'an artificial template and feedback source can be used for the learning phase to build up an appropriate program' (Keele, 1977, p.9). Such feedback substitution techniques have been used as aids in the learning of a foreign language (Kalikow and Rollins, 1973; Kalikow, 1974) and in training the deaf to speak (Nickerson, Kalikow, and Stevens, 1976). In these studies visual displays present transformations of the learner's speech to be compared with a model. Other techniques that have been investigated in skill learning are loop films and videotape (see Holding, 1965). Generally, such systems have been found to be of little use. However, most studies have used only loop films while others only video feedback. According to motor program theory both techniques should be used together — loop films to portray a model and videotape to provide feedback for use in the comparison process. Keele (1977) reports two attempts to apply this idea to the skills of discus throwing and fly casting.

The independence of feedback and program also suggests that for certain skills the template may be established prior to actually performing the skill. It has been suggested that the acquisition of an auditory template prior to movement production may be the basis of the Suzuki method of violin teaching (Keele, 1973; Keele and Summers, 1976). In addition to storing a template prior to actual movement, it also may be possible to store part of the motor program itself. One way of accomplishing this may be through the use of mental practice, a technique that has been shown to improve performance on a variety of skills. The introspective or covert rehearsal of the required movements would aid the establishment of the movement sequence in memory. This idea was tested by Summers (1977b), using a task in which subjects were required to respond as rapidly as possible to events that tended to occur in sequential order. Mental rehearsal of the event order was found to be effective even when movements were not used until later in the task.

The motor program concept, therefore, suggests several ways in which skill learning might be improved. The central element in the acquisition of a skill is the comparison process between response-produced feedback and a model or template of expected sensory consequences. The training techniques described are aimed at improving the quality of the match between feedback and model.

It has previously been noted that one of the distinguishing characteristics of a highly skilled performer is the ability to perform the skill in a number of different ways according to variations in environmental demands. This flexibility in motor behaviour was seen as resulting from the acquisition of a motor schema for a given class of movement. The teaching of a motor skill, therefore, can be viewed as a 'two-stage' process. Initially the teacher or coach must aid the learner in the acquisition of the correct sequence and timing of the movements that comprise the skill, through the use of such training techniques as previously described. Once the performer is able to perform the skill correctly, the next stage is the development of a motor schema containing all the parameters that are needed to generate a unique movement to meet each situation in which the skill is performed. This can be accomplished by providing the learner with practice in a wide variety of situations that not only allow many variations of a movement to be produced but also require the learner to produce movements that meet the exact environmental demands. For example, in teaching the jump shot in basketball, once the player can perform the shot correctly, little is gained from continually practising it in isolation without someone guarding him. Placing the learner in a 'gamelike' situation will allow for the development of a diversified schema from which he will be able to generate a particular sequence of motor commands to meet the specific game situation. The acquisition of a diversified schema is particularly important in the learning of open skills that are performed in a constantly changing environment. Closed skills, on the other hand, because the environment is relatively static, demand a more precise and invariable motor schema that allows for the generation of the same movement sequence over and over. In such skills practice should involve repeated attempts to reproduce exactly the correct movement sequence.

SUMMARY

In this chapter I have attempted to contrast the two major theoretical approaches to motor skills, motor program control and closed-loop control. Evidence has been presented that many motor skills are centrally represented in memory as a motor program. It has been argued, however, that the control of skilled movement requires the integration of both feedback and program processes. Furthermore, the concept of a motor schema was introduced to overcome some of the deficiencies evident in the traditionally accepted views of programmed and closed-loop control. Finally, some of the implications of the motor program concept for skill learning were discussed. More information on learning will be found in Chapter 9.

ACKNOWLEDGEMENTS

The preparation of this chapter was supported by the Australian Research Grants Committee, Project No. A77/15427.

Human Skills
Edited by D. Holding
©1981 John Wiley & Sons Ltd.

Chapter 4

Single-channel Theory

Marcel Kinsbourne

A person's ability to do anything whatever must be finite. An obvious source of limitation is physical, imposed by the inertia of the peripheral apparatus for perception and action. But over and above these peripheral limitations there are central ones that intervene when there is appreciable uncertainty about how to respond at any given moment (James, 1890). Reading is a case in point. The ceiling on a person's maximal rate of fluent reading is not imposed by the reaction time for successive saccades as the gaze shifts across the printed line. Nor is it imposed by the temporal characteristics of pattern perception. Rather it is a central factor, comprehension — the extraction of meaning in memorable form — that limits the rate at which we can usefully read (Jackson and McClelland, 1979).

Humans are adaptive data processors, and the manner in which they process information 'will reflect characteristics largely of the outer environment in the light of the current goal' (Simon, 1969, p.25). It follows that different models will best describe human behaviour in different situations. Should the relevant aspects of environment call for frequent and repetitive ('production line') functions, processing will be parallel and holistic. Such behaviour is best modelled according to control theory. In less familiar situations the predominant processes are associative. Decision theory, for instance, suits such cases. In novel circumstances, problem solving is called for, and this has its own set of appropriate models, in artificial intelligence (cf. discussion by Rasmussen, 1979).

The present topic, single-channel theory, is nested within this continuum. The postulated capacity limitations do not apply to the most completely specified 'automatic' activities. Nor have they been enlightening with respect to the extremes of uncertainty when problem solving. The illustrations that we will consider occupy a middle ground, in which there is sufficient response uncertainty to necessitate central delays (held to reflect the workings of attention), but in which the response alternatives are limited in number and fully specified. As we shall see, in such circumstances the chief problem confronted by the central processing is keeping concurrent or rapidly sequential behaviour apart so that each may run its course uncontaminated by elements irrelevant to it that derive from another processing sequence. Although recent models deal primarily in terms of task difficulty (for instance as expressed in terms of 'workload'), it is task similarity, by virtue of its potential for interference, that becomes the crucial consideration. But a restriction applies in the case of human operators, in contrast to most machines. How difficult a task is, and how similar two tasks are, depends not only on the objective demands of the task but also on the operator's experience. Only within a narrow time frame can stable measurements be achieved. Over time, as performance is repeatedly probed, it changes its characteristics. The observer gains increasing facility in extracting those features that differentiate the tasks, and thus their subjective similarity and their potential for mutual interference decrease. Over time, processing will descend the hierarchy from limited problem solving towards a more automatic, less attention-requiring mode. Thus, it is in the nature of attentive processes to generate their own extinction, as response uncertainty decreases towards the ideal end point at which all contingencies are provided for by fully specified response programs. Our discussion will be limited to performance that is deliberate rather than automatic, but the artificiality of this restriction will become apparent.

LIMITED-CAPACITY MODELS

For many tasks, the limit on performance can be objectively measured. The extent to which a task engages a person is its workload. Workload is a construct that reflects the ratio of the level of performance called for by the task to the limiting level of which the subject is capable (Senders, 1979). The term 'workload' is usually applied to tasks which subjects perform in full consciousness, and as workload increases, subjects experience themselves as focusing attention ever more intently on the task, and as exerting increasing mental effort. These subjective feelings can be rated, and some of their psychophysiological concomitants measured (Ursin and Ursin, 1979). Under such conditions of focussed attention, subjects typically report that they are doing one thing at a time. This unity in conscious experience may be why it is so popular to suppose that performance limits are reached when a limited amount of attention has been fully allocated to the task in question (by dint of exerting maximal mental effort). This subjective bias, in conjunction with the current proclivity for machine analogies, perhaps accounts for the prevalent view of the human 'operator' as a limited-capacity processing device. Following Shannon and Weaver's (1949) analysis, many investigators tested the simplifying generalization that the ceiling on performances in general is the same in terms of information transmitted per unit time (Attneave, 1959). This idea failed to gain empirical support (Neisser, 1967). But another powerful assumption has proven surprisingly durable: that the translation of a signal from a sensory code to a memory or response code involves a limited-capacity channel. In its strong form this is single-channel theory (Welford, 1952; 1959).

Single-channel theory assumes that given a 'main' task, subjects will necessarily devote their full capacity to it (i.e. behave like a single-channel device, such as a computer that at any one point in time processes information from only one terminal). There is no occasion for capacity sharing between tasks, because there is no spare capacity. Easier tasks are completed faster than hard ones, but both easy and hard tasks are performed 'at capacity'.

This model has been so persuasive that the bulk of research has been concerned not to pit its explanatory value against that of alternative models, but, assuming it to be correct, to determine the locus of the postulated capacity limitation within the information-processing sequence–stimulus encoding, response choice, response organization (Sternberg, 1969). Is there a 'filter' before stimuli are encoded (Broadbent, 1958), or at the stage of response choice (Deutsch and Deutsch, 1963)? Again, a simplifying assumption is implicit, that at whatever stage the locus of the 'bottleneck' is, it is at the same stage across tasks. But now that viable alternatives to single-channel theory exist, the attractiveness of assuming an invariant locus for the bottleneck is less, and it is held to be more likely that operations which require attention can be early or late, depending on the demand characteristics of the task (Johnston and Heinz, 1978; Hasher and Zacks, 1979).

Single-channel theory has been pitted against another interpretation of the manner of operation of the limited-capacity processor — the allocatable-capacity model (Moray, 1967; Kahneman, 1973; Norman and Bobrow, 1975; Posner and Boies, 1971). Beyond this, the overriding notion of the operator as a limited-capacity processor has been contested by multichannel processor theory, which regards individual brain mechanisms rather than the operator as a whole, as each endowed with a limited supply of allocatable capacity (Allport, Antonis, and Reynolds, 1972; McLeod, 1977; 1978; Kantowitz and Knight, 1976). It may even be questioned whether the idea that there are specific stable mechanisms basic to all models so far considered, which we will call discontinuity models, is the most useful way of characterizing psychological organization. We will now proceed to trace the course of this progressive retreat from the simple certainties of single-channel theory (Figure 21).

Evidence for single-channel theory

To consider the evidence for single-channel theory we will use as counterpoint its earliest serious rival, allocatable-capacity theory (Moray, 1967). Single-channel theory assumes that workload always corresponds to the limits of capacity. 'Time-sharing between tasks' is by serial attention, not by parallel

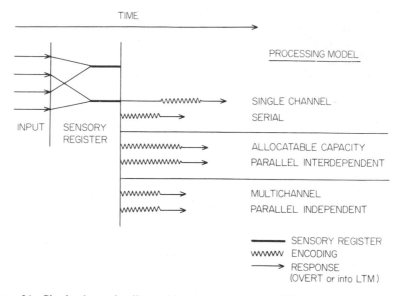

Figure 21. Single-channel, allocatable-resource, and multichannel processing models compared.

division of attention (as with an intermittent correction servo-mechanism, cf. Craik, 1947). In contrast, allocatable capacity theory allows for a division of attention between channels that are in concurrent use. The variant introduced by Kahneman (1973) also makes provision for the mobilization of 'spare capacity' in certain circumstances.

Before evaluating these models, one must confront an obvious objection. It is a matter of everyday experience that people can do more than one thing at a time, and do so constantly. Nor does initiating a second activity (e.g. walking) necessarily detract from performance of the first (e.g. talking). In a strict single-channel view such combinations should not be possible, and in an allocatable-capacity view, though possible, undertaking the dual task performance incurs the penalty of performance decrement in one or both of the concurrent activities. The saving clause that preserves the models in face of these facts exempts from the limitations imposed by a finite amount of available attention those activities which are deemed automatic and thus not necessitating attention (e.g. Bahrick, Noble, and Fitts, 1954; Bahrick and Shelly, 1958). This necessarily follows, though not without logical circularity, from the operational definition of attention as required when two tasks interfere with each other (Keele and Neill, 1978). Attempts have been made to characterize automatic behaviours, as those which are highly familiar (and either incidentally or deliberately practised, and done with little, intermittent, or even no awareness). With practice, task uncertainty is reduced, and control increasingly assumes open-loop instead of closed-loop characteristics (Pew, 1974a; Schmidt, 1975a; 1976a). For purposes of evaluating the limited-capacity models, we will exclude such tasks from consideration.

Single-channel theory can be contrasted with allocatable-capacity theory using paradigms involving timed response or dual-task performance. When two signals follow in rapid succession, the latency of response to the second signal is usually longer than it would have been had there been no preceding signal. Indeed, the delay in second response may exceed the remaining time for which the first signal is processed (Welford, 1959). Not only does the second processing sequence have to await completion of the first, but it would appear that the second processing remains suspended while feedback from the first is monitored. When latency of response to the first signal is increased by varying task parameters, latency of response to the second signal is correspondingly lengthened also. So far the results are consistent with strict single-channel theory. However, sometimes latency of first response is also increased. This seems consistent with parallel capacity allocation to the formulation of the two responses. But it can also be reconciled with single-channel theory. It could reflect a strategy enabling subjects to group their responses. By awaiting both signals, they achieve the economy of integrated response. Overall, these studies do illustrate what has been termed 'psychological refractory period' (Vince, 1948a), and succeed in demonstrating a bottleneck as envisaged by single-channel theory (Bertelson, 1966), though the same data can also be interpreted in quite another manner, as illustrating the impossibility of 'preparing' for both responses prior to the first (Poulton, 1950; Gottsdanker, 1979).

It appears, then, that subjects could not distribute attention between responses. Can they distribute it between different stages of a single response (Moray, 1967)? Suppose that in the sequence stimulus encoding → response choice → response organization, one stage has, by some manipulation, been rendered more difficult. Can the speed of the overall reaction be maintained by simultaneously making another stage easier, releasing allocatable capacity for use in the more difficult operation? The interactions predicted by the allocatable-capacity model do not occur. The manipulations simply have additive effects, as predictable by single-channel theory (Sanders, 1979).

Dual-task performance outcomes are also largely consistent with single-channel theory (Noble, Trumbo, and Fowler, 1967; Trumbo and Noble, 1970; Trumbo, Noble, and Swink, 1967; Kerr, 1973). An extreme case is reported by Klapp (1979) with respect to temporal compatibility. He found subjects quite unable to produce two periodically repeating sequences at the same time unless they were in harmonic relation.

The single-channel model is the most highly developed variant of the family of possible limited-capacity models. Not only is the organism's attention resource limited, but at any one time it has to be committed to one channel only. In its current development, it incorporates, first, a feature analytic device that resolves complex inputs, segregating them into separate channels. The extracted inputs are held in a rapid-decay sensory register, whereupon a filter selects its information sequentially by channel, and passes it on to a limited-capacity, short-term store. There it is available to response, and to long-term memory storage. Much experimental effort has been invested in attempts to validate and further to define these hypothesized stages. And yet, the issues would be transformed if the alternative existing limited-capacity model were preferred. This approach, the allocatable-capacity model, allows of some freedom of distribution of capacity between channels, at the same time.

The simplest construction of dual-task performance would be that the tasks are carried out independently at the same time. According to single-channel theory this would be an impossibility. One would have to assume 'time-sharing' — alternating investment of attention in each channel. Allocatable-resource theory accepts the parallel processing involved, but prediction is complicated (if not made impossible) by two modifying factors working in opposite directions (i.e. resulting in (i) overestimate, and (ii) underestimate of total capacity respectively). (i) On the one hand, increasing workload may result in the mobilizing of 'spare capacity' (Kahneman, 1973). (ii) On the other hand, adding a second task has been seen as not simply additional workload, but as also imposing a clerical necessity — to keep the two programs from intermingling. This expenditure is called 'concurrence set' by Navon and Gopher (1979). On this view, the addition of a second task generates the need for an 'emergent' third task (Duncan, 1979).

These two provisions modify predictions based on limited-capacity models, but do so within the framework of such models. Do they suffice to protect these models from unfavourable comparison with an alternative that attributes capacity limitations not to the operator as a whole but to one of several mechanisms ('channels') at the operator's disposal? Whereas evidence for single-channel processing derives from experiments in which the competing tasks were highly similar, evidence for multichannel processing is most persuasive in situations in which the tasks are very different from one another. Whereas in a paradigm as typically suited to single-channel demonstration as dichotic listening evidence of 'spare capacity' available to the nominally unattended ear has been convincingly presented (e.g. Von Wright, Anderson, and Stenman, 1975), the magnitude of this effect is slight. When more dissimilar tasks are concurrently imposed, the 'spare capacity' effects are enormous.

Multichannel processing

Treisman (1969) suggested that single-channel theory might apply to concurrent use of the same, but not of different subsystems ('analysers'). Allport,

Antonis, and Reynolds (1972) found that pianists could simultaneously sight-read and play an unfamiliar piece of music and shadow an auditory message. Also, having to recall words presented during shadowing did interfere, but pictures for recall did not. Shaffer (1973) found that typists could simultaneously copy-type and shadow, in both cases with minimal detriment to either activity. This ability to perform without capacity restriction is clearly a function of dissimilarity between tasks (and implicitly the use of separate brain mechanisms). McLeod (1977) gave subjects a main visuo-manual tracking task, and a 'secondary' two-choice auditory reaction task. He found much interference when the secondary reaction was also manual, but little when it was vocal. The manual reaction affected the timing pattern of the tracking, but the vocal response had no such influence. He also (McLeod, 1978) found that the interference of auditory probe with visual letter matching studied by Posner and Boies (1971) disappeared if the reaction to the probe is changed from manual to vocal. This invalidates their assumption that the secondary task they used amounted to a neutral probe for unused capacity (see also Shwartz, 1976). These studies are particularly convincing as differences in task difficulty (and therefore conceivably in 'effort') do not obtain. It can, however, be argued that the concurrence cost is less for highly dissimilar tasks because their codes are less confusable. This would account for a relative superiority of dual-task performance in the 'dissimilar' condition, but cannot explain the virtual independence of the two concurrent performances. Further illustrations exist. Treisman and Davies (1973) showed that the difficulty of distributing attention between sensory channels is sharply lessened when, instead of dichotic presentation, one channel involves the visual modality. Brooks (1968) and Baddeley, Grant, Wight, and Thompson (1975) found similar within- versus between-modality effects in performance, as did Kantowitz and Knight (1974). Wickens (1975) cites further instances of what he calls 'difficulty insensitivity' in which manipulating the objective characteristics of the main task will cause corresponding changes in the performance of one secondary task, but not of another. Specifically, those secondary tasks are sensitive to main task effects that rely on the same processor, the activity of which for purposes of the main task is the subject of the experimental manipulation. Again, Brown (1968) had much earlier found tapping most sensitive to concurrent movement tests, and random number generation most sensitive to concurrent perceptual tests.

In summary, there is a confound in the evidence for single-channel theory: the instances of strict capacity limitation involve tasks that arguably compete not only for performing the same operation but for use of the same mechanism in the brain (Allport, Antonis, and Reynolds, 1972). Thus the capacity limitation may be held to apply to the mechanism rather than the operator as a whole. There may be spare capacity elsewhere, untapped by the tasks imposed upon him. When the overlap on brain mechanisms is disposed of, the capacity limitation is similarly eased.

We may now consider the merit of this notion of structure-specific resources (Kantowitz and Knight, 1974; Wickens, 1979). Navon and Gopher (1979) remark: 'Strictly structural models seem inadequate once we realize that processes that use the same mechanism sometimes interfere with each other but seldom block each other completely' (p.233). Should we therefore revive the apparently defunct allocatable-resource model, applying it to the individual structure (mechanism) rather than the operator? Is it the case, as Sanders (1979) suggests, that exchange of capacity may occur only within mechanisms, and not between mechanisms? Probably not, in view of the strong evidence for single-channel theory; we should refer it not to the observer but to the specific mechanism involved. The evidence is thus against allocatable resource within the mechanism (for the same reason that it was considered not to favour allocatable resource within the operator). So at the level of the single mechanism ('channel') the single-channel versus allocatable-capacity debate is revived. Both versions retain their basic weaknesses. Single-channel theory gives a restrictive account of dual-task performance decrement when used in the multichannel processor framework. Only those activities that draw in part upon a common mechanism should show dual-task decrement. Allocatable-resource theory can still postulate an 'executive controller', the concurrence cost of which could account for a wide range of dual-task interference phenomena. But why, then, do some tasks not interfere (call for no concurrence cost)?

EFFORT

If one rejects limited-capacity models, one is left with the task of accounting for the phenomena related to the sense of effort, which Kahneman (1973) had discussed in terms of the allocatable-capacity variant of this family of models. Navon and Gopher (1979) relate the feeling of effort to the 'stress' that accompanies the performance of difficult tasks. But it is not clear that the sense of effort faithfully reflects in its degree the difficulty of the performance. For instance, one may be fully committed to an extremely difficult task of detecting faint signals (e.g. stimuli briefly presented by tachistoscope) and have only a moderate subjective sense of effortful engagement. It seems that the sense of effort is maximally elicited by tasks which are not only difficult but also call for the vigorous maintenance of focused attention. It may be that the 'effort' represents not so much the task performance itself as the suppression of tendencies to take time out from the performance and orient to extraneous matters. There is, as Kahneman (1973) has discussed, good reason for relating the sense of effort to level of reticular formation activation ('arousal'). Easterbrook (1959) pointed out that increased arousal is associated with the restriction of attention to fewer aspects of the environment ('diminished cue utilization'). Physiologically, there is evidence of a positive correlation between ascending reticular activating system activity and the activity of the limbic system, which helps maintain a restricted attentional focus by gating out irrelevant input (e.g. Swonger and Rech, 1972).

As is well known, single-task performance over time is regularly subject to a monotonic decrement in efficiency. At least part of the reason is the increasing incidence over time of lapses of attention (be it in favour of the external events or be it a turning inward of attention). It is subjectively an effortful task to maintain a restricted focus of attention — that is to inhibit attentional dispersion to extraneous matters. Given single tasks, operators may, at least for a time, be able to meet a performance criterion, and yet, profiting from redundancies in the task, intermittently shift attention elsewhere. As the task is made more dependent on faithfully sustained attention, so it becomes more 'effortful'. Is division of attention between impaired tasks merely a special case of the fact that a subjective feeling of effort arises when attention has to be strictly maintained to particular matters, and even minor lapses would impair performance? It does not at this time seem necessary to regard capacity as a variable. It seems a sufficient account of what is known to list those circumstances which facilitate sustained attention (incentives, stimulants) and those which militate against it (fatigue, sleeplessness, sedatives). If we can account for phenomena in terms of disposition of a resource, changes in the amount of that resource need not be hypothesized. In dual-task situations, maintained precision in the disposition of attention is crucial, and this may account for the very 'effortful' subjective feeling that one experiences in such situations.

TASK SIMILARITY AND INTERFERENCE

We have seen that there are some situations in which subjects' performance is well described by a single-channel theory, but others in which it seems to conform to a multichannel processor model. It does not appear that differences in task difficulty or automaticity can explain this. Rather, it is when tasks are most similar one to another that their concurrent performance is most likely to be accomplished successively, or in an alternating fashion. When they are different, they can most readily be accomplished in parallel. Signals in different modalities, responses by voice and by hand, coding in visual and verbal mode lend themselves more readily to a multiprocessing account than do conditions under which modality, coding strategy, and response mode are very alike for the two ongoing performances. The prominence of similarity as an organizing principle naturally highlights a mechanism by means of which it might exert its effect — interference.

While engineering formulations that provide for interference exist (Levison, 1970; 1979) the pervasive use of the currently fashionable term 'channel' may have inadvertently predisposed theorists towards the uncritical assumption that different activities are centrally represented in channels that, machine-like, are literally separate and independent. That view would rule out interference *a priori* as a cause of impaired performance in dual-task situations, and, by default, necessitate a hypothetical construct invoking the limited availability of some commodity or resource, such as 'attention'. But this assumption is not only gratuitous, it is misleading, in that it emphasizes task difficulty, when the emphasis should properly be on task similarity. Multichannel processor models can at least handle similarity dichotomously: tasks are either sufficiently similar to involve the same channels, or not. If the same channel is used, then single-channel theory or allocatable-capacity theory can be applied to it rather than to the total operator) according to the theorist's predilection. Yet in so far as can be judged from the existing literature, we have, not a natural dichotomy, but a set of carefully chosen extreme cases, to dramatize single-channel restrictions on the one hand and multichannel processor flexibility on the other. It remains to map the middle ground, and determine the effect of degree of similarity in concurrent performance.

How do two similar performances interact so as to limit the efficiency of each? According to single-channel theory, two concurrent continuous performances can be sustained only by time-sharing — alternation between channels. The hypothesized alternation could of course occur at such a fast repetition rate that, defying available measurement options, it would stimulate outcomes expected on the basis of allocatable capacity. But, perhaps because this would deprive the model of heuristic value, single-channel theorists have assumed measurable rates of alternation, and attempted to measure them. Under such circumstances, cross-correlation becomes an appropriate investigative tool. The channel switching should become apparent as an increased probability of error on one channel as compared to the other at any point in time. Roldan (1979) ran cross-correlations between two concurrent tracking tasks, one visual, one auditory. They were completely non-significant (although the dual-task situation exacted its price, as evidenced by lowered tracking performance on both channels). He concluded that the cost of dual-task performance was not due to periodic alternating suppression of attention to each task.

Reviewing the argument up to this point, we have a fact — impaired performance when *similar* tasks are performed concurrently or in rapid succession — and a swarm of hypothetical constructs — capacity (attention), concurrence cost (or its synonyms), and the metaphor of the channel. Do we need these constructs, or does what we know suffice to account for what we describe? Specifically, could actual or potential interference account for the whole range of phenomena under discussion?

When two concurrent activities potentially interfere, the logic of speed–accuracy trade-off (see Rabbitt, Chapter 7, this volume) comes into play. If both activities are maintained at their pre-concurrent rate of information transmission, then accuracy will decrease as a consequence of interference. Or, accuracy may be safeguarded by a diminution in rate. Then, systematic error patterns derived from the extraneous activity on the other channel will no longer be apparent, and yet, interference, or, specifically, the threat of interference, was the cause of the lowered rate of information transmission. Applying this line of thought to Roldan's result, we conclude that the absence of cross-correlated incidence of error, although it excludes single-channel behaviour as a determinant, does not compel an allocatable-capacity view. Subjects may have diminished their rate of concurrent tracking in order to avoid interference and to maintain accuracy.

We emerge with a testable alternative to allocatable-capacity theory, and a way of distinguishing the two. If dual-task performance is limited by a limitation in a resource — 'attention' — then, pressed beyond its limit, each performance will break down in the same way it would break down if pressed beyond its limit on an isolated task. The errors suggest impaired control over the workings of the channel, but not any systematic bias. If dual-task performance is limited by interference within a unitary closed system, then the pattern of errors that creep in when performance is pressed will reflect the nature of the competing concurrent task, and will vary with different concurrent tasks. They will reflect the biasing effect of the other activity. When one performance lapses it assumes the characteristics of the other.

Note that any slow-down in information transmission could lend itself to the above alternative interpretations. Even in the classical psychological refractory period situation, the increased latency of response to the second signal (and even to the first) could be attributable not only to capacity limitations but to a safeguarding against interference (i.e. confusion between the reactions, e.g. see Kantowitz and Knight, 1974; 1976). Such confusion would be maximally probable between highly similar acts.

Some evidence on this issue exists. With respect to division of attention on the perceptual side, it is commonplace that lapses in performance on one dichotic channel are largely characterized by intrusions from the other (e.g. Treisman and Geffen, 1968; Hiscock and Kinsbourne, 1978). On the motor side, the same is strikingly true when the pattern of performance breakdown is analysed. For instance, when pianists attempted to play uncorrelated melodies simultaneously with their two hands, 95 per cent of errors reflected the ongoing melodic line on the other 'channel' (Kinsbourne and Hicks, 1978). However, the findings from many more paradigms would have to be analysed to establish the generality of this result. At this stage we can, at least, keep in mind that cross-talk interference between channels is *not* what would be predicted by an allocatable-capacity model. Such findings would be expected not of a system consisting of independent channels, but of one which, though differentiated, is highly linked. Lashley (1951) attributed the tendency of the nervous system to generate only one temporal pattern at a time to the wealth of interconnections, which would lock the entire system into synchrony with one rhythm. In contrast to the discontinuity models that have so far been offered, a continuity model is called for. Do the realities of the relevant hardware, the human brain, permit such modelling?

Interference and learning

It is easiest to perform concurrently those tasks that can most readily be differentiated, or integrated into one. It is in the middle ground between these conditions that interference prevails. The nature of the interference is characteristic — interchanges between channels, leading to confusion errors. In selective attention, information from irrelevant channels intrudes (e.g. Treisman and Geffen, 1968). In concurrent performance, one program becomes dominant, taking over both response facilities (Kinsbourne and Hicks, 1978; Klapp, 1979; Duncan, 1979). Interference is the essence of the problem in division of attention or of performance, and all the experimental findings cited are sufficiently explained as representing the subjects' best efforts to guard against it — to keep inputs separate, to safeguard one motor program from distortion by mingling with another. Viewed in this way, the phenomena of dual-task performance are but a special case of the phenomena of learning. Consider learning as the adaptive shaping of response probabilities. As those response priorities that are innate, and those that are acquired by early interaction with the environment, fail to meet the adaptive goals of the organism in particular contexts, so they are systematically altered until the objective is achieved. The new behaviour is performed against a backdrop of the old. Learning is not *de novo*, but is a continually reshaping of what is already known. The obstacle to learning the new is not ignorance (i.e. primary inability to respond correctly) but obstruction by persistent response tendencies in the old (familiar, probable, but imperfectly adaptive) way. The stimulus for the new performance also tends to elicit the old ('negative transfer') and that has to be suppressed, to permit the new to run its course with unimpaired precision. Time-sharing is a specially dramatized instance of this barrier to learning, for here we are not, as is usual, replacing one response pattern by another, but maintaining two with approximately equal priority. But the issue is the same — differentiation. To explain successful dual-task performance we do not need to resort to the hypothetical construct of available energy (resource, attention, effort). Instead, we must determine how, within a highly linked unitary system (the human brain), patterns of activity *differentiate*.

In learning, however, it is not always a matter of differentiating. The other expedient is to incorporate the new response into an existing pattern (in Piagetian terms, assimilate rather than accommodate). When people learn to perform concurrently activities that initially were highly interfering, it may be that they discovered some new organizing principle which enabled them to integrate ostensibly orthogonal activities into unitary superordinate action programs. Thus one cannot play a 4 per second rhythm with one hand, 3 per second with the other — until one learns to integrate them into a 12 per second time base. Neisser (1980) remarks 'mind has probabilities but no capacity' and cites spectacular cases of concurrent performance of activities that surely share the same structure (reading a story while writing to dictation — with comprehension of both sets of verbal information; Spelke, Hirst, and Neisser, 1976). Thus brain structures or mechanisms as defined in multichannel processor theory, constantly change, under the impact of the very use to which they are put to probe their limitations. This relativism appears not to characterize existing machines. 'No contemporary computer program experiences radical changes in organization as a result of interaction with the environment, as people do when they grow up or practice any skill for a long period' (Neisser, 1980).

Finally, we can broaden our inquiry to the utmost by asking — what, then, beyond physical (peripheral) constraints determines the limits on performance? Why can we not do things faster than we can do them?

The answer could simply be — because we have not sufficiently practised them (Neisser, 1980). What occurs at the asymptote of practice is presumably an information-processing sequence which is maximally efficient because it unrolls in predetermined fashion *without response uncertainty*. But response uncertainty could be inbuilt into a task. Or, as must be much more common in everyday life, it reflects residual ambiguity of choice between the response labelled correct, and other responses in comparable contexts that previously were 'correct' but now are 'incorrect', or responses that are biologically more compatible with the stimulus situation than those called for. In the course of achieving automaticity, a major, or perhaps the major, accomplishment is the ability to eliminate interfering response tendencies (by learning to adapt ever more securely particular responses to ever finer distinctions in stimulation). Ultimately, any discriminable distinction may define a 'channel'. Which ones do is a matter of the subject's life experience in relation to his goals. Viewed in this way, the analogy between channels for information flow in communication systems and the corresponding structures in the human mind is seen to have limited value and to incur the risk of serious misrepresentation. In particular, the idea of gross discontinuity between a limited number of processing channels retreats in favour of virtual continuity (minimal discontinuity) between a great and ever varying number of patterns of response to as many different environmental states.

DEVELOPMENTAL ASPECTS

The ability to carry out dual-task performance is an individual variable, but it has not been shown that this represents a constant across different concurrent task combinations. Different combinations pose different challenges, and can be met by different strategic devices. What, then, are we to make of claims that the very young and the very old are characteristically limited in the ability to do more than one thing at a time?

While it is hard to find any task (other than so familiar as to be automatic) on which old people do not do badly as compared to properly matched younger controls (e.g. Kinsbourne, 1977), it has been suggested that they are disproportionately handicapped in dual-task situations (Craik, 1977). For children, this assumption has been made more explicitly. Multiple-task performance is limited by the restricted 'M-space' of children (Pascual-Leone, 1970). M-space develops, such that after every two years, an additional concurrent operation can be accomplished.

It is difficult to interpret developmental changes in the ability to divide attention because of the great developmentally determined differences in the efficiency with which subjects can perform each individual operation in isolation. According to Case's (1978) analysis, developmental change in M-space is an unnecessary postulate. As we have already discussed, increased operational efficiency (tendng towards automatically) facilitates division of attention between tasks, and clearly adults are more efficient at most things than young children. Case (1978) presents evidence that age-related change in operational efficiency is a sufficient explanation for the increase in ability to divide attention with increasing age. A younger child, trained to a level of operational efficiency that matches the performance of an untrained older child, divides attention equally well. This parsimonious account is limited in its generality by the extreme difficulty encountered in inducing substantive increases in operational efficiency of young children by training (Kurland, 1978). There are biological limits on operational efficiency for single tasks. The question remains — is it then necessary to suppose that there are *additional* biological limits on division of attention between tasks, or do the latter follow from the former? Note also that Case's analysis does not use paradigms in which there is a great degree of similarity between tasks. If it had perhaps the view that dividing attention (i.e. counteracting interference) is itself a skill to develop and to learn (Neisser, 1980) might have been harder to escape. Nevertheless, neurophychological studies support the conclusion that, if operational efficiency is held constant, dual-task effects are not exaggerated in children. In a series of cross-sectional studies of children using an interference paradigm that will be discussed later (pp.83–84), we had children aged three to twelve years perform two tasks simultaneously at the limits of their ability. The expected main effects for age were found, but the measure of interference was invariant across that age range (Hiscock and Kins- bourne, 1978; Hiscock and Kinsbourne, 1980; White and Kinsbourne, 1980).

At any rate, Case's analysis could with advantage be applied also to the case of the elderly. Before we accept that old people are particularly and primarily vulnerable to multitask overload, we need to know whether this impression of disproportionality would survive a correction for operational efficiency of individual tasks.

While it leaves us with unresolved issues, the discussion of age-related phenomena does focus our attention on the biological realities of the system that controls human performance.

Discussing their support of multichannel processor theory, Navon and Gopher (1979, p.249) ask themselves. 'What could convince us to abandon the notion of multiple resources? Like any other theory of metatheory that states the existence of entities whose number and nature are unspecified — the notion of multiple resources is not logically falsifiable. In practice the way to reject [it] — is to repeatedly demonstrate that simpler approaches suffice to capture empirical phenomena.' We will proceed to consider a continuity model that promises such economy. They further wished (p.268) that 'a large body of interference data could be related to some analysis of tasks by components, modalities or mechanisms'. We will now discuss an accumulating body of such data, that contributes towards delineating what Navon and Gopher (1979) call a 'resource space' and what we (Kinsbourne and Hicks, 1978) have called a 'functional cerebral space'. It relies on certain known facts about how the brain works as a functional unit.

THE BRAIN AS A FUNCTIONAL UNIT

The brain is a highly linked system. All of its parts are interconnected, and no more than about five synapses separate any neuron from any other. This linked ground plan is not incidental but fundamental to the brain's mode of action. It reflects the evolutionary origins of the vertebrate central nervous system from the primitive nerve network, and it retains the character of a differentiated net. The differentiation makes discriminative perception and differential response possible. Yet, by virtue of the connectivity, a wide range of present input and learnt responses is able to modify perceptual readiness and response predisposition. Neural models for such a system have been offered (Beurle, 1956; Pribram, 1960; Trehub, 1977). At the behavioural level it is unduly simplistic to model such a system as a single channel. To attribute to it a limited overall capacity ignores its differentiated organization. To credit it with multiple limited-capacity processors misses the point of its essential interconnectedness.

Sherrington (1906), studying neural organization at the level of the spinal cord (in the decerebrate preparation), remarked upon its highly linked nature. Strictly local responses were an analytic fiction. As stimulus intensity is increased, its influence would 'irradiate' to ever wider areas of motor control, generating response patterns that in the limit would leave hardly any of the musculature completely unaffected. No part of the system could be considered insulated from any other, although each part of the system had its own specialization. Sherrington found no need to suppose that the cerebral cortex functions along different lines. Corresponding to, and underlying, each pattern of behaviour is a specific pattern of neuronal activity. Cerebral specialization of function represents the fact that different parts of the cortex are better able to generate certain classes of neuronal firing pattern than can others, which in turn have their own predispositions to a particular patterned activity. But the connected nature of the brain provides for a general spread of whatever is the dominant activity at any time. We suppose that the information is more faithfully relayed to areas that are highly connected to their locus of origin, whereas such information as reaches distant and sparsely connected areas is largely degraded and dedifferentiated from its original specificity. The more difficult the task (in subjective terms, the more demanding of attention), the more cortical mass is implicated in the pre-programming, and the more spread is to be expected. In contrast, very simple, biologically preprogrammed or highly automatized actions are centrally represented to a minimal extent and generate minimal spread. We have called this set of propositions the 'functional cerebral distance principle', referring in this manner to distance within a conceptual cerebral space in which distances depend not on gross brain morphology but on degree of interconnectedness (Kinsbourne and Hicks, 1978).

In the spinal cord Sherrington could document the suppression of one response by a simultaneously triggered competing response. At higher levels of organization, such single-channel behaviour results when two reactions are called for that rely on some of the same cortical equipment. When they do not compete in this 'structural' fashion (Kahneman, 1973) but are nevertheless similar, they interfere without being mutually exclusive. 'Cross-talk' occurs between disparate activation patterns, and so contamination of each eventual response by elements of the other. The ability to keep similar reactions apart grows with development and with experience. Functional cerebral space is thereby effectively expanded. As the full complement of neurons is already present at birth, the basis of this expansion cannot be an increase in the neuronal population. For most short-term effects, we could invoke selective inhibitory barriers and surrounds, and in the long term, synaptic reorganiza-tion. Questions about the role in cerebral function of slow spreading dendritic potentials, and about the chemical mediation of cortical inhibition (gamma-aminobutyric acid?) remain open. Our present task is instead to explain the implication for performance models of the highly linked though internally differentiated nature of the human brain.

We have seen that the most promising organizing principle for the observation that people sometimes behave in single-channel (serial) and sometimes in multichannel processor (parallel) fashion is the effect of differential task similarity. As Navon and Gopher (1979) point out, this can be explained by a *post-hoc* model recovered from interference data for all possible task combinations by means of multidimensional scaling. However, such an empirical approach unnecessarily forgoes help from our existing knowledge about the brain. We can relieve the model of its arbitrary nature by equating degree of behavioural similarity with degree of neuronal interaction. Then one can set up demonstrations to show that, holding similarity constant, the neuronal connectivity remains revealed as the determinant of performance outcome.

Brain basis of dual-task performance

Certainly the relative independence (potential for parallel processing of activity in different modes) is consistent with what we know about the brain. Thus the relative ease experienced in combining a verbal with a visuo-spatial activity can be referred to their representation in separate hemipheres in most people. One may even go so far as to regard each hemisphere as its own limited-capacity processor (Hellige, Cox, and Litvac, 1979). But then again, auditory and visual areas of the brain are separate, although along an antero-posterior rather than a lateral axis, and these two spaces could with equal plausibility be credited with limited-capacity processor status — and so on, for any distinction one might care to emphasize. It is less arbitrary to think in terms of a differentiated but unitary cerebral space.

However, this notion need not be advocated solely on the basis of its simplifying value. It can be subjected to empirical test. This can be done through its predictions of differences in dual-task performance *holding task difficulty and task similarity constant*. The predictors are based on known cerebral specializations in most (especially right-handed) subjects, and in specialization variants in a minority (of non-right-handers). Whereas cognitive mechanisms (verbal, spatial, musical) are unilaterally represented in the brain, each hemisphere controls the contralateral limbs. There the central control facility for one limb will be closer in cerebral functional space to any given lateralized cognitive process than will the other limb. Dual-task performance will be more difficult to sustain when it calls for simultaneous activity by the cognitive processor and the functionally closer (i.e. ipsilateralized) limb than when it involves the limb controlled by the opposite hemisphere.

We can further capitalize on neuropsychological insights by demonstrating different dual-task relationships in similarly tested and equally skilful people who differ in cerebral organization and thus in functional cerebral distance relationships. For instance, some left-handers have hemisphere specialization that is essentially a mirror-image of that prevalent among right-handers (and many left-handers also). But their pattern of cerebral control of limb movements is not different. The model would predict opposite patterns of dual-task interaction in this minority group. Yet other non-right-handers appear to be bilateralized with respect to cognitive functions. The outcome of dual-task combinations should reflect this symmetrical representation (Figure 22).

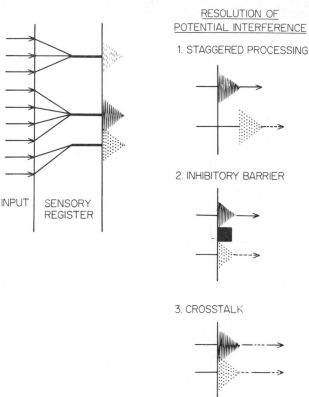

Figure 22. Effect of separation in cerebral functional distance on ability to program concurrent performance.

The brain basis of task similarity (functional cerebral distance concept)

If two activities are non-identical, they must to some extent be based on differing patterns of neural firing. Up to a point one can take a strict localizationist viewpoint, and still explain the interference between similar tasks as rivalry for use of neural elements that their 'action systems' (Shallice, 1978) have in common. But this would imply that, as long as the patterns of neural firing do not actually overlap, there can be no interference. This is blatantly untrue, as we can see if we take the extreme case of rhythm as an instance (Klapp, 1979). Regardless of how disparate the effectors are that we use, we cannot (without intense training) act out two disparate (non-harmonically related) rhythms at the same time. The similarity here is that both tasks call for the beating of a rhythm. But why should the pool of neurons that programs a voice rhythm be thought to overlap with that which programs a limb rhythm? According to the functional distance principle, it does not. Rather, the activity for each locus of programming irradiates, and interference occurs as neuron groups in the two loci tend to resonate to the other rhythm while generating their own.

Contrast this interference view with a single-channel variant — Shallice's dominant action systems. According to the latter model, the action system for one rhythm obtains the ascendancy, the other relinquishes control of behaviour, and the unity of action of the organism is maintained in terms of a single rhythmic output. But this does not necessarily happen. Instead, elements of one rhythm contaminate the other, as is to be expected based on interference.

A further experience will serve to clarify this point. Kinsbourne and Hicks (1978) reported a study in which pianists practised playing unrelated melodies simultaneously with their two hands to the point of flawless performance. When they were then asked to hum along with the melody of one hand, performance suddenly became contaminated by frequent errors (of inter-ference type). Why did this occur? No new melody was imposed. The voice merely joined in an existing melody. Limited-capacity models do not predict this, nor do multichannel processor models. But if we remember the linked nature of the brain, we realize that by recruiting the voice we have enlisted further great areas of the brain in the execution of one melody, thus narrowing the functional cerebral distance between the two loci of programming. The combined hand–voice melody is programmed by more functional cerebral space, and interferes more with any other concurrent activity.

So if we take into account the amount of brain involved in output control, we can refine our predictions to a point beyond that attainable based on similarity considerations alone. If we also take *localization* of brain function into account, we can, still using the same economical functional distance principle, make many further predictions that are quite inaccessible to purely behaviour-based models. Essentially, holding constant task similarity, the model predicts differences in degree of interference depending on whether the two loci in control of the tasks performed simultaneously are highly inter-connected (close in functional space) or not. Specifically, consider task A performed simultaneously with B′ or B″. B′ and B″ are the same task using mirror-image limbs — typically the arms. If the neural substrate for A is lateralized in cortex, and if B′ is represented in the same hemisphere as A, and B″ in the other hemisphere, then there will be more mutual interference between A and B′ than between A and B″.

Using the above logic, it has been possible to demonstrate that in right-handers, in whom voice control is almost invariably left-lateralized, there is more interference between voice and right-hand action than between voice and left-hand action (Kinsbourne and Hicks, 1978). This has been demonstrated using speaking aloud (naming, rhyme recitation, and speaking under delayed auditory feedback (Briggs, 1978)), humming (Hicks, 1975), and covert verbal activity (Hicks, Provenzano, and Rybstein, 1975) as the lateralized main task (A) and dowel balancing (Kinsbourne and Cook, 1971), finger tapping (Bowers, Heilman, Satz, and Altman, 1975), sequential finger movements (Hicks, Provenzano, and Rybstein, 1975), and step tracking (Briggs, 1975) as the ipsilateral or contralateral secondary task (B). In some cases there was no measurable interference between voice and left hand. The effect is greater if either task is made more difficult (Hicks, 1975; Hicks, Bradshaw, Kinsbourne, and Feigin, 1978). In non-right-handed samples, one finds either no asymmetry of interference, or the reversed pattern (Hicks, 1975; Lomas and Kimura, 1976). Non-verbal main tasks do not interfere asymmetrically (Bowers, Heilman, Satz, and Altman, 1975;: White and Kinsbourne, 1980).

These findings are incompatible with single-channel theory, in that concurrent tasks can (if represented sufficiently distant in functional space) be carried out simultaneously without impairment of either performance. They are incompatible with allocatable-capacity theory for the same reason, and also, the dissociation between intra-hemisphere and cross-hemisphere interference would not be predicted on this basis. Multichannel processor theory has no provision for the differential effect of brain organization.

A study which incorporates the essentials of the voice–hand interference paradigm is the one referred to by Kinsbourne and Hicks (1978) in which professional pianists first acquainted themselves with melodies written for each hand, and practised to the point of being able to play them free of errors with both hands at the same time (hands crossed or uncrossed, melodies counterbalanced across hands between subjects). During the experimental phase, they were required to hum along with one or the other hand. Note that the humming was imitative, of a highly familiar melody, and thus did not draw upon the right hemisphere's constructive musical facility. It called only for use of the left hemisphere's vocal output facility. Thus, three control areas were involved in these right-handed subjects: left hemisphere–voice, left hemisphere–right hand, right hemisphere–left hand. Consider the two conditions: (i) hum with right hand; (ii) hum with left hand. In the first condition, both centres in the left hemisphere are engaged in production, the same form of output (albeit in different modes). The unrelated (and potentially interfering) control of the left hand is distantly represented in the other hemisphere. In the second condition, neighbouring areas in the same (left) hemisphere are generating unrelated (interfering) programs. The manual program compatible with voice is controlled from the other hemisphere. According to the functional cerebral distance model, the addition of the humming requirement should interfere much more when in tandem with the left-hand melody. The proximity in functional cerebral space of the voice and right-hand control areas should generate maximal interference with both activities. While in that condition, left-hand performance would be relatively unscathed, overall, across all three effectors, the hemispherically more 'incompatible' first condition should yield better overall performance.

These predictions were all strongly confirmed. Single-channel theory would not have foreseen the ability to perform concurrently. Allocatable-capacity theory would not foresee the differential effects of the two combinations. Multichannel processor theory would have predicted no interference. In the event, the interference origin of the limit on simultaneous performance was strongly endorsed by the results of an analysis of errors, which showed almost all of them to represent intrusions from the competing program.

Should one attempt to salvage the limited-capacity approach by making the additional stipulation that each hemisphere (rather than the whole cerebrum), is in itself an autonomous limited-capacity processor, one is faced with an instance in which an interference difference occurred, but not along inter-hemispheric lines.

We (Kinsbourne, 1975) had subjects perform a multilimb step-tracking task, in which the programs that controlled the movements of separate limbs were unrelated. The pertinent conditions for the present argument are those in which the performance with paired limbs (the two arms and the two legs) is compared with performance of limbs controlled by the same hemisphere (right arm and right leg, left arm and left leg). It turned out (as predicted on the basis of the rich callosal interconnections between homologous points in the premotor cortex) that performance with the limbs controlled by opposite hemispheres was worse (specifically, more subject to interference) than performance based on the simultaneous use of two limbs controlled by the same hemisphere. It is therefore insufficient (even if usually true) simply to say that dual-task performance is better if its control is spread across hemispheres than if it resides within one hemisphere (Dimond and Beaumont, 1971).

We are now in a position to revise the initial claim of single-channel theory in the light of the established facts of brain organization and their impact on dual-task performance. The translation of a signal from a sensory code to a memory code or response code involves a differentiated unitary system. If there is no response uncertainty then no, or virtually no, interference is to be expected, and the operator will proceed at the maximum rate permitted by physical factors limiting rate of information flow through the organism. Response uncertainty may derive from conflicting response tendencies set up by virtue of the design of the task, from pre-existing contrary habits or biological predispositions, or from deliberate concurrent performance of a second activity. In all these cases, the resonse uncertainty is resolved by inhibiting interfering response tendencies.

Thus, while stimulus–response compatibility effects in simple reaction time are small (Callan, Klisz, and Parsons, 1974; Anzola, Bertolini, Buchter, and Rizzolatti, 1977), they are substantial when the entire stimulus and response ensembles in choice reaction time are considered (Brainard, Irby, Fitts, and Alluisi, 1962). If we consider that the problem in response uncertainty is inhibition of a competing response, then, according to the functional cerebral distance model, this should be most onerous (i.e. generate longest latencies) when the competing responses are represented close to each other in functional cerebral space. Thus, it is the relative mapping of the alternative responses that is critical (Duncan, 1977). The outcomes of such studies should be predictable from our knowledge of the relative interconnection of different parts of the brain. This inhibition circumscribes the functional cerebral space available for programming the primary task responses, thus impairing the efficiency with which it is performed. The same process impairs performance of the secondary task. The trade-off between the two is determined by the location of the inhibitory barrier in terms of its overlap with the two control areas. The closer in cerebral functional space the tasks are represented the more interference is to be overcome; and in general, the behaviourally more similar tasks are those closer in functional space.

When functional space is diminished, by neuronal depletion (e.g. in ageing and dementia) or functionally by anxiety or sedative drugs, dual-task performance becomes more difficult and familiar (prepotent) responses become hardest to suppress (e.g. perseverative behaviour increases in incidence). When a cognitive subsystem is damaged, its functional space becomes limited, and the same problems arise within its delimited sphere — slower information transmission, greater vulnerability to interfering cross-talk from concurrent activity, and a tendency towards blocking of adaptive responses by overlearned or biologically prepotent ones — all characteristics of focal brain damage as discussed by Kurt Goldstein (see Kinsbourne, in press).

The present model is economical in that it dispenses with the hypothetical commodity ('attention'), supply of which is 'limited'. It accounts for 'concurrence cost' without the need to invoke the *post-hoc* construct of an executive or clerical facility which is capacity consuming. In its functional emphasis, it typifies the contemporary retreat from the flow charts of the recent past, with their hypothetical stores. In this respect it corresponds in the separate but allied area of memory theory to the levels of processing (Craik and Lockhart, 1972) and encoding specificity (Tulving and Thomson, 1973) approaches, and to pragmatics in language development theory (Tamir, 1979). In its neurological emphasis it extends to higher mental functions fundamental principles of integrative action established by Sherrington (1906) at the sensorimotor level of organization.

CAPACITY LIMITATIONS AND CONSCIOUSNESS

It is the fate of fashionable concepts to be used to explain almost everything. We note without surprise that limited-capacity processing has been repeatedly invoked as the mechanism of consciousness (Atkinson and Shiffrin, 1971; Posner and Klein, 1973; Erdelyi, 1974; Mandler, 1975; Posner and Snyder, 1975; Shallice, 1978). These theorists differ with respect to the locus of this processor, ranging from early in sensory short-term memory (Atkinson and Shiffrin, 1971) to late, in 'action systems' that exert control over responding (Shallice, 1978). But rather than attempt to adjudicate that debate, we will question the underlying assumption. Is there any persuasive reason to endorse conscious experience with limited-capacity properties?

We are subjectively aware of features within the range of our attention (focal and peripheral, external and internal) as well as of our intentions, acts, and emotional state. There are indeed limits on our focal attention (Treisman, 1976) and on our acts (Shallice, 1978) in that in general, they both call for serial processing. But there are no grounds for attributing serial constraints to our peripheral awareness. Indeed the contrary is the case. Treisman has clarified the degree of processing which can be implemented in parallel to enable us to represent that simultaneous wealth of external stimulation and internal state that serves as backdrop ('ground') to the 'figure' created by our favoured attention. Nor has it been shown to be of heuristic value to attribute limited-capacity characteristics to an awareness of our feelings and intentions. So, while it could be disputed whether those aspects of information processing which obey serial constraints are represented in awareness, no case can be made for supposing that they only are so represented. Certainly, unchanging features tend to drop out of awareness — we habituate out the ticking clock, the touch of clothes, the hum of irrelevant conversation. But it would be a gross exaggeration to claim that we are conscious only of the changing elements of the external world. The visual environment, even when static, does not fade from notice, presumably because head and gaze shifts and fine eye tremors counteract sensory adaptation.

Subjective awareness neatly reflects the basic distinction at which we arrived based on empirical evidence: that single-channel theory best describes behaviour focused narrowly within a mode and of a particular manner, whereas multichannel processor behaviour occurs when behaviour encompasses a wide sweep of ultimate modes and *modi operandi*. So with consciousness: that 'coherence of thought and action' that Shallice (1978) scrutinized obtains only in some situations (though they are the ones typically studied by experimental psychologists). Consciousness is not confined to the limited-processing, let alone single-channel mode. It does, oftentimes, adopt this mode, however. By what mechanism does this come about?

At the physiological level, one action system has attained dominance (Shallice, 1978). Does this reflect the controlling influence of a separate attention centre (e.g. LaBerge, 1975)? This type of construct confronts us with the menace of an infinite regress (what informs the attention centre, etc.). More simply, when, by virtue of positive feedback 'contrast' effects (Shallice, 1972; Walley and Weiden, 1973; Kinsbourne, 1974) one action system attains temporary dominance, experience is unified. When we experience ourselves as intending, this indicates dominance of the neural activity that corresponds to what we intend. In that, consciousness is not a process. The workings of the mind are its givens, not its fabric. We are conscious of certain representations that are formulated pending action. Representation, be it of external stimulation, be it of an action plan, does not itself have a controlling function. It gives instead a narrative account of what is happening, but does not make things happen. That is why it is not limited.

The functional cerebral distance principle recognized a distinction between the locally patterned excitation which is the neural basis of representation, and is by its very nature localized, and the spreading patterned excitation that exerts control over behaviour. It is the latter which is subject to interference from comparable alternative excitation, and which generates a fleeting sense of unity of purpose. Multiple representations, in contrast, do not encroach on each other's functional cerebral space, do not interfere, coexist, and endow awareness with its parallel processed richness. Sherrington (1937–38) held that: 'Identity in time and in space suffice.' It instances the 'now' as an integrating factor of the finite mind. He had much earlier arrived at the conclusion that 'pure conjunction in time without necessarily cerebral conjunction in space lies at the root of the solution of the problem of the unity of mind' (Sherrington, 1906).

SUMMARY

This chapter considers possible reasons why human operators are limited in what they can do at a given time, with special reference to dual-task performance. Its point of departure is single-channel theory. This is a rigorous version of possible limited-capacity models, which regards the operator as essentially committed to one activity at a time (with some reservation in regard to highly practised acts). An alternative approach, allocatable-capacity theory, does make provision for sharing of a limited resource between concurrent acts. By and large, findings from paradigms that involve highly similar tasks are consistent with the limited-capacity viewpoint, in the form of the single channel variant. But findings when concurrent tasks are dissimilar are inconsistent with the predictions of any limited-capacity model. An alternative view attributes the capacity limitation not to the operator as a whole, but to each of a set of hypothesized independent processes at his disposal. This multichannel processor model is also inadequate to account for the data, and postulates discontinuities which find no support from present knowledge about how the brain is organized. If we acknowledge the unitary, though differentiated, nature of brain organization, we can conceptualize control of concurrent activities as occurring at loci varying in distance from each other within a 'functional cerebral space'. This model has some predictive value not shared by the others.

Human Skills
Edited by D. Holding
©1981 John Wiley & Sons Ltd.

Chapter 5

Discrete Movements

C. I. Howarth and W. D. A. Beggs

The study of discrete movements has played an important part in the study of skills, partly because they are easy to study, and partly because of the common hope that complex movements may be understandable as an integrated sequence of simpler ones. Because of the ease with which they can be studied a great deal is now known about the characteristics of discrete movements, but the hope that, theoretically, complex movements may be treated as an agglomeration of simpler ones, has not been fulfilled. Indeed, the theoretical traffic has been the other way. Discrete movements are now treated, theoretically, as if they were complex, or as elements of complex movements which can only be understood in relation to the whole context in which they occur.

Discrete movements are easy to study because they have a clear beginning and a clear end. One can measure the length and duration of the movement and the accuracy with which it is made. Most studies of discrete movements have concentrated on the relationships between speed, distance, and accuracy. The effect of other variables such as direction of movement or previous experience, or the quality of the sensory information available, is usually investigated in relation to their effects either on the accuracy of movement, or on the relationships between distance, speed, and accuracy. These things have been studied because they are the easiest things to study.

Since accuracy of movement is the commonest of all measures, it is unfortunate that it has not always been measured in the same way. One should always distinguish between constant and variable errors, since they are not always related to each other in any simple way. Measures which confuse the two, such as the modular mean error (i.e. the mean error independent of its sign) ought never to be used.

Similarly, errors can be measured in different directions. It is important to distinguish at least between errors in the same direction as the movement and errors at right angles to it. Error measured in the direction of movement is related to the accuracy with which a movement can be stopped. Error at right angles to the movement is the error of aiming.

HISTORICAL

The most important early study of discrete movement was contained in R. S. Woodworth's Ph.D. thesis (1899). The seeds of most subsequent developments can be found in his work. He measured accuracy of stopping by asking his subjects to reproduce the length of a line. The movement was recorded on paper which moved at a constant speed at right angles to the direction of movement. As a result, the total time taken by the movement and the shape of the acceleration and deceleration phases were clearly recorded on the paper. He measured accuracy of aiming by the distribution of hits about a target on a piece of graph paper. With this method there was no record of the timing of the movement, so most of his experiments were done on accuracy of stopping.

To control the speed of movement Woodworth used a metronome, ticking at speeds up to 200 beats per minute.

With the eyes open he found that at rates between 40 and 200 beats per minute errors increased with the speed, but not linearly. If E is Woodworth's measure of error, and S is the speed in beats per minute, then a linear relationship would be

$$E = kS \tag{1}$$

where k is a constant which depends on the units in which E and S are measured. Woodworth found in fact

$$E = kS^n \tag{2}$$

where n was a number less than one. This means that as S increases, E also increases, but at a decreasing rate. Figure 23 shows Woodworth's results in the form of a graph.

Below 40 beats per minute, error appeared to be independent of speed. This is also shown in Figure 23.

With the eyes closed, error was independent of speed and the same as the accuracy achieved with the eyes open at speeds above 160–200 beats per minute (see Figure 23). He concluded that movement is controlled by both a 'muscle sense' and by a 'visual sense', and that the latter is more effective at slower speeds.

His early experiments, using repetitive movements, altered speed of movement and repetition frequency together. So he did them again varying the speed of movement and the interval between movements independently. When the interval was constant, then increasing speed decreased accuracy as before. With constant speed of movement, increasing the intervals between movements caused a smaller decline in accuracy. When the two were combined, as when repetitive movements were made in time with a metronome, then the larger effect predominated.

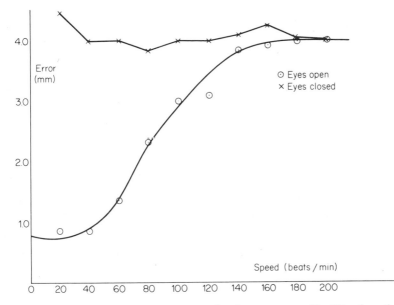

Figure 23. The relationship between speed and error reported by Woodworth (1899).

From these experiments he concluded that there is a control system with:

(a) an 'initial adjustment' which is in some way made more accurately if one has recently made a similar movement;

(b) a 'current control' which is most effective when one can see the movement, and when there is time to make corrections.

These two concepts are still central to theories of movement. (a) is now usually called the 'motor program', while (b) is usually called 'feedback'.

Woodworth also found that each movement had three phases to it, an initial acceleration, a middle phase of relatively constant velocity, and a final phase of deceleration (as in Figure 2, earlier in this volume). Carefully aimed movements had a short, very rapid acceleration and a long deceleration phase during which corrections ('current control') were made as the hand approached the target. At higher speeds these secondary corrections were reduced in number and above 120 beats per minute they disappeared entirely. In unaimed movements the final deceleration phase was less marked, and there were no secondary corrections of the movement.

The effect of practice differed for fast and slow movements. Very little improvement in the accuracy of fast movements was achieved with practice, but at slower speeds a rapid and lasting improvement occurred. This has subsequently been shown (Beggs and Howarth, 1972a) to be almost entirely due to a relative increase in the deceleration phase of the movement, so that the hand of the practised person moves more quickly over the first phase of the movement, but spends more time over the final phase during which corrections are made. The lack of sufficient time to make corrections during the final phase of very fast movements is the probable reason for the absence of improvement with practice.

Woodworth also varied the amplitude of aimed movements and found that the variable error increased with an increase in the length of the movement. This increase was roughly proportional to the square root of the length of the movement. Later workers (e.g. Fitts, 1954) have sometimes assumed error to be directly proportional to length. For constant errors a totally different relationship was found, with near targets being overshot and distant targets undershot.

More recent experiments have added remarkably little to Woodworth's data and analysis. Fitts (1954) reversed Woodworth's procedure and measured the speed with which people could make movements of a fixed accuracy, determined by the size of the target. That is, he measured the speed of free movements of a fixed accuracy while Woodworth measured the accuracy of paced movements. Fitts' procedure is related to many real-life tasks such as putting pegs or bolts into holes of differing sizes, or putting nuts on to bolts with varying tolerances in the thread. Unfortunately, the use of a fixed-size target makes it impossible to distinguish between constant and variable errors. Despite these differences Fitts confirmed many of Woodworth's basic findings, although he used a very different theoretical interpretation.

One aspect of simple hand movements which Woodworth did not investigate was the effect of direction of movement. This was studied by several investigators after the Second World War. Corrigan and Brogden (1948; 1949), Brown and Slater-Hammel (1949), Siddall, Holding, and Draper (1957), and Begbie (1959) all investigated movements of varying direction and extents. They all confirmed Woodworth's findings that longer movements produce greater errors, but found only small and inconsistent effects of the direction of movement. For movements away from the body, Corrigan and Brogden found the greatest accuracy straight ahead, Begbie found the greatest accuracy 35° to the left of straight ahead, while Siddall *et al.* found no effect of movement direction.

Interest in the control of movement revived almost fifty years after Woodworth. During the Second World War the skill with which men controlled machines was intensively investigated. Some of this work was specific to man–machine interaction. However, this work also made psychologists aware of theories of machines, and in particular, of information theory and control theory. Something of the history of the application of control theory has already been described in Chapters 1 and 2, while Chapter 1 also introduced the basic concept in the application of information theory to the study of skills, which is that we should be able to react more quickly to a probably stimulus than to an improbable one. The implications of information theory and of control theory for the study of discrete movements will now be discussed in greater detail.

INFORMATION THEORY

The basic concept of information theory is that improbable messages should take longer to convey than probable messages. An example of this is the inverse relationship between length of words and their frequency of use in English, and indeed in all other languages. The commonest words such as 'I', 'a', 'he', 'me', 'am', 'is', 'the', 'and', 'you', 'are', are all very short words. Long words such as 'antidisestablishmentarianism' are seldom used. Information theory establishes an optimum relationship between the length of a message and the frequency of its use. The way it does this can be demonstrated very simply in relation to the simplest of all codes, the binary code which has only two symbols (conventionally 0 and 1, but any two will do).

For example, if there are only two messages to be conveyed then only one symbol will be needed to distinguish them. So, if only two letters of the alphabet need to be transmitted, the following simple code book will translate them into binary code:

Message		Code
a	. . .	0
b	. . .	1

If we wish to transmit a greater number of messages, then more than one symbol per message will be needed. If we wish to transmit four messages (a, b, c, or d), then the code book could be rewritten:

a	. . .	00
b	. . .	01
c	. . .	10
a	. . .	11

and for eight possible messages it would need to be rewritten again:

a	. . .	000
b	. . .	001
c	. . .	010

d	. . .	011
e	. . .	100
f	. . .	101
g	. . .	110
h	. . .	111

Note that each time an extra binary symbol is added, the total number of possible messages is doubled. If N is the total number of messages, and n the number of symbols in each message, the relationship between the number of symbols per message and the number of possible messages can be represented by the equation:

$$N = 2^n \tag{3}$$

From this equation we can deduce that if we wish to transmit all the letters of the alphabet in binary code, we should need five binary symbols per letter. This would give thirty-two possible messages leaving some over to cope with full stops, commas, question-marks, and so on. Morse code, which translates letters into no more than four dots or dashes, is not in fact a binary code, because it also makes use of spaces in which no dot or dash occurs. It therefore has three symbols, not two.

Equation (3) is usually written in another form:

$$n = \log_2 N \tag{4}$$

which is the simplest form of the basic information theory equation. Since n is a measure of the length of a message and N is the number of possible messages, equation (4) shows how, if one has a greater number of possible messages, the length of each message must be increased. It specifies, for example, the relationship between the number of subscribers linked to a telephone exchange and the length of the number which must be dialled if we wish to be connected to one of them (since telephone numbers use a decimal code the precise equation in that case is $n = \log_{10} N$). This equation also describes the nature of economies of scale, since the length of a message does not increase in proportion to the number of possible messages , but proportionally to its logarithm.

Equation (4) applies only to equally probable messages. If messages are not equally probable, then a modification of the equation is required. It is possible to write a code book with shorter strings of symbols for the more probable messages. However, this is a more difficult thing to do than appears at first sight. For example, if we wish to send only three messages, two probable and one improbable, we might write the following code:

Message		Code
a	. . .	0
b	. . .	1
c	. . .	10

This code would be more economical than using two symbols for each message, but would lead to ambiguity. Here, 101 could be either bab or cb. Ambiguity can be avoided if the beginning of one symbol string can never be mistaken for the beginning of another. This is called the prefix rule. The following code makes use of this rule and is never ambiguous:

a	. . .	0
b	. . .	10
c	. . .	11

Codes which make use of shorter strings of symbols for less probable messages, but which, by making use of the prefix rule are unambiguous, are called 'Huffman codes' after their inventor. It can be shown that there is a limit to the degree of economy which can be achieved by these codes. This limit is given by the equation:

$$n = \log_2 \frac{1}{P} \tag{5}$$

where P is the probability of the message. The simple codes we have been considering do not achieve the degree of economy specified by equation (5) because of their inflexibility. For example, the last code is the only economical three-message binary code which exists. It is most efficient when one message is more probable than the rest, but the same code would have to be used if two messages were probable and one improbable, or if all three were equally probable. More complex code books, with longer message strings and many more messages, are more flexible and approach more closely the limit specified by equation (3). For equally probable messages, equation (5) reduces to equation (2) since in that case

$$1/P = N$$

Sometimes messages are sent through unreliable or 'noisy' channels. When this happens, as with a bad connection on the telephone, the only thing to do is to repeat each message more than once ('I am coming home tomorrow — tomorrow — yes, tomorrow') until the other person has received it. In information theory this is called 'redundancy'.

Information theory was developed by Claude Shannon, working for the Bell Telephone Company during the Second World War (Shannon and Weaver, 1949), although equation (4) was first used by Hartley, also working for Bell Telephones, 1928. It was not long before psychologists realized that the same sort of thinking could be applied to human skills since our movements are controlled by messages sent from the brain to the muscles, often in response to other messages received from the outside world via our sense organs. If these messages are dealt with economically and efficiently then the information equations should specify an upper limit to the efficiency which could be achieved.

The first attempt to apply information theory to human skill was the work of Hick (1952) and independently of Hyman (1953) on human choice reactions. Reaction times are usually measured by getting people to press switches or Morse keys, so that the electrical connection can be used to indicate precisely when the person reacted. This is another aspect of discrete movements which Woodworth did not study, but reaction times had been studied even before Woodworth. In 1880 Merkel had found that if a different response had to be made to different signals then the time taken to respond to a signal increased if the number of possible signals increased. Hick was the first to point out that the increase observed by Merkel was a logarithmic one and that equation (4) could be fitted to the data. Both Hick and Hyman gathered more data showing that equation (4) could be fitted to choice reaction times when the signals were equally probable and Hyman also showed that when some signals were more probable than others, we react more quickly to the more probable signals and more slowly to the improbable ones, as is suggested by equation (5). However, in the latter case the match between equation and data is not so good as when the signals are equiprobable.

These basic findings have been repeated many times and for many different types of response. Some of the more complex data are inconsistent with the simplest of coding mechanisms. For example, it has been found that an improbable message embedded in a series of probable messages will be faster than the same message, with the same probability embedded in a series of improbable messages. Related experiments are discussed in Chapter 7.

In 1954 Paul Fitts attempted to apply information theory to the types of situations which Woodworth had studied. This was one of the most original and interesting applications of information theory to the study of skill, although it is now clear that his ideas were mistaken.

Fitts suggested that the relationship between speed and accuracy of movement could be understood in terms of the length of message required to specify a movement to a particular degree of accuracy. Thus, greater accuracy should be achieved by slow movements because there is time to send a more detailed message to the muscles. As has already been described, Fitts specified the accuracy of the movement by the size of the target. In one set of experiments he used two targets and asked the subject to move backwards and forwards between them as fast as he could. In other experiments he asked people to put pegs in holes as fast as they could. The larger the holes, the faster they could do it. In these experiments he found that the time taken on the task could be predicted by the equation:

$$T = a + b\log\frac{2A}{W}$$

(6)

where T is the movement time, A the amplitude of the movement, and W the width of the target, while a and b are constants dependent on the units used to measure the other three. Figure 24 shows one of his experimental arrangements.

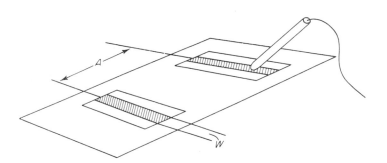

Figure 24. One of the apparatus arrangements used by Fitts (1954). Reproduced by permission of the author.

Fitts suggested that equation (6) was really another form of equation (4), T being determined by the length of the message ('n' in equation (4)). The quantity $2A/W$ represents the number of alternative movements (of accuracy W and of amplitude between 0 and $2A$) the subject might have been expected to make and therefore the number (N in equation (4)) of alternative messages which might need to be sent. There were an enormous number of theoretical implausibilities about this idea and even in Woodworth's data of fifty-five years earlier, some very strong evidence against it.

For example, we would expect the reasoning behind equation (6) to apply to blindfolded movement as well as to visually controlled movement. But Woodworth and many other authors have found that the accuracy of blindfolded movement is independent of speed (cf. Chapter 1).

The same weakness of being unable to account for the lack of any relationship between speed and error in the absence of visual feedback, is exhibited by a new theory recently proposed by Schmidt, Zelaznik, and Frank (1977). They suggest that the error on target is proportional to the force exerted and that the force exerted is inversely proportional to the total movement time. They say explicitly that the relationship between speed and error should not depend on making corrections during the execution of the movement. Since the removal of visual feedback during the course of a movement has such a dramatic effect on accuracy this theory seems unlikely to be correct.

Equation (6) produced a curve similar in shape to Woodworth's equation (2). It is often equally easy to fit a power function (equation (1)) or a logarithmic function (equation (4)) to the same data. Nevertheless, the differences between Woodworth and Fitts are not just theoretical. Their two experimental situations do produce different results. Figure 25 shows some data from Howarth, Beggs, and Bowden (1971) (gathered in an experiment very like Woodworth's of aiming at a graph paper target in time to a

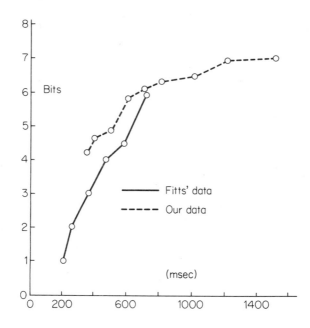

Figure 25. A comparison of data from two experimental traditions. From Fitts (1954) and Howarth, Beggs, and Bowden (1971).

metronome) which cannot be described by Fitts' equation. In general, Woodworth's technique produced much greater accuracy at high speeds, while there is a possibility (as yet unrealized) that Fitts' technique may produce greater accuracy at very low speeds. There are a number of explanations for these discrepancies which will be considered in more detail later.

One of these is the fact that Fitts' method confuses constant and variable errors. We have already mentioned that Woodworth found these two to be differentially affected by length of movement, so that it is unreasonable to expect a simple explanation of the relationship between speed and error in Fitts' experiments. Secondly, there is considerable evidence that subjects do not use the full width of the target when aiming at large targets (Welford, 1968). This is the probable explanation of the longer time which Fitts' subject took over the less accurate movements. They were aiming at a target effectively narrower than the one presented to them.

For these reasons Howarth, Beggs, and Bowden (1971) used line targets and measured accuracy of paced movements only at right angles to the movement. For this situation, Figure 25 shows that equation (6) cannot be fitted to the data. It seems likely that it described Fitts' own data only for accidental reasons which had little to do with the theory. Woodworth's equation (1) did describe our data for reasons which are easily understandable in relation to the kind of theory of intermittent control which has already been described in Chapter 2. This will now be described in some detail.

CONTROL THEORY

Like information theory, control theory developed slowly before the Second World War, more rapidly during the war. Control theory is essentially concerned with the behaviour of machines which have some control of their own behaviour. It made a big impact on the academic community following the publication of Norbert Wiener's (1948) book *Cybernetics*. Cybernetics was Wiener's own neologism derived from the Greek word for the helmsman of a boat. The essential concept of control theory, as described in Chapter 2, is that of feedback, i.e. that in order to control its own performance, a machine must be able to monitor its own output and use that information to govern its future performance.

The application of control theory to psychology did not have to wait until the end of the Second World War. Kenneth Craik (1943) published a book called *The Nature of Explanation* which, among other things, made use of the concept of feedback. His wartime studies of feedback in simple human skills were published after his death (1947; 1948). Basically, Craik claimed that many skilled actions were under sensory control and that when a deviation from the desired performance was detected, then a correction would be made. His most productive experimental situation was a dynamic version of Woodworth's task. The line to be reproduced by the subject was drawn on the same belt of moving paper on which the subject's response was recorded. The task is known as step tracking, but it can also be seen as a way of requiring the subject to make a sequence of discrete movements whose extent and sequential timing can be determined by the experimenter. This led Craik to take an interest in the interactions of movements which follow one another in rapid sequence. Subsequently, these features of skilled behaviour were studied on keyboards which, of course, do not record the movements in the same detail as Craik's step-tracking apparatus (see Chapters 4 and 7).

Subsequent work in the Craik–Woodworth tradition has tended to concentrate on particular elements of the task, such as the motor program, or the rate at which reactions could be made. Very few authors have attempted to put together a coherent control theory account of the basic phenomena which Woodworth observed. One exception is the attempt of Crossman and Goodeve (1963) to derive Fitts' logarithmic function from control theory. It has already been argued, however, that this logarithmic function has little significance.

The most comprehensive attempt to explain the basic phenomena in control theory terms is that of Howarth and Beggs in a series of papers starting in 1970. Their theory was first set out formally in Howarth, Beggs, and Bowden (1971) and is based on the following assumptions (shown below with simplified notation), some of which seemed initially rather implausible.

1. That the angular error of aiming (i.e. the angular variability (a) with which the hand can aim at a target) is independent of the speed of movement.
2. That a is also independent of the distance (D) over which the movement is made. Hence, when a movement is made without correction the error (e) on target will be given by the equation:

$$e \ = \ aD \tag{7}$$

3. That if the movement is visually monitored, errors of aim can be detected and corrected after an appropriate reaction time (τ).
4. That errors detected less than a corrective reaction time before impact on the target will not be corrected, so that the variable error on target e will be determined by the distance away from the target (δ) at which the last correction was made, i.e.:

$$e \ = \ a \bullet \delta \tag{8}$$

5. To a first approximation the *average* distance (δ) at which the last correction of aim is made, can be calculated from the relationship between distance and time as the hand approaches the target. Experimentally Howarth, Beggs, and Bowden (1971) and Beggs and Howarth (1972a, b) found that the final phase of deceleration, as the hand approaches the target, can be described by the equation:

$$d = k \left(\frac{t}{T}\right)^n$$

(9)

where d is the distance of the hand from the target, t the time before impact, T the time required for the total movement (imposed by a metronome as in Woodworth's experiments), and n a number between 1 and 2, being closer to 1 for inexperienced subjects. As usual, k is a constant determined by the units in which d and t are measured.

When t is given the value of the corrective reaction time (τ), equation (9) allows us to calculate the relationship between the distance from the target (δ) at which the last corrective reaction is made, for a given value (T) for the total movement time. Figure 26 shows the significance of this calculation since it is equivalent to reading off from the graph relating time (t) and distance (d) as the hand approaches the target, what is the distance (δ) of the hand from the target when it is one corrective reaction time (τ) before impact.

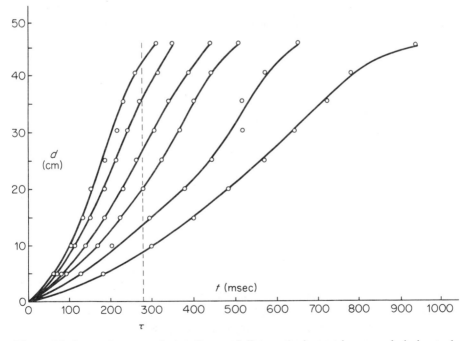

Figure 26. A set of curves relating time and distance to impact in a paced aiming task. From Howarth, Beggs, and Bowden (1971).

By putting the calculated value of δ into equation (8) we can calculate the appropriate value of *e*, the error on target:

$$e = ak \left(\frac{\tau}{T}\right)^n$$

(10)

Howarth, Beggs, and Bowden (1971) found that this equation required one extra term in order to fit the observed relationship between error and speed of movement. As T becomes very long $1/T$ approaches zero so that, if equation (10) is correct, *e* should also approach zero. But for very slow movements, as Woodworth found, there is a lower limit to the accuracy of aiming which they suggested may be related to the minimal tremor of the hand even when we attempt to hold it perfectly still. Howarth *et al.* therefore assumed that both tremor and the error of aiming would contribute to the final error on target and that those two errors would combine independently. Hence the variance of the total error on target (which we can call E^2) should be the sum of the two variances, one due to aiming (e^2 as calculated from equation (10)) and one due to tremor q^2, the 'quaver' factor, which could be determined empirically by measuring the tremor of a stationary hand). Thus the final equation they produced to describe the relationship between speed and error was:

$$E^2 = q^2 + e^2 = q^2 + \left[ak \; \frac{\tau}{T}^n\right]^2$$

(11)

Figure 27 shows some data from Howarth, Beggs, and Bowden (1971) fitted to this equation.

Although equation (11) appears complicated, all of the terms in it can be estimated in more than one way, these ways being determined by the assumptions 1–5 on which the theory is based and by the assumption that q represents normal tremor of the hand. Because there are so many different ways in which the elements of this theory can be tested, and because it has so far passed all these tests, equation (11) must be regarded as the best account we yet have of the relationship between the speed and error of paced hand movements.

For example, *a* can be estimated from the slope of the relationship shown in Figure 27. In this way Howarth *et al.* estimate *a* to be 41′. It can also be estimated more directly from the accuracy of aiming without visual correction using equation (7). Beggs, Baker, Dove, Fairclough, and Howarth (1972) were able to do this by the simple expedient of automatically switching off the room illumination immediately the hand started to move towards the target and switching it back on again when the target was reached. Under these conditions they estimated *a* to be 54′.

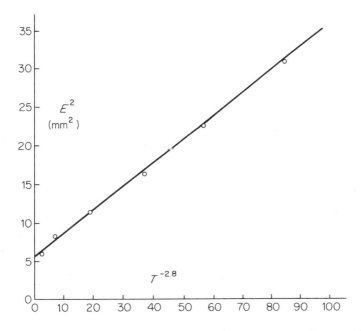

Figure 27. The relationship of error on target and movement speed — predicted and actual. From Howarth, Beggs, and Bowden (1971).

In the same experiment Beggs *et al.* showed that *a* is almost independent of speed, as required by equation (7). This is frequently regarded as the most surprising assumption of the theory: it has in fact been found many times in the past. Woodworth found it for movements made with the eyes closed (see Figure 23). Vince (1948b) confirmed Woodworth's finding except for an increase at very slow speeds. Keele and Posner (1968), on the other hand, found an increase of error for very high-speed movements. Beggs (1971) found a negligible effect of speed on error over the range of speeds he used. In fact all these experiments produced very consistent results as in shown in Figure 28.

The constancy of *a* for movements over different distances was also demonstrated by Beggs, Baker, Dove, Fairclough, and Howarth (1972) since their estimate of *a* was based on the slope of the line relating *E* and the total distance *(D)* of a movement. The degree to which the data could be fitted by a straight line is a measure of the constancy of *a*. Since the straight line accounted for 99.57 per cent of the variance, the constancy of *a* can be regarded as very well established.

The linear relationship, postulated in equation (8), between the distance at which the last correction is made and the error on target *E* was demonstrated by Beggs and Howarth (1970) in an experiment in which the room illumination was switched off when the hand passed through an infra-red beam which could be placed at different distances from the target. They found that, at slow

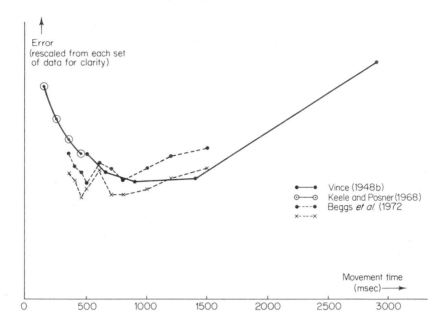

Figure 28. Aiming at a target without visual feedback — a comparison of rescaled data from several sources (Vince, 1948; Keele and Posner, 1968; Beggs, Baker, Dove, Fairclough, and Howarth (1972). © (1968) American Psychological Association. Reproduced by permission of the Experimental Psychology Society and the American Psychological Association.

speeds, error on target was roughly proportional to the distance of the infra-red beams from the target. At faster speeds switching off the illumination had almost no effect at distances less than a critical distance. These critical distances were predictable from a corrective reaction time (τ) of about 290 milliseconds. This estimate of the critical reaction time is close to the estimate of between 190 and 260 milliseconds by Keele and Posner (1968) in an experiment very similar to ours, and rather smaller than the estimates of 400 milliseconds by Woodworth and of 450 milliseconds by Vince. Both of these earlier experimenters asked their subjects voluntarily to close their eyes. The greater difficulty of this procedure may account for the difference.

The value of 'n' in equation (11) can be estimated from the relationship between speed and error of movement, but it can be estimated more directly (as implied in equation (9)) by investigating the trajectory of the hand as it approaches the target. Howarth, Beggs, and Bowden (1971) did so by recording the time at which the hand cut a beam of infra-red light placed at various distances from the target, but which in this experiment had no effect on the room illumination. In this way they estimated 'n' to be 1.4 regardless of the total movement time. This experiment also justifies the form of equation

(9) in which t is measured as a proportion of the total movement time. In a further experiment of the same type Beggs and Howarth (1972b) estimated 'n' to be about 1.26 for unpractised subjects and to approach or even exceed 2 after practice. Figure 29 shows the change in the trajectory of the hand produced by prolonged practice in aimed movement. It can be seen that the main effect of practice is to get the hand closer to the target during the final phase of the movement. As a result, the last correction of aim is made closer to the target so that error on target is consequently reduced. Practice appears to have less effect on the other quantities in equation (11).

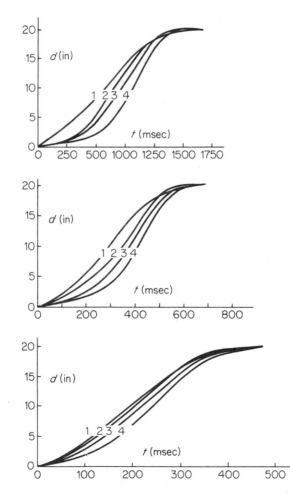

Figure 29. Changes in the approach trajectories of the hand on four successive days of practice (1, 2, 3, and 4) and at three movement speeds (from Beggs and Howarth, 1972). Reproduced by permission of the Experimental Psychology Society.

Beggs and Howarth (1972a) took estimates of a, n, τ, k, and q obtained in different experiments, and by inserting these values in equation (11) attempted to fit the relationship between speed and error of movement. In this way they were able to account for over 90 per cent of the variance.

It should be noted that this theory was developed for paced movements and for variable errors of aiming measured at right angles to the direction of movement. Using unpaced movements in which the accuracy of stopping was the critical factor, Fitts (1954) obtained a completely different relationship between speed and error (Figure 25). In a number of previously unpublished experiments we have attempted to discover which of the differences in our experiments is most important in determining the difference in results. *A priori*, a number of factors would appear to be involved — the nature of the pacing used, external or internal, the presence of one or two targets, and the way in which errors are measured. We believe that our data show that subjects can adopt very different strategies in aiming, which are reflected in the different patterns of errors on different sorts of apparatus.

In particular, as earlier noted by Welford, Norris, and Shock (1969), although subjects do not use anything like the full width of the wider targets in a Fitts'-type task, so that W is not a direct measure of the accuracy of their performance, they can achieve much greater accuracy within narrow targets than when paced by a metronome at the same speed but aiming at line targets. We believe this may be because, just like subjects given practice on line targets, they change the way that their hand approaches the target, reducing δ, and thus minimizing E^2.

A second target is a factor which causes eye movements to occur between targets, and we have shown clearly that there is a large quantitative difference in error scores achieved when fixation or eye movements are used as independent variables in an aiming task.

Equally important theoretically is Beggs' (1971) demonstration that variable and constant errors are affected quite differently by speed, distance, and the difference between errors of aiming and errors of stopping. He has shown that equation (11) can be applied to errors of stopping, i.e. errors measured in the same direction as the movement, provided we ignore the constant errors. When errors are measured at right angles to the direction of movement, and when the movement is a relatively simple one away from the body, then constant errors are very small and largely independent of the speed and distance of the movement. Since, under these conditions, constant errors are unimportant, our theory accounts for almost all of the data. However, as Siddall, Holding, and Draper (1957) showed, when errors are measured parallel to the direction of movement, constant errors can become large. In particular, there is a consistent failure to reach the target (undershooting) at high speeds and for the longer movements. Our theory cannot account for this, but it is yet another factor leading to poorer performance at high speeds in the Fitts situation.

Equations (10) or (11) can be extended relatively easily to deal with continuous movement. Beggs, Sakstein, and Howarth (1974) pointed out that at constant speed 'n' must have a value of unity so that, if we ignore tremor, we should get $e = K/T$, where K includes ϱ and all the other constants in equation (10). This equation resembles those proposed by Rashevsky (1959) to account for the relationship between the speed of cars and the width of the road, and by Drury (1971) to describe the relationship between speed and accuracy of a number of tasks, including driving a fork-lift truck. Both Rashevsky and Drury derived their equations from the assumption that intermittent corrections of aim would be made, but would only become effective after an appropriate reaction time, that is from essentially the same theoretical assumptions on which equation (10) is based. They also assume that, for a given width of track *(W)*, and for a given probability of staying within the track, then the ratio *W/E* must be constant. It is therefore not surprising that all three theories predict essentially the same relationship between speed and accuracy of continuous movement, i.e.

$$S = K' W \tag{12}$$

where S is the speed of movement ($= 1/T$), W the width of the track, and K' is a constant.

Howarth (1978) has shown how the same reasoning can be used to predict the way speed should change when the width of the road changes. He argues that inexperienced drivers do not vary their speed as much as is required by the theory. Although this chapter is concerned with discrete movements, it is an added strength in any theory of discrete movements if it can be easily extended to deal with continuous movements.

Beggs, Sakstein, and Howarth (1972) also asked the same subjects to do three different tasks: walk along beams of various widths as fast as possible; draw a pencil line along straight tracks between 1 and 6 millimetres in width as rapidly as possible; and finally the non-visual, target-aiming task already described. From each of these tasks a measure equivalent to *a* could be derived for each subject, and these were correlated across subjects. To our disappointment, the correlations were very low. Two estimates of 0.29 and 0.50 were obtained for the correlation between beam walking and line drawing. But no correlation at all was found between accuracy of aiming and either of the other tasks. There was a correlation of 0.33 between beam walking and accuracy of stopping in the target-aiming task, but no correlation between accuracy of aiming and accuracy of stopping. These experiments seem to rule out the possibility that *a* is a stable characteristic of a person which determines his performance on many different tasks. A value of *a* can be calculated for many different situations, but represents the person's performance on that task only.

A NEW LOOK AT CHOICE REACTIONS

Beggs, Graham, Monk, Shaw, and Howarth (1972) studied the effect of varying the number of alternative targets in our standard visual target aiming task. A set of up to eight line targets were presented to the subject. Each time he returned to the starting position, one of the lines was indicated, at random, as the next target by lighting a small lamp bulb above it. The subject's movements were paced by a metronome and the accuracy with which the target was hit measured as a function of the number of alternative targets and the speed of movement. Again, equation (11) provided a better fit to the data than the information theory equation (equation (6)). Figure 30 shows the data from this and other experiments, reported in Beggs (1972), plotting E^2 against $(1/T)^{2.8}$. Straight lines are predicted by equation (11). However, the effect of N, the number of alternative targets, is rather a surprise. We had expected it to influence the initial portion of the movement corresponding to the reaction time in Hick's experiments, and so adding an amount to the movement time proportional to log N. There was no sign of this effect, which in Figure 30 would have moved the curves horizontally with respect to one another. Instead there is a clear effect of N on a as indicated by the change in the slope of the lines. The increase in a is proportional to log N.

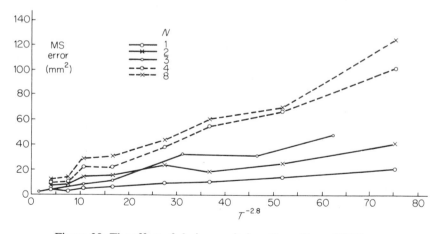

Figure 30. The effect of choice on aiming. From Beggs (1971).

Holding (1968) found that the error of aiming increased proportionally to the logarithm of the delay in aiming. Since the average delay in repeating a response is roughly proportional to N, the number of alternative responses in our experiment, Holding's finding may provide an explanation of our result. To test this idea Beggs (unpublished) has followed Woodworth in varying independently the inter-trial interval and the speed of the individual movements. He found that the effect of delay in repeating a movement is very similar whether or not additional movements are made towards different targets in the intervening period.

The results confirm those of Holding (1968) for the unfilled delay condition up to 3.50 seconds and also in a condition where two non-equiprobable targets were used. It would be tempting to hope that in the case of a large number of equiprobable targets a similar logarithmic relationship holds. Certainly Beggs (1971) found that the data shown in Figure 30 could be reasonably well fitted by a logarithmic function. Beyond this interfit delay, the logarithmic function fails to provide a reasonable fit to the data, which, as inspection of Figure 30 shows, appears to reach an asymptotic value.

In each of these experiments the relationship between error and delay (however caused) can be regarded as a forgetting curve, a fact first noted as long ago as 1892 by Münsterberg. This curve may indicate the loss of positional information over time. A number of experiments have demonstrated that this is a reality both in terms of the remembered position of a simple visual target which disappears (Kinchla and Smyzer, 1967; Findlay, 1974), and in terms of memory for kinaesthetic positions (cf. Adams and Dijkstra, 1966; Pepper and Herman, 1970) (see also Chapters 3 and 6).

INTERSENSORY LOCALIZATION

Howarth (1978) has suggested a new explanation of this rapid loss of spatial information. He has argued that the complex articulation of the body, and the physical separation of the different spatial senses, make it impossible to know completely the relative positions of the different parts of the body, or the positions of all the parts of the body relative to objects in the world about us. The computational and memory problems are too great. Or, at least they are so difficult that it is not worth our while to solve them completely. Instead we make do with 'sloppy' information about the positions of our limbs in space, seeking out more accurate information only when we need it. This information is remarkably specific to the situation in which it is acquired and is rapidly forgotten. It does not generalize to other situations because our basic knowledge of the relationships between parts of the body is not accurate enough to make generalization possible. It is rapidly forgotten because, if we were to remember it all, it would lead to an overload of our memory system.

Howarth argues that the simplest demonstration of the loss of spatial information is autokinesis. In a completely dark room a single point spot of light will appear to wander, irregularly up and down as well as from side to side. Howarth argues that this wandering reflects the loss of position information over time. The generality of autokinesis has been demonstrated by a number of authors such as Jackson (1953) and, most notably, by Fisher (1960, 1961, and 1962). Fisher demonstrated autokinesis in some novel situations. The relative direction of two objects could be perceived either visually (V), auditorily (A) or by kinaesthesis and touch (K). When the two objects were perceived simultaneously by means of the same sense organ no autokinesis was observed. But in all three intersensory conditions, i.e. when one object was perceived by one sense and the other by a different sense (giving three possible combinations VK, VA, and KA) then their relative positions were misjudged in a systematic way, which resembles the conventional experience of autokinesis and which was virtually the same in all three intersensory conditions.

Fisher found that the apparent relative position of two objects changed over time and that the change had two components to it. The first was a rapid random variation about a relatively fixed value. The second was a relatively slow but much longer change of relative position. This latter, relatively slow, change seems to be what is perceived as autokinesis when we view a spot of light in the dark. Conventional autokinesis is an example of visual kinaesthetic (VK) intersensory localization, since the posititon of the body relative to the room is perceived kinaesthetically.

Fisher also found systematic relationships between the various errors in intersensory localization of a kind which had been suggested on theoretical grounds by Howarth (these ideas are described in some detail by Howarth, 1978). Fisher's principal findings were:

1. That over short periods of time there was a consistency between the constant errors in the three types of intersensory judgement such that if a visual stimulus was judged to the left of a kinaesthetic and kinaesthetic to the left of auditory, then inevitably the visual would be judged to the left of the auditory.

2. Each of the three intersensory localizations had a characteristic variance which was a measure of the rapid random variation. The three intersensory variances are also consistent in that each can be treated as the sum of two variances characteristic of the appropriate senses. These were slightly less than 1° for vision, slightly more than 1° for kinaesthesis and about 3° for hearing.

Recently, Auerbach and Sperling (1974) have found a similar consistency in constant and variable errors.

It now seems likely that the quantities which Fisher called constant and variable errors are not so different as he imagined. It is more likely that both are different time samples of essentially the same loss of information over time which Holding (1968) and Beggs (1971) have studied. Kinchla and Smyzer (1967) have argued that this loss of information is analogous to diffusion or Brownian motion and that the increase in error is not proportional to the logarithm of time, but to the square root of time (or, to put it another way, that the variance of the error increases linearly with time). In their experiment two flashes of light were displayed with a varied time interval between them, so that unlike the experiments discussed so far, the judgements were intrasensory (i.e. within one sense modality) rather than intersensory (i.e. comparing information from one sense with another). Nevertheless, the same mechanism could be responsible for the loss of spatial information over time in both intra- and intersensory localization.

We now believe that it is possible to regard '*a*' in our aiming experiments as a kind of intersensory accuracy, representing either the accuracy with which a visual position can be related to a motor program, or perhaps, more plausibly, the accuracy with which the position of a visual stimulus can be related to the position of a kinaesthetic stimulus. Fisher's estimate of $1° 24'$ is only two or three times greater than our estimates of between $41'$ and $56'$ for '*a*'. The difference could easily be accounted for by the lack of any opportunity to recalibrate the system in Fisher's experiments. In the aiming experiments there is almost continuous opportunity to relate the two sensory systems or the sensory and motor systems.

OTHER FACTORS DEGRADING INTERSENSORY JUDGEMENTS

Although intersensory judgements clearly deteriorate with time, there are other factors which interfere with them. For example, Carr (1910) and Gregory and Zangwill (1963) have shown that unidirectional autokinesis can be induced as an after-effect of strong aversion of the eyes. If there are after-effects of eye movements one would expect a restriction on eye movements to reduce the extent of autokinesis. Matin and MacKinnon (1964) have shown that this is indeed the case.

Similar after-effects can be induced in kinaesthesis. A common party trick is to exert strong pressure in one direction on someone's arm. When the pressure is released and the arm relaxed, it tends to move 'of its own accord' in a direction opposite to that of the original pressure. Hick (1953) has studied this phenomenon under the name of the 'after contraction'.

There are also after-effects of limb position without any strong muscle tension. For example, Selling (1930) and Nachmias (1953) asked their subjects to hold out both hands horizontally at the same level. Then, with the eyes closed, one hand is raised above the head and then returned to the original horizontal position, with the instruction to make both hands level with each other as before. Both workers found that the hand which had been moved was held several degrees higher than the hand which had not moved. Jackson (1954) demonstrated this kind of 'postural persistence' for postures other than those which are held against gravity, and has shown significant effects after as little as 5 seconds.

Since the body is almost always in motion, these effects of 'after contraction' and postural persistence must create continual difficulties in relating different parts of the body. However, the greatest difficulty is the complex articulation of the body, the physical separation of the different spatial senses, and the compounding of these problems by the variable weightings which are put upon the limbs. The simplest way to vary the weight on a limb is to change the direction in which gravity acts upon it by changing the attitude of the body. The forces acting upon the arms are quite different when we are bending down from what they are when we are standing upright. In addition, we may hold weighted objects in our hands, or wear clothes which hamper our movements in various ways.

All of these factors lead us to suspect that the most important factor affecting the accuracy with which we can make discrete movements is the adequacy of our knowledge of the starting position of the body, of the position of objects in space near to it, and the relationship between these sources of positional information. Many of the features of skilled movement can be seen as strategic adaptations to our lack of reliable spatial information.

STRATEGIES IN THE CONTROL OF MOVEMENT

Perhaps the most important strategy is the one we have already described, i.e. the continual monitoring of movement and the intermittent correction of errors. For relatively slow movements i.e. movements lasting longer than a 0.25 second, these corrections can be made during the course of the movement itself, leading to the relationship between speed and error enshrined in equation (11). For faster movements, corrections can be made only between one movement and the next. An additional consequence of this strategy (for relatively slow movements) is the need to bring the hand as close as possible to the target at the moment that the last correction is made. This explains the change, with practice, in the shape of the relationship between time and distance as the hand approaches a target (see Figure 29).

Of perhaps equal importance are the strategies which enable us to 're-calibrate' the different spatial senses relative to each other. This 'recalibration' is usually very quick provided we are given appropriate information. For example, our colleague, Dr A. D. Heyes has shown that, when people with poor hearing are first given two ear-level hearing aids they can localize sounds quite well, but their auditory 'space' is narrow compared with visual or kinaesthetic space (Hayes and Gazeley, 1974). That is, they will judge sound 90° to the right of straight ahead to be only 45° to the right, while a sound 90° to the left will be judged only 45° to the left. The auditory 'space' can be expanded until it is coincident with visual or kinaesthetic space by merely shaking a matchbox at arm's length and at various positions around the head (A. D. Heyes, personal communication). Simultaneous visual, kinaesthetic, and auditory information about the position of the matchbox leads to a rapid recalibration of auditory space.

There have been many studies of the recalibration of the spatial senses after an artificially induced discrepancy such as that produced by the wearing of prism spectacles. The experiments of Held and Hein (1958) and of Held and Freedman (1963) have led to a very large literature on adaptation to the wearing of prism spectacles. Most reviewers interpret this literature as showing two effects of the greatest importance:

1. That the recalibration which is learned can be very specific to the situation in which it occurs.
2. That the recalibration occurs more easily when active movements are involved.

Howarth (1978) has argued that the second finding is an accidental consequence of the first, so that the specificity of adaptation results in a greater effect of active experience on active testing. With passive testing one might expect a greater effect of passive learning. Templeton, Howard, and Lowman (1966) have shown that passive experience can lead to correct judgement of the passively placed position of the hand after only sixteen trials; Pick and Hay (1965) have also demonstrated passive adaptation.

Examples of specificity of adaptation are, for instance, the experiments of Harris (1963) and Hamilton (1964) on the effects of wearing prism spectacles. They showed that learning to point correctly with one hand produced no transfer of learning to the other hand. Harris also showed that there was no effect on auditory localization of a learning experience which concentrated attention on the visual and kinaesthetic senses. Hardt, Held, and Steinback (1971) showed that even after adaptation of the felt position of the hand had occurred, after wearing prisms, no adaptation was shown when the subject was asked to return his hand to a remembered position, i.e. one taken up by the hand before adaptation occurred.

One can explain the lack of transfer from one situation to another by the lack of any stable relationship between the different spatial senses. Transfer could only occur if there were a stable framework. In the absence of a stable framework learning is situation specific.

Howarth (1978) has suggested that one of the functions of 'warm-up' activities in athletics and sport is to give the different spatial senses and motor systems the opportunity to 'recalibrate'. Some of these activities merely stretch the muscles and stimulate the circulation of the blood. Others, which typically resemble, and may be identical with the activities for which they are a preparation, are the ones which are best adapted to the 'recalibration' of the various systems. When practising, athletes often say they are 'getting the feel of things', or that 'things are beginning to click into place', these phrases are at least consistent with Howarth's suggestion, although they are not evidence for it.

Finally, we have to consider what is likely to happen when different spatial senses give conflicting information. Because of the ubiquity of the autokinetic phenomenon, we are usually unaware of real differences in direction of as much as 30° (Jackson, 1953). A familiar example of this is ventriloquism where the ventriloquist's voice (when his lips do not move) appears to come out of the dummy's mouth. By a simple extension of the ventriloquism situation one can discover how the discrepant information is combined. The two sources, visual and auditory, may appear to come from the same place, but where is that place? By asking the subject to point (without being able to see his hand), or to judge the position of the combined auditory/visual stimulus relative to a kinaesthetically perceived stimulus, one can get an estimate of where the combined stimulus is. Fisher (1962) did the latter experiment and found that the judged position of the combined stimuli was between the positions of the visual and auditory stimuli, but closer to the position of the visual stimulus. When the subject was told that the visual and the kinaesthetic stimuli were in the same place, their combined position was approximately midway between the two positions. Moreover, the variability of the judgement was independent of the actual separation of the stimuli. These experiments are discussed in greater detail by Howard and Templeton (1966) and by Howarth (1978). The most economical interpretation of these results is that the apparent position of an object, perceived by two different senses, corresponds to a weighted average of the information from the two senses, where the weighting is determined by the relative accuracy of the two senses. Pick, Warren, and Hay (1969) and Howard, Anstis, and Lucia (1974) have obtained essentially the same conclusion from rather different experiments.

SUMMARY

The basic argument in this chapter is that many of the characteristics of discrete movements can be seen as consequences of the poor and transient information which our spatial senses provide about the disposition of our bodies in space.

The effect of delay, or of intertrial interval on the accuracy of pointing, is a direct expression of the decay of spatial information with time. The effect of increasing the number of choices on the accuracy of pointing or on any kind of reaction time may have the same explanation, although this is not as well established as one would like.

The relationship between accuracy and speed of movement is almost entirely a consequence of a strategic adaptation to inadequacies of spatial information. Since movements are inevitably not made with perfect accuracy we will, if possible, detect and correct any errors in them. Because of this, the relationship between speed and error of movement is entirely determined by the shape of the function relating time and distance from the target as the hand approaches the target. The effects of practice are seen to be largely due to a strategic change in the trajectory of the hand which enables the practised person to get nearer to the target before the last correction is made.

There are other ways in which we attempt to overcome the deficiencies of our spatial senses. The most important of these are the strategies we use to improve the quality of the information available to us in a situation in which accurate information is needed. Some of these are best understood by investigating directly the accuracy of spatial information as, for example, in the phenomena of autokinesis, ventriloquism, and spatial learning. But these phenomena all have a direct influence on skilled behaviour. This is particularly easy to demonstrate with discrete movements since, with their fixed beginning and end, it is so easy to measure their timing and accuracy.

Chapter 6

Motor Memory

Gerald J. Laabs and Roger W. Simmons

The preceding chapter (Howarth, Chapter 5) laid the groundwork for considering the storage of sensory information related to motor movement. Of all the sensory information available to the human information processor, that obtained from the kinaesthetic, proprioceptive, and visual senses is the primary subject of motor memory research.

Although the history of motor memory can be traced back to about the turn of the century (e.g. Woodworth, 1899), research in the area did not began in earnest until the late 1960s following the emergence of verbal short-term memory as a distinct research area. Several information-processing views of attention and memory were proposed during this period, and movement reproduction began to be viewed as an information-processing activity. As a shift occurred from the study of perceptual-motor learning to the study of information processing related to motor activity, motor memory became a separate research area and the perceptual side of perceptual-motor skills was de-emphasized. Although perceptual processing was put in the background, it is a very important part of the processing that occurs prior to or concurrent with the storage of information related to motor movement. In fact, perceptual-motor memory is a better heading for the research discussed in this chapter than motor memory.

The focus of this chapter is on the processing and storing of the sensory information associated with simple motor activity, primarily over the short term. Although a variety of paradigms will be encountered along the way that will contribute to our understanding of motor memory, the data will come primarily from studies that involve the reproduction of slow positioning movements. First, the reproduction paradigm will be discussed in terms that specifically acknowledge the perceptual processes involved in remembering a motor act. Next, recall data will be reviewed with two questions in mind: (1) To what extent is a perceptual process being studied rather than, or along with, a memory process? (2) What is it that is stored or encoded when a motor movement is made? After that, current theoretical notions and recognition memory will be examined. Finally, progress in the research area of motor

The opinions expressed in this chapter are those of the authors and do not necessarily reflect those of the Navy Department.

memory will be reviewed by comparing its developmental stages with those of verbal memory.

MOVEMENT REPRODUCTION PARADIGM

Reference Task

Consider the following general task. A standard stimulus is presented to a participant, and he or she is asked to make judgement either immediately or after some period of delay by varying another stimulus until it matches the standard. No feedback is given, and the error associated with the response is the performance measure.

This task description fits a variety of perceptual judgement studies because it is basically the psychophysical method of adjustment. It also fits most of the motor memory studies in which a movement is presented and later reproduced. Figure 31 shows an arm-positioning apparatus that forces the participant to rely on kinaesthetic/proprioceptive information and schematically illustrates the reproduction of a standard constrained by a mechanical stop.

Error Analysis

There are two classes of errors that can occur in the repeated reproduction of a standard stimulus: (a) systematic or constant error, which indicates the direction of the difference between a reproduction and the true of physical value of the standard; and (b) variable error, which indicates the spread or dispersion of a set of reproductions.

In the psychophysical judgement paradigm, a standard stimulus is presented repeatedly and the mean judgement is calculated to obtain the indifference point or point of subjective equality. When this quantity is compared to the standard, constant error is obtained. In most psychophysical experiments an attempt is made to reduce or counterbalance constant error. There are studies specifically designed to examine how perceptual judgements are made, however, that focus on the analysis of constant error (usually termed time-error or time-order-error). The standard deviation of the judgements is also calculated and used as a measure of discriminability. Because standard deviations get smaller from one experimental session to another, participants are usually given preliminary practice in making judgements to reduce or eliminate this effect.

In the movement reproduction paradigm, a standard or criterion movement is presented repeatedly and the algebraic or signed error of each reproduction is calculated. The result is a distribution of deviation scores which can be fully characterized by the statistically independent measures of mean algebraic or constant error and the standard deviation of the algebraic error or variable

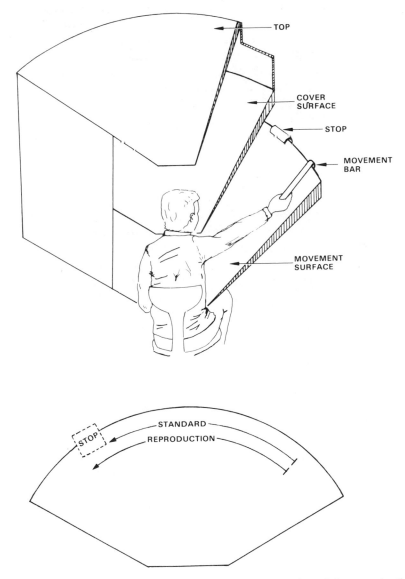

Figure 31. Arm-positioning apparatus and schematic representation of the reproduction paradigm for a standard constrained by a stop.

error. In motor memory studies (as well as some perception studies), these measures are the dependent variables of interest rather than factors to be controlled. Unfortunately, the measures have been used interchangeably. This creates a problem because inconsistencies will occur whenever an independent variable has a differential effect on the two measures (see Laabs, 1975a).

Although constant and variable error are the measures reported in recent motor memory studies, the most popular retention measure of earlier studies was the average deviation of the unsigned error or absolute error. The exclusive use of this measure has been questioned by several investigators (e.g. Laabs, 1973; Schmidt, 1970; Schutz and Roy, 1973) because absolute error is a weighted combination of constant and variable error. This makes absolute error results difficult to interpret: to the extent that different independent variables have different effects on constant and variable error, absolute error will be ambiguous.

One situation in which the use of absolute error may be appropriate is when the restrictions on feedback usually imposed in motor memory studies are lifted (see Newell, 1976a and Schmidt, 1975a for arguments in favour of using the absolute error measure). The provision of knowledge of results in a motor memory study shifts the focus of the study from retention processes to other aspects of motor learning. Assuming that both constant and variable error are reduced during motor learning, a composite score such as absolute error or Henry's (1974) composite error, or a statistical method that evaluates the combination of several dependent measures (Roy, 1976), may yield more information on change than a separate analysis of these errors.

Methodological Problems

The interchangeable use of dependent measures is not the only potential source of conflicting findings. In response to Stelmach's (1974a) review of motor short-term memory, Gentile (1974) pointed to four often-ignored variables involving the presentation of standards that make data interpretation difficult: (1) method of presentation; (2) return movements after presentations; (3) relative length or position of standards; and (4) repetition of standards over an experimental session. Although these methodological problems have become the variables of interest in more recent research, they are present in one or form or another in a large number of experiments covered in this chapter. Nevertheless, consistencies in the research findings are evident.

Conceptual Framework

Because constant and variable error appear to reference different processes, we will categorize the data according to the dependent measure used. In accordance with Laabs (1973), variable error is viewed as an index of forgetting because it is reduced with practice in psychophysical judgement. When memory traces are strengthened in an analogous motor memory situation, variable error will decrease; when memory traces are weakened (forgotten), variable error will increase. Likewise, constant error is viewed as an index of perceptual processing because it is sensitive to factors associated with a frame of reference in psychophysical judgement, such as adaptation level (Helson, 1964). When this contextual framework operates in an analogous motor memory situation, constant error will be affected. Constant error may also change with forgetting, but this is seen as a reflection of more fundamental perceptual processing that is allowed to become more prominent as memory traces are weakened.

Before we start our discussion of the data, we must integrate our view of perceptual-motor memory within an information-processing framework. To recapitulate a general view of human information processing as discussed in one of the earlier chapters (Kinsbourne, Chapter 4), information is seen as flowing through five sequential stages: (1) sensory transduction; (2) storage of this 'raw' information in sensory memory; (3) patten recognition, which depends upon contact with long-term memory; (4) storage of the recognized information in short-term memory; and (5) final storage of encoded information in long-term memory. Our main assumptions concerning this information flow are based on the notion that contact with long-term memory is a non-attentive process (e.g. Keele, 1973). We assume that the first three processing stages operate, for the most part, automatically. That is, they are free from the need for extensive processing capacity. These stages also define the perceptual processing related to criterion movement presentation which is indexed by constant error. The maintenance or further encoding of information in short-term memory and the transfer of information from short-term to long-term memory that occur during the last two processing stages require processing capacity. These functions make up the motor memory processing which is indexed by variable error.

BIAS IN REPRODUCTION

This section draws an analogy between the perceptual processing involved in motor memory and perceptual judgement, and is based on constant error results only.

Empty Interval Effects

A common finding for perceptual judgement studies is a negative shift in constant error over an empty comparison interval (negative time-error or time-order-error). Although this shift may not occur at shorter intervals (less than 3 sec), it is usually present at longer intervals (Needham, 1934).

Several motor memory studies report a similar effect, a shift in the direction of 'undershooting', over an empty retention interval (e.g. Faust-Adams, 1972; Herman and Bailey, 1970; Kelso, 1977a; Pepper and Herman, 1970, Exp. II;

Stelmach, 1969). Examination of a variety of other studies that also included an empty delay reveals non-significant effects, but trends in the appropriate direction (e.g. Burwitz, 1974a, 1974b; Diewert, 1975; Duffy, Montague, Laabs, and Hillix, 1975; Hagman, 1978; Keele and Ells, 1972; Laabs, 1973; Marshall, 1972, Exp. II; Marteniuk, 1973; Pepper and Herman, 1970, Exp. I; Roy, 1977; Stelmach, 1970; Stelmach and Walsh, 1972, 1973; Stelmach and Wilson, 1970; Williams, Beaver, Spence, and Rundell, 1969, Exp. II; Williams, 1971). Although the effect appears to be relatively weak, it is well established.

When the trend towards a negative shift in constant error over an empty interval is observed in motor memory studies, it is often taken as an indication of forgetting rather than perceptual processing. Negative time-error and time-order-error in perceptual judgement studies also have been explained in terms of memory changes. There are situations under which the usual direction of the empty-interval effect is reversed, however, which would not be expected if the effect is a reflection of memory decay.

A central tendency effect may replace or obscure the usual negative constant-error shift over an empty interval. This effect, in which small stimulus intensities are overestimated and large stimulus intensities are underestimated when an individual is presented with a series of stimuli along the same dimension, has been reported repeatedly since the early beginning of psychophysical research. For example, Woodrow (1933) had participants compare successive weights, and found that constant error was negative for both a 100- and 200-gram standard when determined in separate experiments. When a series of standards ranging from 100 to 200 grams was used within one experiment, he found that constant error was positive for the lighter standards and negative for the heavier standards.

The central tendency effect for movement length was demonstrated by Hollingworth (1909) in a forerunner of modern motor memory studies. The central tendency effect also occurs for movement position (e.g. Fitts, 1947). The effect has been found in most of the recent studies of motor memory in which a series of movement lengths or positions is included as a variable (e.g. Duffy, Montague, Laabs, and Hillix, 1975; Faust-Adams, 1972; Hagman, 1978; Hall and Wilberg, 1977, 1978; Keele and Ells, 1972; Kelso, 1977a; Kerr, 1978b; Laabs, 1973, 1977; Marteniuk, 1973; Patrick, 1971; Salmoni and Sullivan, 1976; Stelmach, 1970; Stelmach and Wilson, 1970; Wallace, 1977).

Of particular relevance to this discussion, is the finding that the central tendency effect increased over a comparison interval in a perceptual judgement study (Needham, 1935). Laabs (1973) has reported a similar effect in a motor memory study for both movement distance and end-location. These results imply that shifts in constant error over an empty interval are dependent upon the range or context within which judgements or reproductions are made and only indirectly upon memory decay, which seems to allow perceptual processing to become more prominent.

Assimilation Effects

One of the most prevalent findings in perceptual judgement studies is a shift in constant error as the result of stimulation given either prior to a comparison judgement or interpolated between the standard and the judgement. When using one of the psychophysical methods, constant-error changes are generally in the direction of the level of stimulation and are termed 'assimilation'. In perceptual judgement experiments using rating scales, changes in classification are usually in the direction away from the level of stimulation and are termed 'contrast'; but the point of subjective equality shifts in the direction of the level stimulation yielding a true assimilation effect. Movement reproduction studies show similar assimilation effects.

Prior Movements

An assimilation effect due to prior stimulation was shown in a psychophysical judgement study by Turner (1931). He found that if a comparison of weights was preceded by a heavy one, the constant-error shift was positive (i.e. constant error increased); if it was preceded by a light one, the shift was negative (i.e. constant error decreased).

In motor memory, there are only a few comparable experiments. Craft and Hinrichs (1972) conducted a series of experiments involving the presentation of a standard and an interfering movement, followed by a reproduction. The assimilation effect was found when the interfering movement preceded the standard. Identifying the standard either before or after the presentation of the two movements did not change the effect. In a similar experiment, Craft (1973) found the assimilation effect over an immediate and 20-sec delay, but not when a 20-sec interval was introduced between the interfering movement and standard. In contrast, Herman and Bailey (1970) studied force reproductions that were preceded by smaller or larger forces, and found no shift in constant error. In their study, the standard was presented with concurrent visual feedback via an oscilloscope and the direction of the force application of the prior stimulation was opposite to that of the standard, which may have contributed to the conflicting finding.

Interpolated Movements

If stimulation occurs during the interval between the standard and comparison stimuli in a perceptual judgement study, assimilation usually results. For example, Philip (1947) reported that the constant error associated with judgements of time duration over an empty interval shifted in a negative direction with a short interpolated duration and in a positive direction with a long interpolated duration.

A large number of motor memory studies report assimilation due to interpolated movements (e.g. Craft, 1973; Craft and Hinrichs, 1971; Herman and Bailey, 1970; Laabs, 1974; Patrick, 1971; Pepper and Herman, 1970, Exp. III; Stelmach and Kelso, 1975; Stelmach and Walsh, 1972, 1973; Trumbo, Milone, and Noble, 1972). The general findings are illustrated in a study by Laabs (1974) in which the effect of interpolated movements was assessed separately for movement distance and end-location. He found that the lengths of interpolations determined the assimilation effect for distance reproduction and that the end-locations of interpolations determined the assimilation effect for location. Other studies have shown that assimilation can be enhanced by an increase in the difference between interpolation and standard (Trumbo, Milone, and Noble, 1972), an increase in the duration spend at the interpolated end-location (Stelmach and Walsh, 1972), and the later temporal placement of the interpolation within a retention interval (Stelmach and Walsh, 1973). Conversely, the assimilation effect can be offset by strengthening the 'trace' of the standard through repetition or increased sensory feedback (Stelmach and Kelso, 1975).

Some of the studies cited above required the interpolated movement to be remembered, others did not; yet similar assimilation effects were found. In contrast, variable error of reproduction increases only when an interpolation has to be remembered, as we shall see in the next section. Thus, constant and variable error appear to be affected differently by the same independent variable, and in a way that is consistent with the notion that bias in reproduction is not a function of processing-capacity availability, but recall is.

Presentation of the Standard

Return movements after the presentation of the standard have been identified as a source of a potential constant-error effect. That is, investigators who use return movements rather than having the participant disengage his or her hand from the movement apparatus unknowingly may be including an interpolated movement in their studies, which can cause assimilation. Based on the limited evidence available, it appears that the effect of return movements depends upon the cue that is used to guide the reproduction. In the only systematic study of return movements, Marteniuk (1977) allowed the distance cue to be reliable. He found a negative shift in constant error over an empty retention interval for disengagement, no change in constant error for active returns, and a positive shift in constant error for passive returns. On the other hand, Stelmach and Walsh (1972, 1973) carried out two different experiments involving the reproduction of end-location and found the same biasing effect due to interpolated end-location in both, even though return movements were used in one study and not the other. Thus, interpolated distances in the form of return movements neither cause large constant-error shifts nor appear to pose a difficult methodological problem when the reproduction cue for the standard is end-location. When the cue is distance, however, the return movements probably should be interpreted as practice.

There is another factor sometimes associated with return movements that may affect the constant error of end-location reproduction. That is, participants are often required to hold on to the movement bar after completing the return movement rather than disengage from the apparatus. The potential for this action to cause assimilation when the location cue is being used has not been considered. Evidence that it may occur comes from a study by Craske and Crawshaw (1974) who found that holding an unseen hand at a position shifts the verbal estimate of a later position.

A novel perceptual judgement study by McClelland (1943) points to another presentation procedure that may affect constant error, that is, whether the experimenter or the participant defines the standard. The purpose of McClelland's experiment was to demonstrate that the usual negative constant error observed in psychophysical judgement studies is due to comparing the lower stimulation level of the first stimulus, caused by the gradual ending of stimulation, to the full stimulation of the second stimulus. He found negative constant error for visually presented lines when a light was turned off (gradual fading of stimulation); positive constant error when stimulation was ended abruptly with a shutter. The prediction for motor memory studies is that a constrained (experimenter-defined) standard will show relatively more overshooting than a preselected (participant-defined) standard, the reproduction of which is schematically illustrated in Figure 32 (cf. Figure 31). Most of the studies which compared these methods found no main effects for constant error, and the trends varied across the conditions of the studies (e.g. Jones, 1974a; Kelso, 1977a; Marteniuk, 1973, 1977; Roy, 1978; Roy and Diewert, 1978; Stelmach and Kelso, 1977; Stelmach, Kelso, and McCullagh, 1976; Stelmach, Kelso, and Wallace, 1975). In the next section we shall find that these same studies have shown large main effects for the comparison of constrained and preselected movements using variable error. Here is another case in which a potent independent variable for recall apparently does not have the same strong effect on the perceptual processing involved in motor memory.

Another source of a potential constant-error effect encountered during the presentation of the standard is the instruction to participants to use only part of the cue information available. The remaining cues are seen by the experimenter as being irrelevant to the task, but they still exert influence on the perceptual processing involved in motor memory. This is demonstrated in studies that rendered either the distance or end-location cue unreliable when the other was to be used and found assimilation due to the irrelevant cue (e.g. Kerr, 1978b; Laabs, 1973). Shea (1977, Exp. II) and Wallace (1977) have also shown that irrelevant direction information and misleading verbal labels, respectively, affect constant error. In general, the constant error shifts towards

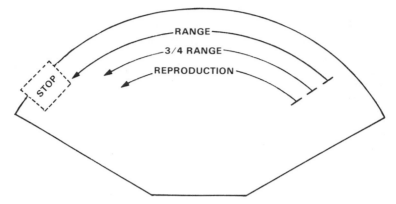

Figure 32. Schematic representation of the reproduction of a preselected standard defined by having the participant produce a portion of a movement range.

the information present in the irrelevant or invalid cue. Nevertheless, the primary or relevant cue still has the most effect on performance.

An example of a corresponding finding for perceptual judgement is reported by Behar and Bevan (1961). They found that anchors exerted the maximum effect on judgements of time intervals when they were in the same modality as the standard; they also found the effect of visual stimuli on auditory judgements was significant, as was the effect of auditory stimuli on visual judgements. Other studies have demonstrated the influence of multiple anchors in perceptual judgement (e.g. Steger and O'Reilly, 1970; Turner and Bevan, 1962). This suggests that there are either multiple inputs to a single frame of reference or that there are multiple frames of reference in perceptual judgement studies. The operation of a frame of reference, other than the one given primary focus by the experimenter, is consistent with both the results of the motor memory and perceptual judgement studies we have cited.

Contrast Effects

In a few studies of perceptual judgement, contrast rather than assimilation has been observed primarily when the intensity of the prior or interpolated stimulation has been extremely different from the standard. In one study, Christman (1954) found that judgements of pitch did not shift in the direction of a preceding higher or lower tone of long duration as an assimilation effect predicts, but shifted in the opposite direction. The only related movement study is one concerning movement averaging using the production method (Levin, Norman, and Dolezal, 1973). The longer movements of the pair to be averaged were given more weight in the averaging process (i.e. the productions were longer than the average), especially when the judgements were preceded by a series of reproductions of much smaller movements. These results represent a contrast effect.

In another perceptual judgement study, Platt (1933) compared judgements of sound intensity and of weights after an empty interval with those after an interval containing an extremely small interpolated stimulus. According to the assimilation effect, the usual negative constant error observed over an empty comparison interval in perceptual judgement should be lessened with the interpolated stimulus. The opposite effect, contrast, was observed. No motor memory study has systematically examined the effects of either extremely larger or smaller interpolated movements. The operation of a contrast effect, however, may have contributed to the failure to find assimilation under all interpolated conditions in some motor memory studies (e.g. Stelmach and Walsh, 1972, 1973) and other isolated failures to find predicted constant-error effects (e.g. Kerr, 1978b; Stelmach and Kelso, 1973).

The only clear case of contrast in movement reproduction was found by Laabs (1971, Exp. III) in an experiment requiring concurrent information processing during the recall of end-location. Signals coming from the bar being moved by the participant during recall defined either a location, or a distance to be remembered and recalled after the reproduction of the standard was completed. The constant error in reproduction of the standard was significantly more positive when the concurrent task information was stored than when there was not concurrent task. Since all of the concurrent task input necessarily occurred to the left of the left-to-right reproductions, these results represent a contrast effect similar to that found in perceptual judgement involving simultaneous presentation of stimuli.

Interpolated Mental Activity

The results discussed so far demonstrate context effects in motor memory, but touch only lightly on the effect of changes in processing capacity. An examination of studies that include retention intervals filled with mental activities such as counting backwards, should give us an indication of the potency of the effect of processing-capacity availability on constant error.

There are several studies that included an interpolated mental activity and reported a significant retention interval effect for constant error (e.g. Faust-Adams, 1972; Herman and Bailey, 1970; Kantowitz, 1972, Exp. I, IV; Kelso, 1977a, Exp. II; Pepper and Herman, 1970, Exp. II, III). The general finding is a constant-error shift in the positive direction with an interpolated mental activity as compared to an empty delay. There are also several similar studies which report no significant effects (e.g. Burwitz, 1974a; Diewert, 1975; Kantowitz, 1972, Exp. II, III; Keele and Ells, 1972; Laabs, 1973; Marteniuk, 1973; Roy, 1977; Stelmach, 1970; Williams, Beaver, Spence, and Rundell, 1969), but most do show the positve shift trend. The effect seems well established, but relatively weak. If this constant-error effect is related to competing demands for processing capacity, it is not nearly as strong as the variable-error effect also shown in several of the cited studies.

Further examination of the studies cited above suggests that perceptual context is a primary factor with processing-capacity availability determining its prominence. For example, Keele and Ells (1972) found that an interpolated digit classification task increased the central tendency effect rather than causing a positive constant-error shift for both smaller and larger movements. Laabs (1973) found similar trends in his data for both an interpolated counting task and a spatial reasoning task. Both of these studies, as well as several others (e.g. Kelso, 1977a; Marteniuk, 1973; Stelmach, 1970) indicate that the major contribution to positive shifts in constant error with interpolated mental activity comes from the relatively small movements. Although it might be claimed that only smaller movements require processing capacity (variable-error evidence for this claim will be presented later), these results can be explained in perceptual terms. This can be done by adopting Pepper and Herman's (1970) proposal that interpolated mental activity raises the general tension level. If an increase in tension level leads to an increase in the value of a frame of reference such as an adaptation level (instead of combining with the memory trace as Pepper and Herman propose), operation of the new frame of reference will result in relatively large positive shifts in constant error for the smaller movements and relatively small negative shifts in constant error for the larger movements.

Although a processing-capacity explanation for the positive shift in constant error with interpolated mental activity cannot be ruled out completely, it can be concluded that the constant-error measure is relatively invulnerable to processing-capacity changes as opposed to perceptual context effects. Mikkonen (1969) goes one step further and explains the time-error and time-order-error of perceptual judgement studies solely in terms of changes that take place in the way stimuli are perceived and judged. Based on the analogy we have drawn between motor memory and perceptual judgement, the constant error of motor memory studies can also be explained without recourse to a memory function. Nevertheless, it is interesting to speculate that constant error may be indexing recognition memory along with the automatic perceptual processing. Recognition memory is distinguished from recall primarily in that performance on a recognition test is highly susceptible to changes in context, and that the similarity of the item to be remembered (standard) and distractor items (interpolations) is the major dimension of interference. This seems to be a fair summary statement of the constant-error results we have presented.

RECALL MEMORY

This section highlights the relationship between motor memory processing and processing capacity, and will be based primarily on variable-error results.

Unfortunately, variable error has only been reported in more recent studies. Consequently, absolute-error results also will have to be used. Because of the interpretation problems associated with absolute error, we will make it a point to indicate when only these data are available or when these data are specifically being discussed.

Reproduction Cues

There is a wide array of information inherent in a movement that can be used as a cue for later reproduction, such as distance, end-location, force, and direction. A common experimental procedure is to isolate one cue, or a combination of cues, and force reliance on this information to the possible exclusion of other information. It is important to point out that the data to be discussed are based on the reproduction of constrained (experimenter-defined) standards, usually achieved by inserting a mechanical stop, rather than preselected (participant-defined) standards which had different retention characteristics.

Location versus Distance

Two of the more prominent cues available for the reproduction of a movement are its distance and end-location. Separation of these cues is accomplished by using different starting points for the standard and the reproduction which makes one or the other cue unreliable at recall (Figure 33). Several of the earlier studies compared a condition in which both cues were reliable (no change in starting point) with conditions in which only one or the other of the cues was reliable. The absolute-error results of a comparison of the combined cues with the distance cue (Posner, 1967) indicated that neither were rehearsable nor affected by interpolated digit-classification tasks (there was a hint that location information might be rehearsable). This was consistent with results for the distance cue in an earlier study (Posner and Konick, 1966). A group of studies that followed showed a similar lack of absolute-error effects due to interpolated mental activity, but did find some interference for interpolated motor activity (e.g. Faust-Adams, 1972; Kantowitz, 1972, Exp. IV; Stelmach, 1970; Stelmach and Bruce, 1970). All of these studies allowed both cues to be reliable.

Keele and Ells (1972) compared the combined cues with the location cue and found both were rehearsable: reproductions did not deteriorate over an empty retention interval and were adversely affected by an interpolated digit-classification task. A group of studies that followed showed some adverse affects of an interpolated activity that required limited processing capacity, namely, remembering an interpolated movement (e.g. Stelmach and Walsh,

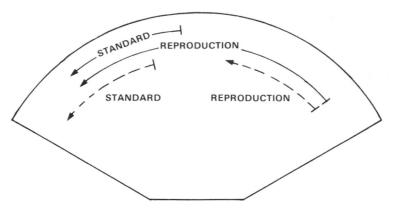

Figure 33. Schematic representation of the separation of the cues of end-location (solid lines) and distance (dashed lines) in movement reproduction.

1972, 1973). These studies allowed both cues to be reliable, but asked participants to reproduce location.

A study by Laabs (1973), which compared the location cue with the distance cue, cleared up some of these apparently conflicting results. He found different retention characteristics for these cues: distance showed a deterioration over an empty interval and no additional interference from interpolated mental activity; end-location showed little forgetting over an empty retention interval but a strong interference effect when processing capacity was taken up by an interpolated mental activity. Although there are some discrepancies to the notion that end-location is sensory encoded and distance is not, several studies have confirmed that the separated cues are comparable at immediate reproduction (e.g. Hagman, 1978; Hagman and Francis, 1975), that the location cue is better retained after a delay (e.g. Laabs, 1974, 1977), and that the location cue is more subject to capacity interference (e.g. Diewert, 1975; Laabs, 1976).

One discrepant study (Marteniuk and Roy, 1972) indicated that the location cue is superior to the distance cue at immediate reproduction but repeated the same movement over twenty trials, which may have allowed the sensory-encoded cue to be learned. This interpretation is consistent with Zahorik's (1972) finding of improvement over thirty-one learning trials when participants used the location cue but not when they used the distance cue. Other discrepant studies (Diewert, 1975, 1976) that suggest distance is rehearsable did not eliminate the strategy of counting, which has been shown to result in retention characteristics resembling that of end-location (Laabs, 1973). Even in these discrepant studies, end-location turns out to be the best source of reproduction information.

Once an encodable cue is isolated for study, a further procedure based on the distinction between structural and capacity interference (see Kahneman, 1973; Kerr, 1973) can be used to determine the specific nature of the coding involved. Capacity interference is caused by competing demands made on the limited-capacity, central-processing mechanism presumably involved in information processing. Structural interference, on the other hand, is caused by competing demands made on some specific perceptual, memory, or response mechanism. Thus, task interference that is over and above that expected from capacity demands, can be used to make inferences about encoding.

Motor memory studies have only recently begun to use this technique (e.g. Diewert, 1975, 1976; Hagman, 1978; Laabs, 1976). In one experiment, Laabs (1976) found that remembering the distance or end-location of an interpolated movement interfered equally with location reproduction, indicating the presence of capacity interference but not structural interference. In another experiment, Diewert (1975, Exp. I) found that an interpolated kinaesthetic judgement interfered with distance retention but a similar visual judgement did not. This finding supports structural interference for distance information but not capacity interference. The notion of structural interference with a perceptual mechanism explains the deterioration apparently caused by interpolated motor activity in several of the earlier motor memory studies which allowed the distance cue to be reliable.

Long versus Short

The general conclusion that distance information is neither rehearsable nor influenced by changes in processing capacity may be contingent on the length of the movement to be reproduced. Where length of movement has been included as a variable, differences in retention have been found in distance conditions (e.g. Diewert, 1975; Faust-Adams, 1972; Hall and Wilberg, 1978; Kerr, 1978b; Laabs, 1977; Posner, 1967; Posner and Konick, 1966; Roy and Kelso, 1977). The general finding is that absolute or variable error increases as the movements get longer.

This finding does not necessarily mean that shorter movements are processed differently from longer movements, because it can also be explained in terms of a decrease in discriminability as expected in accordance with Weber's law. On the other hand, there is some evidence, primarily based on absolute error, that suggests shorter lengths may be rehearsable and subject to capacity interference (Keele and Ells, 1972; Posner and Keele, 1969; Stelmach, 1970; Stelmach and Wilson, 1970). Unfortunately, the results of these studies are equivocal because length and position were allowed to covary. In a more recent study, Laabs (1974) found that an interpolated movement only provided interference (presumably structural interference) for longer distances but not shorter distances or end-locations. One explanation for these apparent differences in codability according to length is that a short but not long distance may be easily recoded as two points in space, which are sensorily encoded similar to end-location.

Overall, the context variable of length that has such potency for constant error appears to have a much less pervasive effect on variable error. More research is needed to establish that shorter distances are rehearsable and subject to capacity interference.

Active versus Passive

Another source of proprioceptive/kinaesthetic information inherent in a movement, whether a standard is presented actively or passively, does not seem to result in differentially retained cue information. The general finding is that there is little overall difference in reproduction of constrained standards in terms of absolute and variable error (e.g. Jones, 1972, 1974a; Keele and Ells, 1972; Kelso, 1977a; Stelmach, Kelso, and Wallace, 1975; Whitaker and Trumbo, 1976). When the constrained movement conditions of these studies are examined more closely, however, it is clear that passive locations are rehearsable and subject to capacity interference (e.g. Keele and Ells, 1972; Stelmach, Kelso, and Wallace, 1975). Likewise, Jones' (1974a) results suggest that passive distances are neither rehearsable nor subject to capacity interference. Thus, the end-location of actively or passively presented standards seems to be one of the more important characteristics in the representation of movement in memory. One exception to the general active/passive finding showed that constrained distance when actively presented was reproduced better immediately and after a 20-sec delay than when passively presented, but was not differentially affected by interpolated activity (Roy, 1978).

Force and Direction

Movement force is a prorioceptive/kinaesthetic cue that can be manipulated by having participants either push or pull a stationary transducer (isometric force) or by adding weight or tension to the usual reproduction movement (rotary force). Pepper and Herman (1970) investigated isometric force and reported no decrease in absolute error over a 60-sec retention interval in one experiment. In another experiment, they found a significant decrease in absolute error with interpolated mental activity (the rest condition also showed a decrease, but it was smaller than that due to the interpolation). These results indicate that force is rehearsable and subject to capacity interference just like location information, but Pepper and Herman provided visual feedback via an oscilloscope so that the task is not analogous to the constrained movements we are discussing. When visual feedback was removed in different study (Fowler and Notterman, 1975), force retention more closely paralleled distance retention in that absolute error decreased over time. Several motor memory studies that investigated reproduction under tension tend to support the conclusion that force is not rehearsable (e.g. Jones, 1974a; Keele and Ells, 1972; Stelmach, 1968). These studies found no change in forgetting as measured by absolute or variable error with added tension.

Movement direction is an easily isolated cue that has been the subject of some interesting attempts to examine the nature of encoding. One study (Dickinson and Higgins, 1977) adapted the release from proactive interference paradigm from verbal memory and demonstrated that movement direction is a relevant encoding characteristic. Wallace (1977) used a technique in isolating the location cue in which the standard and reproduction are made with different limbs. He found that the alteration of movement direction hampered switched-limb reproduction but not same-limb reproduction, which also indicates the importance of the direction cue. Finally, Diewert (1976) and Hall and Leavitt (1977) report evidence that direction is rehearsable and subject to capacity interference.

Cognitive Encoding

So far we have been discussing the encoding of proprioceptive/kinaesthetic information inherent in a movement. Some reproduction cues (e.g. location, direction) appear to be rehearsable and subject to capacity interference, others do not (e.g. distance, force). Although the 'raw' sensory information of the latter cues do not appear to have a comparable sensory-encoded form, it does not mean they cannot serve to guide reproduction: all that needs to be done is to convert this information into another form, that is, cognitively encode it.

The most obvious cognitive encoding involves verbal labelling, but there are also other means to convert sensory-unencodable information to a rehearsable form. We have already implicated counting (a time-based form of verbal labelling) in the recoding of distance, end-locations in the recoding of short lengths, and visual guidance in the recoding of force. A recent study by Diewert and Roy (1978) confirms the recoding of distance in terms of end-location and counting. The choice of strategy depended upon the relative ease with which the location cue could be used. A somewhat surprising result was that when distance was recoded as a single digit it was not only rehearsable, but also *not* subject to capacity or structural interference from interpolated counting. In contrast, Laabs (1973) found that similar interpolations interfered with distance retention for counters. One of the reasons for the excellent performance of Diewert and Roy's counters may be that the same length (hence the same digit) was repeated on all trials.

The use of verbal labelling has often been offered as an explanation of motor memory results, but the number of studies that have specifically investigated this form of cognitive encoding is very small. Whitaker and Trumbo (1976) demonstrated that participants could use a familiar metric system to accurately label distance and, likewise, could accurately produce distances when given only the verbal metric. Shea (1977) provided participants with labels to help in the reproduction of movements for which both location and distance cues were reliable. He found increased forgetting over an empty retention interval with no labelling or irrelevant noun labelling, and little forgetting with relevant labelling of end-location (positions on a clock face). In a more extensive study of labelling using the location cue, Ho and Shea (1978) compared no-label control groups to those provided with a label or required to make up their own. As might be expected from the use of the location cue, they found that all groups showed little forgetting over an empty retention interval but a strong interference effect when processing capacity was taken up by an interpolated mental activity. The control groups showed significantly more interference than the experimental groups, however, and when members of the experimental groups forgot their labels their performance was similar to that of the no-label controls. Participant-provided labels resulted in better performance than the experimenter-provided labels.

All of the above studies indicate the extreme importance of controlling the cognitive strategies of participants in motor memory studies designed to investigate encoding.

Movement Preplanning

The conclusion that distance information is neither rehearsable nor subject to capacity interference when experimenter-constrained standards are reproduced (Figure 31), does not hold when standards preselected by the participants are reproduced (Figure 32). Using the distance cue along and in combination with the location cue, Jones (1974a) found different retention characteristics for these different presentation methods: constrained standards showed a deterioration over an empty interval and no additional interference from interpolated mental activity; preselected standards showed little forgetting over an empty retention interval, but a strong interference effect when processing capacity was taken up by an interpolated mental activity. In general, preselected movements are reproduced better than constrained movements (e.g. Jones, 1972; Kelso, 1977a; Marteniuk, 1973; Roy, 1978; Stelmach and Kelso, 1977; Stelmach, Kelso, and Wallace, 1975; Wallace and Stelmach, 1975).

Although Jones (1972, 1974a) did not include a location condition in his studies, he concluded that preselection and not end-location information underlies movement rehearsal. This view does not account for the finding that constrained end-location is rehearsable and subject to capacity interference (e.g. Laabs, 1973). Furthermore, studies that show preselected location is reproduced better than constrained location (Stelmach and Kelso, 1977, Exp. III; Wallace and Stelmach, 1975) indicate the importance of preselection but do not provide evidence against the importance of the location cue. In fact, recent studies showing that preselected location is reproduced better than preselected distance attests to the importance of the cue (Stelmach, Kelso, and Wallace, 1975; Roy, 1977). A study by Kelso (1977b), in which participants were deprived of proprioceptive feedback through the use of a pressure cuff, provides evidence of the central encoding of location information. Under normal preselected conditions there was no difference in the absolute error of immediate reproduction of location and distance. Under nerve block conditions, however, location reproduction was superior to distance reproduction. Variable error showed similar trends, but only for larger movements. Constant error shifted in different directions and amounts under the two conditions yielding the more dramatic absolute-error results.

Similar to constrained findings, short preselected movements are better reproduced than long ones (Stelmach, Kelso, and Wallace, 1975; Roy and Diewert, 1978). This may be due to the superiority of location encoding for both methods of presentation. In contrast to constrained findings, active preselected movements are reproduced better than passive ones (Jones, 1974a; Kelso, 1977a; Stelmach, Kelso, and McCullagh, 1976; Stelmach, Kelso, and Wallace, 1975). This finding indicates the apparent importance of efference or outflow in preselection.

Central Monitoring of Efference

Jones (1972, 1974a) was the first to offer an explanation of the preselection effect in terms of an efference-based mechanism. His position is that when a preselected movement is made, the resulting efferent discharge is stored in the form of an efference copy. Movements are reproduced by monitoring efferent commands and matching them to the stored copy. Thus, internal feedback underlies the superior preselected reproduction; the absence of this feedback and reliance on non-centrally represented proprioceptive feedback causes the poorer constrained reproduction. In support of this position, Jones and Hulme (1976) present evidence that a secondary task during the presentation of a standard negatively affects constrained reproductions, which presumably involves feedback processing, but not preselected reproductions. Carlton's (1978) recent study of movement rate production, however, only partially supports this position since only fast movements, like those used by Jones, were unaffected by a secondary task. Slow preselected movements were adversely affected. All of the results discussed earlier that indicated location information is crucial to accurate reproduction also rules against Jones' position. Of course, it can still be argued that proprioceptive information or inflow, although sometimes used, is not necessary for movement control.

Sensory Presetting

A less restrictive efference explanation of the preselection effect is one that proposes that outflow facilitates the sensory encoding of proprioceptive information (Kelso, 1977a; Kelso and Stelmach, 1976; Stelmach, Kelso, and Wallace, 1975). This position holds that when a preselected movement is made, two sets of signals are generated: (1) the efferent discharge to the muscles; and (2) a simultaneous central discharge from the motor to sensory centres that presets the sensory systems for the anticipated inflow. Because sensory processors are prepared to receive the proprioceptive feedback, superior encoding results. The prominent role given to proprioceptive feedback overcomes arguments made against the strict outflow position.

Cognitive Strategy

Roy and Diewert (1975, 1978) explain the preselection effect in terms of an encoding strategy adopted by participants when they are given prior information about the termination of a constrained distance. They found that the preselection effect was eliminated when the total movement range was presented to participants who were then told they would move to a stop defining half of the range. Roy (1978) replicated this finding and showed that when prior information was not available the preselected movement effect reappeared. He also showed a preselection effect when presenting prior information with passive movements. Since little or no efferent information is available with passive movements, a cognitive strategy rather than an efference-based mechanism was implicated. As an alternative, prior information may allow efferent commands to be generated. Kelso's (1977a) finding that reproduction of passive preselected and constrained standards differ when actively but not passively reproduced, supports this view. It remains to be seen whether prior information can improve passive reproduction of a passive preselected standard or if active reproduction is required.

Visuo-spatial Structuring

Most motor memory studies eliminate vision to force participants to remember kinaesthetic/proprioceptive information. When vision was allowed in some motor learning studies, learning was more efficient in terms of absolute error and performance was better on subsequent recognition trials or reproduction trials without knowledge of results (Adams and Goetz, 1973; Adams, Goetz, and Marshall, 1972; Adams, Gopher, and Lintern, 1977). Similarly, when vision was allowed in some motor memory studies that used absolute error, reproductions did not deteriorate over an empty retention interval and were adversely affected by an interpolated mental activity (e.g. Burwitz, 1974a; Kantowitz, 1972, Exp. II; Posner, 1967; Posner and Konick, 1966).

The improved performance in motor memory with vision may be due to the provision of either concurrent feedback during the movement or information about the end-location of a movement. There are several studies that indicate it is the latter information that is important. For example, Holding (1968) found a decrease in absolute error with longer durations of target exposure for ballistic aiming, which supports the conclusion. Again, a recognition memory study by Faust-Adams (1975) showed that vision during a series of three movements did not improve the judgement of which of the last two movements was the same as the first, but 4 sec of prior vision did. A recent learning study (Smyth, 1978) supports this finding in that visual guidance groups made larger errors than groups which received visual information only at the termination of the movement. Likewise, a study of ballistic movements found more absolute error with vision of the hand than with vision of the target (Whiting and Cockerill, 1974). All of these results suggest that information about the termination of a movement is the important contribution that vision makes. Therefore, it is reasonable to conclude that vision is probably important in the movement preplanning process.

A few studies indicate that we must be cautious about this conclusion. Kelso and Frekany (1978, Exp. I, II) suggested that vision does not enhance preplanning because they found that vision during the presentation of the standard *only* did not help reproductions. In a learning study, Newell and Chew (1975) found that a decrease in absolute error, due to a dot of light at the start point or on the movement bar, disappeared after about five trials. They also found that the only group to continue to learn was the one that viewed the apparatus. They concluded that extraneous surround cues were used.

The above results suggest that, as an alternative to providing end-location for preplanning, vision in motor memory may provide a spatial structure in which movements can be remembered and reproduced. The precision of the spatial representation would be related to the availability of vision and the perceptual richness of the environment. Russell (1976) has proposed that this structure may be a space coordinate reference system to which all modalities can provide inputs. The auditory and kinaesthetic/proprioceptive senses have less spatial resolving power and presumably lead to less precise spatial structuring. This, in turn, yields the poorer recall for movements without vision. A related proposal is that the spatial structure may be an integrated visual/kinaesthetic store (Connolly and Jones, 1970). A number of recent studies (e.g. Diewert, 1975, 1976; Diewert and Stelmach, 1977; Salmoni and Sullivan, 1976) provide only weak support for this concept.

One other major effect of vision on the processing of kinaesthetic/ proprioceptive information should be discussed. Because visual feedback is such a potent variable in motor memory, it can sometimes lead to poorer performance than if only kinaesthetic/proprioceptive information is used. This was demonstrated in a motor learning study (Smyth, 1978) in which one of the visual guidance groups also moved to a stop. When the stop and visual guidance were removed during test trials, the absolute and variable error was worse for this group than for a non-vision group who made their practice trials to a stop. Klein and Posner (1974, Exp. II) provide further evidence that vision seems to dominate kinaesthesis when information from both senses is available, and this dominance occurs even when the visual information is irrelevant and could be ignored. They found that the processing of the kinaesthetic pattern information was impaired by the presence of visual pattern information whether or not the participant knew which modality would be used in reproducing the movement pattern. An apparent exception to this finding is reported by Kelso and Frekany (1978, Exp. III) for preselected movements.

THEORETICAL FORMULATIONS

Theoretical efforts have concentrated on the more global topics of motor control and learning rather than motor memory. What theorization that has occurred is embodied in two models which are specific to the reproduction paradigm.

Models of Motor Memory

Pepper and Herman's Shrinking-trace Model

The first attempt at modelling motor memory was made by Pepper and Herman (1970) who tried to accommodate the following constant-error findings: (1) an increase in relative undershooting over an empty delay; (2) a shift in constant error towards the physical value of an interpolated motor act; and (3) an increase in relative overshooting with the interpolation of a mental activity. They proposed a dual-trace model that assumes the decay of a memory trace for intensity or extent of a criterion movement (shrinking trace) and postulates interference with the memory trace through assimilation of proprioceptive stimulation. The proprioceptive stimulation may be either in the form of an interpolated movement or 'general changes in the level of muscle tension' resulting from an interpolated mental activity. The assimilated memory trace, which is continually updated, represents the mean effects of the proprioceptive simulation arising from the standard, the interpolated motor act (if there is one), and the prevailing level of muscle tension. Stelmach and his associates (Stelmach and Kelso, 1975; Stelmach and Walsh, 1972, 1973) proposed a refinement to this assimilation that emphasized the relative decay states of the standard and interpolated memory traces which are assumed to be assimilated at the time of recall.

Laabs' Perceptual-motor Memory Model

As an alternative to the Pepper and Herman (1970) model, Laabs (1971, 1973) proposed an information-processing model of motor memory that incorporated both the constant- and variable-error measures. Constant error was proposed as an index of perceptual context effects, and an assimilation notion similar to that of the shrinking-trace model was retained. One of the main assumptions is that a reproduction is made in reference to the memory trace of the standard and the adaptation level of the set of movements presented. The assimilated memory trace represents the weighted effects of the memory of the standard and a referent movement (adaptation level or levels) with the weighting determined by the relative strength of the memory trace. As the memory trace decays or becomes subject to interference, more reliance is placed on the referent movement. This leads to the central tendency effect for a series of movements and to assimilation effects due to interpolated activity. Another assumption is that as the memory trace decays or becomes subject to interference, it is less able to be reproduced accurately. This leads to greater inconsistency in reproduction, and variable error was proposed as an index of forgetting. Marteniuk (1973) and Marteniuk and Diewert (1975) provided some support for this model in direct comparisons with the Pepper and Herman model.

Theories of Motor Control and Learning

Closed-loop Theories

Adams (1971, 1976) applied the closed-loop notions of error detection and correction to learning data on slow positioning movements. This resulted in a theory that defined two memory states: the perceptual trace and the memory trace. The memory trace, representing recall memory, is a 'modest motor program' which has the purpose of only initiating the movement. This trace develops as a function of knowledge of results and practice. The purpose of the perceptual trace, representing recognition memory, is to control the progress of the movement. This trace develops as a function of response-produced feedback. To complete a movement, response-produced feedback is matched against the perceptual trace. For slow positioning movements, this means a movement continues until the individual 'recognizes' that it is correct. Adams' theory has led to a large number of motor memory studies which investigate two primary areas: (1) the formation of the perceptual trace as a function of the quality and quantity of feedback (e.g. Adams and Goetz, 1973;

Adams, Goetz, and Marshall, 1972; Newell, 1976b; Stelmach, 1973); and (2) the differentiation of the memory trace and perceptual trace (e.g. Newell and Chew, 1975; Schmidt, Christenson, and Rogers, 1975).

Using Adams' (1971) theory as a base, Schmidt (1975a, 1976a) constructed a theory that incorporated Pew's (1974b) schema concept. He proposed that three schema are generated: (1) a response or recall schema which leads to the specification of a motor program; (2) a recognition schema for expected sensory consequences analogous to the perceptual trace; and (3) a schema for labelling the error between expected and actual sensory consequences of a movement which feeds into the recall and recognition schema. Several recent motor memory studies (e.g. Levin, Norman, and Dolezal, 1973; McCracken and Stelmach, 1977; Moxley, 1979; Newell and Shapiro, 1976; Williams, 1978; Williams and Rodney, 1978) support the plausibility of the schema concept. More emphasis is given to the motor program in the schema theory than in Adams' theory.

Open-loop Theories

The main competition to the closed-loop version of motor learning is an open-loop system based on the concept of a motor program (Keele, 1973, 1975; Keele and Summers, 1976). The motor program is seen as a centrally stored plan for a movement which, in the absence of an error, can be exercised without feedback. Feedback is monitored, however, to ensure that the movement is progressing as planned, and it is used to modify an ongoing program if required or to make subsequent changes to the program. The emphasis placed on the operation of the motor program as opposed to the use of feedback is exactly the opposite of the emphasis placed on these concepts in closed-loop theory. Thus, one of the major differences in these theories is in role ascribed to feedback which was discussed in an earlier chapter (Summers, Chapter 3). Motor memory research related to the motor program theory has focused on the representation of the program (e.g. Summers, 1975, 1977a).

RECOGNITION MEMORY

Most motor memory studes have focused on movement reproduction, which we treated as movement recall. According to closed-loop theories of motor learning (Adams, 1971; Schmidt, 1975a), the studies we reviewed involve a recognition process instead of a recall process. The question that needs to be answered is whether or not slow positioning movements are governed solely by a recognition process. The increasing interest that has been shown in separating and studying the recall and recognition processes should help resolve this issue.

On the Recognition Process

There are three different procedures that have been used in efforts to experimentally separate the recall and recognition processes, each of which manipulates variables that are assumed to related to recall and recognition as represented by Adams' (1971) perceptual trace and memory trace.

Ballistic Movements

This procedure assumes that a ballistic movement is completed so fast that it is carried out using the memory trace only, without influence of response-produced feedback or the perceptual trace. Therefore, only the recall process is assessed by the movement error. The recognition process is assessed by examining the estimation of movement error made after movement completion, which is when the perceptual trace is proposed to be operating.

Studies of ballistic movements (e.g. Koch and Dorfman, 1979; Newell, 1974; Newell and Chew, 1974a; Rubin, 1978; Schmidt and White, 1972; Schmidt and Wrisberg, 1973; Schmidt, Christenson, and Rogers, 1975) usually present a number of practice trials with knowledge of results and then withdraw this feedback somewhere in the series of trials. There are two variables that seem to lead to a differential effect on the measures of recall and recognition, lending support to the existence of the two hypothetical memory states. One variable is the amount of response-produced feedback: Schmidt and Wrisberg (1973) and Newell and Chew (1974a) found a decrement in response recognition but not recall primarily when visual feedback was withdrawn along with knowledge of results. Another variable is the delay in presenting knowledge of results: Schmidt, Christenson, and Rodgers (1975) found recall was unaffected by the delay while recognition deteriorated. In contrast, Koch and Dorfman (1979) investigated the very same variables and found no decrements in the recognition process.

The recognition measure (i.e. correlation or absolute difference between actual and estimated error) used in all of the above studies has been criticized on a number of grounds, but most recently because it can be affected by subjective criteria for reporting error and thus confounds individual differences with sensory sensitivity. To overcome this criticism, Rubin (1978) used a signal detection measure and found that error detection was poorer in comparison to actual performance as in the other ballistic movement studies.

Auditory Feedback Without Movement

Newell and his colleagues (Newell, 1976b; Zelaznik and Spring, 1976; Zelaznik, Shapiro, and Newell, 1978) have developed a procedure that attempts to develop the recognition mechanism in the absence of overt responses by providing only the auditory feedback associated with a rapid timing task. The general finding is that participants who have had the benefit of auditory feedback (or of more varied auditory feedback), as opposed to those who do not, show a reduction in absolute error over a subsequent series of production trials without knowledge of results. It is assumed that performance improves in the absence of knowledge of results through the development of a recognition process. Alternatively, open-loop theory suggests that a rudimentary or partial motor program may be developing instead of the perceptual trace or recognition schema of closed-loop theory.

Passive Movements

The procedure proposed by Kelso (1978) to separate recall from recognition is the comparison of passive and active production movements. Only recognition is used in passive production because the hypothetical memory trace would remain inactive. It follows that if all slow positioning movements are governed solely by recognition, then both active and passive production of a standard should be performed equally well after the standard is learned. Similar to the ballistic movement studies, Kelso (1978) presented a number of practice trials with knowledge of results and then withdrew this feedback. There were no apparent differences in the absolute error of production on the acquisition trials, but after the knowledge of results was withdrawn the performance using active production deteriorated greatly while that using passive production remained stable. The conclusion that can be drawn from these results is that some additional (or separate) process is involved in active slow positioning movements over and above recognition, namely, recall in the form of central monitoring of efference or motor programming.

Accepting this interpretation of active versus passive movement production means that recognition is superior to recall (as is the case in verbal memory); while accepting the interpretation of the ballistic movement studies indicates the opposite, that recall is superior to recognition. The answer to this discrepancy will require further research.

Comparison of Recall and Recognition

A more direct approach to studying motor recognition memory uses a recognition paradigm. A standard is presented in this paradigm, and, either immediately or after some period of delay, the participant is required to indicate whether a comparison movement is the same as or different from the standard (same/different procedure) or which of two comparison movements is the same as the standard (forced-choice procedure). This is schematically illustrated in Figure 34.

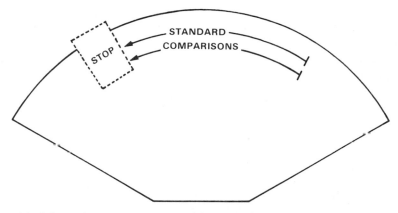

Figure 34. Schematic representation of the recognition paradigm for a standard and comparison or comparisons constrained by a stop.

Marshall (1972) was one of the first investigators to compare recall and recognition by using both a reproduction and recognition task. The reasoning behind this study was that if slow positioning movements are governed solely by a recognition process, then recall and recognition measures from parallel experiments should have the same functional relationship with the same variables. Using a two-interval, forced-choice recognition paradigm, he found that increases in reinforcement in the form of repeated standards positively affected both recall and recognition. He also found detrimental effects of delay for both recall and recognition; however, the loss for the recognition measure was very small. These parallel results were taken as support for the proposition that recall is fundamentally a recognition process. The additional finding that the mean proportion of correct recognitions increased with increases in length while reproduction accuracy as measured by absolute error got worse, calls for caution in accepting the notion the recall is solely a function of recognition.

Because of the increased memory load associated with presenting two comparison movements in the forced-choice procedure, Kantowitz (1974) used the same/different procedure. The major independent variable is the area under the memory operating characteristic calculated from the same/different judgements and associated confidence ratings. Kantowitz (1974) found that recognition of movements when using the visual modality was superior to that when using only the kinaesthetic modality. He also found that recognition performance deteriorated over an unfilled interval, but did not show further deterioration when the interval was filled with a paced tapping task. This finding is somewhat characteristic of the retention of constrained distance and indicates that recognition, in either the visual or kinaesthetic modality, may not be subject to the information-processing constraints that are associated with the retention of constrained location or preselected movements.

More recently, Laabs (1975b, 1978) conducted several studies that used the same/different procedure in examining encoding variables. One set of experiments (Laabs, 1978) used each of the methods of preselected and constrained presentation of the standard in separate experiments that combined both recall and recognition trials. Including both kinds of trials provided the opportunity to see if delay has the same effect on these processes. It also allowed a more simple and direct test of the proposition that slow positioning movements are solely governed by a recognition process. If the proposition is true, then a reproduction of a standard on a recall trial ought to elicit a 'same' judgement when presented later as a comparison movement on a recognition trial. To the extent that 'different' judgements are elicited, the theoretical proposition must be reconsidered. In both experiments, the variable of delay appeared to affect recall and recognition differently. In regard to the direct test, the proportion of 'same' judgements on trials where previously made reproductions served as comparisons were at the chance level in both experiments. This is further evidence that slow positioning movements are not solely governed by a recognition process.

Laabs (1975b) also conducted an experiment designed to parallel a previous recall study (Laabs, 1973) to see if the delay variable would interact with the reproduction cue in recognition as it had in recall. The interaction did not occur, suggesting that delay does not affect recognition and recall in the same manner when reproduction cues are controlled. Recognition when using the location cue was much better than when using the distance cue, as might be expected from Kantowitz's (1974) results on the visual modality and the apparent relationship between location encoding and visual structure. Although there was a slight trend for recognition to deteriorate over an empty retention interval, no statistical difference was found. In contrast, Marshall (1972) and Kantowitz (1974) did find significant deterioration of recognition over an empty retention interval, but the amount was small so that the question of how much recognition deteriorates over an empty interval is still open.

A more important question is whether or not recognition is relatively impervious to processing demands as suggested above. A group was run during the Laabs (1975b) experiment, but not reported, which allows examination of this question. This group had its retention interval filled with a counting task and its performance did not differ from that of an empty-interval control group. This result is in opposition to that of the parallel recall study (Laabs, 1973) which found location information is affected by information-processing activity while distance information is not. Apparently, processing demands do not affect the recognition process to the same degree as they affect the recall process.

When the findings of the studies that experimentally manipulated recognition and recall information, and those just discussed that used a recognition paradigm are considered as a whole, there are grounds for a reasonable doubt that slow positioning movements are governed solely by a recognition process. Obviously, there is a need for more research to refine the concept of the recognition process and to determine more precisely the relationship between the recognition and recall processes.

COMPARISON WITH VERBAL SHORT-TERM MEMORY

To summarize the research in the area of motor memory, we will review the area from a somewhat different perspective.

Early motor memory research tried to establish a correspondence between the verbal and motor domains. When inconsistencies could not be ignored, subsequent research focused on differences between these domains. Currently, research seems to be focusing once again on the similarities between the domains with an increase in the adaptation of verbal memory paradigms to the study of motor memory. Along the way motor memory has shared many conceptualizations with verbal memory.

In the Beginning . . .

Verbal Memory

The seeds for the elaborate verbal memory research area and the acceptance of the use of the information-processing framework in that research were planted in the late 1950s. For example, Broadbent (1958) presented a model of information processing that specifically set aside a sensory store and a short-term store. Sperling (1960) followed with persuasive evidence for a separate sensory store with a very brief trace duration. At about the same time, Brown (1958) and Peterson and Peterson (1959) reported their classic work on short-term memory. In these studies, massive forgetting of single items occurred in a matter of seconds when the retention interval was filled with a mental task. This led to the belief by some that there is also a separate short-term memory that decays very rapidly if it is not continually updated through rehearsal, and that this memory structure is different from long-term memory, which is subject to interference but not decay. Not everyone accepted this notion (e.g. Melton, 1963), and a central issue in the verbal memory research area became the distinction between the short-term and long-term components of memory. Initially, studies focused on the investigation of interference effects to see if the new short-term component was really different from the long-term component. Efforts were devoted primarily to defining the conditions for the occurence of proactive interference, that is, the negative effect of a prior item-recall sequence on a subsequent sequence (e.g. Keppel and Underwood, 1962; Loess, 1964; Peterson and Gentile, 1965). Now let us turn to the motor area.

Motor Memory

About five or six years after the initial verbal short-term memory studies, the question was raised as to whether or not motor short-term retention would obey the same laws as verbal short-term retention. The research goal was to provide evidence for a parsimonious, single short-term memory system. This goal was sought even though it was known that verbal and motor long-term memory were different (i.e. well-practised continuous tasks are retained extremely well over the long term as compared to verbal responses). In one of the first studies in motor short-term memory, Adams and Dijkstra (1966) found rapid forgetting over an empty retention interval and decreases in forgetting with increases in practice. At about the same time, Posner and Konick (1966) found similar forgetting over both an empty retention interval and one filled with a mental task. These results were interpreted as being consistent with the decay explanation of verbal short-term memory. However, motor memory was different in that it appeared it could not be rehearsed over an empty retention interval and it was not differentially affected by the difficulty of the interpolated mental task as was verbal memory. Moreover, neither of these studies showed proactive interference, and they were followed by other studies that sought to demonstrate this verbal memory effect.

In general, no proactive inhibition effects were found even when intertrial intervals were very short, allowing maximum interference from previous item-recall trials (e.g. Montague and Hillix, 1968; Schmidt and Ascoli, 1970a). The proactive inhibition that was found to occur appeared to be related to the presence of an information-processing demand during the presentation of the standard and retention, such as the requirement to hold prior movements in memory and reproduce them after standard reproduction (e.g. Ascoli and Schmidt, 1969; Schmidt and Ascoli, 1970b; Stelmach, 1969). In addition to interference from prior movements, a number of studies also investigated interference from interpolated movements. Some results supported retroactive interference due to the similarity of the interpolated activity (e.g. Williams, Beaver, Spence, and Rundell, 1969; Stelmach and Bruce, 1970; Kantowitz, 1972) which is consistent with verbal memory results, others did not (e.g. Schmidt and Stelmach, 1968; Stelmach, 1970). Thus, the search for similarities in the verbal and motor domains led to the reluctant conclusion that there may be separate short-term memories for verbal and motor information. Notice, however, that the structure of short-term memory was adopted without question in the study of motor behaviour.

Growing Up

Verbal Memory

Because the question of whether or not interference affects the short-term and long-term components of verbal memory in the same manner was answered in the affirmative; alternative evidence for this dichotomy was sought. Evidence was gathered along several lines: (1) apparent differences in encoding depending upon the length of the retention interval (e.g. Kintsch and Buschke, 1969); (2) interactions between a variety of variables and different parts of the serial position curve that is typically found in recall (e.g. Glanzer, 1972); (3) specific memory deficits in brain-damaged patients (e.g. Milner, 1970); and (4) the notion that short-term memory has a limited capacity (e.g. Miller, 1956). When evidence from all these lines of research were taken together, a fairly strong case was made for a multiple-trace model of verbal short-term memory. Additional research was concerned with the relationship between the short-term and long-term components of verbal memory (e.g. Waugh and Norman, 1965). This carries us up to about the mid-1970s; let us turn to the motor area to see what happened during this period.

Motor Memory

By the early 1970s, most researchers had accepted that motor short-term memory was different from verbal short-term memory. Thus, replications of verbal memory research in the motor domain declined, and the important questions regarding the short-term/long-term dichotomy were never entertained. No one ever got around to asking specifically whether or not motor short-term memory is different from motor long-term memory or what the relationship is between these two hypothetical components of motor memory. Research on motor memory continued unabated. Instead of searching for evidence to support a multiple-trace model of motor memory, however, emphasis was placed on demonstrating the variables that apparently affected motor short-term memory. The encoding process became the main focus of the research. A number of previously inconsistent results became understandable with the finding that different encoding or storage processes were involved for different reproduction cues (e.g. Laabs, 1973) and for different methods of presenting the standard (e.g. Stelmach, Kelso, and Wallace, 1975).

During this period the motor memory research area turned inward on itself and began to struggle with issues such as the appropriate measures for retention, and effect of the methods of studying motor memory on experimental results. What were previously methodological artefacts became the important variables in motor memory. During the same time, theoretical formulations of motor learning (e.g. Adams, 1971, 1976; Schmidt, 1975a, 1976a) were presented, which set in motion a whole new line of research in which movement recognition and recall were the main topics. Motor memory began standing on its own without relying on continual comparison with verbal memory. Motor short-term memory was still compared to verbal short-term memory whenever the results were consistent, and reference was made to the importance of research showing the apparent unity of the short-term memory concept. On the other hand, when the results were not consistent with verbal results, reference was made to the importance of research showing that the two domains were different. Thus, the sharing of conceptual structures and processes appeared to be a matter of convenience.

New Directions

Verbal Memory

Recent reviews of verbal learning and memory indicate that the area is taking on a new (or maybe an old) look, with a trend away from a multiple-trace to a unitary model of verbal memory (e.g. Peterson, 1977; Postman, 1975). While most everyone seems to accept the existence of a sensory store (see Holding, 1975 for a notable exception), it appears that the acceptance of the short-term/ long-term dichotomy was too hasty. Some of the evidence for the distinction between these components did not hold up very well and conceptualization turned away from structures to processing. For example, Baddeley and Hitch (1974) proposed a working memory as an alternative to the structural short-term memory store. Working memory is a central control system with a limited-capacity work space that is allocated between storage and control processes. This system is used for such diverse information-processing activities as reasoning, language comprehension, free recall, and visualization. Another alternative to the structural conceptions of short-term and long-term memory is the concept of levels of processing proposed by Craik and Lockhart (1972). They suggested that memory can be conceived as a by-product of perceptual processing, with the duration of the memory dependent on the depth of processing carried out on the stimulus. There are two types of rehearsal in this approach: maintenance rehearsal to keep information at a given level and elaborative rehearsal to transfer information to a new and deeper level. The amount of material analysed and the depth to which it is analysed is determined by the limited capacity of the human information-processing system. Both of these approaches are conceived, not as theories, but as flexible frameworks for verbal memory research that allow change and development, while at the same time suggest specific testable hypotheses.

Motory Memory

A glance at the studies of motor short-term memory that are being reported currently indicates that the research area is once again trying to establish a correspondence between verbal and motor memory. Of course, this might be only a matter of convenience, as noted above. Nevertheless, there is ample justification to search for a unitary set of laws that can be applied to both verbal and motor domains. This search is one direction in which motor memory research is going as evidenced by studies of the release from proactive inhibition (Dickinson and Higgins, 1977), incidental learning (Dickinson, 1977, 1978), levels of processing (Ho and Shea, 1978), directed forgetting (Burwitz, 1974b; Dickinson, 1975), spacing variables (Marshall, Jones, and Sheehan, 1977) and serial position effects (e.g. Magill and Dowell, 1977; Wrisberg, 1975; Zaichkowsky, 1974). Another direction is that pointed out by the current models of motor memory and other theoretical formulations related to motor memory. Regardless of which direction is taken, the question that remains to be answered is 'What purpose does motor short-term memory serve?' The studies that are done within the current theoretical formulations related to motor memory will provide part of the answer to this question. For those studies done outside of current theoretical formulations, there is a need carefully to examine the results in relationship to some overall framework such as that provided by the verbal memory research area or some other research area such as perceptual judgement as suggested in this chapter.

SUMMARY

Our organization of the motor memory research area presents a clear distinction between the perceptual (and perhaps recognition memory) processes and the recall processes involved in movement reproduction.

The data on bias in reproduction reveal an often-ignored relationship between perceptual judgement and motor memory. The corresponding effects in these two areas include: (1) negative constant-error shift over an empty interval (i.e. time-error or time-order-error), (2) central tendency effects; (3) assimilation due to prior stimulation; (4) assimilation due to interpolation; (5) assimilation due to presentation method; and (6) contrast effects. In addition, the effect of interpolated mental activity on constant error in motor memory studies can be explained in terms of perceptual processing. In general, perceptual processing in motor memory is highly vulnerable to context effects and relatively invulnerable to changes in processing capacity.

The recall data for constrained criterion movements indicate that some reproduction cues are sensorily encoded and rehearsable (e.g. location, distance), while others are not (e.g. distance, force). Cognitive strategies, such as verbal labelling or counting, can also play a role in the encoding of movement information. Cognitive strategy may have a part in the reproduction of preselected criterion movements, but there is strong evidence that an efference-based mechanism is involved in such movement preplanning. Visuospatial structuring is also implicated in movement preplanning.

Movement recognition appears to be more related to the perceptual processing in motor memory than to the recall. Like bias in movement reproduction, movement recognition seems easily affected by context but not by the availability of processing capacity.

Our view of perceptual-motor memory shares an information processing orientation with verbal memory, and we hope that it might provide a useful conceptual framework for future motor memory research.

Chapter 7

Sequential Reactions

Patrick M. A. Rabbitt

Tasks of sequential reaction, such as keyboard tasks, present both timing and accuracy problems. As it will appear, the problems of accuracy and its relation to speed have been relatively neglected. However, concern with reaction-time issues goes back to the beginnings of modern psychology.

Wilhelm Wundt set up the first laboratory for the study of human experimental psychology in 1879, in Leipzig. His main research programme was to continue the studies of simple and choice reaction time begun by F. C. Donders ten years earlier. In one form or another this programme has been energetically pursued for the last 100 years in all the major psychological laboratories of the world. Yet in all this time the simplest possible question about human performance at reaction-time tasks has hardly ever been asked and has never satisfactorily been answered. We still cannot explain why people become faster and more accurate when they are practised on very easy choice reaction tasks, and indeed we have no useful models to explain any kind of change in performance at any simple psychomotor task.

This is a curious neglect since practice probably has more effect on mean reaction time (RT) than does any other variable so far investivated. For example, I, like many other investigators, have collected a great deal of data on the effects of prolonged practice on choice reaction times (CRTs) which I have not published because there is no useful model to interpret them. A group of subjects was practised on two-choice, four-choice, and eight-choice task in which S–R compatability (spatial mapping of signal lamps on to response keys) and signal discriminability were varied. Changes in RT due to twenty days' practice were four times as great as any changes due to variations in the number of signal and response alternatives (information load), S-R compatability, signal discriminability, or any interaction between these variables. Indeed after forty days' practice, involving some 40,000 responses on each task, speed and accuracy continued to improve while variations in CRT due to variations in information load, compatability, and signal discriminability had little or no effect. It is possible that if I had been able to practise my subjects for longer, I should have replicated Mowbray and

Rhoades' (1959) classic results and found that CRT no longer increased as the number of signal and response alternatives rose from two to eight. I might also, eventually, have confirmed Crossman's (1956) hypothesis that, if subjects are given enough practice, effects of particular variations in S–R compatability may be entirely abolished.

It has been obvious (to all of us) for the last twenty years that variations in the number of signal and response alternatives, S–R compatability, signal discriminability, signal repetition effects, and sequential effects usually studied in CRT tasks (Bertelson, 1965; Rabbitt, 1968a) account for a much smaller fraction of RT variance than does extended practice. There is also excellent reason to suspect that the effects of all these other variables are evanescent if enough practice is given. Yet all existing models for choice reaction time still concentrate only on these relatively trivial and temporary sources of variance. The trouble seems to be that all current models for human performance are descriptions of a system in a hypothetical 'steady state'. None describe systems which are subject to any sort of *change*, whether change brought about by practice, by maturation, by ageing, by diffuse brain damage, by disease such as schizophrenia, by stress, or by ingestion of drugs. The main models now debated allow us no way to discuss any of these effects (e.g. see Audley 1960; 1973; Audley, Caudrey, Howell, and Powell, 1975; Falmagne, 1965; Henmon, 1911; Laming, 1968; McGill, 1967; Pike, 1973; Stone, 1960; Snodgrass, Luce, and Galanter, 1967; Theios, Smith, Haviland, Traupmann, and McCoy, 1973; Vickers, 1970; Welford, 1968): they are all essentially 'static' models.

LIMITATIONS OF STATIC MODELS

In my view the trouble can be traced back to the uncritical, tacit adoption of the assumption of sequential, independent, successive processing stages made by F. C. Donders in 1868 to justify his decomposition of measured mean CRTs into additive components. The class of models resting on this assumption may be termed linear independent sequential process systems (LISPS).

Donders (1868) felt it reasonable to suppose that a subject required a certain measurable period of time to identify any signal presented to him as a particular member of a set of signals between which he had to distinguish. He further supposed that until the subject had completely identified a signal he could not begin the process of selecting an appropriate response to it. It followed that overall mean RT represented the sum of the latencies of at least these two successive and independent processes. This assumption allowed Donders to compare RTs in three tasks. In task (a) only one signal was ever presented and subjects always made the same response to it. In task (b) any one of five signals might appear and subjects had to choose the appropriate one of five different responses accordingly. In task (c) any one of five signals might appear, but subjects had to respond only to one of them and to ignore the onset of the others. Donders argued that the difference in RTs for tasks (a) and (b) gave an estimate for the time required to choose between five different possible responses rather than to make the same response; while the RT difference between tasks (c) and (a) gave an estimate of the time required to identify any of five different signals rather than simply to register the onset of a signal repeated on every trial. Note that Donders' assumptions were quite arbitrary, and could not be tested by his experiments. Note further that the logic of his experimental manipulations was faulty on two grounds. First, aside from problems of signal recognition the mean RT would be shorter in task (a), in which subjects might expect a signal to respond on every trial, than in task (c), when a signal requiring a response occurred only on one trial in five. Second, in task (b), subjects indeed had to discriminate each signal from each of four other possible signals since they had to select an appropriate response to each of them. In other words they had to discriminate a set of five signals into five subsets of one signal each. However, in task (c), subjects only had to discriminate one critical signal from four other possible distractor signals. They did not have to discriminate the distractors from each other. Thus, they only had to discriminate a set of five signals into two sub-sets of one signal and of four signals. Consequently, difficulties of discrimination between signals in tasks (b) and (c) were not comparable and the equation $X \mathrm{RT}\, b - X \mathrm{RT}\, c$ = response choice time was invalid (see Rabbitt, 1971).

Models of this kind can serve as extremely sophisticated frameworks (e.g. Briggs and Swanson, 1970) within which data from CRT experiments can be analysed. Because they are based on very rigid and clearly stated assumptions they allow us to construct intricate functional descriptions of hypothetical perceptual-motor processes. I shall nevertheless argue that the simplicity and rigidity of the assumptions on which they are based prevents them from handling aspects of CRT data which are more informative than simple mean RT, prevents them from giving any account of the way in which subjects control their performance in CRT tasks and, consequently, prevents them from discussing the most critical aspects of *changes* in performance within or between individuals.

Failures to consider accuracy

A first limitation of all the models we have discussed is that they are based only on computations of arithmetic means of overall observed CRTs. They take no account of accuracy. Indeed a necessary condition of application of Sternberg's (1969; 1975) techniques for decomposing RTs is that error rates should be minimal, and identical in all conditions compared, even if this means that subjects must be given more practice at some conditions than at others. Note how this demand actually obliges us to disregard any *other* effects which practice might have beyond increasing accuracy. Overall mean RT is partitioned to give estimates for each of a number of hypothetical sequential processes (signal encoding time, memory search time, response selection, and production), but there is no rationale for deciding that particular errors represent failures at one point rather than another in this chain of hypothetically independent events, nor even any way of comparing the contributions made to overall errors by each of these independent events. Obviously, if any one process in a linear sequence fails, input to all succeeding processing stages will be corrupt and identification of any unique point of failure in the chain will be uncertain.

More seriously, Sternberg's and Brigg's decomposition models do not predict the large differences between mean RTs for correct and incorrect responses usually observed in CRT tasks. In most tasks mean RTs for errors are much faster than mean RTs for correct responses. This difference is usually explained by the assumption that people need some minimum time to identify a signal correctly and to select an appropriate response to it. Errors are assumed to become increasingly probable as RTs fall below this necessary minimal time, so that on average error RTs will be faster than correct RTs. Over some critical band of RTs speed and accuracy appear to trade off against each other (Pachella and Pew, 1968; Pew, 1969; Rabbitt and Vyas, 1970; Schouten and Bekker, 1967). Distributions of RTs for correct and incorrect responses can be compared to derive speed–accuracy trade-off functions for various tasks and for various subject populations, and there is a choice of several plausible models to explain such functions (Ollman, 1966; Yellott, 1967).

The linear independent sequential process (LISP) models which we have discussed treat overall RT as the simple sum of independent latencies for successive processes. The existence of speed–error trade-off functions (SETOFs) makes it questionable whether this assumption can be correct, or even useful. For example, we must assume that each of these hypothetical independent processes will require its own characteristic minimum time for successful completion. Each process may also have a different *range* of latencies over which speed and accuracy can be exchanged (i.e. a different SETOF with possibly a different slope constant (see Rabbitt and Vyas 1970).

We have seen that the critical assumption for LISPS is that processing times are independent for each stage. This can be true only when all stages have more than enough time for completion — that is, when speed and accuracy are not traded off. Where speed and accuracy are traded off two things may happen. First, subjects may set themselves to complete all stages in some fixed time. In this case any increase in the time taken by one stage, on one trial (due, perhaps, to random fluctuations in processing time from trial to trial) must reduce the amount of time available for successful completion of all other stages. Processing times for stages will, therefore, not be independent.

Second, each stage may be completed after consuming some criterial time for accuracy, and it may be argued that these times will be independent because processing at each stage must terminate in order for processing at the next stage to begin. That is, each stage may be regarded as having, and observing, a separate and independent SETOF. This will not do either. Rabbitt and Vyas (1970) point out that subjects *cannot, ab initio*, recognize their SETOFs but must make and detect errors before they can learn to recognize and avoid the fast, limiting RT bands at which errors become intolerably frequent. Thus, in order to adjust performance and to avoid errors, subjects must adjust RT from trial to trial. If overall SETOFs are determined by a sheaf of SETOFs for each of a number of independent component processes, subjects must not only learn to control overall RT but also to partition overall RT so as to preserve the accuracy of each of a number of processes, all of which take different times to complete. In order to distribute overall mean RT among component processes in this way, subjects would have to be able to monitor accuracy of each component process independently in relation to its own, idiosyncratic, mean completion time and SETOF. In short, they would not merely have to know whenever errors occurred *somewhere* in the train of successive processes, they would also have to know *in which particular process* the failure occurred. There is no evidence that this is possible.

Note that any other line of explanation sacrifices the assumption of independence on which all such models depend. If we assume that subjects do *not* discover and set time limits for accurate completion of *each independent* process, but rather discover, set, and adjust time limits for the completion of *all processes*, it follows that time limits for individual processes are not independent because they are set in relation to a common criterion for accuracy.

Failures to discuss changes in distribution of RTs from trial to trial.

LISPs are based on obtained differences between mean RTs and do not predict changes in trial-to-trial variance in RT within or between subjects and tasks. This greatly limits their usefulness because task variables such as the number of signal and response alternatives or S–R compatability and signal discriminability, intrasubject variables such as practice and fatigue and intersubject variables such as age or diffuse brain damage all affect RT variance much more strikingly than they affect mean RT.

In particular, shifts in computed arithmetical means of RT, on which LISP models are based, typically do not reflect any shift of an RT distribution along the RT axis. They rather merely reflect changes in the positive skew of distributions; e.g. practised subjects make fewer very slow responses and more fast responses, but the latencies of the *fastest* responses which they make may remain invariant with practice. The picture is, therefore, of a system which improves average performance by reducing trial-to-trial variation rather than of a system which alters its maximum capabilities over time.

Failures to describe accurate regulation of set to respond to discrete continuous tasks

In real life people often have to respond to continuous series of events rather than to discrete signals. These events may occur at more or less predictable intervals. To perform optimally a man must learn the characteristics of such sequences and accurately predict and estimate time intervals in order to prepare himself to respond at precisely the moments when signals fall due (see Rabbitt, 1969; 1979a, b). Even in simple RT tasks, when fore-signals are used, subjects seem to need a fixed, minimum time (fore-period) to prepare themselves adequately for onset of a signal to respond (Karlin, 1966; Klemmer, 1956; Nickerson, 1965; Davis 1957). As fore-periods grow longer they become less accurate at estimating fore-period duration and so predicting the moment of signal onset. At all fore-period durations they make effective use of sequential properties of sequences of successive fore-periods in order to optimize their prediction (Nickerson, 1965; Possemai, Granjon, Reynard, and Requin, 1975). To do this people cannot behave like the simple, passive information-processing channels assumed by LISP models. They must rather actively and flexibly control their sets throughout long series of events. LISP models do not allow for control of this kind. They rather consider each transaction of signal identification and response production as a passive, independent process without considering that subjects may use overall supervisory control to order these transactions in time so as to anticipate events and so maximize sensitivity of signal detection and facilitate response production. In short, even in very simple RT tasks, subjects can be shown to exercise a degree of the predictive control which is so important in tracking (see Hammerton, Chapter 8, this volume).

This is an important limitation, since recent work shows that changes in the variance of CRT which are brought about by differences in the efficiency with which temporal control of set can be established are quite as great as those introduced by most other parameters which have been investigated (Rabbitt, 1969; 1979a).

Failures to describe control of information encoding and response production

Subjects can exercise very flexible control over the units in which they encode information and the complexity of the response sequences which they emit. For example Chistovitch (1960) and Chistovitch and Klass (1962) showed that people who shadow speech adopt various strategies at various times, monitoring and reproducing individual phonemes, words, or entire phrases as best suits task demands. Both the size of the 'chunks' in which they encode input (deduced from the lag between received and emitted messages) and the complexity of the sequences emitted (judged by units of output) vary with message speed, with experimental instructions, and with message discriminability.

Subjects are able to exert flexible control of input and output in this way by reference to information available in long-term memory which allows them to recognize and use redundancy in continuous input, and provides them with motor programs for the emission of complex response sequences rather than merely for discrete motor acts. The best examples of this are a series of brilliant studies by Shaffer (see Shaffer, 1973; 1975; Shaffer and Hardwick, 1970) who investigated how highly skilled typists transcribe continuous text. He showed that they exercise adaptive control by determining the rate at which they process input, by choosing the size of unit in which they sample this input, and by alternating sampling of input with emission of responses in order to achieve a remarkably fast and very constant rate of responding.

The point, once again, is that LISP models do not consider how subjects exercise this complex control let alone how they *learn* to do so. Shaffer's elegant studies show that this control improves with practice and so must be learned. We may go beyond these experiments to suggest that breakdown of performance with brain damage or in response to stress may reflect loss of this high-level, learned control. Let us consider how far LISP models can account for change in performance with practice, and what additional assumptions may be necessary to explain the data we have discussed.

Descriptions of practice effects by LISP models

As we have seen, LISP models assume that in order to identify a signal and choose a response to it a person carries out a fixed series of processing operations $P_1 \ldots P_2 \ldots P_3 \ldots P_n$, each of which takes a finite time $T_{P_1} \ldots T_{P_2} \ldots T_{P_3} \ldots T_{P_N} \ldots$ so that

$$RT = T_{P_1} + T_{P_2} + T_{P_3} \ldots + T_{P_N}$$

Thus, if total observed RT reduces with practice this can only be because some or all of these or all of these component processes take less time. If performance becomes more accurate with practice this can only be because some or all of these processes improve in accuracy.

This is a very simplistic model of practice since it assumes that early and late in practice precisely the same events occur in precisely the same order, the only difference being that they occur faster and more accurately. Models of this kind can be made slightly more sophisticated if we adopt a suggestion by Crossman (1959) that the sequences of events which occur between reception of a signal and emission of a response to it may be regarded as activating 'pathways' through a hypothetical information coding network. Crossman's suggestion is that early in practice any one of a number of different pathways through a network may link a particular signal to the particular necessary response. Some of these pathways will be slower than others. Thus, early in practice, when all pathways are employed with equal probability, variance in RT from trial to trial will be great and overall mean RT will be slow. Crossman (1959) suggests that as practice proceeds a mechanism (which he does not discuss) causes 'more efficient' (i.e. faster) pathways to be selectively preferred to 'less efficient' (i.e. slower) pathways. Both RT variance and mean RT are thereby reduced. Further, the asymptotic shape of practice curves can be predicted from these assumptions.

This is an ingenious and useful concept which may well guide later thinking, but it needs to be greatly extended before it can account for many results. First, it is precisely the *active* selection of 'more efficient' rather than 'less efficient' techniques of information processing ('pathways') which a good model of practice should describe. If this is left as an *ad hoc* postulate we do not get very far. Second, Crossman's model does very well as an account of how an individual may improve with practice, attain greater speed and accuracy and so contribute less to overall RT variance. But many recent studies show that with extended practice subjects do not simply carry out the same information-processing transactions faster and more accurately in the same way, but rather find new and more efficient ways to identify signals and select responses to them.

Fletcher and Rabbitt (1978) found that after practice subjects cease to identify the symbols to which they respond as particular entities and begin, instead, to respond to constancy and change between successive displays. This of course carried the important corollary that a response is always selected in relation to the last response made (same or different to last response) and not merely as a particular motor act triggered by a particular signal. Kristofferson's (1977) data from signal classification tasks show that subjects cannot use the same cues in order to discriminate complex signals from each other both early and later in practice. Rabbitt, Cumming, and Vyas (1979) obtain similar results in a series of visual search tasks. They also show that as practice proceeds subjects may change their perceptual encoding strategies and identify signals by two successive decisions rather than by a single decision. Signals are first identified as members of a particular class (target class rather than background class) and only when once located are they further analysed to determine which particular target set member they are. Even if we only consider how particular signals are recognized it is clear that subjects do not simply retain and improve the same strategies of signal recognition, but rather develop new and more efficient ways of dealing with particular discriminations.

In all the cases which we have considered it is clear that changes in performance with practice must be regarded as active progressions towards determined goals rather than as gradual improvements in the passive system which Crossman's (1959) model describes. This realization is unhelpful unless it provokes us to put forward, and test, active rather than passive models. Let us consider a very simple control process model which explains some data from elementary, self-paced, serial choice response tasks.

A 'TRACKING' MODEL FOR MAINTAINING SPEED AND ACCURACY

Shaffer's typing studies are concerned with tasks in which skilled subjects clearly learn to exercise adaptive control over very complex performance (Shaffer, 1973). They learn to determine the rate at which they process input (text) and to use, or discard, redundancy which determines the size of perceptual samples which they take of that input. Their improvement with practice is partly due to the fact that they learn to alternate sampling of text with production of responses. They learn to emit responses at a very fast, and remarkably regular, rate irrespective of variations in redundancy of input. In order to explain how these complex activities are integrated with each other we must postulate overall control and time-sharing. It may seem that we do not need these complex assumptions if we consider very simple tasks in which signals occur one at a time, and a discrete response is made to each before the next appears. Here the unit of input (one signal) and the unit of response output (a single finger movement) are determined by the task. Straightforward LISP models may seem quite adequate to described such situations.

In fact, even very straightforward serial self-paced tasks present subjects with problems of active control over their performance. In all such tasks the invariable experimental instruction is, 'Go as fast as you can and make as few errors as possible.' In the author's experience 95 per cent of subjects immediately retort to this bland instruction, 'Yes, but which matters more? Speed or errors?' The author is ashamed to have ignored this excellent question for over fifteen years. Subjects who ask it, precisely define the control problem which they face in such tasks. They are concerned to point out to the experimenter that they can *actively choose* whether to respond fast and make more errors or to respond slowly and improve accuracy at the expense of speed. In formal terms they are saying that they can *actively choose* how to structure their RT distributions in relation to their SETOFs. This implies that either know, or can discover, what their SETOFs may be for a particular task.

This last point is critical since SETOFs will vary from task to task (Pachella and Pew 1968; Pew, 1969; Rabbitt and Vyas, 1970). Faced with a novel task a subject cannot, *ab initio*, deduce his SETOF for that particular situation. He must rather *discover* just how fast he can respond without making an error. It is useful to consider just what a subject needs to know, and just what control he must have over his own behaviour in order to do this.

Subjects need at least two different kinds of information in order to adjust their performance to task demands. First they must know when they make errors, otherwise a SETOF could never be recognized. Second, to profit from their recognition of errors, they must know just how fast each incorrect response was. They must also be able to vary their response speed accurately to respond a little slower, or a little faster, than a response which they have recognized as fast but inaccurate or accurate but unnecessarily slow. They must be accurate in estimating, reproducing and adjusting their brief reaction times.

In a number of discrete RT tasks, as in continuous self-paced serial choice response tasks and in continuous tasks with preview (e.g. typing) subjects very rapidly detect most of the errors they make (e.g. Burns, 1965; Long, 1976; Rabbitt, 1966a, b; 1968b; 1978b; Rabbitt and Vyas, 1970). Subjects can even detect errors which have occurred two or more responses previously (Rabbitt, 1979a) and, apparently, can detect some errors due to failures of perceptual analysis as well as errors due to failures of responses selection and execution (Rabbitt, Cumming, and Vyas, 1978).

It is interesting to arrange computer print-out of trial-to-trial variation in CRT during continuous, self-paced serial response tasks so that response speed is plotted as a function of trial number. From such graphical plots it is immediately apparent that subjects respond faster and faster from trial to trial until an error occurs. They must then immediately recognize the error because responses following errors are typically very slow indeed (see Rabbitt, 1969). After an error, slow responses continue for three or more trials. Responses then again speed up to approach the risky, fast RT band at which errors are likely to occur (Rabbitt and Vyas, 1970). The general picture is of a system which gradually reduces RT from trial to trial until an error occurs, then slows RT to avoid this limit to accurate performance, and then once again 'tracks' a critical RT band at which speed can be maximized without risking accuracy. Thus the SETOF for any particular task is actively *discovered* by commission and detection of errors and is subsequently 'observed' by adjusting response speed so that RTs approach, but do not transgress it. The system is not concerned to control overall mean RT directly. Mean RT is controlled by adjustment of RT variance between a lower limit determined by the SETOF and an upper limit determined by an internal 'clock' which warns the subject when he is responding unnecessarily slowly.

This is a description of a system which actively adapts to improve its performance with practice. We have not merely described a system which can 'learn', but have suggested *what* it learns, *how* it learns, and *what information it needs* in order to learn. The model makes predictions for the effects of prolonged practice on the *distributions*, as well as the *arithmetical means* of RTs, and makes further predictions for changing relationships between the distributions of RTs for correct responses and the distributions of RTs for incorrect responses. On the first point we must predict that as subjects become more practised they learn more precisely to estimate their safe lower limit of responding and more precisely to control their RTs from trial to trial to observe this limit, but not to rise far above it. This is just what happens. On the second point we have assumed that subjects establish their SETOFs for particular tasks and then learn to avoid those rates which cause errors. It would follow that they would transgress SETOF limits early but not late in practice. As a consequence, if we derive SETOFs by *post-hoc* comparisons of the distributions of subjects' correct and incorrect responses (as we must, Rabbitt and Vyas, 1970), SETOFs should be obtainable from RT distributions early in practice when subjects make fast errors, but not late in practice, when they avoid making fast errors. To put this another way, the difference in the means of RT for errors and RTs for correct responses must reduce with practice. Again, this is what happens (Rabbitt and Vyas, 1979 in press). Finally, on the model we have proposed, subjects can regulate their lower limits of RT by identifying and so observing their own SETOFs. When a SETOF is transgressed there is likely to be immediate feedback, since an error will probably occur. There is no such precise feedback when subjects respond unnecessarily slowly. They can only compare response speeds against some internal clock which tells them when they are taking too long to respond. It would follow that subjects have precise feedback from which they can judge when they respond too fast, but that their recognition that they are responding too slowly depends upon the accuracy of an internal 'clock' (i.e. on time estimation). Two consequences follow. First, RT distributions should be markedly skewed, with a sharp cut-off for fast responses and a straggling 'tail' of slower responses. This is the case. Second, if subjects are provided with external feedback (such as an elapsed-time signal) which informs them when they are slow, they should be able to shape the RT distributions accordingly and reduce arithmetical means of RT, without increasing errors, by shaping the distribution of RTs to avoid unnecessarily slow responses. Again, this is just what happens (Rabbitt and Vyas, 1979).

It is important to recognize that the system we have described is flexible, and can adapt equally well to a variety of different task demands other than those expressed by the curiously ambiguous instruction, 'Go as fast as you can and make as few errors as possible.' If speed is stressed, and errors are inconsequential, subjects may abandon error detection and simply respond more or less at random approaching their limiting rates of response production (Rabbitt and Vy as, 1979). If accuracy is stressed and there is no demand for speed, subjects are faced with a new control problem. They can no longer 'track' the lower limit of accurate RT in order to maintain a distribution of RTs with the least possible variance avoiding errors. Since the task now demands that they never transgress the fast RT band at which errors become more probable they must restrict the speed of their fastest responses, not by detection of errors and avoidance of the RT band in which they occur, but rather by reference to some independent internal timing device or 'clock'. In consequence, we might expect that the sharp lower cut-offs to RT distributions observed under speed–accuracy optimization instructions will be replaced by a straggle of RT variance representing uncertainties as to which cautious 'clock-settings' are most appropriate for the task (see Figure 35). In fact this is just what happens (see Rabbitt and Vyas, 1979).

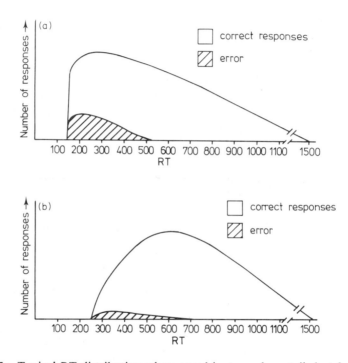

Figure 35a. Typical RT distribution where speed is stressed, curtailed at fast reaction times by observation of SETOF limits.

Figure 35b. Typical RT distribution when extreme accuracy is stressed and subjects avoid the SETOF limit, thus having no feedback to shape the fast tail of their RT distribution.

As we have seen, this model is specifically derived to describe how extended practice at a task changes performance. It is important to note that it can also describe the way in which performance changes as a result of intrasubject variables such as fatigue or stress and intersubject variables such as chronological age.

Old people have considerably slower mean RTs than the young. The surprising point is that old and young people may have almost identical mean RTs for errors (Rabbitt and Vyas, 1979). Previous models have concentrated on the first detail but ignored the second (e.g. Birren 1977). If we consider only the first detail we might assume that old people respond more cautiously than the young, seeking to avoid their SETOFs by a larger margin so as to guarantee high accuracy at the expense of speed. However, their error RTs show that this is not the case and we may be tempted to conclude that old people are, in fact, much more brash than their juniors and attempt to reduce their RTs by responding as fast as possible irrespective of increases in error rate. But this does not do either since old people, on average, do not make more errors than the young.

In terms of the model which we have discussed, a further possibility is that old people, unlike the young, cannot recognize the errors which they make and so do not know when they sacrifice accuracy by responding too fast. However, their low error rates contradict this, and Rabbitt and Vyas (1979) find that old people detect their errors as accurately as their juniors. The key seems to lie in the fact that trial-to-trial *variance* in RTs greatly increases as people grow older. It seems that old people lose precise control over their response speed and that when they attempt a slight increase in speed to reduce RT without sacrificing accuracy they begin to respond much too fast, overshoot their SETOFs by a large margin, commit errors, detect their errors and react to them by immediately responding much too slowly. Thus, they add responses to the lower and upper limits of their RT distributions. Their fast errors are much too fast and their cautious responses are unnecessarily slow. Thus, this model suggests the particular change with age which reduces flexibility of adaptation and optimization of performance.

It is also possible to reinterpret classical data on the effects of various stresses on performance of continuous self-paced choice response tasks with the context of the same model. Wilkinson (1959) pointed out that subjects suffering from loss of sleep may occasionally make single, very slow responses (blocks), but their overall mean RTs do not increase as performance continues over a half-hour run. They seem to 'spurt' between blocks to maintain a relatively constant overall mean rate of responding. This picture of increasing drift from a fast, tight optimal RT distribution with intermittent attempts to maintain constant mean response rate would be well described by the simple system we have discussed. Broadbent (1972) points out that three other stresses — noise, heat, and alcohol ingestion — affect performance in a different way from loss of sleep in that they cause increases in errors without changing overall mean RT or producing blocks. Broadbent explains this by suggesting that noise, heat, and alcohol all degrade processes of perceptual identification of signals but do not affect response selection, timing, or execution.

Since the experiments which Broadbent quotes were done without benefit of apparatus now available *error RTs were never measured*, and the changes in RTs which he discusses are changes in overall RT during a run. Thus the data for noise, heat, and alcohol are consistent with the idea that under the influence of these stresses SETOFs remain stable but subjects lose time control of their response speed. *RT distributions* may be affected, and errors may increase while mean RTs remain approximately constant.

The difference between predictions from Broadbent's and the present hypothesis lies in his contention that input from signals will become poorer, or will become intermittent, because of distraction. In this case a SETOF obtained from distributions of correct and incorrect RTs produced by subjects who suffer from the effects of heat, noise, or alcohol should be displaced towards a slower RT band in comparison with a SETOF obtained from subjects responding under optimal conditions (see Figure 36).

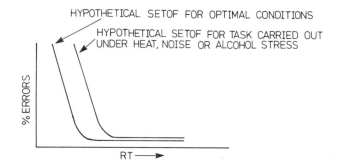

Figure 36. Hypothetical SETOFs for optimal conditions and for task carried out under stress.

This is to say that if subjects suffering from the effects of noise, heat, or alcohol consumption attempt to respond at their normal rate they will make more errors. This can be checked by examining RT distributions obtained in all these conditions, calculating SETOFs from them, and examining the spread of the actual distributions of correct RTs in relation to the derived SETOFs. If RT distributions under normal and stressed conditions are the same, while SETOFs differ, this will be evidence that Broadbent may be right. In this case we may further check to see whether heat, noise, or alcohol reduce the efficiency of error detection so that subjects suffering from these do not discover that their SETOFs have shifted.

An alternative possibility is that heat, noise, and alcohol, like old age, deprive people of fine control over the timing of their responses. In this case errors might occur because subjects under these stresses behave like old people and when trying to track their SETOFs respond much too fast and so tend to make fast errors (see Figure 37). Once again examinations of the distributions of actual RTs against derived SETOFs would show whether this is what happens. SETOFs would be identical for stressed and unstressed conditions, but stressed conditions would

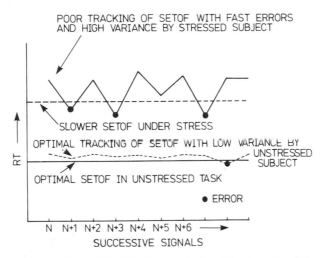

Figure 37. Tracking of SETOFs by stressed and unstressed subjects.

show much greater RT variance and much poorer control of RT from trial to trial.

Note that these hypothetical models for changes in performance under different stresses are not mutually exclusive. It is quite possible that both changes in response timing and changes in observation of SETOFs occur concurrently, but in different degrees for different stresses. This might at last allow us to distinguish between the effects of noise, heat stress, and alcohol in ways which Broadbent's model does not allow. This would be a relief because it offends intuition and common sense that we still cannot distinguish the effects of three such dissimilar conditions on a simple task.

Two further general points can be made. First, in order to describe the effects of practice, old age, fatigue, noise, heat stress, or alcohol consumption any model must incorporate the idea that these conditions change the efficiency of one or more parameters of human performance. Current models of performance on simple tasks have considered only two possible changes in performance parameters — mean RT and accuracy. The present model substitutes for these a wider range of more sensitive parameters, i.e. $\overline{X}$ correct RT, $\overline{X}$ error RT, SETOF, relation of the fast tail of the correct and error RT distributions to the calculated SETOF, and degree of positive skew of the entire distribution of correct and incorrect RTs. It must be emphasized that the advantage of the SETOF model does not simply lie in the fact that it allows 'profiles' of the effects of practice, age, stress, etc. to be constructed in terms of more rather than fewer performance indices. Models of this type should be preferred because they allow us to discuss how people *adapt* to changes in one or more of these performance parameters in order to maintain as high a level of efficiency as possible.

The second point is that if we discuss human beings as purposive systems which strive to maintain performance between defined parameters, or as systems which exercise choices between various optional strategies of adaptation to task parameters, or which adapt to their own changing efficiency, we do not therefore move further from our data. On the contrary, models of this kind oblige us to consider *more* rather than *fewer* data, they make more rather than fewer predictions for empirical results, and they allow us to design a wider range of convergent experiments in terms of which we can assess differences between tasks and between the individuals who carry them out.

We may now go on to consider other details of performance in simple tasks which oblige us to recognize that subjects are not simple, passive systems which emit each separate response as a direct transform of information conveyed by a particular signal. We have seen how the timing of each of a continuous sequence of responses, more than other factors, creates control problems for which subjects have to actively seek solutions. Let us consider two other simple tasks which illustrate how people meet different forms of this problem of temporal control.

MANAGEMENT OF TEMPORAL CONTROL

Adaptation to irregularities of signal onset

In most simple serial self-paced tasks subjects can accurately predict the moment at which each signal will arrive. This is because the interval between successive signals (S–S interval) or the interval between each response and the next signal (R–S interval) is very precisely controlled by the experimental equipment and remains constant throughout a task. Rabbitt (1969) held R–S intervals constant during runs of 300 successive signals and responses, but varied R–S interval duration from 20 msec to 200 msec between runs. He found that overall mean RT reduced by 30 msec to 60 msec as R–S intervals increased between these limits. This regression of RT on R–S interval duration was strikingly similar to that observed in simple RT tasks in which intervals between warning signals and signals to respond (fore-periods) were varied over the same range (see Davis, 1957; Nickerson, 1965). It seems that both in simple RT tasks and in choice RT tasks with R–S intervals subjects require a minimum time, greater than 220 msec, to prepare optimally to respond to each signal. When fore-periods or R–S intervals are as short as 20 msec subjects cannot attain optimal preparation by the moment of onset of the response signal. However, as R–S intervals or fore-periods increase to 220 msec preparation gradually approaches optimum and RTs decline.

In most real-life tasks signals do not occur at constant, predictable intervals and subjects have to keep pace with irregular series of events. Rabbitt (1979a, b) investigated the effects of varying R–S intervals unpredictably from trial to trial within the range of 20 msec to 200 msec and the range 20 msec to 1600 msec. He found that the negative regression of RT on R–S interval duration between 20 msec and 200 msec remained exactly the same whether R–S intervals were constant and predictable or variable and unpredictable during a run. However, when R–S intervals were 800 msec or longer subjects responded faster when successive R–S intervals were identical than when they were different.

Rabbitt (1979b) pointed out that the absence of any effect of R–S interval irregularity over the range 20 msec to 200 msec was consistent with the idea that subjects need at least 220 msec to attain optimal preparation for an expected event. If R–S intervals are shorter than this it does not matter if they vary unpredictably from trial to trial because subjects can gain nothing from being able to predict correctly or to time accurately the next R–S interval. All they can do is to mobilize their preparation as fast as possible on each trial. The level of preparation they attain at the moment of signal onset will simply depend on the speed of this mobilization and cannot be improved by prediction.

In contrast, when R–S intervals or fore-periods are 800 msec or longer we must assume that subjects always have enough time to maximize preparation for each signal. Since, presumably, maximum preparation once briefly attained cannot be indefinitely maintained, RTs will be fastest if subjects can arrange to attain their point of maximum preparation to coincide precisely with the moment of onset of the signal they expect. To manage this they must:

(a) correctly predict the moment of onset of the next signal;
(b) accurately estimate the passage of time so as to achieve the necessary coincidence.

If all fore-periods or R–S intervals used during a task are equiprobable subjects can manage prediction (a) with only a chance level of accuracy. In this case they can only optimize time estimation (b), and any prediction strategy which helped them to do so will optimize performance. In this case it may be strategic for them to expect fore-periods or R–S intervals to repeat on successive trials. This is because this expectation will prove false no more often than any other. However, when it proves correct, it may have the advantage that a subject can most accurately estimate a time interval which he has just experienced. A number of experiments on the effects of repetitions and alternations of fore-period durations in simple RT tasks can also be interpreted as demonstrations that subjects use this strategy to optimize time estimation when accurate prediction is impossible.

Several features of this model must be contrasted with other, passive, models of human performance. First, a number of experiments show that the efficiency of information processing is not invariant at any moment, but changes with momentary fluctuations in arousal and attentional selectivity. In order to optimize performance subjects must plan ahead to ensure that their information-processing systems are maximally efficient at the moments when signals occur.

A second point is that to achieve this advance planning subjects must store and use a great deal of information. For example, subjects must be able to sample long sequences of events in order to recognize, and use, complex properties of the distributions of time intervals between them; (see Nickerson, 1965). Subjects must also be able to make accurate estimates of the durations of different time intervals, store this information about relative and absolute interval durations, and access it as necessary in order to control the timing of their expectancy.

A final, most crucial, point is that the system we have described to account for the results of these very simple experiments is adaptive in one unique respect. It adapts to its own limitations. It bases optimization of performance on optimization of one parameter (time estimation) when optimization of another (accurate advance prediction) becomes impossible. If accurate advance prediction becomes possible the advantages of accurate time estimation may be abandoned in order to capitalize on this. An interesting experiment would be to arrange sequences of R–S intervals or fore-period durations so that alternations between two different interval durations are more common than repetitions of interval durations. As bias shifted in this direction we would predict that RTs for particular R–S intervals or fore-periods would become faster on alternations than on repetitions. In brief, faced with a situation in which its own limitations as a statistical predictor, or as a clock, force the system to abandon the possibility of optimization in terms of both parameters, the system adjusts and does the best it can by trading off one against the other.

Adaptive time-sharing of signal identification and motor programming

We cannot describe complex real-life skills such as driving or air traffic control without discussing how subjects manage their allocations of attention over time in order to interrogate a number of different sources of information in a strategic order and with strategically biased frequencies (Baron, Kleinman, and Levison, 1970; Moray, 1978). It is less generally recognized that accurate time-sharing of this kind, particularly time-sharing between the identification of signals and the control of responses made to them, is necessary even in very simple tasks.

Rabbitt and Rogers (1965) showed this in a task in which subjects made reaches of varying extents to press touch switches mounted immediately below signal lights on a console 45.7 cm long. Two conditions of a continuous task were compared. In the first condition the sequence of events began with the ignition of a signal lamp (A) on the extreme left of the console. As soon as the subject had switched it off by touching the switch immediately beneath it, either lamp B (48cm to the right) or lamp C (45cm to the right) came on. These events occurred unpredictably with equal frequency. The subject then had to move his hand as fast as possible from A to switch off either B or C as necessary. As soon as he did this lamp A lit again, he moved his hand to switch it off, and the cycle continued in this way for 300 trials. In a comparison, condition lamp A was followed by either lamp B or lamp D (10cm to the right), and the same cycle of events occurred.

The point was to compare RTs for moves from A to B between the first condition, where this required a choice between two, very similar reaches (i.e. 48cm and 45cm) and the second condition where this required a choice between two very different reaches (i.e. 48cm and 10cm).

Early in practice young subjects showed no difference in RTs to initiate reaches to B between these two conditions. However, as practice progressed RTs to initiate reaches to B became faster when the choice was between similar reaches than when the choice was between different reaches. This happened because when the choice was between very similar reaches, as soon as a subject touched A he could begin to make a reach of correct amplitude to get to the general vicinity of B or C without waiting to discover which of these lights had, in fact lit up. They could then decide which light was on during the course of this ballistic movement, and to modify the termination of the movement to home in on the correct touch switch. In the second condition they could not do this since they had to discover which lamp had lit before they could begin to program an appropriate response to answer it.

Subjects required practice to achieve this precise alternation between initiations of a reach, identification of a signal, and modification of the reach to touch the correct switch. Old subjects carrying out the same tasks never learned this skill, and took the same time to initiate reaches to B in both conditions.

Thus we have an example of a system which learns to program itself to use dead time during a ballistic movement to identify a signal and to begin to direct the termination of that movement. Apparently, young subjects shifted with practice from this sequence of events:

1. identify signal;
2. initiate ballistic reach to terminate precisely at signal;
3. terminate reach at signal;

to the more efficient sequence of events:

1. initiate ballistic movement of approximately the right amplitude;
2. identify signal during movement;
3. modify termination of movement to touch key.

Again we see that as subjects become practised they do not merely improve their performance by going through the same information-processing transactions in the same order, ever faster and more accurately. Even in this very simple task they improve by exercising adaptive control over the sequence in which they perform successive transactions, and actively seek out new and more efficient ways of scheduling sequences of operations. Good examples of other ways in which people reschedule the order in which they make a series of component decisions, so as to improve the efficiency with which they make very simple choices, appear when we consider how they decide which of two limbs to use to make a simple reach.

Attentional control and choice between limbs

Rabbitt (1978a) found that people can respond to signal lights on a console faster when they make all reaches with the same hand than when they have to answer some lights with the right hand and others with the left. Subjects also respond faster when they have to make successive, different movements with the same hand than when they make a movement with one hand followed by a movement with the other (Rabbitt, 1965; 1978a). When successive movements are made with the same hand both right- and left-handed subjects respond equally fast with either hand. In contrast, when successive movements are made with different hands, all subjects respond slightly faster with their dominant hands.

Rabbitt (1978a) suggested that these effects can be explained if we assume that repetition of a response facilitates only those processes responsible for its execution. With this assumption choices between responding limbs may be made by a sequence of decisions which can be conveniently illustrated as a sequence of instructions such as that found on computer programs.

Instructions	*Instruction content*
Step 1	Is key in range of dominant hand?
	If yes, go to Step 3
	If no, go to Step 2
Step 2	Is key in range of non-dominant hand?
	If yes, go to Step 4
	If no, go to Step 1
Step 3	Complete reach to key and go to
	Step 1 to test new event
Step 4	Complete reach to key and go to
	Step 1 to test new event.

A system controlled by such a sequence of instructions would show 'dominance' in the limited sense that each new sequence of tests would always begin with a test to discover whether the dominant limb could be used. This would be quite an adaptive way to control decisions since apparently the choice between limbs takes a finite time and by developing the habit of using the same hand (or paw) for most responses an animal would save time and increase efficiency.

For our present purposes this is another demonstration that human beings can adapt to their own limitations in order to increase their efficiency. On the model we have discussed they do not do this merely by increasing the speed and accuracy with which they carry out in turn each instruction in a hypothetical sequence, but also by altering the sequence in which decisions are taken and by *altering the conditional branching of the sequence* in order to initiate some tests before others. Changes in the efficiency of such a system, whether these represents improvements in efficiency due to 'learning', or loss of efficiency due to old age, stress, or injury, are likely to appear as new patterns of regularity in performance rather than as simple changes in speed or accuracy.

We have seen that even in the simplest perceptual-motor tasks decisions necessary to produce appropriate responses may be made in more or less efficient sequences. The effects of such variations in planning of overall control of response sequences appear when we consider how people produce length sequences of familiar responses which must be 'played off' from information stored in long-term memory.

Control of responses by information stored in long-term memory

Consider how people produce very familiar sequences of responses — for example, how they manage to recite the alphabet aloud. The problems here are rather different from those considered in the previous chapter. Obviously the names of letters of the alphabet, and their conventional ordering, are stored in a man's long-term memory and he can access them whenever he wishes at any moment throughout a long lifetime. In order to recite this familiar sequence correctly he requires two different kinds of information. First, as we have seen, information about the entire sequence must be available, and must be accessed in long-term memory. Second, he requires some prompt from short-term memory to tell him what he has just done so that he can index long-term memory picking up the point he has reached in the sequence and deciding what letter to name next.

Each letter of the alphabet is unique so that in order to decide which letter to produce next a person need only remember the last letter he spoke. However, not all sequences are of this type. If sequences contain recurrent elements the problem becomes much more difficult. For example, consider a sequence of this kind:

A, B, C, D, B, E, D, B, F . . .

Here, even if a man can recall that he has just uttered 'D' he will not know what letter to name next unless he can remember the last two letters he spoke. If he just uttered 'B' he will be able to continue unless he remembers his last three responses.

With Anderson and Heptinstall I have carried out pilot experiments which suggest that young adults can maintain very accurate performance on sequences of the first kind in spite of very high levels of distraction (successive serial subtractions from large numbers). However, while sequences of the second kind were flawlessly reproduced without distraction, they could not easily repeat them when distracted by subsidiary tasks. They paused after repeated items and often went into recurrent 'loops' (e.g. from the example above 'B, C, D, B, C, D, B, C, D . . .') These delays and failures seem to indicate that the process of 'running control', or 'indexing' of an overlearnt sequence held in long-term memory by means of information held in short-term memory had failed due to attempts to keep up with a subsidiary task. Increased demands on short-term memory load bring about failures in performance. Time-sharing of the interlocked processes we have discussed remain to be investigated. Once again it is obvious that we cannot discuss even commonplace, and apparently very simple tasks in terms of rigid sequences of operations. We have to assume dynamic, active, adaptive control of a number of interlocked systems all of which, acting together, must adjust to any change in task characteristics. It follows that changes in the efficiency of any one of these systems (i.e. long-term memory storage of sequences of necessary condition, short-term memory capacity, speed and accuracy of short-term memory indexing of long-term memory programs, etc., will not result in a simple decrement of some corresponding 'index' of efficiency, but rather in a readjustment of an integrated system. The point is that this readjustment will occur as the response of an entire adaptive system to some particular change in its efficiency. It will not occur, and may not be recognized, as a change in efficiency of any single parameter of performance.

SUMMARY

Over the last 100 years models for the processes by which people recognize signals and make responses to them have failed to consider how performance may change. The most striking instance of this is the absence of any discussion as to how performance on very simple tasks improves with practice. Absence of models for change has also prevented discussion of improvement of performance with maturation, or the gradual impairment of performance by old age, by the onset of illness such as schizophrenia, by diffuse brain damage, and by a variety of stresses.

One reason why models for simple tasks have been so limited is that they have, either tacitly or overtly, considered human beings as linear independent sequential process systems of limited capacity. To discuss changes in performance in terms of such systems we are forced to make the very crude assumption that particular, independent component processes become faster or slower, or become more or less accurate. Models of this kind do not allow us to discuss how the systems which they describe may adapt to task demands, *and to their own changing limitations*, so as to maintain optimal performance. A large number of experiments show that human beings actually do adapt in this way. The recognition that people can learn to monitor and select their own speed–accuracy trade-offs, and can achieve high-level control of other information processes, makes possible a new class of adaptive models.

Human Skills
Edited by D. Holding
©1981 John Wiley & Sons Ltd.

Chapter 8

Tracking

M. Hammerton

When you drive a car along a road, avoiding alike the kerb and the centre-line, you are carrying out a typical tracking task. It is typical in all the definitive respects: the path, the control, and the 'score'. The road is outside your control: it imposes a demand upon you; and you may have much (as on a motorway in daylight) or little (as in a country lane at night) forewarning of what that demand may be. You are producing your response via a mechanism — the steering of your car — which is characterized by some precise relation between the movements you make and the response of your vehicle. Your object is at all times to keep your error — which may roughly be defined in this case as the extent to which you overrun either kerb or centre-line — at zero.

These three characteristics were used by Adams (1961) to define, more formally, the class of tracking tasks. In his words:

'(1) A paced (i.e. time function) externally programmed input or command signal defines a motor response for the operator, which he performs by manipulating a control mechanism.

(2) The control mechanism generates an output signal.

(3) The input signal minus the output signal is the tracking error quantity, and the operator's requirement is to null this error . . . The measure of operator proficiency ordinarily is some function of the time-based error quantity.'

This definition stands.

Investigations into tracking began with severely limited and practical aims in view. Although there is a 'pre-history' of tracking dating back to the 1930s or earlier, it was not until the demands of war became pressing that the systematic study of tracking problems was vigorously pursued. The object of these early studies was simply to find how to make it as easy as possible for operators to point guns in a desired direction. The urgency of this problem was especially pressing in air warfare, where targets move very rapidly and guns have to be swung correspondingly fast; and the Second World War saw a number of studies of this kind (e.g. Tustin, 1944).

However, narrow and immediate though their aims were, these early researchers found themselves at once faced with problems of more general interest. The attention of academic psychologists was drawn to those matters largely by the work of Craik (1947; 1948), since when both theoretical and immediately applied work has continued in parallel.

A little reflection will soon produce a number of reasons why tracking studies have theoretical interest. A tracking task may be devised to require almost any degree of visual-motor skill from trivial simplicity to insuperable difficulty. Further, the task is definable in strictly mathematical terms (of which a little more later) and the subject's performance is measurable to any desired degree of precision. Both track and response may, in principle, be approached and described in terms of information load and of control theory — branches of applied mathematics combining great power and elegance. The task readily be combined with others, to enquire whether and how far subjects can combine performance of more than one task at a time, and, if so, how this is done. Also, the laboratory task may often be given a large measure of face realism, a characteristic beloved by both naïve subjects and by grant-awarding bodies.

TYPES OF TRACK

Although the possible variety of tracks which might be presented to subjects is infinite (for once the word is used literally) laboratory workers have generally found that a small number of types is adequate for their purposes; and some account of the main ones is called for. First, let us consider an ultra-simple tracking apparatus. Let us suppose that a roll of paper has some curve drawn along it, and that the roll can be made to move beneath a sheet of board, in which is a slit of variable width (see Figure 38). The subject is asked to keep the point of a pencil on the curve as it passes under the slit. The curve (track) can be so prepared as to have any desired degree of complexity and predictability; and, by varying the width of the slit, the extent of foresight allowed the subject can be controlled at will. The speed with which the roll moves, and the nature of the excursion of the track also affects the task difficulty.

Nowadays, electronic devices of more or less complexity are used to present points or lines on a cathode ray oscilloscope (CRO), whereon the subject controls another spot or line; but the idea is essentially the same.

The simplest type of track is the *ramp*. This is a simple line, usually straight (see Figure 39); and when pursued through the slit in the basic equipment we described would require a simple movement at constant speed. Ramp tracking is rare in the real world: Poulton (1974) mentions the operator of a TV camera in the centre of a circular race-track. It is, however, of theoretical interest in that, since it requires a constant response, any alterations in response characteristics must reflect limitations in the operator.

A *step function track* is more complex. Here the track consists of segments

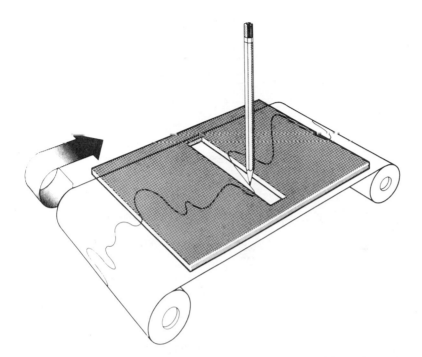

Figure 38. A very simple equipment for tracking studies. A subject tries to keep the point of his pencil on the track drawn on the roll of paper.

parallel with the overall direction of travel joined by segments at right angles to it (see Figure 39b). Again in our basic equipment, the task presents itself as a series of abrupt jumps spaced by fixed-position waiting periods.

The *sine-wave track* is outwardly simple, but of great and subtle importance. This is the indefinitely repeating waveform shown in Figure 39c. The lateral distance between peaks and troughs is called the amplitude *(a)* and the distance between corresponding points on repeating waves is called the wavelength (λ). (It is often more useful to use the frequency (ν) than the wavelength, the frequency being the number of wavelengths which pass a given point in unit time.) In our simple equipment, the required response is a back-and-forth movement of smoothly and continuously changing speed.

Sine waves are of basic importance, partly because they enable performance to be studied when variable rates of response are required, but more because — as was shown by the great French mathematician Fourier, in the nineteenth century — *any* curve can be produced by combining a sufficient number of sine waves of various λ and *a* values. Complex sine waves, therefore, include all real-world tracking situations; and tracks of any degree of complexity and (to the subject) predictability can be produced by such combinations.

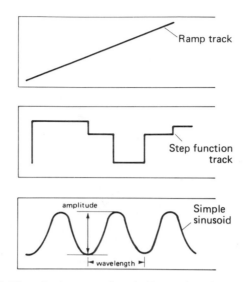

Figure 39. Three basic types of track. For explanation see text.

Pursuit and compensatory displays

In the equipment we described above, the arrangement is of the kind known as *pursuit*. In this type of display the subject simultaneously observes the track, his own output, and his error, if any: if the task were presented on a CRO he would see a moving (target) spot, the spot he controls, and the distance between them — i.e. the error. However, another form of display is possible: he could be shown the current error only. On the CRO there would be a mark, usually in the middle of the screen, representing the position of zero error, and a moving spot whose distance from the zero point represents the current state of the error. A display of this kind is called a *compensatory* display.

Numerous studies, pioneered by Poulton (1952) have attempted to decide which form of display produces the best results — i.e. the smaller overall error measure. The results of over forty such studies, tabulated and discussed by the same writer (Poulton, 1974) unequivocally point to the superiority of pursuit displays. The only caveat which has to be entered is that, as Poulton himself remarks, not every possible variety of task has been examined; but the presumption is strong that pursuit is always to be preferred. This conclusion is not *a priori* surprising, for two evident reasons. In the first place, the pursuit display provides the subject with more information at all times: he sees, as we have remarked, both input and output; whereas in a compensatory display only the difference between them is shown. Secondly, as the reader will readily discern, in the compensatory mode he has to make apparently reversed control movements. Suppose his track is veering to the right of where it should be. He will then observe a spot moving to the right of centre of the screen, which will demand a leftward movement from his control. This can be disturbing.

More elaborate modes of display will be adverted to later.

Order of control

So far we have only discussed the simplest kind of linkage between the subject's movements and his output — namely a pencil. Real systems — such as a car's wheel — are usually more complex than this; and the degree of complexity is broadly indicated by what is called the *order of control*. What is meant by this can best be understood by considering the control movements required by the different orders in a specific case.

Let us suppose that a subject sits facing a CRO upon which is a movable spot of light and two fixed vertical lines a fixed distance apart. Initially, the spot rests upon one of these lines; he is required to move it to the others and to do this he uses a control in the form of a joystick. The order of control decides the movements which have to be made to achieve this end; and for the moment we shall assume an ideal subject who acts with perfect economy and precision.

Suppose that the deflection of the joystick from centre directly controls the position of the spot, i.e. for any value of deflection of the stick there is a corresponding position of the spot. This is called *zero order* or positional control. In this case (see Figure 40) the operator makes a single movement of his stick, from its initial to its final position, and keeps it fixed there.

Secondly, suppose that, if the stick is held in its central position, the spot remains stationary wherever it happens to be, and that it moves away from that position in the direction in which the stick is moved and at a speed proportional to the extent of the deflection: twice the deflection produces twice the speed. This is called a *first-order* or velocity or rate control; and, as appears in Figure 40b, it requires at least two movements for the same task. The first deflection gives the spot a velocity in the required direction; the second, back to centre, stops the spot when it has reached its target.

Thirdly, let us consider the more complex and difficult situation known as *second-order* or acceleration control. (British students especially often find this confusing, because of our unfortunate habit of calling the speed control of our cars an 'accelerator'. It is, in fact, a velocity control with variable lag.) In this case, when the stick is in the central position, the spot keeps the velocity which it already had: this may be, as in the case we are imagining, zero. Any deflection of the stick produces an acceleration of the spot, i.e. a change of velocity, in the direction of, and proportional to that deflection. Thus, if the stick is held in some deflected position, the spot will steadily increase its velocity in the direction of that deflection, and will soon disappear off the screen. A minimum of three movements is therefore required for our task (see Figure 46c). The first step will cause an acceleration in the desired direction. If the stick were then merely returned to its central position, the spot would go on moving past its target with the speed it had attained; i.e. the stick must be given a deflection equal and opposite to its first one. If the operator's judgement and timing were exact — which we are supposing — the spot would just have stopped as it reaches its target, when he will return the stick to centre, having the spot stationary where it ought to be.

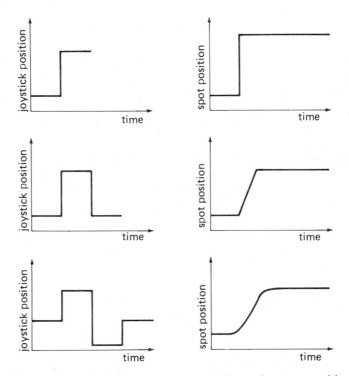

Figure 40. Movements required to move a controlled spot from one position to another with three orders of control. Position control (a) requires a single movement; velocity control (b) requires two; acceleration control (c) needs three.

Augmented displays

In the discussion so far, we have tacitly assumed a single display of a straightforward type, be it pursuit or compensatory. However, the skill of modern instrument designers, with the resources of advanced electronics at their disposal, can provide a variety of displays for special purposes.

We have remarked that second-order controls are very difficult to master; but sometimes their use is unavoidable: the dynamics of the machinery involved allows nothing less. Even more complex controls are compelled in some cases: the steering of a submarine, e.g. is essentially a lagged third-order system. When this cannot be avoided, it is as well to provide the controller with more information. This is generally referred to as an 'augmented' display; and two kinds are especially to be recommended, namely rate-augmented and predictor displays.

In a *rate-augmented display* the controller sees not only the current state of things (either in pursuit or compensatory form) but also the rate at which it is changing. Thus, in one of the most familiar applications, the pilot of an aircraft who wishes to reach or maintain a particular height will have not only his altimeter — giving the current state of affairs — but also a rate-of-climb indicator. This latter gives the rate of change of the situation, which greatly helps in smoothing out the approach to the desired value. It is not intended here to go into any mathematical detail; but we will merely observe that if the 'output' is x, then the rate of change is dx/dt. This is always one control order down from x, so that an operator who finds x peculiarly difficult to handle may find the rate much easier to handle.

A predictor display, as its name implies, shows the operator his current position and the way that position will change over the next few seconds (or longer period in a slow-responding system). This can only be done with the help of advanced electronic equipment. It requires a special-purpose computer which holds a mathematical representation of the system, and continuously calculates the effect of current operator behaviour very much faster than the actual effects take place. This calculation has to be performed in a time which is negligible compared to system or operator response; hence the need for a computer. Since this effect will itself be a function of any changes in the operator's behaviour, the predictor usually has one of two assumptions built in: either it assumes that the operator slowly returns his control to the central position during the time of the prediction, or it assumes that the operator keeps his control where it is at the current instant. The writer does not know of any experiment which investigates which of these two is the better; but Kelly (1962) convincingly demonstrated the advantages of a predictor display in a complex system.

Present-day predictor displays usually look something like Figure 41 with time as one axis and system state (or error, in a compensatory display) as the other. However, there is no reason why future systems should not incorporate holographic presentation in three dimensions, with two output variables in a viewing plane and the future represented as increasing depth. The idea is attractive.

Preview

Common sense and experiment alike affirm the value of preview, i.e. of being able to see what is coming next. Poulton (1957c) showed that, the more

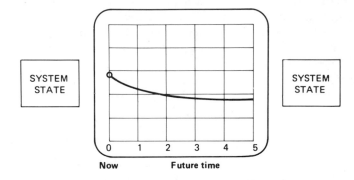

Figure 41. A predictor display.

preview of a track an operator got, the less his error. He also speeded up when the experimental conditions allowed it. The desirability of supplying any controller with the maximum amount of information on forthcoming demand is evident.

The reader will already have thought that no real system has such perfect and immediate response as we have supposed (though purely electronic systems can approach it very closely indeed). Neither do real operators possess such immaculate skill and judgement. Real systems exhibit some degree of lag. Some finite time elapses before the demand signalled by the control movement is achieved: this has the effect of rounding and slightly flattening response curves such as those shown in Figure 40. Also, however, they make the judgement of when to make or cancel a demand more difficult; and this is especially the case if the lags are long. This naturally brings us to another question.

OPTIMAL CONTROLS AND DISPLAYS

We have talked about controls which produce movements or change in velocity in proportion to the extent of their deflection. Clearly, a control can be very sensitive indeed: we may imagine a first-order control such that the merest touch gives maximum velocity. Such a device would be pretty useless; for few if any operators could refine and control their movements enough to halt movement with sufficient precision. On the other hand, supposing that we were using a wheel rather than a stick, we could arrange matters so that a couple of full turns were necessary to obtain a moderate velocity. Such a control would present no difficulty; but equally we could hardly expect subjects to perform their tasks at record speed, because of the time taken to get things going. It would seem reasonable, therefore, to suppose that some intermediate level of sensitivity were optimal. But there is a catch here: in presenting our imaginary extreme cases, we changed from a joystick-type control to a wheel; and if we do not, we are forced to other conclusions. Let us examine our task with more precision.

Let us define the sensitivity of the control as the movement produced (cm for a zero order, cm sec^{-1} for a first order, and so on) divided by the movement made (cm deflection, e.g. for a stick). This value is variously named 'gain' or — which I prefer — display/control ratio (D/C ratio). Let us consider the elements of the simple acquisition task we have discussed already. The operator has to get his spot to the target area, and there to stop it. Assuming a first-order control with a particular maximum velocity (and all real systems have such an upper limit) it is evident that the more rapidly the operator can reach maximum velocity, the more rapidly will the gross movement — i.e. the movement to the target area — be accomplished. Thus the gross movement requires a high D/C ratio. However, he there has to stop; and every real operator has a certain amount of tremor and a certain liability to positioning error; and if every such slight error or movement sets his spot in motion it will take a long time to settle down. Thus the settling or adjustment phase calls for as low a D/C ratio as possible. The result of those two conflicting requirements can be seen in Figure 42.

This diagram appears in many textbooks and is part of the 'received wisdom' of the subject. It is also highly misleading.

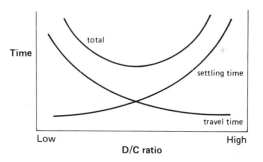

Figure 42. The components of acquisition time. When the D/C ratio ('sensitivity') is indefinitely variable, there will generally be an optimum value in the roughly U-shaped relationship between acquisition time and this ratio.

A joystick can have only limited travel — say 30°–40° upon either side of centre at most. Therefore, with any real system, there is a downward limit to the D/C ratio given by maximum deflection for maximum output. Moreover, the rapid flick required to reach maximum deflection is virtually constant, unless the stick should have very heavy spring or frictional loading. In other words, for a joystick control, it is not possible to move down the D/C axis below the flat part of the travel–time curve. The curve therefore, is of the truncated, roughly J-shaped form of Figure 43; and we assert that, for all controls of joystick type, the lowest possible D/C ratio is best (see Hammerton, 1963, also Poulton, 1974).

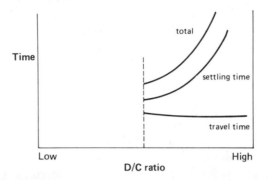

Figure 43. When D/C ratio has only a limited possible range (as is the case with many practical controls, such as joysticks, levers and pedals) the optimum value is generally the lowest obtainable.

It is surprising how persistent is the misleading conclusion of Figure 42; though the writer doubts whether any other reason needs to be cited than the sheer inertia of the printed word. An unfortunate consequence is that the very conclusion offered has to be rediscovered again and again: this is still being done (Labuc, 1978).

We have discussed in a little detail the arguments related to optimum sensitivity for controls of the joystick type; but this by no means exhausts the optimization questions which might be asked. For example, are joysticks best? If they are, are movement or pressure sticks best? Is a thumb control to be preferred to a hand control, or vice versa? What is the optimum order of control? Further, do these optima vary with the task (remember that we have only discussed a very simple one-shot target acquisition)?

Only tentative answers can be given to some of these questions. Chernikoff, Duey, and Taylor (1960) present data which strongly favours first-order control systems, which is entirely in agreement with the present writer's observations; but their experimental design was open to criticism (Poulton, 1973). Thus we can only assert the superiority of first-order controls as probable; though it must be added that its superiority over higher order systems is hardly open to doubt. That human beings find great difficulty in predicting and judging accelerated motion has been notorious for a century (Gottsdanker, 1956). Similarly, as has been pointed out by Poulton (1974), it is possible that continuous tracking of very rapidly swinging paths may be easier with a slightly higher than minimum D/C ratio: the matter has yet to be studied.

The quite general argument adumbrated above seems to require the superiority of joysticks over almost any other kind of control; and the present writer, together with the late A. H. Tickner, looked into the type of joystick which is to be preferred (1966). We concluded that hand controls were marginally better than thumb controls, which were vastly better than large sticks swung by the whole forearm. This is entirely in accord with common sense, of course; but it deliberately and specifically ignored the possible need to apply brute force: such a need should be eliminated in any well-designed modern system.

We referred above to pressure controls. These may not be as familiar to all readers as others; but their name is in fact self-descriptive. A pressure control is one which does not move and whose output is proportional to the force exerted upon it by the operator. It invariably (as far as the writer's experience goes) incorporates a form of spring centring — i.e. it returns to an equivalent of zero position when force is removed — and is generally operated by means of a piezoelectric crystal. The obvious advantage of such a system is that its D/C ratio is almost indefinitely variable; its drawback is that pressure feedback — i.e. the sensation of effort the operator is exerting — is almost certainly less precise than is the visual and positional feedback available with moving controls. Evidence carefully amassed and weighed by Poulton (1974) appears to indicate the superiority of pressure controls, especially in more difficult tasks — a conclusion emphatically endorsed by Mehr (1970).

Another question which arises, and which has given rise to some curious confusion, is that of display compatability: what is the best relationship between movement of (or direction of pressure on) a control and the movement of the display? The answer is entirely conformable to common sense, and has been known for a long time (e.g. Regan, 1959): move the control right and left to move the display right and left, move the control forward and back to move the display up or down. This unsurprising conclusion often draws the query: 'What about aircraft?'; but it should not be forgotten that aircraft are controlled from inside; and the horizon, which is effectively the display, does indeed move up as the stick moves forward.

These comments, of course, apply to a sensibly arranged system where the operator sits with his control before him and facing his display. Not every system is sensible (alas); and there are cases where an operator has no choice but to look at a display which is not in the same direction as his control. (A military application at once springs to mind here. The controller of a guided anti-tank missile may be in a helicopter with his control-stick in front of him and his target well off to one side.)

This question has theoretical as well as practical interest, and that in a different field of psychology. The question is: what is the preferred frame of reference for skills learning: is it spatial or located in the operator's body? Put differently, would it be better to have to move a control parallel to the desired display movement irrespective of the location of the display, or if the display has to be moved left (say) is space, should the control be moved to the left of the operator's body? (See Figure 44.)

For simple situations at least, it seems that the body frame is what matters: the operator should always have to move his hand to his left in order to move the display to its left.

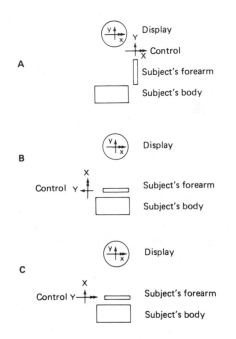

Figure 44. Schematic plan view of an experimental set-up to investigate the relative importance of space — and body — frames of reference in control tasks. In A, the control (a thumb joystick) is correctly oriented both to the spatial frame (the face of a CRO) and the body frame (the subject's forearm). In B, orientation is correct for body but not for space; in C, orientation is correct for space but not for body.

Alternative presentations

All the studies we have discussed involve the operator watching a display at the centre of his visual field, and doing something about it. This is not always possible; e.g. a pilot bringing his aircraft in to land may not wish to take his eyes off the runway to monitor his instruments more than he can possibly help. The change in accommodation of the eyes takes, and therefore results in a dead time of, 1 to 2 sec. One method of dealing with this which modern technology can supply is the 'head up' display. Here the necessary data are projected either upon the aircraft's windscreen or on the pilot's helmet and focused at infinity: he should be able to keep them in view while watching the ground. (Test pilots have assured the writer that this does not wholly solve the accommodation problem: it is difficult to see why not.) Another method is to use peripheral vision.

If you are looking at a display in front of you, you will not find it easy to read a dial (say) out of the corner of your eye. It is relatively easy, however, to note whether and how fast a light is flashing, or how bright it is. Only a few studies have been conducted to look into the effectiveness of such peripheral markers (e.g. Ziegler, Reilly, and Chernikoff, 1966), but they seem to indicate that some coded flashing system (e.g. the faster the flash rate, the larger the error) could function satisfactorily. Perhaps this possibility merits further study.

A little work has been done on using auditory instead of visual demand signals in tracking. As we all know, we can (roughly at least) localize the unseen source of a sound; and the human auditory system is highly sensitive to changes in the pitch and quality of a sound. Also, simple reaction time to an auditory stimulus is much shorter than to a visual stimulus (this makes good evolutionary sense: if you can hear something, it must be nearby). The possibility of using an auditory display for the second of two quantities which have to be followed simultaneously has, therefore, found some advocates.

Ellis, Burrows, and Jackson (1953) had their subjects track one variable visually, while a second was presented by representing upward errors by a high note (2.3 kHz) and downward errors by a low note (170 Hz). The magnitude of the error either way was represented by the rate at which the tone bleeped. The results indicated that satisfactory performance could be obtained in this way. It will be remembered that the German wartime *Knickebein* aircraft guidance system operated on a similar basis: to the right of the path the pilot heard a stream of Morse dashes, to the left a stream of dots, along the correct path a continuous note (Jones, 1978). It seems to have been entirely satisfactory, so long as no one was interfering.

It seems, then, that subsidiary tracking tasks can well be monitored by hearing. Little use of this is at present made in practical systems; but, again, the matter might be worth pursuing.

A variety of other forms of subsidiary tracking have been tried from time to time. Poulton (1974) refers to skin vibration and mild electrical stimulation. Not surprisingly, perhaps, they have attracted little attention; though there is no *a-priori* reason to doubt that a more intense electrical stimulation could be, at least, an infallible emergency signal.

It is worth noting that all the moderately successful non-visual tracking systems which have been tried are analogous to compensatory rather than to pursuit tracking. It is reasonable to suppose that this is because the non-visual senses have insufficient discrimination to keep simultaneous track of both target and current status: at best they can apprehend the direction and approximate magnitude of an error.

MEASUREMENT OF TRACKING PERFORMANCE

In order to make statements about 'better' or 'optimal' tracking controls and devices, it is necessary to have some measure of performance. In the very simple acquisition task discussed above, nothing more complex is required than the time required, after leaving the initial position, to come to rest on the target. However, in more complex continuous tracking tasks time measures are rarely satisfactory. For example, suppose we used time-on-target as our measure (i.e. the actual length of time, or the proportion of the operating time, for which the subject is on or within a permitted distance from the target track). This has only one virtue — that of simplicity. It has, however, the fatal drawback of showing no difference between an operator who is (say) on target half the time and very near it the rest, and one who is on target half the time and wildly out for the rest. Clearly, a better measure must be sought.

Consider the imaginary data presented in Figure 45. With modern electronic equipment it is a simple matter to keep continuous track of the subject's error and present an integrated value (in cm^2) at the end of the experiment. This again, however, does not differentiate between the operator who makes one huge error but is otherwise perfect and the one who is never far off but never quite on. Two measures are generally used which provide the bulk of the information required: these are the modulus mean error (MM) and the root mean squared error (RMS).

Figure 45. In general, a subject's track will differ from the required one. Here we see a reasonable effort, error being shown by vertical hatching: there are problems in producing a measure for the overall error.

In MM, no account is taken of the direction of error; but the value of the error (cm) is measured at successive time intervals, and the mean of all these values is taken. In formal notation, if an error at some measured instant is $\pm x$, and n such measures are taken,

$$\mathrm{MM} = \frac{\Sigma |x|}{n}$$

In RMS, each error is squared, and the square root of the mean of the squares is taken. With the same notation,

$$RMS = \sqrt{\left(\frac{\Sigma x^2}{n}\right)}$$

These two measures correlate very highly together, and either is very useful and valid. For certain statistical purposes, RMS is to be preferred, for it lends itself more readily to use with parametric statistics, but there is usually no compulsion to use such statistics; so the student may please himself. Poulton (1974) recommends the use of *relative* RMS or MM error scores. These are defined as the error (RMS or MM as the case may be) divided by the error that would be obtained if the operator simply did nothing and multiplied by 100. In other words, the ratio of actual to zero-action error expressed as a percentage. This clearly has utility in comparing the results of different experiments and different equipments.

In all these measures, only one error quantity is considered at any instant — what we have termed x. However, it is sometimes the case that a subject may be following a track well-nigh perfectly, but a trifle late. If we follow the ultra-simple experimental picture we started with, we would observe, in such a case, that his error in a direction at right angles to the direction of movement of the roll (x as we have called it) would vary a lot, while his error along the direction of movement (y, let us say) would be a small constant. The former (x) may be called amplitude error, the latter (y) tracking lag. It may be desirable to measure them separately; in which case the experimenter will produce two values, either of MM, RMS, or relative errors.

MODELS OF TRACKING BEHAVIOUR

By this time the reader may have thought that these several findings are no doubt interesting, and very useful if you wish to design a control system, but that they are lacking in generality. Is there not, he may well ask, some adequate theory of tracking behaviour which would enable us, having measured, perhaps, various constant terms, to predict the outcome of all these experiments? Unfortunately, there is not; though not for want of heroic efforts.

Most of the efforts to reach a theoretical understanding of tracking behaviour have stemmed from two extra-psychological areas, namely the theory of servo-mechanisms and information (or communication) theory. The immediate attractiveness of the servo-mechanical approach is obvious (and is endorsed in Chapter 2). To say that a human being controlling a mechanism is acting as part of a closed-loop servo system is, in a sense, trivial. (Poulton, 1974, refers to compensatory control systems as 'open loop' — a terminology which seems to the writer to be slightly misleading.) Some part of the world — i.e. the system — is not as desired; the human operates upon it; he perceives the effects of his operation as the display; and performs a further or different operation, and so on. The system or device he is using will generally have some definable characteristics of its own, which may be very simple — as, for example, a hammer — or of the greatest complexity, as in some advanced vehicles. This state of affairs can quite validly be portrayed in the kind of diagram shown in Figure 46; and the servo language is clearly an acceptable one. But that alone is not enough.

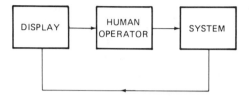

Figure 46. Any tracking task can be treated as a closed-loop control set-up; and (in principle at least) the mathematics of control theory can be applied.

Each of the 'boxes' in Figure 46 — or any like it — has the characteristic of changing its output systematically in response to a change of input — as, for example, the flow of electric current in a circuit will change as a controlling resistance is altered. The theory of servo-mechanisms (see e.g. Brown and Campbell, 1948) is a branch of applied mathematics which offers a powerful set of techniques — technically known as transfer functions — for describing such changes and hence for describing and predicting the behaviour of the systems they make up. Also, when an element is a 'black box', as a human operator is, methods exist for deriving its transform by examining its response to a known input or sequence of inputs (see e.g. Teasdale and Reynolds, 1955).

In the first flush of enthusiasm for servo methods, much research was directed towards finding 'the transfer function of the human operator' — not the confident definite articles. Tustin (1944) wrote: 'The object . . . was to investigate the nature of the subject's responses . . . and to attempt to find the laws of relationship of movement to error. In particular it was hoped that this relationship might . . . permit the well-developed theory of linear servo-mechanisms to be applied to manual control.' Such an aim, if achieved, would not only make it possible to synthesize optimal system designs, but on a theoretical plane it could have immense value in guiding studies of brain functioning and the search for the physiological mechanisms involved. Alas, the attempt failed.

The first important catch lies in the use of the word 'linear' in Tustin's remarks above. It means, simply, that the transform must be of the type which can be described by a class of mathematical functions known as 'linear differential equations'. This type of expression cannot cope with an intermittent response; and it soon became evident that, in many cases, human operator responses are intermittent (Poulton, 1950).

There are, indeed, methods for coping with non-linear systems. They involve finding the best linear equation — i.e. the one which leaves the least amount of the data unaccounted for — and adding a 'remnant' non-linear term for the rest. These methods have neither the beauty nor the generality of linear equations, but they can, nevertheless, be very useful in particular cases.

This has been particularly urged by McRuer and his several co-workers (e.g. 1967), who were able to construct reasonably successful descriptions of their data. However, in order to do this, expressions of considerable complexity were required, involving at least five, and in some cases nine undetermined constant terms. Now an expression with nine undetermined and independent numbers in it can be made to fit just about anything after the fact, but can predict nothing before it. (In this context Poulton, 1974, approvingly quotes the common saying that 'an equation with 2 constants in it can be made to fit an elephant, and one with 3 constants can make its tail wiggle'.) It is therefore difficult to argue that our general understanding has been advanced by these studies, impressive though their mathematical sophistication undoubtedly is.

There are further difficulties. In almost any situation, human operators display a remarkable ability to learn at least the overall statistical characteristics of the task. They can also learn to master control systems which, at first, were insuperably difficult; but such learning tends to be unstable. Thus, Garvey (1960) showed that subjects could, in effect, acquire an extra order of integration — enabling them to cope with an order of control one higher than they could before — but that they lost this ability when their attention had to be divided. Similarly, the learning of general task characteristics may, in any particular trial, be counteracted by fatigue and boredom. Thus, it would seem, one cannot hope to do more than find the transfer function (be it never so complex) of a well-practised, well-motivated operator who is not yet very tired or bored. It is hard to avoid the conclusion reached more than twenty years ago by Birmingham and Taylor (1954) that '*The* human transfer function is a will-o'-the-wisp, which can lure the control system designed into a fruitless and interminable quest.' This is yet another problem which will be adverted to below.

Both the track and the operator's output can be treated as signals or messages received and transmitted over time. It is not surprising, then, that a number of workers have tried to see whether information theory could help our theoretical understanding. During the 1950s many psychologists became very enthusiastic about the application of this theory to their subject. This was not at all unreasonable; for, after all, a very great deal of human activity may validly be described as the processing of information of more or less complexity. However, the theory of information (or communication, as it is more properly called) has certain constraints which make its application to psychology very difficult (see, e.g. Pierce, 1962), and most of the attempts to use it proved sterile.

Nevertheless, its application to tracking studies seemed *a priori* reasonable, since both input and output take a form which seems to lend itself to information measures. However, despite some ingenious attempts and a lot of disputation, no formulation has succeeded in commanding general acceptance. It is perhaps significant that in his formidable survey of the area, Poulton (1974) does not even index information theory.

Why should so many attempts to find a generally applicable and acceptable theory have failed to deliver the goods? Consideration of an experiment which was actually conducted for another purpose (Hammerton and Tickner, 1970) may help to cast some dark on the matter.

In this study subjects sat facing a TV screen, which bore on it a central vertical graticule. They used a thumb joystick which controlled the movements of a TV camera which could move back and forth parallel with and facing a horizontally moving target. The control was a first-order one with a small lag, which was not difficult to use; and the movements of the target were determined by the sum of three sine waves: this pattern of movement repeated after about 2 min, which was a good deal longer than each testing run.

Before and behind the target were screens. In one condition these were painted with a landscape, so that the target seemed to be running along the top of a cliff, backed by rolling downland; in the other condition they were matt white. This was the *only* difference between the two conditions: the target courses were statistically identical in the two cases; and identical responses were available, which would have produced identical data. Nevertheless, the results of the two conditions were very markedly different. It therefore seems to the writer that any comprehensive theory of tracking behaviour, in whatever terms, must take account of the purely local characteristics of the visual background of the input. The literature of the field is far too extensive for any man to be able to claim with confidence that he has not overlooked any relevant paper: the writer can only aver that he knows of none which attempts this.

What of computer models? The amazing power and versatility of modern computers has naturally attracted persons interested in tracking problems; but simulations so far lack generality. Given an ingenious programmer (and many members of that respected profession are very ingenious indeed) a machine can be made to mimic any particular piece of human tracking behaviour. The programmes produced so far, however, do not generalize to other tasks and other operators. In any case, the criticism advanced above also holds.

Virtually all the studies we have referred to so far were laboratory studies, using more or less artificial situations and displays, all of which were a few tens of centimetres from the subject. How well do these results apply to real-world tracking situations? Also, since the use of simulators for training is becoming ever more important (Institute of Measurement and Control, 1977), how much does a skill learned in a restricted 'artificial' environment help in coping with the 'real thing?'

TRANSFER OF TRAINING

There can be little doubt that the optimizing conclusions cited above hold, at least as rank orders; although a caveat has to be entered to the effect that the real world seems to be rather a good place to do tracking in. Steering a ship is, after all, a heavily damped third-order system; but it is not usually of insuperable difficulty. The questions which arise concerning applying a skill learned on an indoor simulator to a real situation, however, involve psycho-logical problems of deep significance. Suppose that it is indeed the case that persons who master task A subsequently master task B more rapidly than those who have never attempted A (an effect known as the transfer of training); why should it be, and what conditions may enhance the effect? Like many interesting questions in psychology, this one is difficult: the phenomenon itself it not easy to measure: more than one possible explanation is in the field; and these answers, further discussed in Chapter 9, are not necessarily mutually exclusive.

It should be made clear that we are not, in general, concerned with starting with an easy task and proceeding to a less easy one. Indeed, Holding (1962) concluded that 'task difficulty' was not a useful concept at all for examining transfer between tracking tasks: it is doubtful whether it ever is.

Consider a 'typical' transfer experiment. A control group, which we shall call C, learns some task B, their initial and final performances providing by subtraction or ratio a measure of skill acquired. A matched experimental group, which we shall call E, learns some task A, and then learns task B. Evidently we need some formula for comparing E's performance on task B with that of C. We may, as we shall remark in a moment, require other information, but let that suffice for the moment.

Simple and straightforward though this seems, literally hundred of formulae have been proposed (e.g. Murdock, 1957). Broadly, however, they fall into two classes: there are those which are concerned with *savings*, and there are those which are concerned with initial or *'first-shot'* transfer performance. Savings measures answer, more or less directly, the question: how much training time (or, how many training trials) are saved in learning task B by the prior learning of task A? First-shot measures answer the question: how does the prior learning of task A affect *initial* performance on task B?

It is important here to remember that these classes of measures really are dealing with different things. It has usually been tacitly assumed — though not, so far as the writer knows, explicitly stated — that the two classes cor-relate almost perfectly one with the other — that a very high savings measure automatically implies a very high first-shot measure. Unfortunately, as the writer showed (1967) this is not the case: it is possible to combine a saving of some 70 per cent or more of training trials with a *negative* first-shot measure. In other words, though E-group trainees may take less than a third as long to attain proficiency in task B as do those from group C, their initial performance initial performance can be worse than if they had no prior training at all.

It is evident upon very slight reflection that there are some practical situations in which this would be disastrous, and others in which it would not be a serious drawback. Thus it is necessary to be very clear what we need from a simulator, and hence what measure of its performance is appropriate, and to design the simulator so as to maximize its effectiveness. 'Effectiveness' in any real situation is, of course, an economic as well as a purely technical matter; and the costing is far from being a simple exercise. It is necessary to ask: what is the running cost per hour of the simulator as compared to that of the real equipment? Does even a poor operator of the real equipment produce some useful output which can be set against cost? Is he, on the other hand, likely merely to waste raw materials, or even damage the plant itself? And so on. It is considerations of this kind which decide whether the user is after a very high 'first-shot' transfer, or whether he will be satisfied with a substantial saving of training time.

When the need has been established, the simulator must be designed; and there is now a good deal of information available to guide the designer. Much, though not all of this information derives from studies of aircraft cockpit simulators, for the very obvious reasons that aircraft are very expensive to build and run, that their misuse can be disastrous, and that, consequently, funding for research into training methods has often been generous. The results may be summarized quite simply: very simple devices can produce remarkably good savings measures; but if you want good first-shot transfer, then you must pay for it in terms of more complex fidelity to the real situation. Curiously, perhaps, this result is more unequivocally shown by laboratory than by field studies.

Let us consider the question of what is transferred in a visual-motor skilled task. The trainee learns to make some set of appropriate motor responses to various discretely or continuously varying signals, which are usually visual. Let us suppose that a simulator has been made which presents the 'bare bones' of this situation — for example, a particular dial with a pointer as the input signal and a lever to move in response. In general, the real situation will be more complex than this; and the trainee, when first he uses the real equipment, will be getting a whole host of other signals, many of them unfamiliar. These will include the relevant signals; and he has to learn to ignore and discard a lot of others among which they are found: this situation is known as 'stimulus compounding'. The need to cope with it probably accounts for the poor, or even negative first-shot transfer which can, as we have noted, sometimes be associated with very good savings measures.

Where savings are the chief requirement, it is remarkable how simple some effective devices are. Even in flying, noticeable reductions in dual-control hours were reported (Flaxman, Matheny, and Brown, 1950) using nothing more elaborate than an 'artificial horizon' consisting of a line on a board held up by an instructor. Not unreasonably, though, we might expect that, if we want good first-shot transfer, we must provide *in the learning situation* a fair sample of those irrelevant 'compounding' stimuli with which the trainee will eventually have to live. Such an expectation was amply borne out in a series of studies the writer conducted some years ago (Hammerton, 1967). Precisely comparable field data are hard to come by. There is, indeed, ample evidence (e.g. Caro, Isley, and Jolley, 1975) that elaborate simulation — including such refinements as projected scenery and multiple-axis cockpit motion — produces very good transfer indeed A strict comparison with less complex devices is — as far as the writer's knowledge goes — wanting. The reasons for this are very simple: it has become usual, when introducing a new type of aircraft, to make the most complete and elaborate simulator possible, so that no one even tries a simpler one; and, when an elaborate simulator is used to replace a simpler one, the amount of training time used on it is promptly cut down — without first carrying out the expensive comparative study. One must suppose that the responsible authorities are so convinced by the laboratory studies already cited that they do not consider more extended tests to be necessary. If they are so convinced, they are probably right, for once.

What light do these several findings cast upon the theory of transfer? Three theories have been propounded at various times. The traditional view was that the training task (task A in our summary) exercises some part of the brain, just as lifting weights exercises sets of muscles; and in consequence the subject approaches task B with a stronger, fitter brain. However, other alternatives are now more popular.

Thorndike (1903) propounded the most extreme view: task A can help with task B only in so far as there are elements of performance which are common to them both. There is an attractive simplicity about this, as about so many of the ideas propounded by the early behaviourists. However, it rules out — or seems to — any notion of 'generality' in learning; and a contrary view is that it is precisely such general principles, explicit or implicit in task A, which are of use in task B. The celebrated study of Hendrickson and Schroeder (1941) may be cited as supporting this view. They found that a prior study of refraction did not show any advantage when aiming at underwater targets; but that an advantage did show when the depth of water was changed: subjects with knowledge of refraction adapted more rapidly than those without.

(There is also what may be called the cynics' or 'test' view: task A is not the slightest use in learning task B; but it is a good test of potential for task B. In other words, in order to do well at task A, you need the very abilities that will stand you in good stead when tackling task B.)

At first sight, it might be argued that the 'common element' theory is supported by the data we have discussed. However, it is worth noting that the poor 'first-shot' transfer recorded in some experiments indicates that it is precisely these common elements that the learner fails to extract from the second situation. It cannot be claimed that these results are decisive; but, besides bringing to light the previously unsuspected phenomenon of different savings and first-shot transfer, tracking studies give some support to the 'general principles view'. It should not be forgotten, however, that the traditional or 'exercise' theory has never, to the writer's knowledge, actually been disproved. It has only become unfashionable.

TRACKING AND CHANNEL CAPACITY

A vital question (already raised in Chapter 4) for those who wish to understand human skill is: to what extent can we do two things at once? Put more formally, what are the limitations on our rate of processing input demands and output responses? For many years, the view which was most generally accepted was that of Broadbent (1958), which suggested that all these operations passed through a single central channel, whose capacity had, naturally, some upper limit. This model held that we can indeed do only one thing at a time; and that when we appear to do more we are either switching smartly and economically between tasks, or are leaving one of them, which must be highly overlearned (e.g. riding a bicycle) to a purely automatic system. Later work modified this view to suppose that there is indeed a single limited channel, but that it can, as it were, be divided between various tasks, provided none of these is overwhelmingly difficult.

Continuous tracking tasks afford an elegant means of testing this theory. A fairly difficult task of low predictability certainly absorbs a great deal of capacity, but uses as input only the eyes (vision) and for output only one hand. The subject can still hear, speak, make one-handed gestures, or otherwise respond to a variety of visual stimuli. These facts were utilized by McLeod (1977) in a study which should become a classic.

His subjects were presented with a decidedly difficult second-order tracking task, for which they used a hand joystick. The difficulty was increased by making the control asymmetric: the D/C ratio in one direction was less than in the other by 20 per cent. At the same time a second task easy in itself, was presented: this was to decide whether a short bleep of sound was of middle (1 kHz) or high (3 kHz) pitch. One experimental group indicated this decision by pressing an appropriate button with their free hand; another simply stated which sound it was.

The beauty of this experiment is that in stimulus or perceptual uncertainty the two groups were identical; the only difference was in the modality of the output of the second task. However, it was found that there was a marked decrement in tracking performance when, but only when, the choice response was made manually.

In a further experiment, the same tracking task was performed simultaneously with mental arithmetic (questions and answers being spoken) of two levels of difficulty. It appeared that performance on the tracking task was independent of the difficulty of the arithmetic.

The conclusion appears to be compelled that two processes employing the same output mode (manual, in this case) are indeed on a single channel; processes involving different output modalities are on separate channels. A multiprocessor, as opposed to a single-channel model seems required by these data: a result of fundamental importance.

THE STATUS AND FUTURE OF TRACKING STUDIES

Some years ago the writer wondered whether tracking studies were in the process of being automated out of existence. To some extent this has happened. The progress of microelectronics has made it possible to eliminate human controllers from many situations where, a few years ago, a highly trained operator was essential. The difference between the command-guided Soviet SAM-2 missiles and their SAM-7 and SAM-9 successors, which only need to be launched in the general direction of their target, will come immediately to the thoughts of the informed.

There remain, of course, wide areas where the controller has not been, and for some time is not likely to be, eliminated: road transport and air transport are the most obvious and numerically the most important cases. Yet even here, we may ask, are there problems sufficient to justify prolonged research programmes? After all, the major prescriptions, as we have seen, can already be given; and it would be difficult to justify, on straightforwardly applied grounds, elaborate investigations of new systems, unless they contained features thought likely to modify available conclusions, or to be of a nature where even the faintest improvement must be sought.

Are there applied areas where more needs to be known? The only one which seems important, other than tying up some of the loose ends we have already indicated, is the effect of prolonged vigilance upon tracking skills. The extensive literature on vigilance studies suggests that operators may modify their criteria of being 'on target' over time. How this tendency may best be met and overcome has not yet received much attention.

However, the function of science, as has justly been observed, is not to make things, but to make sense of things. It cannot be pretended that anything like a full theoretical account of tracking behaviour can be given. For reasons given above, the writer does not believe that a full account can be attained in terms either of control theory or of information theory. It is a challenge to control theorists to extend their theories to include intermittent or variable systems within their range; but even if success crowns such an enterprise, it must be combined with an account of how human beings incorporate background features into their assessments of speed and relative position. At present this can be done only in general terms, which it would be difficult to combine with formal control equations.

Advantage may be taken, however, of the large empirical body of data on tracking tasks, and of the powerful and informative measures which exist for assessing performance on them. We have already adumbrated the way in which these have been used to settle an important issue in the study of channel capacity. It needs little imagination to see that they might be used in such areas as attention and motor learning. They are already being used in studies of the sequelae of some neurological diseases; and it is reasonably hoped (Downing, personal communication, 1978) that they may pinpoint the nature and area of deficiencies which afflict some sufferers.

If such studies appear auxiliary and tangential, they may nevertheless prove valuable.

SUMMARY

Tracking studies began in the 1940s with the most strictly practical ends in view. These early studies, however, raised questions of great theoretical interest concerning the functioning of human beings as elements in closed-loop control systems, and as processors of information. High hopes were entertained that formal descriptions of human behaviour in servo- or information-theoretical terms would enable optimal designs to be derived mathematically and would cast an important light on central human functioning. These hopes have not been realized to more than a very limited extent; and there is reason to suppose that they cannot be, with the mathematical tools now available.

Nevertheless, the original object of tracking work — the finding of specifications for optimal control orders, displays, and sensitivities has substantially been achieved. It is evident that zero or first-order control systems are to be preferred wherever possible. The superiority of pursuit over compensatory displays is firmly established, except where a non-visual auxiliary system is contemplated. Hand controls are in general to be preferred; and with the possible (and somewhat doubtful) exception of pressure-operated controls following a complex track, the lower the D/C ratio the better. Ordinary control systems can therefore be optimized virtually by rule of thumb.

Some tracking tasks, especially piloting aircraft, necessarily involve some difficulty, and the consequences of failure are grave. Great attention has therefore been paid to the design and use of tracking training devices and simulators. This work has produced important results in the measurement and understanding of transfer of training; and, again, enables broad rules to be laid down for the design of simulators.

It is not clear whether classical tracking studies will retain their importance in applied psychology: automation and microelectronics have enabled the human controller to be removed from many advanced systems. The established knowledge and informative measures available, however, can be used to investigate many fields of general importance. They have already made substantial contributions to our knowledge of human channel capacity, and may prove useful in a number of other areas.

Human Skills
Edited by D. Holding
©1981 John Wiley & Sons Ltd.

Chapter 9

Skill Learning

K. M. Newell

Skill learning is still very much the Cinderella of experimental psychology despite its strong roots in the discipline. Learning, by and large, is synonomous with verbal learning, with skill acquisition representing an area of study which, at best, might generate a chapter for inclusion in a learning text or a lecture or two in a learning course. Similarly, the field of perception continues, in the main, to develop in isolation of concepts of actions, despite the obvious conceptual links between knowing and doing. It is to be welcomed, therefore, that ideas on human skills have an opportunity to converge, and in particular, that current issues in motor skill learing may be given an overview and synthesis.

Over the last decade there have been significant changes with respect to the major lines of enquiry within the field of learning. Of these changes two trends in particular stand out as having had a potent impact upon the field (Estes, 1976). First, there has been a shift away from the study of learning *per se*, towards the related but independent construct of memory. Second, there has been considerable research interest in *what* is learned and *how* information is transformed and organized in memory, in contrast to the traditional concerns for the conditions that influence learning and retention. These changes in orientation have been stimulated in part by general developments in cognitive psychology which have been facilitated through advancements in the separate subareas of, for example, information processing, language development, and artificial intelligence.

Students of motor skills have not been oblivious to these changing orientations in learning. Indeed, Pew (1974a) has argued that the current *zeitgeist* in motor skills has switched its focus from the traditional 'product'-oriented issues to a concern for the 'processes' which determine the development and maintenance of skilled performance. While this claim as a generalization is undoubtedly premature, it is clear that there is a growing appreciation in motor skill learning of the cognitive approach. For example, we have seen the emergence of process-oriented theories of motor learning (Adams, 1971; Schmidt, 1975a) together with a considerable effort to understand the manner in which movement cues are coded and organized (cf. Stelmach, 1974b). Generally, however, advances in the process orientation to skill learning have been slow and patchy, not the least because there is still only a rather small group of active researchers in the skill-learning area.

This chapter attempts to reflect some of these changing orientations to skill learning through intertwining traditional and current approaches to both theoretical and practical issues. Unfortunately, synthesis of current trends to skill learning may be a little premature, because although the influx of new viewpoints to skill learning holds the potential of broadening and strengthening the theoretical base of empirical operations, it also has the effect of spreading rather thin the thrust of research effort on each particular issue. The result, as Gentile (1972) observed, is that the literature has taken on something of a supermarket quality in that it contains a sprinkling of papers on most issues but nothing of substance on any one particular issue. Many of the traditional issues in skill learning have disappeared from the current literature not because closure has been brought to these issues, but rather because of the faddish nature of skill-learning researchers who have moved quickly on to the in-vogue issues of the day.

The basic and traditional research issues in skill learning remain, however, even if the current interpretations or orientations for explanation are different (cf. Bilodeau, 1966; Newell, 1977). As with any chapter, boundaries for discussion need to be sought, particularly with a topic as wide ranging as skill learning. This chapter will focus on three comprehensive issues which have had, and continue to have, a significant place in both the theory and practice of skill learning. Initially, we will examine the role of information in skill learning, then we will tackle conditions of practice, and finally discussion will focus on the generalization of skill.

INFORMATION AND SKILL LEARNING

With reinforcement interpretations of skill learning in large part put to rest, the most pervasive theoretical and empirical issue over the last decade has been the role of information in skill learning. Although informational interpretations of knowledge of results (KR) and feedback have predominated (e.g. Annett, 1969; Newell, 1976c), the function of information in skill acquisition needs to be considered in a much broader framework than in terms of the mere description of the complete action. Information processing is a continuous operation for the performer, and as such prevails prior to and during action, not only on completion of the act.

In this section we examine recent interpretations of the various avenues through which information is, or can be, made available in the acquisition of skill. Throughout, it needs to be borne in mind that the usefulness of the various modes of presenting information to the performer will vary with both person, task, and situational variables. For example, the age of the performer may determine the rate of information processing (e.g. Connolly, 1970; Welford, 1961), together with the appropriateness of each specific mode of presentation. The long-held assumption that information-processing capacity increases with maturational development has, however, been challenged recently by some provocative findings of Chi (1978) in favour of strategic and knowledge factors as principal causes of developmental differences in performance. Similarly, the nature of the skill, whether open–closed, gross–fine, discrete–serial–continuous, etc. together with its complexity (Hayes and Marteniuk, 1976), may well interact with the skill level of the performer in determining the rate of information processing and the difficulty of the task. Further, the environment itself affords certain task-relevant information such that the information processing of the performer should not be considered in isolation of the performance cues available naturally in the surround. To facilitate discourse, we will consider the role of information in skill learning in three sections: namely prior to, during, and on completion of action, although as we shall see, the effectiveness of information processing in any one section is highly dependent upon the manner in which information is available throughout the skill-learning process.

Information Prior to Action

Before attempting any action, the performer ideally should have knowledge about the goal of the act, together with some understanding of the way(s) through which the goal can be accomplished. In short, the performer needs to know what to do and how to do it. For the adult there are many occasions where one has a clear idea of the goal of the task despite the fact that one has not participated in it previously. Usually, this knowledge comes from observing other performers, either live or on television, or of course it could come through reading or hearing descriptions of the task. Less likely is an understanding of the possible ways through which the goal of the task can be achieved, although this knowledge or some hypotheses about it, may also be known *a priori* by the learner. The key issue for the teacher or trainer is identifying and implementing the most effective means of supplementing the learner's knowledge about the goal and appropriate movement pattern(s). For the theorist of skill learning, the central questions are why certain modes of information presentation are more effective than others and how subjects process task-relevant information at different stages of the skill-learning process.

The most popular methods for conveying information about the goal and appropriate action sequence(s) are verbal instructions and demonstrations. Unfortunately, despite the prevalence of their use, no systematic attempts have been conducted to examine the influence of instructions in skill learning since

Holding's (1965) discussion of the topic. Instructions, appropriately conveyed, can obviously be useful in transmitting information relative to the goal of the act, but their effect in relaying information about the action pattern to perform, is less clear. Usually the instructor focuses on kinematic descriptions of the action, although this can be supplemented with statements about principles or the strategy underlying the potentially appropriate action pattern. Judd's (1908) early example of transfer of principles in the throwing of darts to targets under different water levels suggested that practice was necessary to realize fully the potential of utilizing knowledge relevant to certain principles of action. More recent studies have found immediate performance benefits from a knowledge of action principles (e.g. Hendrickson and Schroeder, 1941), suggesting an intricate relationship between knowing and doing.

Arguably, knowledge of movement invariants or rules of action are not particularly useful to either the performer or teacher. Pew (1974b) for example, has shown that subjects failed to recognize a repeated stimulus pattern in tracking, even though they continued to reduce tracking error over sixteen days of practice. One is also reminded of Polanyi's (1958) classic illustration of tacit knowledge, whereby the proficient cyclist has no idea of the rule to be observed in bicycle riding and it would seem that knowledge of it would probably not help one either learn or teach the skill. This, indeed, may be the case where the rule to be observed is complex and rather abstract, but in skills where the action rule is meaningful and translatable into a representative action, knowledge of it, together with relevant feedback, could be beneficial. Unfortunately, there have been few attempts to understand the rule(s) or structure(s) of action plans (Newell, 1978).

To instil in the learner the nature of the goal of the act together with the action(s) that will accomplish the desired outcome, instructors inevitably resort to demonstration to supplement instructions. This is accomplished either live by the instructor, or a filmed demonstration may be given with or without augmenting instructions. Despite the frequency with which demonstrations are employed in the variety of skill-learning contexts our understanding of this process is very poor. In fact, if we were to judge the effectiveness of demonstrations by the empirical literature one would wonder why they are generally accepted as facilitating the skill-learning process at all. Even in sports, where a visual-aid market flourishes, there is little or no evidence that film loops facilitate the learning of skills.

The earliest systematic investigation into the effects of demonstrations on skill learning was by Sheffield (1961; Sheffield and Maccoby, 1961). The focus of this research was the impact of what Sheffield called utilization and demonstration variables on the effectiveness of filmed demonstrations in skill learning. Utilization variables referred to the way in which demonstrations interacted with practice conditions, whereas demonstration variables referred to features of the filmed demonstration itself, such as camera angle, speed of the film, etc. The general finding of Sheffield's work was that the effectiveness of the filmed demonstration varied with the nature of the task. In complex assembly-type tasks, films facilitated the acquisition process and seemed most effective when the action sequence could be broken up into its natural components, whereas in other tasks no clear trends emerged for task-utilization variables. As might be expected the research on demonstration variables suggested that the film should reflect the action as veridically as possible to the observer.

There has been little theoretical or empirical advancement with respect to the use of filmed demonstrations in motor skill learning since the work of Sheffield in the early 1960s. Sheffield's notions about symbolic representation have been incorporated to some degree into Bandura's (1969) stimulus-contiguity social learning model, but the acquisition of social behaviours reflects a rather different theoretical process than that of motor skill learning. Research has continued on task-utilization variables, for example the spacing of the demonstration over practice trials and the influence of the social status of the demonstrator. Considered overall, however, the empirical work in the area has been sporadic and lacked the guiding arm of theory relevant to skill acquisition.

Presumably, the fundamental reason for employing demonstrations is to transmit information to the learner about the goal of the act and the potential movement pattern(s) that may be generated to complete the act. Intuitively, films would seem particularly useful for conveying information about how to perform the skill because instructions alone would seem sufficient to convey information about the goal of the act. Why then is the research equivocal regarding the usefulness of film loops and demonstrations in general? A major reason is the failure of many researchers to realize that information, like beauty, is in the eye of the beholder. That is, unless the film reduces uncertainty on the part of the learner no information is being conveyed. Many film-loop studies seem to forget the knowledge state of the performer and assume that information load is a function of the task alone. As was indicated earlier, many learners of skills, particularly sports, know what to do and how to do it, through, for example, television, rendering the film-loop or demonstration by the trainer or coach somewhat redundant.

Additional problems with film-loop studies fall under Sheffield's banner of task-utilization variables. In many skill-learning situations the film loop is shown in a separate room and some considerable time and distance from the site of ultimate performance so that the information conveyed might be forgotten through decay or interference by the time the performer attempts to put into practice this newly gained knowledge. The time gap between demonstration and practice can be reduced through a live demonstration by the instructor, but this can raise other problems such as an imperfect demonstration and so on. An additional confounding factor in assessing the impact of films is that after the first performance trial, KR is usually available to the learner. KR can be such a potent variable as to provide, within a few trials, all the information necessary for the performer to generate an appropriate action plan. This would seem to be particularly true in open skills where the movement pattern is a means to an end and not the goal of the task. Thus, even when information conveyed by demonstration can be put into practice the benefits may only be fleeting and exist for the initial trials of practice.

In complete contrast is the situation where the learner cannot put into practice the information conveyed by the demonstration, for example the circumstance where the response strategy employed in the demonstration is just too difficult for the learner to generate without considerable practice. Here the learner may attempt the strategy demonstrated (i.e. show the right form or movement pattern), but as a consequence, produce a resonse outcome which is very poor, and certainly of lower performance than if he had employed an alternative strategy (see Martens, Burwitz, and Zuckerman, 1976, Exp. 2). Presumably with sufficient practice, the subject would be able to produce a higher performance outcome from the strategy demonstrated than the alternative strategy which produces immediate performance gains but holds limited long-term potential as an effective response strategy. Getting the learner to understand this knowledge–action conflict and the long-term benefits to be derived from learning the appropriate strategy can be a difficult task for the instructor.

Recent interpretations of demonstrations explain the benefits to be derived under an information-processing label, but overall this merely seems to provide a theoretical umbrella under which the empirical work can be respectably conducted. There have been no systematic attempts to assess the interaction of the state of the performer and the nature of the task and its impact upon the information transmitted by either a film-loop or live demonstration. As a result, the information-processing notion remains a rather global and nebulous explanation for the effectiveness of both demonstrations and instructions in motor skill learning.

Instead of viewing a competent performer either live or on film, an alternative and as yet largely unexplored approach, is the provision of the kinematic details of the action. That is, the learner might be given the displacement, velocity or acceleration curves of the key joint-linkages of an expert performing the skill. Whether this approach would be more useful with beginners or the advanced learner is an empirical question. Extrapolating from the progression–regression hypothesis of the tracking literature (Fuchs, 1962), it may be that as one gets more skilful, the learner would benefit from a 'demonstration' of a higher derivative of the movement-displacement pattern. If research shows kinematic or even kinetic modes of demonstration to be useful in skill acquisition, it would seem sensible to link this method of prescription with a compatible form of description. This is an issue to which we will return.

Although demonstration usually implies visual demonstration, there are additional means under the banner of demonstration through which information about the act can be conveyed. For example, sounds are sometimes generated as a natural consequence of action or they can be artificially imposed. Recently, it has been shown that audition can be an effective medium to 'demonstrate' the response (Newell, 1976b). In these experiments, subjects heard the sound associated with the linear timing response to be learned, prior to being asked to perform the criterion response under no-KR conditions. In rapid responses, subjects showed a systematic reduction of movement error over the initial no-KR trials presumably because they could evaluate the sound produced from the movement generated against the auditory reference established in the 'demonstration'. The principle under examination was analogous to that in some bird-song experiments (e.g. Nottebohm, 1970) and the Suzuki method of training for the violin (Suzuki, 1969) which suggests the use of an auditory reference mechanism in the development of bird song and violin skills, respectively. It could be, therefore, that in certain tasks, auditory demonstrations of the criterion action provide a useful addition or alternative to the traditional visual means of conveying information.

A form of prescribing action that is unknown, in large part, outside of the dance and physical education world is that of movement notation. In essence, movement notation is analogous to a musical score in that it details through symbols the movements to be generated in an action sequence. The movement score specifies not only the limbs and actions but also the timing and weighting of each movement. Given the range of movements that humans can generate, the various forms of movement language (e.g. Eshkol and Wachmann, 1958; Laban, 1956) are rather extensive and, like other languages, require a considerable outlay of time and energy to learn the vocabulary and syntax. Attempts have been made to computerize the movement-notation systems, but whether this approach to detailing the goal of an act, together with the appropriate movements, becomes as useful and popular as the musical score, remains to be seen. Movement notation also can be used as a form of description, or feedback, but its principal contribution seems to be as a method of prescription in movement art forms.

There are then, a variety of means through which action information can be supplemented to those cues naturally available in the environment. The various forms of prescription outlined seem to have various degrees of influence in facilitating the acquision of skill. The current focus has been the informational properties of prescriptions for action, but this does not preclude their potential in motivating the learner to achieve in the learning situation. Furthermore, the various forms of prescription outlined tend to impose upon the learner a set approach to the acquisition of the skill rather than allowing the learner to establish for himself the most appropriate response strategy. Structured forms of prescription are probably appropriate when the goal is the training of a high level of competence in a specific task. On the other hand, a discovery approach to skill learning might be appropriate in educational settings because it seems more likely to develop an active thinking learner to the task, and as a consequence, facilitates the acquisition of related skills (Singer, 1977).

Information During Action

Actions may be modified while they are unfolding and this error detection-correction process is the cornerstone of the closed-loop principle. The facility with which this process occurs is a function of a variety of factors, including the degree of practice of the performer, richness of feedback available, and the nature of the task. Sometimes the feedback which is intrinsic to the task is rather restricted (e.g. no visual feedback and limited proprioceptive feedback) making the pick-up of relevant information difficult. As an aid to the learner, this action information feedback (Miller, 1953) may be supplemented by augmenting the feedback intrinsically available from the task, or by forcibly guiding the learner's action by some means (see Armstrong, 1970a and Holding, 1970 for comprehensive reviews of augmented feedback and manual guidance procedures).

Early work on augmented feedback was stimulated by the desire to improve military skills such as tracking and gunnery operations. The outcome, however, of a series of studies in the 1950s on the pedestal sight manipulation test (PSMT) and pursuit rotor proved to be somewhat equivocal. The performance benefits of augmented feedback did not in many cases remain when the augmented feedback was withdrawn, suggesting that it is a performance rather than a learning variable. This is particularly the case when the task itself holds few intrinsic cues because it tends to focus the learner's attention towards the augmented information. And when the intrinsic proprioceptive cues are augmented this has the confounding effect of requiring a change by the subject in the output commands necessary to produce a similar response.

It may be that visual augmented feedback is useful to skill learning if the visual cues bear a one-to-one correspondence to the appropriate dimension of the movement itself (Fox and Levy, 1969). Additionally, more persistent effects of augmented feedback may be found in the later stages of learning when the performer can evaluate more accurately the intrinsic feedback provided through proprioception, but this again is an empirical issue. Considered overall, then, the augmented feedback studies are rather inconclusive, and there has been little research effort of late to alleviate this state of affairs.

In contrast, manual guidance in the form of forced response or physical restriction (Holding, 1965) shows some benefits to the learner in the early stages of learning. In the forced response mode, the learner is passively moved through the appropriate spatial–temporal details of the action by the instructor or by a machine. In the physical restriction mode, the learner actively generates the response, but the action is constrained spatially by certain physical properties of the equipment (e.g. a golf-o-tron machine) or by the instructor. One of the early benefits seen to be derived from guided practice is that it reduces the likelihood of the learner making errors with the result being that he is less likely to develop bad habits.

The benefits of errorless learning, however, vary according to the kind of error being made by the learner. Manual guidance would seem to be most appropriate for the reduction of selection errors (Schmidt, 1976b), that is, the generation of fundamentally inappropriate actions to the task at hand. Continued practice of inappropriate actions could ultimately impede the rate and level of skill acquisition, although knowledge of potentially, inappropriate actions might be useful (e.g. Von Wright, 1957). In contrast, execution errors, that is, variations in the spatial–temporal details of fundamentally appropriate actions, may not be detrimental to skill acquisition and may even be beneficial. There are some suggestions that experiencing a range of responses in the 'ball-park' of the task criterion may facilitate both the retention of the skill (Williams and Rodney, 1978) and the transfer to a similar task (Newell and Shapiro, 1976). These findings are consistent with the theorizing of the schema point of view (Pew, 1974a; Schmidt, 1975a), but the variable and errorless practice findings to date are far from clear cut, making generalizations even from the same task problematic.

There are further practical and theoretical problems with the guided practice techniques. Some skills, via their very nature, are just impossible for the instructor to guide the learner in any reasonable fashion. Even in situations where it is possible for the instructor to approximate the spatial and temporal features of ideal actions, recent laboratory work on active and passive movements suggests there might be some limitations to this approach (see Kelso and Wallace, 1978). A major conceptual problem with the forced response mode is that it eliminates the learner's need to select an appropriate response and as a consequence, the control aspects associated with the output of the movement. This has been a criticism of the guidance techniques used in physical therapy with cerebral palsied patients (Jones, 1974b).

Thus, theoretically and practically, the benefits of guided practice appear to depend on the nature of the task and the mode of response guidance. In general, it seems that what one gains on the roundabouts (proprioceptive feedback of an ideal response) one can potentially lose on the swings (efferent command of an ideal response). Only further research will determine where the weight of evidence actually lies for guided practice. It would seem, however, that judicious use of manual guidance in practice could realize the potential benefits without accruing the penalties which are likely to occur with long-term passive responding.

Information After Action

Knowledge about the outcome of action has long been known to be a most potent variable in learning, whether it be in the form of a score representing actual performance or the error of performance against the task criterion. The contemporary theoretical interpretation of its effect is that KR provides information to the performer who evaluates this in relation to the goal of the task and the movement produced as a precursor to actively deciding on the degree to which the action plan need be modified on succeeding trials (e.g. Adams, 1971). Although the informational role of KR is the prevailing theoretical perspective, direct empirical support for this position is not as strong as advocates of this approach indicate. This situation is probably due, however, to poor experimentation rather than any apparent shortcomings of the informational interpretations of KR.

The KR literature is immense and given a recent review of this work (Newell, 1976c), a full treatment here would be redundant. The major focus of this section, therefore, will be on potential future avenues of KR research, together with alternative forms of providing response outcome information to the skill learner. It should go without saying that information about response outcome is essential to skill learning, although the relative effectiveness of the various means of presenting KR is still not clear.

In a number of respects KR theory has developed beyond its point of useful application to the practical setting in that many of the findings hold more academic than operational relevance. For example, despite the fact that delaying KR within the intertrial interval has not been found detrimentally to affect rate of acquisition, it would seem wise in practice to provide KR as soon after completion of the response as possible. This would maximize the learner's ability to associate the response outcome information (KR) with the input and output factors of the response produced, and also increase the possibility of reducing the length of the interresponse interval, which itself seems to influence the rate of acquisition (Denny, Allard, Hall, and Rokeach, 1960). The degree of precision of KR should be sufficiently detailed without being too demanding of the learner and there should be a sufficient post-KR period to allow the learner time to complete information-processing activities (Rogers, 1974). And even though the performer can estimate his performance without KR after considerable practice (e.g. Newell, 1974), it would be advisable to ensure that outcome information is always presented to the learner, and/or that the learner always seeks to ascertain the outcome of the response if this information is available directly from the environment.

Most of the research that has generated the foregoing principles of KR has taken place on unidimensional tasks, such as linear positioning and timing responses, which facilitate the potency of a single score as the form of outcome information. The effectiveness of KR in its traditional mode would presumably be reduced in a response where the characteristics of the action goal are defined on more than one dimension. In this situation, the KR from each dimension can be condensed to form a single score or it can be reported individually to the performer. In the former case, the concoction of an amalgamated dimension tends to make the task more difficult, while in the latter approach subjects tend to improve on the dimension (e.g. speed versus spatial accuracy) emphasized by the instructions (e.g. Malina and Rarick, 1968). A full examination of the effectiveness of KR on multidimensional tasks would clearly be appropriate.

In addition to knowledge of response outcome, the learner may also benefit from knowledge of the movement pattern which produced the outcome, or knowledge of performance, as Gentile (1972) has labelled it. This type of response information would seem particularly useful in those closed skills where the generation of a specific kinematic pattern is essential. This information is usually conveyed through a verbal description of features of the action by the trainer, although technological advances have made videotape feedback a popular teaching tool in a variety of skill-learning situations.

As with demonstration film loops, the evidence in support of the effectiveness of videotape as a medium for feedback is not as compelling as manufacturers of these items might advocate (see Rothstein and Arnold, 1977 for a review). Again, the lack of empirical support for the benefits of modern technology is probably due to poor experimentation combined with an overemphasis conceptually of the role of videotape in skill learning, rather than any shortcomings in its practical utility. Through providing a veridical picture of the action just completed, the videotape replay probably conveys too much information to the learner. This information overload can be compounded by indiscriminate verbal assessment of the performance by the instructor. The videotape replay should not be taken as a substitute for verbal instructions but a supplement to the key points that need to be conveyed to the learner. It is possible that videotape is more useful with the experienced performer because information about the appropriate gross adjustments to action may be conveyed as easily from verbal instructions as they are from a videotape picture. In addition, the use of videotape in group instructional settings probably leads to an overly long intertrial interval for each individual learner.

Videotape as a form of feedback may be more beneficial when it is shown in conjunction with a taped demonstration by an expert performer, than when it is shown alone. By the same token, this combined use of prescription and description may maximize the potential of film loops as a form of demonstration. Some evidence for this can be found in the fact that the majority of demonstration loop studies which have facilitated the learning of sports skills have also employed videotape feedback (Brumbach, 1969). With the development of split screen techniques it should be possible to refine the effectiveness of videotape feedback when used in conjunction with filmed demonstration of the criterion act.

Rather than present the picture of the whole body to the learner, it might be useful in certain tasks to present the time displacement, velocity, or acceleration curves of the key limb segments. In a variety of skills, performers produce rather consistent action patterns and kinematic information may prove to be a most potent form of feedback. A recent experiment by Hatze (1976) illustrates the potential of this approach. Subjects were required to lift their right leg through a 20° range in the sagittal plane as rapidly as possible. On the initial trials, subjects received traditional KR in the form of time to complete the movement. This produced the usual performance gains and after a number of trials the reduction of movement time showed signs of asymptoting. At this point, Hatze showed the subjects, on completion of the act, a time–velocity curve of their performance in conjunction with a derived time–velocity model of their optimum performance. As Figure 47 shows, this produced an immediate reduction in movement time, and performance approached the projected optimum for the subject. This example clearly highlights the potential of kinematic information as a form of knowledge of performance, although whether it would be more effective at one stage of learning than another is unclear. Certainly, from the Hatze study kinematic information seems beneficial in tuning the action at the more advanced stages of practice. Whether kinematic or kinetic information would be the most useful form of feedback would probably be determined by the relative contribution of these parameters to the demands of the act.

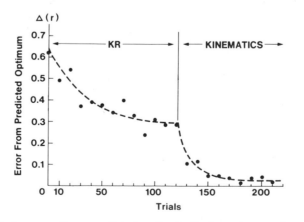

Figure 47. Timing error from predicted optimum for leg raise as a function of form of feedback over trials. Adapted from Hatze (1976). Reproduced by permission of the author and the University Park Press, Baltimore (©1976).

The link between prescription and description in skill learning can also be made through the medium of sound. Sometimes tasks generate sounds naturally or sound can be augmented to provide additional feedback about the response. When the response is rapid this information can probably be used only to adjust the response of the following trial since it is often completed before error detection and correction procedures can be completed. Recently, Lionvale (quoted in Keele and Summers, 1976) employed this technique in teaching subjects to cast in fly-fishing. A potentiometer on the fishing-pole recorded its time displacement pattern and the pitch of a sound generator varied directly according to the displacement pattern. No statistically significant benefits were shown in this study, but the trends suggest that augmented auditory feedback could be beneficial in learning certain tasks. In essence, sound was another medium of presenting kinematic information, but it has the disadvantage that subjects will eventually have to be weaned from the augmented sound.

In summary a few major themes for practice emerge from the foregoing discussion of the various forms of presenting information to the skill learner. First, that methods of prescription should be used in conjunction with forms of description. In other words, knowledge of what to do and how to do it should be linked with what happened and how it happened, and vice versa. Intuitively, this link will be ideal if it is made in the same language, e.g. kinematics to kinematics, outcome scores to outcome scores, etc. although what is the most useful form of prescription and description for the different stages of skill acquisition in the various types of skills remains to be determined. Second, in making this link, we need to investigate more thoroughly the complete range of media available through which to convey information to the learner. The failure unequivocally to demonstrate the benefits to be derived from modern information-conveying apparatus seems to be due to shortcomings in the experimental investigations rather than the potential of the equipment. In short, we need to apply to all forms of information presentation the same industry that we have applied to KR research, but hopefully with greater ingenuity. As the empirical examination becomes more precise it is to be hoped that this broader attack on the role of information in skill learning will have its influence both on the practice of skill learning and the development of theorizing about this process.

From a theoretical perspective, the information-processing framework is often appealed to on the basis that it possesses the appropriate network of explanatory constructs for the effect of the foregoing variables on skill learning. And yet ironically, the information-processing approach, both conceptually and empirically, has had little or no concern for skill learning or, more generally, for the development of adaptive behaviour. As a consequence, the few attempts to relate information-processing notions to skill learning appear to monitor changes in the way the performer organizes and executes responses that are concomitants of learning, rather than an examination of the fundamental contribution to the determinants of skill acquisition (e.g. Welford, 1968). Adams' (1971) theory has made a start in going beyond this by incorporating a learning perspective into the information-processing framework, but in doing so it has operated at rather superficial level from a mental events perspective. Some such compromise seems essential, however, if we are to advance our knowledge of skill learning, because if we wait to understand the processing of information and the control of movement, as a prerequisite to introducing into our conceptual frameworks the process of learning, we are likely to wait a very long time indeed.

CONDITIONS OF PRACTICE

A good deal of the research in the preceding section on the role of information in skill learning was conducted in relatively sterile and artificial conditions. It seems that the drive for the control of experiments through internal validity has been achieved through compromises with respect to external or ecological validity. And yet, as any teacher or trainer will attest, the creation of an appropriate learning environment is essential to the effective learning and performance of motor skills. Obviously, a variety of factors converge to create the ideal conditions for learning skills. Unfortunately, contextual constraints to skill learning have rarely been considered, leaving the key issues, both theoretically and practically, the distribution and nature of the practice.

Distribution of Practice

Most of the research on conditions of practice for skill learning has focused on the spacing or distribution of practice either between or within sessions. Distribution of practice can have effects upon both the learning and performance of skills and it gained theoretical significance through its association with Hull's (1943) theoretical postulates of reactive and conditioned inhibition. During the 1940s and 1950s many distribution-of-practice studies were conducted on the pursuit rotor, and the general finding was that some degree of distributed practice was superior to massed practice. Since this time, empirical investigations of practice schedules have declined, and currently they are few and far between.

A significant factor in explaining the impact of distribution of practice relates to the definition of massed and distributed practice. If distributed practice refers to the situation when the time between trials is longer than the duration of the trial itself (Schmidt, 1975b), then only experiments utilizing continuous skills like the pursuit rotor pertain to the issue, because in discrete skills, the pauses between trials are inevitably longer than the trial itself, even under the most speed-stressed conditions. If, however, we reserve massing to relate to the compressing of more trials into a given time space in comparison to some longer intertrial interval condition, then massed versus distributed practice remains a general issue.

The majority of research has focused on the trial spacing within a session, rather than the duration or spacing of the practice sessions. Compressing trials within a session enables more practice and, although this can have the effect of depressing performance to some degree, this does not necessarily mean that learning is inhibited, as the demonstration of improved performance or reminiscence at the introduction of the next practice session often reveals. Massing the trials within a session is probably useful, therefore, as long as the introduction of fatigue or boredom does not lead to the continued production of an inappropriate action.

The distribution of practice sessions can be equally effective in influencing acquisition rate and have profound effects upon the time and energy required to train someone in a skill. A recent experiment by Baddeley and Longman (1978) illustrates both of these points. They trained post office workers on a typewriter keyboard which controlled a letter-sorting machine under four different practice sessions. There were one- and two-hour practice sessions conducted either once or twice per day. Figure 48 shows the rate of correct keystrokes for the four conditions. The beginning point of each curve represents the time taken to learn to touch type all the keys. The results show clear benefits for the one-hour per day group in both learning to touch type and subsequent typing performance. These benefits need to be considered in light of the fact that the actual length of training time was considerably longer for the one-hour per day group (almost three months) as opposed to the two-hour twice-day group (four weeks). The optimal practice distribution, therefore, will depend on the unique interaction of the time available to reach the performance criterion, together with the type of skill and the age and skill level of the performer. The explanation of these distribution of practice effects remains a significant issue for contemporary theoretical accounts of skill learning.

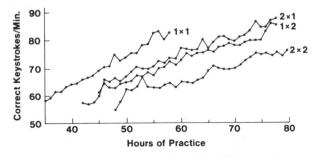

Figure 48. Rate of acquisition of typing skill as a function of training schedule. Adapted from Baddeley and Longman (1978) in the journal *Ergonomics*. Reproduced by permission of the authors and of Taylor & Francis Limited.

Whole and Part Methods of Learning

In the same way that practice sessions can be split into different phases, action patterns may also be subdivided into smaller components. These parts of the whole skill may be practised independently or in sequence with other parts of the skill to form two teaching techniques commonly known as the whole-part-whole and progressive stages methods, respectively. In the former method, individual parts of a skill are practised separately before being incorporated back into the total skill. In the latter method, the individual parts of the skill are separated and put back together again over practice sessions in some cumulative fashion until the total action is complete. Like a number of issues surrounding conditions of practice, generalizations regarding the practical utility of these techniques are not founded on strong evidence (see Holding, 1965 for that which is available) and theoretical interpretations of their effects are even more hazardous.

As a general rule, it would seem that, where possible, the skill should be practised in total. Thus, when the basic action sequence can be approached by the learner it should remain in contact for the practice sessions. When, however, the complexity of the action sequence is so demanding that even a basic approximation of it is beyond the scope of the learner, some breakdown of the skill into parts is probably inevitable and desirable. Many assembly or serial tasks can be partitioned conveniently into meaningful and fairly independent parts. Practice of isolated action components can be useful, although where the timing of the whole sequence is crucial, the refinement of each part would be inappropriate. In other words, part practice should only be long enough to master the fundamental action of that part.

Whether the progressive stages or whole-part-whole method is most appropriate for handling the break-up of skills will inevitably depend upon the make-up of the skill. Where the performance of one part is relatively independent of performance on another part, such as in a number of assembly serial-type tasks, the whole-part-whole procedure is probably most appropriate. When, however, performance of one part of a skill is in large part dependent upon the performance of a proceeding part(s), such as in gymnastic routines, the progressive stages procedure is probably most appropriate. These generalizations only represent guidelines, as the experience of the trainer will ultimately determine the most appropriate procedure for breaking down skills in the learning situation.

Mental Practice

A less obvious form of practice is that of mental practice where the performer mentally rehearses or imagines performance of the motor skill. A number of studies have shown benefits of mental practice, although as might be expected, it tends to be less effective than actual physical practice (Richardson, 1967a, b). The facilitatory effects of mental practice vary with the nature of the skill and the skill level of the performer.

A recent experiment by Minas (1978) sheds some light on both the practical benefits and the theoretical explanations for mental practice. Subjects were required to learn to throw balls of different weights and textures into a fixed sequence of target bins under different physical and mental practice conditions. The central result was that mental practice with feedback facilitated the learning of the appropriate sequence of action but did not improve the performance outcome of each individual throw. In other words, the learning of the symbolic component of the task was facilitated but not the actual production of the action. Mental practice then, could be a most useful aid in the initial stages of learning serial (e.g. typewriting) or sequential (e.g. gymnastic routines) skills, although physical practice is clearly required to refine the action sequence.

The explanations for the mediating effects of mental practice have revolved around two rather distinct hypotheses. One view, following Jacobson (1932), is that mental practice generates some degree of muscle activity in the appropriate muscle groups controlling the action and that this innervation facilitates subsequent overt performance. The contrasting view is that mental practice is the covert rehearsal of strategies or symbolic components of the task and it is this, as the Minas (1978) results suggest, that facilitates learning. This latter hypothesis is compatible with recent cognitive explanations of action and implies that the stronger the symbolic nature of the task the more likely mental practice is to facilitate learning. It is surprising that the move towards process-oriented explanations of motor learning has not yet revived empirical activity on the role of mental practice.

Other Practice Factors

As has already been indicated there are numerous factors which need to converge to maximize the conditions of practice for the learner. We have managed in this section to mention only the traditional concerns of practitioners and theorists. It should be apparent that there have been no major gains in our knowledge about conditions of practice since Holding's (1965) summary.

One final point needs to be made about practice conditions and our knowledge of the effect of various variables on acquisition, and that is the current trend of researchers to observe performance over very short practice periods. Pew's (1974b) recent long-term tracking study is a welcome and imaginative exception, but gone are the days when skill-learning sessions resembled long-term practice (e.g. Crossman, 1959; Seibel, 1963). Contemporary testing sessions can be characterized as one-shot operations with at best about 100 trials for each subject. While observation of this initial period of practice captures some of the major changes that occur with skill learning, it would be rather naïve to imagine that this is a sufficient period of observation on which to base any comprehensive theorizing. Clearly, the theoretical need for longer-term sampling of performance should have a stronger influence over operational pragmatism than it currently enjoys.

GENERALIZATION OF SKILL

If there was no link between knowing and doing, and no increment in knowledge with experience, the acquisition of even the basic skills necessary to survive in this world would be rather a tedious undertaking. Fortunately, by all accounts this is not the case. A cardinal principle of adaptive behaviour is that experience influences, and in some cases determines, the manner in which one learns new skills. The issue of skill generalization, and specifically the principles of transfer of training are, therefore, at the heart of learning theory *per se* and the educational process in general.

One cannot, however, invoke the concept of transfer without appealing to the related construct of retention. It is this dual theoretical focus, together with its obvious practical implications, which places generalization to the fore as an issue in motor skill learning. Modern theoretical notions on generalization had their origins at least as early as Thorndike's ideas of identical elements (Thorndike and Woodworth, 1901), while practical implications of generalization became more important as twentieth-century technological developments increased the range of skills that can be learned, together with the payoffs and penalties associated with their successful or unsuccessful execution. In the main, there have been two relatively independent theoretical approaches to the generalization of skill; a learning-theory approach which has its origins in the all-encompassing behavioural learning theories of the early twentieth century and, an individual-difference approach which emerged in the 1950s.

Learning Theory versus Individual Difference Approach

Traditionally, learning theory explanations for the transfer of skill have centred on the degree of similarity between tasks (e.g. Osgood, 1949). The principal dimensions on which similarity has been evaluated for transfer effects include: stimulus and response characteristics; task difficulty, and response strategy (for reviews of this task-characteristic approach, see Briggs, 1969; Holding, 1977). Unfortunately, many empirical tests of theorizing about transfer have been fraught with methodological problems such as design inadequacies and inappropriate or insensitive scoring systems. In addition, the results of transfer tests tend to vary according to the type of task investigated.

Nevertheless, the general view of transfer from the learning-theory perspective is that the more similar the response to tasks with the same or different stimulus the more likely positive transfer, while the more dissimilar the response to tasks with the same or similar stimulus, the more likely negative transfer. The empirical findings are not completely in accord with this generalization, particularly on the issue of negative transfer, which despite the face validity of its occurrence in our everyday activities, has been a phenomenon difficult to demonstrate in the laboratory setting.

In contrast to the learning-theory approach to transfer is the individual-difference approach (Fleishman, 1962; Henry, 1958), which indicates that skill is specific and not general. This view does not deny the transfer of elements of skills, but suggests that each skill has certain features which are peculiar to the task at hand and that these can be picked up only through practice in the task itself. Hence, repetition of an action can only improve performance relative to that respective act (Henry, 1958). Further, the artisan or sportsman can only transfer his skill to another task if he possesses the specific abilities required to perform that task. According to this view, therefore, the generalist or all-around performer, does not possess a general motor ability, but rather possesses many specific abilities which increase the probability that he will be competent in a broader range of acts.

The learning-theory and individual-difference viewpoints also differ in their experimental approach to the issue of skill generalization. The former rests its case on findings from the experimental manipulation of group means while the latter relies on the correlation of an individual's scores generated from each task investigated. Thus, one can observe transfer in the form of positive or negative shifts in mean group performance due to the effect of prior practice on another task, but this does not imply that a significant correlation (positive or negative) will result between an individual's performances on the tasks. In fact, all the evidence from the individual-differences approach indicates low correlations for an individual's performances across even the most similar of tasks (see Marteniuk, 1974), suggesting that skill is a specific and not general ability.

The distinction between the two approaches to transfer has been emphasized because at first glance the individual-difference viewpoint might appear to represent conflicting ideas and results to those derived from learning theory. On reflection it should be seen as complementing rather than contrasting the traditional approach to skill generalization. In essence, the individual-difference approach serves to remind us as to the limitations of inferences that can be advanced from group means in that individual performance predictions from prior task experience cannot be made with any degree of certainty.

Theoretical Issues in Transfer

With the general wane in interest of traditional issues in skill learning, skill generalization and transfer of training do not enjoy the same degree of theoretical and empirical activity that they once did. In fact, it is difficult to discern the prevailing theoretical viewpoint for transfer or skill generalization. In many respects, transfer of training still seems to have the notion of identical elements as its umbrella explanatory construct under which the operational focus is biased towards the similarity of task characteristics. The outcome of this development is that transfer is explained and predicted on an operational basis rather than on theorizing about the coding and storage of information about action. As there have been several recent reviews from the task-characteristics perspective this section will attempt to relate the findings from this approach to theoretical issues underlying the transfer of skill.

The only theoretical stimulant to issues in the transfer of skill this last decade has been as a consequence of the revival and application of notions of schemata to skill learning (Pew, 1974a; Schmidt, 1975a). Schema was a popular construct in British psychology during the first half of the twentieth century and was applied in a direct, although superficial manner to theorizing about action (Bartlett, 1932; Head, 1920). Overall, current theorizing about the role of schemata in skill learning is still far from sophisticated, but the intuitiveness of this view holds considerable appeal, and as a consequence it has generated a number of empirical examinations in the last few years.

An issue central to skill generalization which schema theory attempts to meet head-on is how we can produce what appears to be an infinite variety of actions from a finite action experience. In short, this is what Schmidt (1975a) has referred to as the novelty problem. The theoretical significance of this issue is most pertinent to open skills where the changing environmental contingencies modulate, or even drastically alter, the action generated from trial to trial. And, even when the kinematics of the action appear to be relatively consistent, one never merely repeats something old, as Bartlett (1932) observed in his now well-known reflections on the tennis stroke.

What, then, is the reference for action? Traditional associationistic arguments for some isomorphic representation of each movement or action do not account for the generative nature of skill. Even if they did, such views would create the additional problem of the infinite number of action representations that would be necessary to store in memory for the range of acts we have undertaken or will undertake in our life-span. Although this is largely a default argument, there being no evidence that that brain is not capable of this, it seems much more parsimonious to postulate an abstract representation of action. This approach intuitively accounts for the storage problem and provides a generative mode of representation for skill action.

Schemata are seen to be the abstract representations of actions. In Schmidt's (1975a) theory, practice develops the strength of the abstract representation of four fundamental response features: initial conditions, response specifications, outcome of actions, and the sensory consequences. The schemata relate to classes of actions and the abstract prototype stored in memory supplies the essential response invariants for each action within the action class. Presumably, as the action plan unfolds, it becomes more concrete through successive differentiations which supplies the added details peculiar to the evolving action. Schmidt (1975a) has proposed separate schemata for the processes of recall and recognition, although it seems intuitive and more parsimonious to propose a unitary schema, or constancy function, for both perception and action (Turvey, 1977).

A key prediction of schema theory is that the abstract representation of a class of actions becomes stronger the more variable the precise instances of it from previous actions. The operational implication of this is that practice which is variable will develop a schema which is more impervious to decay and more flexible or generative in production. Of course, response variability is a natural product of performance even at a single task criterion. What variable practice refers to here, therefore, is practice at a range of tasks or a single task with a variety of response criteria. The predictions about variable practice are significant for the acquisition of open skills in particular, owing to the greater demands on response innovation, and the fact that in some situations, such as ball games, the performer invariably has only one opportunity to perform each specific action. It seems ironic, therefore, that to date, tests of the schema variability of practice notion have all been conducted from the perspective of closed skills.

Unfortunately, we are no more certain of whether benefits accrue from variable practice than we were prior to the recent schema theories of skill learning. Most of the related experiments have compared transfer performance to a single criterion after original practice to either a range of task criteria or practice of a single criterion in the linear positioning or timing paradigms. Some evidence had emerged indicating that variable practice leads to better performance on transfer to a task criterion outside the range of initial practice (e.g. Newell and Shapiro, 1976), although the boundaries of response similarity within which the transfer effect occurs have yet to be determined. Variable performance also seems to lead to a more persistent performance on transfer to a task criterion in the absence of KR (e.g. Williams and Rodney, 1978). Although these findings and others are supportive of the schema position, none of the data are terribly convincing and it has to be concluded that the benefits of variable practice have yet to be unequivocally established. It has been suggested that schemata development might be more appropriately assessed in children than adults because the latter may already have formulated appropriate schemata for the task under examination (Schmidt, 1975a), but this remains a *post-hoc*, although intuitive argument.

The recent schema variability of practice experiments are operationally similar to the early pursuit rotor studies which varied the speed of the target to be tracked from original practice to transfer (e.g. Lordahl and Archer, 1958). In these studies, the metrical specifications for action differ between the originally learned task and the transfer task, but the structural prescription for action is fundamentally the same (Turvey, 1977). A structural prescription refers to the qualitative ratio of activity in the muscles which tends to be invariant with respect to absolute activity level. A metrical prescription, on the other hand, specifies the absolute activity level of the muscle groups involved and in essence provides detail to the general structural prescription specified. These are two prescriptions which are seen to determine the details of the motor program or coordinative structure defining the action of the muscle groups which are constrained to act as a unit (Turvey, Shaw, and Mace, 1978).

The distinction between structural and metrical prescriptions has some potentially interesting repercussions for skill generalization. For instance, does generalization only occur across metrical prescriptions within a given structural prescription, or is transfer possible across structural prescriptions? A related question is whether, and to what extent, these prescriptions for action are generalizable across different coordinative structures. Of course, these questions can be begged by raising the more fundamental question of when does a metrical adjustment require a structural adjustment? (Newell, 1978.) The theoretical distinction as outlined, however, provides a sound basis upon which to begin unpacking the definition of an action class which is at the heart of understanding the boundaries of schemata rules and abstractions for response generalization.

The recent schema studies which have manipulated the distance, time, or force characteristics of the same action essentially reflect changes in the metrical prescriptions. On this basis, it seems that positive transfer occurs to metrical changes of a common structural description (e.g. Newell and Shapiro, 1976), although as indicated previously, the metrical boundaries of this positive transfer are not clear. As a consequence, it is difficult to define different structural prescriptions and hence the assessment of whether transfer occurs across structural prescriptions. Certainly, the bilateral transfer studies suggest that positive transfer may be made across different coordinative structures when they have the same structural prescription (e.g. Cook, 1934). Negative transfer, on the other hand, seems to occur principally to a structural change, particularly when the time constraints of response initiation are demanding (Adams, 1954). Thus, when a similar stimulus requires a structural change in the action of a group of muscles constrained to act as a unit around a joint, such as in reversing the roles of the agonist and antagonist muscle groups, the potential for negative transfer occurs.

The rhythm or timing between discrete actions also seems to be a fundamental aspect of the structural prescription. Rhythmicity within sequential actions can be difficult to acquire, and once it is, it can be equally difficult to eliminate, as many musicians will attest. A good example of this negative transfer is to be found in a study by Summers (1975) on the role of timing in motor programs (see also Summers, Chapter 3, this volume).

Subjects initially learned a set temporal rhythm between key presses of 500–100–100 msec or 500–500–100 msec. Once the tempo was acquired subjects were then asked to forget the learned timing sequence and depress the keys as rapidly as possible. The transfer results demonstrated that the original tempo learned still remained to a considerable degree between the key presses, whereas it was not evident in the groups which had constant or random temporal intervals in original training. Thus, a study which was originally conceived to investigate the role of timing in motor programs turns out to be one of the best demonstrations of negative transfer in the contemporary literature.

As an aside, it is worth noting that the negative transfer demonstrated in Summers's experiment is revealed from rather precise measurement of the skill. The use of inappropriate or insensitive recording measures may have masked laboratory incidents of negative transfer that we all know occur in our everyday activities. In addition, it might, as Holding (1976) has suggested, be better to focus on errors resulting from movement rather than level of performance. Sometimes errors in selection of the appropriate action do not lead to noticeable decrements in performance, while sometimes they do. Only measurements sensitive to these considerations will isolate subtle incidents of negative transfer when overall performance appears unaffected.

While the preceding brief discussion of the representation of actions may be seen as preliminary, esoteric, and somewhat divorced from the practical problems of skill transfer it will be advances theoretically, rather than operationally through a task-oriented approach, which will have more general and lasting influence on our understanding of skill generalization. Although, of course, this does not deny the significance of the latter role, particularly when theory is not very well developed. The invariants of action abstracted in the form of schemata clearly need to be elucidated further, as do the boundaries of structural and metrical prescriptions. As developments occur here, ramifications for transfer in the practical situation will likely emerge and possibly provide a more comprehensive line of thinking than that currently in existence through the task-oriented approach.

SUMMARY

Perhaps the one central theme to emerge from the foregoing discussion of skill learning is that the field is in a state of flux. The last decade has witnessed the inflow of ideas and experimental approaches outside the traditions of learning theory, but as we have seen, the potential of these has yet to be fully realized. Indeed, it seems unlikely that the new conceptual ideas on skill learning will ever develop if the empirical examination of theoretical issues in the acquisition of skill continues its steady decline. In the same vein, we seem no closer to resolving the traditional applied problems of skill learning. There have, of course, been some isolated studies reported in the literature which attempt to deal with problems peculiar to a specific task in a certain contextual setting, but again investigations of such issues as conditions of practice and the variables which facilitate the learning process are few and far between. In short, closure has not even been approached on any of the traditional theoretical or applied problems of skill learning.

ACKNOWLEDGEMENTS

I would like to thank D. H. Holding, J. D. Schendel, and H. N. Zelaznik for their helpful comments on earlier drafts of this chapter.

Human Skills
Edited by D. Holding
© 1981 John Wiley & Sons Ltd.

Chapter 10

Handicap and Human Skill

Clark A. Shingledecker

A common characteristic of all skills is that they require coordinated physical and mental activity involving the entire chain of sensory, perceptual, and motor mechanisms which underlie behaviour. When this organization is disrupted by some factor affecting one or more components of the chain, skilled performance deteriorates. Temporary decrements in human performance can often be attributed to task demands which exceed the inherently limited ablities of the individual, or to the actions of physiological, situational, and environmental stressors which can effectively reduce his capacities even further. In general, the acute breakdown of skill produced by these conditions can be alleviated or avoided by reducing the mental workload placed on the human operator or by protecting him from the stressor. Other deficits which arise from more enduring changes in the individual result in a chronic breakdown of skill. One example of this class of problems is the deterioration of skill caused by impairments of sensory and central capacities which accompany the normal ageing process. The reader interested in the effects of ageing on skill will want to consult the book by Dr. Sanford which appears elsewhere in this series.

CHRONIC HANDICAPS

This chapter is concerned with the chronic breakdown of skill which occurs when a receptor or effector component of the chain of mechanisms responsible for skill is lost or impaired because of disease, injury, or congenital malformation. Owing to the permanent nature of sensory and motor disability and to the fundamental way in which these conditions affect the organization of skill, many research efforts for the handicapped are aimed at the development of equipment which will permit them to acquire skill by some alternate means. During the last thirty years the rapid development of technological capability has engendered the production of a number of prosthetic and orthotic devices intended to replace human limbs or to restore their function, as well as a large catalogue of sensory aids to supplement or replace defective visual and auditory systems. Unfortunately, sophisticated engineering solutions have often failed to alleviate the deficits in skill suffered by the handicapped because the design of sensory and motor devices has been undertaken with insufficient consideration of the human user, particularly with regard to the central mechanisms which underlie skill.

A general model of human performance has emerged from skills research which provides a framework for the understanding of the mechanisms of skill and which can serve as a useful conceptual approach to the problem of re-establishing skills that have been impaired by sensory or motor disability. Derived from theories of communication and control engineering, this model draws an analogy between the human operator and an information-processing device that receives inputs from the environment through a number of sensory channels and transmits information back to the environment via a group of effector mechanisms. Intervening between these input and output processes are a set of hypothesized mechanisms which select input channels, store and transform information, choose responses, provide commands for the motor systems, and feed back response information.

Two general features of this model illustrate important characteristics of human skill. First, like other processing devices, the human has a finite capacity to transmit information so that the speed and accuracy with which information is gathered, processed, and converted to an appropriate response is determined by the limited abilities of the sensory, perceptual, and motor processes that are responsible for skill. A second characteristic shared by human and inanimate information processors is that when taken together the individual processing mechanisms form an interdependent system. In the case of the human operator this implies that an alteration in a sensory or motor component may have considerable effects on the demands placed upon the central mechanisms and on the activities they will be required to perform.

These basic characteristics of the human as an information processor indicate that the structure and function of the mechanisms of skill should be given primary consideration when attempting to design motor or sensory aids. Unfortunately, surprisingly little is known about the way in which the human nervous sytem accomplishes the universal yet complex behaviours such as locomotion, manual control, speech perception, and reading which are most seriously affected by handicap. Nevertheless, in recent years there have been increasing numbers of attempts to apply contemporary theory and knowledge of the general nature of skill to the understanding of sensory-motor disability and to the development of suitable prostheses and aids. This growing emphasis on the fundamental bases of skill has been especially apparent in work on motor impairment.

MOTOR IMPAIRMENT

Persons impaired in motor function through the absence or loss of an extremity by amputation or by dysfunction of the motor system as a result of spinal injury, stroke, cerebral palsy, or neuromuscular diseases such as poliomyelitis represent one of the largest proportions of the severely handicapped population. Until approximately thirty years ago these individuals had only a few body-powered aids available to them. These were both heavy and difficult to use and were severely limited in their ability to restore the complex level of functioning observed in the normal arm or leg. The recent introduction of externally powered devices has radically improved the potential utility of prosthetic equipment, but it also presented problems which call into play a number of skills variables. The initial difficulty that beset designers of powered devices concerned methods by which the equipment could be controlled by the disabled individual.

Motor Control

The human upper extremity is a complex system of joints with a total of thirteen degrees of freedom of movement. Combined with the hand, this system permits rapid and accurate acquisition of objects in space and an almost infinite number of patterns of movement. Biomechanical research has shown that only two of the thirteen degrees of freedom could be eliminated without seriously affecting the performance of everyday manual skills (Hancock, 1970). With the complexity and versatility of this system in mind it is not difficult to recognize that attempting to devise a method by which an amputee could control a prosthesis which even remotely approximates the capabilities of an intact arm is an exceedingly daunting task.

In order to eliminate the awkward body movements used to control conventional prostheses, two alternate types of control have been devised for externally powered devices. One of these utilizes small movements in residual muscles to operate pull switches. Although sites for the location of these controllers are limited, this problem is often solved by using only a few muscle sites with multiple-position switches. The second type of control used for powered prostheses and orthoses is an electromyographic (EMG) potential derived from minute voluntary contractions of residual muscles. These signals are detected by transducers mounted on the surface of the skin and are amplified to act as control sources for electric motors. The EMG control of prostheses was originally suggested by Reiter (1948) and was first employed for this use in an artificial hand displayed by Russian scientists at the 1958 World Fair in Belgium.

Both switch and EMG methods of control have been used in systems to provide artificial hand prehension for below-elbow amputees, and in more complex devices which replace elbow flexion and extension, humoral rotation, and sometimes limited shoulder movement. Comparisons of amputee performance with the two types of control have favoured the EMG method. Carlson (1970) and Peizer, Wright, Pirello, and Mason (1970) found that in tests of grasping objects and placing them in various positions, subjects with powered hand prostheses were able to perform more quickly and with fewer compression errors with EMG control. However, the latter study also showed that the advantage of EMG control diminishes with higher level amputations where prosthetic hand and elbow components must be used together. Nevertheless, in all cases patients preferred EMG control because of reduced fatigue and because the EMG control was less ambiguous than the switch control.

The control problems that arise with pull switches were delineated by Peizer, Wright, and Pirello (1970) in an evaluation of an electric elbow and mechanical hand prosthesis in which a single pull switch operated by shoulder flexion was used to control movement. Shoulder excursion of $\frac{1}{8}$ inch with minimal force produced elbow extension while further movement of $\frac{1}{8}$ inch produced elbow flexion. Continued pull bottomed the switch and operated the terminal device. Even after extensive training with the prosthesis, subjects found it difficult to avoid inadvertent operation and experienced considerable difficulty in hunting for control positions. Control discrimination with the EMG method appears to be better because a larger number of spatially separated sites can be used to provide signals. Rae and Cockrell (1971) found that many locations on upper trunk muscles were relatively free of unwanted EMG activity in the absence of voluntary contraction and were able to generate sufficiently high potential differences to provide control signals for an upper extremity prosthesis.

The discriminability of controls is not the only factor influencing the ease with which prosthetic controls can be used. Regardless of the method of control, as the number of functions to be performed by the artificial limb increases, the total number of control locations or levels of control at a single site also increases. Since the speed at which humans can respond is reduced as the number of equiprobable alternative responses increases (Hick, 1952), it is apparent that a multiple degree of freedom device with many control functions will tax the information-processing abilities of its user. This problem of multiple controls and the limited channel capacity of human operators was well illustrated in a review of a prosthesis which required the amputee to operate a system of nine control switches which had to be selected, actuated, and turned off individually (Groth and Lyman, 1961). Evaluation revealed that the decision load placed upon the user was excessive and that, even in simple tasks, performance was degraded.

Two general methods of EMG control have been used with externally powered prostheses. One of these, known as digital or on-off control, produces movement of the device in a single direction and at a fixed rate when EMG activity exceeds a preset threshold value. In the second type of EMG control system individual muscle sites control different functions and the amplitude of activity at each site determines the force or rate of movement in a proportional manner (Staros and Peizer, 1972). Although a number of digital, proportional, and hybrid systems have been devised, little research has been conducted to determine an optimal system for the non-manual control of prostheses.

The skills literature provides fairly precise information regarding the capacities needed for manual control. An important source of limitation to motor output is the rate at which responses can be made. A number of studies indicate that the human motor system is capable of producing a maximum of ten responses per second (Fitts and Posner, 1967, p. 78). In most cases, however, this upper limit is not reached because the human operator is acting in a closed-loop fashion. That is, he is using information about the results of his ongoing actions to modify his responses. This activity introduces computational time lags and reduces response rate. It appears that this lag is inherent to the human information-processing system and perhaps that a basic refractoriness or intermittency is responsible for the single channel nature of skilled performance (Welford, 1968). Estimates derived from reaction-time studies (Hick and Bates, 1950) and from measurements of movement corrections in tracking performance (Hill, Gray, and Ellson, 1947) indicate that, for manual control, humans can generate approximately one control change per 0.33 second. In terms of information theoretical measures, this indicates that the rate of information transmission from the manual system is 3.03 ($\log_2 n$) bits/second.

In comparison to the muscles of the intact arm and hand, the muscle sites available for the control of prostheses on the trunk and upper body would be expected to have coarser control and a lower capacity to transmit information because they are innervated by larger motor units and because these muscles have less practice in the development of fine motor skill. This was confirmed by Lucaccini, Freedy, Rey, and Lyman (1967) in a study which showed that the upper trunk muscles display an average increase in reaction time of 0.25 second over the manual case. Assuming a proportional increase in the rate of generating control signals, this indicates that the maximum rate of information transfer for non-manual control is reduced to 1.72 bits/second. On the basis of these data Freedy, Lucaccini, and Lyman (1967) reviewed the information requirements of a number of possible control systems which could be used to operate an arm prosthesis capable of movement in three dimensions that would mimic the movement characteristics of the intact arm when transporting an object between two points in space. Analysis of position, velocity, and frequency controls indicated that the information demands for simultaneously controlling the three dimensions of movement in a trajectory similar to that observed in a normal arm would be excessive. The only system which appeared to fall within the capacity of non-manual control was a form of digital control that would require the user to discriminate three levels of muscle contraction. Using this system the operator would merely initiate an action and then supply a signal for deceleration at the appropriate time during the movement.

The actual rate at which information can be transferred in manual control is strongly influenced by the compatibility of the code which relates the way in which the control device is actuated to the observed results of the control change. Numerous studies of control–display compatability have indicated that wide variations in the rate of information transmission can be produced with alternate stimulus–response codes (Fitts and Posner, 1967, pp. 104–106). Although prosthesis designers have often stressed the importance of 'naturalness' in device control, very little research appears to have been done to investigate compatibility in non-manual control. One obvious form of compatibility relevant to prosthesis control has been demonstrated in the reported naturalness of artificial hands controlled by residual muscles in the forearm that would normally control extension and flexion (Reswick, 1972). However, even in cases where this type of compatibility cannot be achieved, it is likely that the investigation of alternate spatial configurations for control transducers and of various kinds of voluntary activity that can be generated at single sites will reveal differences in the ease with which handicapped persons can generate signals to control different dimensions of movement.

Sensory Feedback

The provision of precise analogue control by EMG methods has been an elusive goal for the designers of prosthetic equipment. One factor which has contributed to the difficulty of this task has been that only a rough neurological relationship exists between EMG activity and voluntary muscle contractions (Mason, 1970). Devising a technique to overcome the inherent imprecision of the control signals that can be produced by the user of a prosthesis is a problem which demands some consideration of the manner in which the intact limb is normally controlled by the nervous system.

Two general theories have been put forward to describe the way in which movement control is achieved. In its strictest form, the outflow model suggests that proprioception plays no important role in motor control (Summers, Chapter 3, this volume). Practice establishes learned patterns of motor impulses in the brain which are 'tuned' by experience to permit accurate movement. The inflow model (Moray, Chapter 2, this volume) states that feedback from both exteroceptors and interoceptors is necessary and that it is the constant interplay between motor output and feedback information about the state of a limb which permits the performance of skilled movements. While neither model can account for all of the observed phenomena, in most cases the weight of the experimental evidence supports the inflow view. The profound effects of delay and spatial displacement of visual feedback conclusively demonstrate the necessity of this information in many skilled tasks (Smith, McCrary, and Smith, 1963). Although methodological problems limit the investigation of the role of kinaesthetic feedback in movement control, numerous studies which have either partially blocked kinaesthetic cues or have enhanced them by the manipulation of control constants illustrate its importance (see Trumbo and Noble, 1973).

Intact human limbs are richly supplied with muscle, tendon, and joint receptors as well as pressure receptors in the skin which can provide precise feedback information about the position of the limb in space and direct data on resistance and strain. Although all prosthetic devices severely degrade these sources of feedback, the problem is exacerbated in modern externally powered equipment. Earlier body-powered devices were cumbersome but they contributed direct feedback about the state of the prosthesis by muscle tension and force cues available to the amputee's stump. In contrast, electrically powered devices transmit little or no information back to the user and he is forced to rely upon vision and noise cues from the motor in order to function in a closed-loop fashion. Although these cues are useful, they cannot be monitored at a low level of awareness. Furthermore, complete reliance on vision and audition for feedback renders these systems unavailable for the reception of other task information. Finally, evidence which suggests that motor learning depends upon a shift from exteroceptive visual control to kinaesthetic control indicates that the absence of proprioceptive feedback will retard normal skill development (Fleishman and Rich, 1963).

In view of the psysiological and behavioural evidence for the importance of feedback in normal motor control, designers have endeavoured to include substitute sensory feedback systems in powered prostheses and orthoses. These systems sense grasp force, hand position, or elbow position and display this information to the skin either by electrical stimulation or mechanical vibration. A number of experimenters have reported improvement in prosthesis control when hand position and grasp force feedback were supplied. Rohland (1975) compared patients' ability to reproduce reference pressures on a pinch meter when using an artificial hand with and without supplementary electrocutaneous feedback from a pressure detector located in the fingertips. Errors with feedback were shown to be ten times smaller than without. Nevertheless, these errors remained two to three times larger than those produced by the users with their intact hands. Prior and Lyman (1975) provided grasp force and hand position feedback to amputees' stumps via a single concentric electrode. Force was represented by the width of a constant-current pulse while pulse repetition rate was used to code position. Tests of patients' abilities to duplicate forces up to 15 pounds and to identify blocks of different sizes without vision indicated that the addition of electrocutaneous feedback substantially improved performance with the prosthesis. However, average performance with supplementary feedback was only 40 to 60 per cent as accurate as that obtained with the intact hand.

Just as compatibility is an important factor in control selection, a powerful factor influencing the effectiveness of artificial feedback in prostheses appears to be the coding of the information displayed to the user. An attempt at producing high physiological compatibility has involved the direct stimulation of afferent nerves which normally carry feedback from the intact limb. Clippinger, Avery, and Titus (1974) implanted several below-elbow amputees with stimulators located on the medial nerve of the forearm. A strain gauge in the terminal device was used to transform prehension force to an electrical signal which stimulated the nerve. Although no objective performance data were collected with the device, nearly all subjects reported perceptions of hand movement when the frequency of stimulation was varied.

Very little research exists to indicate which of the many possible forms of tactile display is most compatible for the presentation of feedback about limb position and movement. However, some inferences can be drawn from research on attempts to develop tactile communication codes. Geldard (1961) reviewed a number of possible codes for vibratory stimulation and found that the high spatial resolution of the skin made locus a desirable coding dimension. In addition, he indicated that cutaneous movement was a promising secondary dimension for tactile communication because of its vividness. Alles (1970) described a tactile display which incorporated both spatial and motion cues. The system made use of the phantom sensation which appears when two spatially separated vibrators mounted on the skin are modulated appropriately. The phantom position or motion of the vibratory display across a line segment of skin can be controlled by modulating the time of onset of the vibrators, their phase relationships, or their amplitudes. Alles found that the display was easily learned and that unimpaired subjects could use the system to match display position to elbow position with a high degree of precision. Results from a simple tracking task indicated that the display also provided accurate information on the direction and rate of movement. Mann and Reimers (1970) applied this system to the problem of presenting position feedback in an EMG-controlled elbow. Results from tasks in which unilateral amputees were required to match the position of the prosthetic elbow to that of their intact elbow and to locate targets on a panel without direct visual information revealed a 50 per cent reduction in errors over the no-feedback condition and performance equal to, or better than, that achieved with a cable-operated elbow.

Motor Programs and Adaptive Aiding

Figure 49 illustrates some of the artificial motor control and feedback connections which would have to be incorporated in a prosthesis that would provide the level of functioning observed in an intact arm. Although designers have begun to develop systems which approach this degress of sophistication, the user of such complex devices often finds that he must devote his full attentional capacity to the execution of a simple reaching movement. Hence, reducing the mental effort demands of operating an artificial limb is one of the greatest problems facing rehabilitation researchers (Wilson, 1965). It is likely that this problem will be solved in part by the continued development of more compatible control methods and displays for the provision of supplementary feedback. However, it is improbable that these improvements alone will be sufficient to permit disabled persons to achieve independent movement control at the low levels of effort experienced by non-handicapped individuals. In

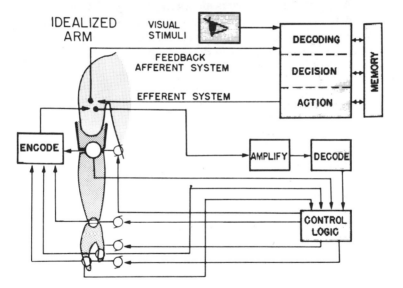

Figure 49. Idealized schematic representation of the machine and human components of a completely controlled arm prosthesis system. From *Bulletin of Prosthetics Research* (*BPR*, **10–8**, 1967).

addition to the fact that compatibility is neurologically 'hard wired' in to the sensory–motor system, other features of the unimpaired human information processor act to reduce the decision load of motor control. One way in which this is accomplished is by the presence of internal feedback and reflex loops in the peripheral nervous system (Geldard, 1972). These feedback loops regulate reflex responses and play an important role in the control of ongoing voluntary responses without the involvement of central processing mechanisms. A number of prosthetic devices have been designed to mimic this feature of the motor system. Pressure, force, position, and velocity have been automatically detected and used to stabilize the action of a prosthesis or to control secondary aspects of operation which would otherwise demand a portion of the user's limited channel capacity. An example of the use of this sort of local feedback is a system in which the incipient slip of an object held by an amputee in a prosthetic hand is detected and used to control prehension force. As the object begins to slip a signal is fed back to cause the hand to grip tighter until the slip is prevented (Reswick, 1972).

Another reason why the unimpaired individual can engage in motor behaviour while economizing on conscious effort is that his central processing mechanisms seem to be able to operate in both a closed-loop and an automatic mode. Highly overlearned movement patterns may be stored as motor programs which can be run off on command (see Summer, Chapter 3, this volume). This automatization reduces decision load by eliminating the need to continuously monitor feedback. The design of aiding subsystems to assume a portion of the decision and control load of a prosthesis is essentially an attempt to provide the handicapped user with an artificial motor program. Freedy, Hull, and Lyman (1971) introduced an experimental computer control system for a prosthesis which worked to unburden the operator by 'learning' through observation of tasks being done and progressively assuming the majority of the responsibility for movement control. The system, based on a maximum-likelihood decision principle, is able to learn a variety of tasks and can predict unexperienced patterns of movement from rules extracted from redundant portions of a task. In the pilot evaluation a three-degree-of-freedom arm was controlled by EMG transducers mounted on the chest, abdomen, and shoulders of a normal subject. Two tasks requiring the movement of sixteen small blocks to specified locations on a table-top were chosen to test the performance of the aiding system. Measures of the system's effectiveness in unburdening the operator are shown in Figure 50. Following approximately two hours' practice on similar tasks, performance on the experimental tasks was recorded in terms of the proportion of trial time during which the machine and the user were in control of the arm. It is interesting to note that by substituting the labels *automatic control* and *feedback control* for *computer time* and *override time* in the figure, these data present a feasible theoretical picture of the development of a motor program in normal skill acquisition.

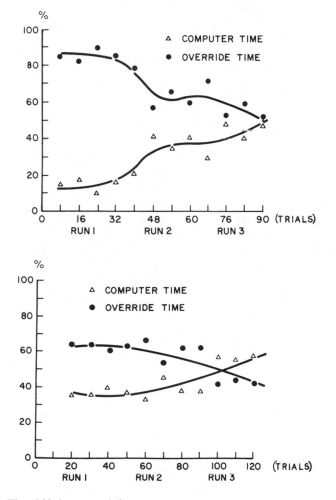

Figure 50. The shift in control from the operator to the computer as a function of of practice on two manipulative tasks using an adaptive aiding system for artificial limb control. From Freedy, Hull, and Lyman (1971). Reproduced by permission of the authors, who worked under a VA contract with UCLA (Dr. J. Lyman, principal investigator), and the *Bulletin of Prosthesics Research*.

SENSORY IMPAIRMENT

A mystique has always tended to surround popular conceptions of persons suffering from the major sensory disorders of deafness and blindness which is not apparent in attitudes concerning individuals with severe motor impairments. This view has been expressed in a number of ways, but in all cases it is characterized by the belief that the handicapped person somehow possesses supernatural or at least extraordinary sensory and cognitive abilities that automatically accrue to him by the loss of visual or auditory input. For the most part, these notions seem to be based on casual observations of successful deaf and blind persons who appear to be engaging in skilled behaviours thought to be impossible without the rich supply of information provided by the visual or auditory senses. Although the more bizarre beliefs that the blind and the deaf are endowed with powers of extra-sensory perception or with especially high intelligence have been discounted on rational grounds, the general idea continues to survive in the form of the sensory compensation hypothesis.

Briefly stated, this hypothesis suggests that the deprivation of visual or auditory sensation produces a biological enhancement of the powers of residual sensory systems. Unfortunately, the experimental evidence has failed to confirm the hypothesis. In direct comparisons, the thresholds of sensitivity and powers of discrimination of the tactile and auditory senses of the blind have been shown to be equivalent to, and possibly even poorer than, those of the unimpaired population (Axelrod, 1959; Rice, 1970). At the neurophysio-logical level, Russian researchers cited by McDaniel (1969) have presented evidence which indicates that the blind display reduced cortical excitability and disinhibition of subcortical structures in comparison to sighted subjects. Myklebust (1964) showed that a similar *negative* compensation may occur with deafness. Because persons with sensory deficits do not automatically acquire abilities which permit them to engage in skills normally served by audition or vision, considerable effort has been directed towards the development of efficient methods of employing alternative sensory systems. The following sections of this chapter discuss the profound effects of auditory and visual impairment on human performance and examine the skills variables which contribute to the success of attempts to restore skill by the application of sensory aids.

Deafness

Auditory impairment is one of the least obvious yet most prevalent physical handicaps. In the United States alone it has been estimated that 8.5. million people have a significant degree of hearing loss and that there are over 900,000 people who cannot perceive speech without the use of some form of sensory aid (Levitt and Nye, 1971). Deafness is a broad term which encompasses a variety of hearing disorders. The most common symptom of most of these auditory impairments is an absolute loss of sensitivity of hearing either in specific frequency ranges or across the entire audible spectrum. However, additional deficits often include various forms of distortion of the acoustic signal, an abnormal growth of loudness with increases in signal amplitude, and the perception of buzzing or ringing in the ears.

Although audition plays an important background monitoring role in a number of skills, the overwhelming significance of language skill in nearly all aspects of human behaviour has prompted rehabilitation researchers to focus the bulk of their attention on the improvement of speech perception in hearing impaired persons. As in many perceptual–motor skills, the communication of ideas and concepts between individuals requires the use of a code. The listener's task is to decode the stream of sound waves produced by the speaker into the units of a language code and then to interpret the meaning which the speaker has intended to convey. The complexity of the listener's task is magnified by the fact that there is no simple relationship between the phonemes, or basic units of spoken language, and the speech sounds which impinge upon the ear. The acoustic cues for successive phonemes are intermixed in the speech stream to such an extent that definable segments of sound do not correspond to segments at the phoneme level.

Despite its intricacy, the speech code is the most universal, efficient, and compatible code yet devised for the communication of ideas. Speech can be followed at rates as high as 400 words per minute (Orr, Friedman, and Williams, 1965). In addition, the perception of speech is highly resistant to disruption so that with normal hearing meaningful speech can often be recognized when embedded in noise of a greater intensity than the speech wave itself, when the speech signal is curtailed by filtering out its high- or low-frequency components, when it is distorted by various methods, and even when up to 50 per cent of an utterance is deleted by time sampling (Denes and Pinson, 1963).

If information was conveyed in speech only by the analysis of the cues present in the acoustic signal received by the ear, the speed and accuracy of listening skills would be very poor indeed. Fortunately, the inherent limitations of the listener are circumvented by the fact that speech is perceived by the use of multiple cues. The speech signal itself contains multiple acoustic cues for the recognition of individual phonemes so that not all of the signal needs to be received for adequate comprehension. More importantly, a large part of the perception of speech is given by the knowledge of what the incoming signal *probably* is rather than by an exhaustive analysis of the stimulus itself. This knowledge is derived from a number of sources. In normal discourse the listener quickly builds up expectations about what is being conveyed by the speaker from the general speech situation and the context of the message. Furthermore, the listener normally has a detailed knowledge of the structure of the language in which the speaker has coded his message. Prior to receiving any signal the listener knows both the range of permissible phonemic units of the language and the rules which determine how these units can be combined to form words. Likewise, his knowledge of the grammar and syntax of the language restricts the way in which these words can be combined to form phrases and sentences. The multiple acoustic cues present in the speech signal added to those provided by the knowledge of language and those derived from the context of the speaker's message allow the listener to predict the content of connected speech quite accurately. In fact, the combined cues are far in excess of what is actually needed for the recognition of speech. However, it is this redundancy itself which permits the perception of speech at remarkable rates and under extremely variable listening conditions.

The congenitally deaf person has the primary disadvantage of being at least partially unable to make use of the basic structure of language to facilitate speech perception. Even when hearing loss is partial the fact that these persons often have a deficient knowledge of the statistical, syntactic, and semantic properties of the language code limits their ability to anticipate the form and content of speech. Although the individual whose hearing loss occurs after he has acquired language skills is able to use the structure of the code, the redundancy of the speech stream is reduced because his impairment reduces the amount of relevant stimulation that he receives. Consequently, whether he relies on his residual hearing or the minimal cues available through lip reading, the deaf individual is less likely to extract all of the information from the speech signal. This effect is cumulative so that the deaf person's uncertainty about contemporaneous input is raised even further by his inadequate knowledge of the situational information normally derived from preceding discourse. Finally, since the hearing-impaired person must recognize speech on the basis of degraded sensory evidence, a large part of his limited processing capacity must be devoted to retaining information in short-term memory while it receives more complete analysis than would be otherwise necessary. In combination with the other factors this extra processing severely reduces the spare capacity that the deaf person has available to deal with the information currently arriving in the speech signal.

The most common approach to the problem has been to make use of residual hearing whenever possible. The conventional hearing aid is designed to overcome a loss in auditory sensitivity by linear amplification of the speech signal. Although this procedure seems to be simple enough, the choice of suitable levels of amplification for different frequency ranges is often quite difficult to make. For example, it is often found that the best speech perception is obtained when the greatest amount of amplification is provided for frequency regions where threshold elevation is least (Levitt and Nye, 1971). Furthermore, even when sufficient residual hearing appears to be available, simple amplification does not always result in an adequate improvement in speech perception.

In cases of profound hearing loss, methods must be devised to present speech information to alternate sensory modalitites. Visual displays of speech have existed for a number of years with the most common type consisting of some form of graphic array. These devices may indicate the presence of certain aspects of the acoustic signal such as the position of vowel sounds or certain high-frequency consonants, or they may present a picture of the entire frequency spectrum of the speech wave on a television screen (see Levitt and Nye, 1971, Chapter 3). Although these devices appear to be useful as speech-training aids for the congenitally deaf, complex spectrographic representations are of little use for the perception of connected speech in real time. The eye excels at perceiving static spatial displays, but tends to be unable to distinguish events occurring in rapid succession. Because of this it is not surprising that vision has difficulty in dealing with a complex graphic display designed for interpretation by repeated scanning when it continuously changes with the rapidly varying speech signal (Sherrick and Cholewiak, 1977).

Although complex visual displays have proven to be of limited value, it is clear that vision is capable of acting as an input channel for speech. Lip-reading is a skill acquired by many deaf individuals. Messages conveyed by lip-reading constitute an optical language encoded in the changing shape of the mouth and relative positions of the teeth, tongue, lips, and jaw which accompany the production of speech. The speech-reader's task is complicated by the fact that only about one-third of the forty-odd meaningful sounds of spoken language are visible, even to the careful observer. As a result, accurate lip-reading requires an extensive use of contextual and structural cues which can lead to an excessive processing load for the deaf individual (Pauls, 1964).

In order to reduce the effort of speech-reading, Upton (1968) developed a device mounted in a spectacle frame which presents additional speech information via a seven-segment LED display projected on the speaker's face by virtual imagery. The signal processor of the device selects aspects of the speech signal which are not easily derived from the observation of the articulatory movements of the speaker and displays each feature as a flash of light from one of the LED segments. Tests of the aid indicate that dividing visual attention between the speaker's lips and the rapidly flashing display is a difficult perceptual task in itself. However, after extended training with one deaf subject, lip-reading scores were improved by 19 per cent when the aid was used (Gengel, 1977). Furthermore, the subject reported that communication was easier and more relaxed with the aid. Thus, although evidence for the efficiency of the Upton aid is meagre, it appears that this device may reduce the processing demands of lip-reading by increasing the redundancy of the incoming signal.

Any display designed to use vision to present speech to the deaf individual has the primary disadvantage of occupying a sensory channel which is important to the execution of numerous skills often performed in conjunction with speech perception. An alternate sensory substitute that does not suffer from this disadvantage is the tactile sense. The possibility of speech communication by touch has been an appealing notion to researchers because the skin shares some psychophysical properties with audition, including sensitivity to vibration and the ability to resolve temporal sequences of events. Unfortunately, over fifty years of research on this problem has failed to produce a method of presenting speech information to the skin by means of vibratory display. Although a number of approaches have appeared promising in early work with limited test materials, none have been able to produce acceptable recognition of connected discourse.

One of the most obvious reasons why the development of tactile displays of speech has proved to be an extremely difficult task is that in comparison to audition the cutaneous sense is much more restricted in terms of vibratory sensitivity and power of discrimination. Although the range of frequencies over which the skin can respond is quite large, the absolute threshold of vibratory sensitivity rises sharply above 1000 Hz (Bekesy, 1959) and the skin's ability to discriminate frequencies deteriorates rapidly above 200 Hz (Goff, 1967). It has also been shown that the skin responds more slowly than the ear (Bekesy, 1959) and that in order to discriminate two successive events it requires an interval at least five times longer than does the ear (Gescheider, 1970). In an attempt to bypass these temporal limitations some researchers have coded the speech signal in a spatial form using devices based on the vocoder principle (Dudley, 1939). Vocoders divide the frequency spectrum of speech into a number of channels by means of a set of band-pass filters. The output of each channel is a voltage proportional to the amount of acoustic energy fed into it. This apparatus has been used to drive a set of spatially separated vibrators at a frequency perceptible by the skin.

A variety of tactile vocoders have been developed which differ in the selection of pass bands and the number of channels into which the frequency spectrum is coded. However, none of the devices have proven to be adequate for more than learning simple discriminations among a restricted set of speech sounds. A limiting factor in the use of tactile vocoders has been the masking phenomenon which tends to occur when multiple skin loci are vibrated simultaneously. In their study with a ten-channel vocoder which stimulated each of the fingers of both hands, Pickett and Pickett (1963) found that simultaneous masking often prevented subjects from identifying speech sounds specified by vibrations on several fingers. Thus, problems of spatial discrimination must be added to the list of psychophysical limitations of the skin as an input channel for speech.

A second hypothesis which has been forwarded to explain the failure of both tactile and visual displays for speech is that speech perception is biologically tied to the auditory system. Liberman, Cooper, Shankweiler, and Studdert-Kennedy (1968), argued that the auditory channel contains a special mechanism for decoding phonemes from the complexly intermingled acoustic cues present in the speech wave, and that no such decoder is available to the other senses. Although this notion has had much influence on theoretical conceptions of speech perception, its practical validity is placed in doubt by considerable evidence that deaf–blind persons trained in the Tadoma method are able to perceive connected speech tactually by placing their hands on the face and neck of a speaker (Alcorn, 1945; Reed, Durlach, Braida, Norton, and Schultz, 1977).

Kirman (1973) has suggested that the explanation both for the success of the natural tactile–kinaesthetic display used by the deaf–blind and for the failure of artificial tactile displays of speech is that they differ in their ability to permit the skin to extract larger linguistic units from the speech stream. Kirman contended that techniques which seek to preserve the individual perceptual identities of the tactually coded elements by separating them spatially and temporally inevitably lead to slow communication rates because they reduce the probability that the skin will be able to organize the stimulus patterns produced by the speech wave into words and sentences. This argument indicates that a useful tactile display of speech would have to make use of aspects of tactile perception which facilitate the integration of information into meaningful perceptual entities.

A display which may satisfy this condition presents spatially coded information which temporally unfolds across the surface of the skin. Research on the cutaneous display of letters (Bliss and Linvill, 1967) and geometric forms (Bach-y-Rita, 1967) by matrices of vibrators has shown that when these stimuli are scanned so that they appear to move across the skin, identification is superior to the situation where the entire spatial pattern is presented statically. Kirman proposed that the phenomenon of tactile apparent movement could be used to provide the spatio-temporal framework for the perceptual integration of speech in the same way that the successive movements of the jaw and lips and the continuous variation of perceived laryngeal vibrations permit the perception of speech by the Tadoma method. Such an organizing framework could be achieved by using dynamic tactile patterns to represent such things as the continuous movement of formant resonances over time produced by changes in place of articulation during speech, or the continuous change in the amplitude envelope of the acoustic signal which reflects the segmentation of speech into syllables and patterns of stress.

Although a device incorporating these features has not yet been tested, the issues raised by Kirman (1973) indicate that the solution to the problem of developing compatible techniques of sensory substitution to restore receptive speech skill in the deaf will require a more complete understanding, both of the way in which information is transmitted by speech and of the methods of coding and display which make the best use of the abilities of different sensory channels to integrate information into meaningful perceptual units.

Blindness

Vision's primacy among the human senses and its central role in the execution of the vast majority of skills makes blindness potentially one of the most handicapping conditions that can be experienced. Reasonable estimates can be made of the prevalence of blindness in Western countries from statistics which have shown that in the United States at least 1.7 million people suffer from severe visual impairment, and that over 40 per cent of these people cannot read print or use vision to guide themselves during foot travel in the environment (Mann, 1974). The importance of these basic skills of reading and mobility to the rehabilitation of the blind cannot be underestimated. The blind individual who does not have access to the printed word or who is unable to travel independently is often relegated to a life-style characterized by passive reliance on others. In contrast, the visually impaired person who does acquire adequate reading and mobility skills enjoys a high degree of personal freedom and is able to pursue educational and vocational goals which otherwise would be unavailable to him.

The development of standardized non-visual alternatives for print began in France in the late eighteenth century with the introduction of the first embossed tactile codes. The earliest of these codes consisted of raised print letter shapes. Many simplified analogue alphabets were created to improve the legibility of individual characters, but by the late nineteenth century most of these printing systems were superseded by Louis Braille's punctiform code. Braille slowly gained universal acceptance as a substitute for print, partially because it appeared to be simpler to read, but primarily because it could be both read and written by the blind with comparative ease.

In modern Braille the elements of printed language are coded as tangible characters composed of one to six raised dots arranged within a matrix of two columns and three rows. The most commonly used Braille system, known as Grade 2 Braille, contains 263 elements assigned to the 63 possible characters. In addition to the 24 letters of the alphabet, Braille characters for numbers and contractions of certain letter groups are formed from the remaining 39 patterns and through the use of adjacent characters to modify the meaning of individual cells.

Despite its long history of acceptance and use by the blind, Braille is by no means an ideal substitute for visually presented print. The reading rates attained by the majority of Braille readers are disappointingly slower than those of sighted print readers. Numerous studies have shown that typical average Braille reading speeds range between 70 and 90 w.p.m., depending on the experience of the reader and the difficulty of the test materials (e.g. Meyers, Ethington, and Ashcroft, 1958). Print is normally read by the sighted at rates four to five times faster than this.

One of the more obvious factors that may limit the rate of information transfer by the Braille code is its low redundancy. Failure to perceive any of the dots in a character or to identify accurately the position of dot patterns in equivocal characters often leads to confusions among Braille letters. In contrast, Kolers (1969) has shown that most print types are highly redundant so that the reader need not perceive an entire letter shape to identify it correctly.

A second problem with the Braille code that has emerged from the important series of studies by Nolan and Kederis (1969) is that the visual print and tactual Braille reading processes differ in a very basic way. Although both experienced print and Braille readers are able to use their knowledge of the statistical constraints and grammar of written language as well as general context to identify the content of a passage, the unit of recognition for the Braille reader is much smaller than that of the print reader. Recognition times for whole words printed in Braille are longer than the sum of the recognition times for the individual letters which comprise the word. This result is in complete contrast to the comparable findings for print reading and indicates that most Braille readers do not perceive whole words from the flow of dots which pass beneath the finger. Instead, larger linguistic units must be tediously constructed from an exhaustive analysis of individual Braille cells. This mode of perception is time consuming and forces the reader to retain the information acquired from individual characters in his limited-capacity short-term memory while further evidence is collected to identify a word. As a consequence, both the speed and accuracy of reading are likely to be impaired. Taenzer (1970) presented evidence in support of this explanation of the difficulties of Braille reading by showing that when sighted readers are forced to perceive printed letters individually, reading rates similar to those of blind Braille readers are obtained.

In addition to low reading speeds Braille has the disadvantage of providing only indirect access to print. Transcribers, in recent years aided by computers, must be employed to perform the translation, and this process inevitably limits the availability of Braille reading material. The purpose of direct translating reading aids is to provide the blind with immediate access to print. These devices detect the light reflected from a page and present the reader with an auditory or tactual analogue of the patterns produced by printed letters. The Optophone provides an auditory display of the contours of a line of print as a probe consisting of a single vertical line of photodetectors is passed across individual letters (Coffey, 1963). The display is designed so that the presence of letter strokes in the beam of any of the detectors is coded as a unique tone. When the probe is scanned across a line of print, the output of the Optophone is an intricate series of tonal patterns which uniquely specify individual letters.

Although several years of research have been invested in the development of the Optophone and other similar devices, only a small number of users have been able to achieve any measurable success at interpreting this sort of display.

Considering the fact that the Optophone reader is required to make exceedingly difficult discriminations among complex tonal patterns it is not surprising that even after extended training reading rates rarely exceed 12 w.p.m.

The Optacon (Bliss and Linvill, 1967; Bliss, Katcher, Rodgers, and Shepard, 1970) is a direct-translation device which displays a tactile image of printed text to the reader's fingertip. Although raised print letters were rejected in favour of Braille long before the development of the Optacon, the results of a considerable amount of psychophysical research were taken into account in the design of this aid in order to maximize the accuracy and rate of reading tactually displayed letter forms. The Optacon display is a densely packed array of 144 vibrating points. Experiments conducted by the inventory showed that optimal legibility was obtained at a vibratory frequency of 200 Hz and when 24 stimulating points were used to represent the vertical dimension of print letters. Bliss and his colleagues also found that reading speed was higher when letters flowed beneath the fingertip in a manner similar to the display presented by a Times Square lighted sign than when they were presented statically. The six-column width of the display was chosen on the basis of data which indicated that reading rate was enhanced when entire letters were within the field of view of the reader's fingertip. Typical reading rates with the Optacon in its present form range from 12 to 50 w.p.m. after extended training and practice. However, speeds equivalent to those attained by average Braille readers have been observed in some cases.

The relatively slow reading rates normally achieved with Braille and available direct-translation aids could be attributed to a basic inability of the cutaneous and auditory senses to make efficient use of the sort of information presented by written language. However, the apparent efficiency of these input channels for numerous other skills makes it more likely that the problem stems from a failure to display print information to the skin or the ear in an optimal manner. As a result of poor compatability the Braille, Optaphone, or Optacon user is forced to engage in extra intellectual activities which place an excessive load on his limited information-processing system. Since the task of gathering raw information from the display involved such a high degree of mental effort, the blind reader has little spare capacity to devote to the cognitive activities such as inference, anticipation, and interpretation which are the hallmark of the skilled print reader.

The problem of sensory substitution for reading skill is simplified by the fact that a compatible alternative for the print code is readily available in the speech code. Records and tapes presenting oral versions of written text have been used successfully by the blind for a number of years. Like Braille, such recordings provide only indirect access to print. However, recent developments in optical character recognition and speech synthesis indicate that direct print-to-speech translation devices will become available in the near future. Although the reading rates of blind persons almost certainly will be improved by the design of such devices, it is doubtful that they will prove to be an ideal substitute for visual print reading. As Foulke (1969) has noted, one of the important features of skilled print reading is the reader's ability to control the rate of input and to scan selectively the textual material according to his informational needs. Because of the purely temporal nature of the speech display, the person who reads by listening cannot easily engage in the rapid skimming and selective scanning behaviours which enhance the efficiency of visual print reading. Such limitations make it apparent that any attempt to develop a device which will permit the blind to read as quickly and accurately as their sighted counterparts will not only have to optimize the compatability of the code used to present print to an alternate sensory system, but also ensure that the format of the display allows the user freely to control his exposure to the reading materials.

MOBILITY SKILLS

The difficulty with which reading skills are acquired and practised by the blind is undoubtedly a serious impediment to rehabilitation. However, the single greatest handicap that is produced by the absence of visual stimulation is the impairment of independent movement in the environment. Although a blind individual may gain a number of special intellectual and occupational skills, it is unlikely that they will be of significant value to him if he has insufficient travel skill to give him access to the places in which these abilities can be meaningfully exercised. Mobility, as this skill has been termed, can be defined as the ability to travel from one place to another safely, comfortably, gracefully, and independently (Foulke, 1970). Thus, mobility refers both to the ability to move through space without disruption because of accidental contact with obstacles, and to the ability to orient with the environment in order to achieve purposeful or goal-directed movement.

Efforts to assist the blind in acquiring mobility skill have consisted of the development of sensory aids and associated training techniques. The two most common mobility aids in regular use by blind pedestrians are the long cane (Hoover, 1950) and the dog guide (Ebeling, 1950) (see Figure 51). When properly used the long cane acts as a tactual–kinaesthetic extension of the traveller's arm which explores the surface of the path into which his next step will carry him. Dogs have been specifically trained as guides since 1916, and a limited number of blind persons who have the physical stamina and are able to tolerate the inconveniences of caring for an animal are able to use a dog guide to improve their mobility. Unfortunately, neither the dog nor the cane is an ideal mobility device. Not all blind persons are able to learn to use these aids effectively, and even when training is successful, the safety and efficiency of the blind traveller does not approach that of his sighted peer.

Figure 51. Traditional and electronic blind mobility aids. The long cane, the dog guide, the Nottingham Obstacle Detector (bottom left), and the Sonic Guide.

As a result, during the past twenty years numerous designers have attempted to devise electronic sensory aids to enhance blind mobility skill. These devices emit ultrasound or coherent light and convert the energy reflected from objects in the environment to some form of auditory or tactual display. Most of these devices have never reached significant levels of development. However, a few have survived and are either in production or in the final stages of evaluation (Figure 51). The simplest electronic aids which indicate whether a clear path exists ahead of the pedestrian and provide some range information include the Pathsounder (Russell, 1971), and the Nottingham Obstacle Detector (NOD) (Armstrong and Heyes, 1975). More complex aids such as the Bionics Laser Cane (Benjamin, 1970) and the Sonic Guide (Kay, 1972) attempt to supply a more complete view of the environment by informing the traveller of specific environmental features or by providing a display enriched with azimuthal and textural cues. Regrettably, the electronic aids which have been subjected to thorough evaluation by blind pedestrians have failed to live up to the expectations of their creators.

An important reason why adequate solutions to the mobility problem have not yet been found is that relatively little research has been conducted to analyse the behaviour of blind travellers or to investigate the perceptual processes which underlie mobility skill. Leonard (1972) noted that it is curious that experts in the field of human performance know very much about the behaviour of astronauts in their working environment but very little about the performance characteristics of the common pedestrian. One reason for this disparity of knowledge is that, in many ways, the measurement and analysis of an astronaut's performance is a fairly simple problem. Essentially, he works in an enclosed, highly structured environment in which most of the stimuli presented to him and his responses are clearly observable and quantifiable. In contrast, mobility is a complex, open skill in which task demands continually change as the traveller enters new portions of space. The information displayed to his senses is not well constrained so that is difficult to determine which environmental stimuli are important to his performance. In addition, response sequences in mobility tend to be highly integrated so that the quantification of output is an arduous task.

Because of these difficulties the problem of assessing and analysing the blind pedestrian's performance has been approached in a variety of ways. A large proportion of the research which has been conducted on blind mobility skill has been in the form of practical evaluations of mobility aids. Unfortunately, because of inadequate experimental design, the use of device-specific indices of performance, and a reliance on subjective measurement, this work has provided only very meagre insights into blind mobility (Shingledecker and Foulke, 1978).

An alternative approach which has made significant contributions to the understanding of blind mobility is represented by the body of research conducted to isolate various component subskills which contribute to overall performance. One of the most notable examples of this type of experimentation was a series of studies conducted to investigate the fabled 'facial vision' of the blind (Supa, Cotzin, and Dallenbach, 1944; Cotzin and Dallenbach, 1950). Results showed that this ability is attributable to the learned use of reflected high-frequency acoustic cues usually produced by the traveller's footsteps, and that the differential pitch of the original and reflected sounds is the important dimension of the cue. These results were extended by Kohler (1964) who replicated the earlier findings and described the way in which guiding sounds and sound shadows are used to complement echo location. Other studies of the subskills underlying mobility have included Juurmaa's (1973) preliminary work on spatial orientation skills and Cratty's (1971) psychophysical studies of the veering tendency displayed by blind subjects as they attempt to walk in a straight line, and of their ability to detect gradients, path curvature, and geographical direction.

Although subskill studies have contributed much to our knowledge of the basic sources of information that the unaided blind pedestrian is able to call upon in a mobility situation, this approach cannot provide a complete description of the quality of overall mobility performance in actual travel situations. A methodology for the assessment of mobility performance which permits whole task measurement was described by Armstrong (1975). In this technique, a number of behaviourally defined objective measures derived from the task goals of safety and efficiency are used to evaluate the performance of blind subjects as they travel over prescribed routes. Safety measures include the frequency and nature of body contact with objects in the environment and the frequency of departures from the pathway. Measures of efficiency consist of the assessment of behaviours which lead to reasonably rapid progress and which provide the most accurate route to a travel goal: walking speed; the continuousness of progress; and the accuracy of navigational decisions. This methodology has been used successfully to evaluate the contribution of several sensory aids to mobility performance.

A common starting point for the analysis of complex skills in human performance research is to attempt to assess the information-processing demands placed upon the individual. Upon initial consideration this approach may not appear to be meaningful for blind mobility because it is often thought that it is simply the lack of sufficient information which makes the blind pedestrian's task difficult. However, if the absence of visual input alters the mobility task so that extra processing activities are necessary to achieve safe and efficient performance, it is likely that the increased processing load or mental effort demanded by the task may be an important factor in accounting for deficient mobility performance.

The possible sources of excessive processing load for the blind traveller are numerous. For example, it is apparent that the increased difficulty of selectively attending to single sources of information presents an additional load for the blind pedestrian who must often rely on the relatively inefficient auditory system. Another process which is disproportionately loaded for the blind traveller is short-term memory. Unlike his sighted counterpart, he has few immediate cues available to permit him to monitor his present position in relation to the beginning and end of a route. Thus, he must often maintain a running memory span of the number of turns made or of the number of streets crossed in order to achieve orientation. An even more important difference between the blind and sighted pedestrian that may have an effect on the processing demands of mobility is that the blind traveller receives very little information about upcoming events, while the sighted person normally has full knowledge of the near environment. Laboratory studies of tracking skill have shown that as subjects receive increased preview of the course that they are following or as they gain practice on a course with recognizable regularities, performance improves (see Holding, Chapter 1, this volume). These results illustrate the importance of advance information in complex skills. When forthcoming stimulus events are unpredictable, processing overloads result because the performer's limited-capacity decision-making mechanism lags behind the incoming information. However, when future events can be directly observed or when they can be anticipated from memory, the decision-making apparatus can work ahead of immediate motor output and thereby permit accurate performance.

The blind pedestrian is in much the same position as the subject in a tracking experiment with limited preview. Because he often receives only limited and degraded information about the space ahead, the blind person can experience momentary periods of overload during which large amounts of information are encountered. Instead of continuously working ahead of his immediate spatial position, the blind traveller tends to receive sporadic information that must be interpreted and acted upon within a very brief period of time if his performance is to remain both safe and efficient. Although with sufficient practice on a particular route the blind individual can begin to rely on a memorial representation to anticipate events, the success of this strategy depends on the questionable quality of the 'cognitive maps' that he has been able to construct and on the problem of forgetting.

The validity of the notion that extra information-processing demands are placed upon the blind pedestrian and that these demands are partially responsible for poor blind mobility performance, was tested in an experiment conducted by the author in which a secondary task (as discussed Kinsbourne in Chapter 4, this volume) was used to assess processing load as blind and blindfolded sighted subjects walked over routes in a simulated travel environment (Shingledecker, 1978). The secondary task was a two-choice reaction-time (RT) problem which required the subject to respond to vibratory pulses presented to his wrists by pressing the appropriate button on a panel carried in his left hand. After baseline mobility and RT performance had been recorded, the subjects were randomly divided into three groups and were then required to perform the mobility and RT tasks simultaneously.

In the dual-task condition one of the groups walked the same route with which they had received five practice trials. A second group walked an unfamiliar route of equivalent complexity. The third group walked the identical unfamiliar route, but received preview of turns, steps, and kerbs. Preview was presented in the form of brief verbal messages spoken to the subject by an experimenter who followed him over the route. It was hypothesized that subjects who had prior experience with a route and those who received preview of an unfamiliar route would produce better mobility performance than those who had no basis for anticipation. Furthermore, if the ability to anticipate reduces the momentary processing load of the mobility task, more 'spare channel capacity' should have been available to those subjects who had some form of advance information. Thus, it was expected that their performance on the RT task would show less impairment than that of the subjects who had no basis for anticipation.

The results of the experiment were in agreement with these predictions. Mobility performance as assessed by the measures outlined by Armstrong (1975) was improved under dual-task conditions by both practice and preview. More importantly, the effects of anticipation were clearly shown in the errors made by the subjects on the secondary task (see Figure 52). Subjects who were unable to anticipate upcoming events failed to respond to the vibratory stimuli significantly more often than those who received preview or those who could predict environmental events from memory. Secondary task performance was also shown to vary as a function of the momentary information-processing demands of the travel environment. Decrements in RT performance for all of the groups tended to occur at points along the routes which required subjects to detect landmarks, locate changes in direction, and maintain a straight course while crossing a street.

This experiment provided objective evidence to support the hypothesis that human information-processing limitations are a significant impediment to blind mobility skill, and that the provision of anticipatory information can reduce the extra processing load incurred by the loss of vision. These findings indicate that a major design criterion for mobility aids should be the incorporation of preview information. Although most designers have implicitly adopted this criterion, few of them have considered the problem of excess processing load when making decisions about the type and amount of advance information that should be gathered from the environment or about the way in which this information should be displayed to the blind pedestrian.

An inspection of the characteristics of current mobility aids reveals two distinct design philosophies. The first of these contends that a viable mobility aid should gather very little information from the environment and should

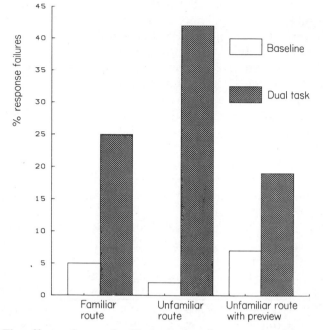

Figure 52. The effects of route familiarity and environmental preview on a secondary task performed during blind mobility. Original figure from data presented by Shingledecker (1978).

display that information to the user in a simple manner. The NOD and the Pathsounder were developed under this philosophy. Both are intended only as supplementary sources of travel information and warn the user of objects in his path via an easily learned auditory display. The alternative approach to the design of mobility aids can be characterized by a belief that a device should gather a great deal of information and that as much of that raw information as possible should be displayed to enable the user's brain to select and interpret it as needed. Devices which have attempted to embody this principle include a prototype aid, the Tactile Visual Substitution System, which uses a television camera to drive an array of vibrators fixed on the user's abdomen or back (Bach-y-Rita, 1972), and the currently available Sonic Guide.

The potential problems associated with this form of mobility aid can be appreciated by examining the Sonic Guide, a binaural sonar system which is mounted in a spectacle frame. The distance of objects within its range is coded by the pitch of the auditory display, while the azimuthal position is coded by the relative intensity of the signal in the user's left and right ears. All of the objects which are simultaneously present within the wide beam of the device contribute to the display, and the reflective characteristics of these objects further modify the nature of the signal received by the user.

It is obvious that the output of the Sonic Guide is extremely rich in information about the traveller's world. Unfortunately, the expected improvement in mobility resulting from the use of this aid has not been fully realized. Although some blind persons have been able to achieve better performance, others have shown very little change or even a deterioration in travel skill (Airasian, 1972). Additional evidence has shown that long cane skills may suffer when, as recommended, this aid is used in conjunction with the Sonic Guide (Armstrong, 1972).

Findings such as these are congruent with the results of the experiment described earlier in this section. Devices which attempt to display a complete and therefore complex view of the travel environment may, in fact, increase the already high cognitive processing load of the blind mobility skill. The problem of limited-processing capacity and the effective further reduction of this capacity by the absence of vision is one which must be a primary consideration in the design of future hardware to enhance mobility skill.

SUMMARY

An overview of the advances in modern physical science which have made it possible to design and build the sorts of prostheses and sensory aids described in this chapter indicates that there are few insurmountable technological barriers to the development of any aid that a disabled person might require. In fact, it is not difficult to conceive of a time in the near future when our technical knowledge will be sophisticated enough to produce the equipment that would be needed to construct the Bionic Man of science fiction fame whose prosthetic receptors and effectors not only meet but exceed the functional capabilities of intact sensory and motor organs. Despite these immense physical resources, many devices intended to restore skill to the handicapped continue to have only limited value because designers often have been forced to rely on introspection and intuition to determine the appropriate characteristics of prosthetic equipment and sensory aids. As a result, the human user's information-processing capacities and limitations which are ultimately responsible for skill have not been sufficiently taken into account.

The problem is perhaps best illustrated by returning to an analogy presented in the introductory section of this chapter where the human operator was conceptualized as an information-processing device similar to a computer. Like a computer the human operator can be described as a central information-processing device along with a set of peripheral input and output devices. The computer's input devices corresponding to human sensory systems might be a paper-tape reader and a keyboard. Its output peripherals analogous to human limbs or vocal apparatus could be a line printer and a graph plotter. One task that the computer might be called upon to perform would be to receive some data via its paper-tape reader, organize the data, and provide a frequency distribution of the data by drawing a curve on the graph plotter. A mechanical failure of the graph plotter would produce a breakdown of this 'skill'. A student who decides to substitute the line printer for the graph plotter in order to get his job done, simply by instructing the computer to address the printer rather than the plotter, is likely to be rather disappointed. Although the printer has the mechanical ability to plot a graph by printing a series of points to represent the data and axes of a figure, to do so it requires different instructions than those needed by the graph plotter. The eventual success with which this 'motor' substitution could be made would depend on the computer's ability to provide interpretable commands to the line printer, the availability of an appropriate program in the computer's memory, and the computer's capacity to meet the information-processing demands of the task.

In order to be successful at the task of restoring skilled performance, the designer of devices for the disabled, like the computer operator, must be aware of the mechanisms of skill and of the strategies of information processing that dictate the way in which these mechanisms are used. The development of efficient ways to use substitute sensory systems and to design effective sensory and motor aids require consideration of the entire information-processing chain. The sensitivity and powers of discrimination of sensory systems must be understood, the decision-making capacities of central processes must be taken into account, and the properties of motor control must be appreciated if useful solutions to the problems of handicap are to be found.

Chapter 11

Final Survey

Dennis H. Holding

The previous chapters have covered a great many substantive issues, contributing between them nearly all the basic information needed to assemble a comprehensive account of human skills. It seems appropriate for this chapter to try to complete the picture in three different ways. First, the fact that the individual chapters have been written by different hands makes it more than usually important to provide a brief review of the most salient issues, with some attempt to exhibit the links between separately treated topics. Next, it seems necessary to introduce a little of the material which has been excluded from consideration so far. Probably the most relevant category of information not supplied in the previous chapters is material concerned with the breakdown of skills, since clues about the organization of skills are provided by the manner of their disintegration. Finally, there is a brief attempt to forecast the directions which research on skills seems likely to follow.

SALIENT ISSUES

We have seen that feedback is of central importance to the development and maintenance of skilled activities. An open-loop system, in which an input leads to a response output without reference to the consequences of any prior output, can operate well only in a highly predictable environment. As Moray points out in Chapter 2, it is only the skilled performer who can afford to 'go open-loop' since, for him, most action sequences are relatively predictable. Feedback mechanisms can be analysed in considerable detail, from the relatively passive systems of early theory to the more dynamic 'filtering' systems of modern control theory, providing well-elaborated models for human performance. The fact that human operators can apparently use a variety of transfer functions, although viewed with despondency in Chapter 8, may instead be regarded as a potentially advantageous kind of flexibility; one might expect to see more experiments directed at finding out when and how humans select different strategies for closed-loop performance.

At the same time, it is now clear that humans operate in at least a temporarily open-loop fashion much more often than was once supposed, using motor control programs which specify in fair detail the characteristics of learned movement sequences. The evidence is that many coordinated movements can still be executed when feedback has been eliminated, either by direct intervention or by the speed demands of the task. We have also seen that there is evidence for the preprogramming of movements, even when feedback is available, from studies in which the preparation time for complex action is shown to exceed the times for simpler movements. As Summers suggests in Chapter 3, incorporating the motor program concept into a fuller account of skilled performance may require something along the lines of Schmidt's (1975a) schema theory. This kind of concept calls for the representation in memory of integrated networks of information, relating the goals of human actions both to motor command sequences and to correlated data from the various sensory systems. The flexibility of this approach seems promising, although it remains to be seen whether the theory can be made sufficiently precise for explicit testing.

It should be stressed that the feedback and motor program concepts are complementary, rather than antithetical. In fact, even at the time when motor skills theory was primarily concerned with feedback mechanisms, Licklider (1960) drew attention to the possibilities of a 'conditional' servo system. Such a system contains predictor elements which allow for open-loop operation as long as the output is in line with the target or 'intention' of the activity, but will switch into corrective feedback whenever a significant discrepancy appears. Feedback is also viewed as functioning to adjust the overall parameters under which the system operates, which is fully compatible with current thinking. However, the practical problem for research is to determine exactly when the human operator is making use of feedback cues.

A useful example is given by Wilke and Vaughn (1976), who tried a reaction-time probe at various points during a dart-throwing movement. Reaction to a photographic flash bulb took 307 milliseconds during the period immediately before the movement, when most of the information processing takes place, fell to 274 milliseconds as the subject's arm was drawn back ready for the throw, and continued to decline through successive segments of the movement down to 178 milliseconds immediately after the release of the dart. Notice that the greatest attention demand, as implied by the lengthened reaction time, arises at the stage when preprogramming is presumed to occur but, also, that the reaction times are still elevated while the movement is in progress. This in turn implies that monitoring of the movement, probably by proprioceptive feedback, is still taking place well after the initial motor commands have been formulated and the movement started. Subsequent research of this kind can be expected to clarify matters further.

The reaction-time method used in the dart-throwing experiment is a form of the secondary task technique discussed by Kinsbourne in Chapter 4. The usefulness of this kind of method, further underscored by the work on blind mobility in Chapter 10, is for practical purposes almost independent of its implications for the single-channel concept. However, the status of limited-capacity hypotheses has obviously been jeopardized by some of the complications arising in recent research. In fact, the investigation of processing capacity may turn out to have been a mistaken approach. Meanwhile, the chances seem good that we can reach a fuller understanding of the implications for information processing of the multiple interconnection of cerebral neurons. The idea of functional cerebral distance seems to resolve a number of discrepant findings, subsuming problems like the hemispheric sharing of attention under the same explanation that accounts for the interference between tapping to two simultaneous rhythms.

When we return to the behavioural problems of discrete movements, we find that the link between the perceptual and the motor elements of skills needs emphasis. Recent work on ball-catching, for instance, draws attention to the need for studying dynamic rather than static visual acuity (Sanderson and Whiting, 1978). The spatial senses, particularly vision and proprioception, need continuous recalibration with respect to bodily movements, and continuous adjustment for reliability in the way that information from different sources is combined, in addition to their recurring use in monitoring and correcting movements. Howarth and Beggs, in Chapter 5, show that the allocation of these functions may be viewed as strategies which human subjects vary, and which they learn to improve. Traditional problems, such as the exact form of Fitts' (1954) law for the relationship between the speed, amplitude, and tolerance limits of reciprocating movements, seem also to involve perceptual factors; a case in point is that speed and accuracy are related differently in the absence of visual feedback.

Although there are some studies of the retention of tracking skills, most of the analytic work on motor memory has used discrete movements. In most cases, the task has been to reproduce a previously experienced movement, whether active or passive, after varying delays. Movement information is apparently best coded for storage in terms of location cues, although it is unclear to what extent the effect might be modified by imagery. In Chapter 6, Laabs and Simmons consider the possibilities of various storage models, including the two-stage version in which temporary, short-term codes are subsequently abstracted into a higher-order schema. Obviously there are many parallels between motor and verbal memory, which suggests that will be profitable to explore a depth-of-processing approach. The chapter offers some support for this approach and — certainly where verbal labels for movement locations are used — it can be shown that loss of movement accuracy relates to the depth of processing.

The instructions for quite long sequences of responses can be stored in long- or short-term memory. Accessing these stored instructions is one of the problems for sequential skills, where the predominance of keyboard tasks also ensures that analysis cannot neglect verbal mediation. This is a developing area of research, involving issues which range from the thorough analysis of human errors and error correction to the elaboration of models of choice behaviour. The particular contribution of Chapter 7 is to show how the concepts of modern control theory, which we first encountered in the discussion of feedback mechanisms, can deal with the constantly changing parameters of human performance. Serial choice reaction tasks and, in fact, all tasks which involve continuous response selection, are subject to performance changes which require careful specification. As Rabbitt confirms, the effects of various stresses, practice, and learning effects are such that the human operator is clumsily represented by steady-state models.

The same may be said for tracking tasks where, as we saw, transfer function analysis ran foul of various non-linearities. However, Hammerton's job in Chapter 8 has been largely to explain the accumulated empirical data. A great deal is known about the advantage of pursuit over compensatory forms of tracking tasks, about the performance associated with different orders of control, and about the merits of various kinds of control design. Enough is known about the technology of tracking to produce extremely serviceable simulators when difficulty, danger, or expense make training on live equipment undesirable. The crucial question for any simulator is how well its training transfers to the real task, although the issue is not simple. The scores on initial transfer may not reflect later performance and, as Holding (1976) illustrates, a transfer model for overall scores may be very different from a model predicting negative transfer in the form of intrusive errors.

Transfer of training is one of the central issues in learning, since most skills must be generalized for practical use. Newell, in Chapter 9, contrasts the individual-difference approach to transfer with the traditional theoretical view, making the additional point that information-processing ideas have been under-used in explanations of transfer. The basic problems for the acquisition of skills, prior to transfer, are usefully classified as concerning the effects of information before, during, or after action, and the effects of different conditions of practice. Before action, information about goals and techniques may take the form of instructions or demonstrations, or perhaps special written notations, with varying effects. Information during action may be action feedback, or one of the forms of direct guidance, while information after action raises all the problems of the research on knowledge of results.

In general, it is difficult to reach broad conclusions on these learning issues although, for practical purposes, perhaps our current knowledge concerning the conditions of practice is barely adequate. Thus, the spacing and length of learning trials can be shown to affect training time, as can the use of whole versus part learning strategies, and mental practice. However, there is no way of knowing, for theoretical satisfaction, whether for example the Baddeley and Longman (1978) two-hour practice group might have practised proportionally less within the session than the faster learning one-hour group. There are many similar loose ends; one cannot avoid concluding that, in the learning area as in the tracking area, many problems have been abandoned rather than solved.

In contrast, the growth of the knowledge needed to remedy handicaps seems reasonably promising. To some extent, engineering technology has out-stripped the corresponding information on the sensory and motor control characteristics of the human user of various aids, but the gap may be closing. To some extent, piecemeal selection of aids is being replaced by remedial techniques which take into account the entire information-processing system. The formulation of research questions about the handicapped has been greatly helped by recent, more sophisticated approaches to skills analysis. Thus, for example, it is possible to ask whether blind mobility is hampered by requiring an overload of information handling as much as by a deficit of stimulus information, and to answer the question by systematic use of the secondary task technique. Shingledecker raises many issues in Chapter 10, such as the importance of preview and anticipation, which exemplify in practical form the theoretical concerns of earlier chapters. In fact, considering and analysing handicaps can be seen to improve our general understanding of the ways in which skills function. Studying blind mobility, again as an example, has shown us a good deal about what is involved in normal travel from place to place.

THE BREAKDOWN OF SKILLS

Apart from the direct effects due to handicaps, skills may suffer deterioration as a result of drug action, because of fatigue or other stresses, or as a consequence of ageing processes. Each of these areas has a considerable research literature, represented elsewhere in this series, but it is possible to give a brief indication of the kinds of skill difficulties suggested by breakdown under these different circumstances.

Drugs

The effects of various drugs on human performance are considered in detail by Warburton (in press). Many of the issues are rather specialized, but there are one or two illustrative points which may be made. The traditional classifica-tion separates out those drugs which stimulate from those which depress functioning of the central nervous system. The stimulants have been little used in the detailed analysis of motor skills, although it is known that drugs like amphetamine tend to produce compulsive and repetitive motor behaviour, with increased precision in simple tasks. In general, we may assume that the stimulants will tend to enhance the effects of arousal noted below in the discussion of stress.

An example of a nervous system depressant, which tends to inhibit cortical function, is provided by nitrous oxide. Using this drug, Legge (1965) showed that handwriting became larger as the dose was increased, as shown in Figure 53. It seems that the perception of the movement of one's hand, by vision and by proprioception, is impaired by the drug; the increased size of writing compensates for this effect, perhaps because the new visual size is appropriate for a subjectively more distant visual stimulus. Legge's analysis of stylus movements to a reference mark showed that the errors made were least when both the stylus and the target were perceived visually, and somewhat greater when both were perceived proprioceptively, but that the greatest variable error occurred with mixed modalities. Thus, combining visual and proprioceptive information seems to constitute an additional stage of processing for the subject, and one which is particularly sensitive to disruption by the drug.

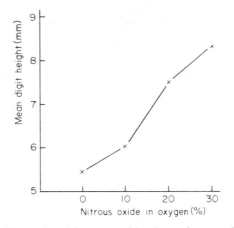

Figure 53. Handwriting size increases with drug dosage. From Legge (1965). Reproduced by permission of the author and the British Psychological Society.

Alcohol is also classified as a depressant drug, despite its use as a 'stimulant', and it, too, causes larger handwriting, together with other kinds of exaggerated movement. Drew, Colquhoun, and Long (1958) showed that heightened levels of blood alcohol produced successively greater amounts of steering-wheel movement in a simulated driving task. With high alcohol dosages, the subjects also tracked less accurately, often steering more towards the middle of the road in order to compensate for their variability, which was particularly evident in cornering. There were no consistent effects on driving speed, which seemed to depend on personality characteristics.

In addition, drugs and other substances may produce a number of toxic effects. Thus, the presence of lead in the blood tends to lengthen response times in vigilance tasks, and to slow down measures of eye–hand coordination

(Morgan and Repko, 1974). Inhaling methylene chloride has the effect of impairing a wide range of performance measures, including indices of sensory functioning (Winneke, 1974), probably as a result of a general depressant effect. Evidence of this kind is accumulating, and will eventually contribute more fully towards the understanding of skills.

Stress and Fatigue

Various environmental and individual stresses, such as heat, noise, or loss of sleep, have adverse effects on human performance. A volume surveying these effects, together with those due to fatigue, has been prepared by Hockey (in press). The consequences of many stresses may be linked in different ways to the concept of arousal.

Loss of sleep, for example, presumably results in a state of reduced arousal. It affects the rate of responding in many tasks like serial reaction, makes for errors or gaps in performance, and causes missed signals in watch-keeping. Of course, the opportunity for sleep will restore arousal and performance to normal levels. However, if arousal is further increased by some form of stimulation, performance may again deteriorate. Hence, it has been proposed that performance is related to arousal by an inverted U-shaped function, such that both under- and over-arousal are detrimental (Corcoran, 1965).

This idea may explain some of the confusing effects of noise, which may in different circumstances be adverse, beneficial, or neutral (Loeb, in press). Noise seems to be arousing, so that its use will improve performance after loss of sleep by raising arousal to an optimal level, whereas in other circumstances it may damage performance, perhaps by causing overarousal. Noise effects will also interact with the level of arousal as it varies during the normal day, and with other factors, in a complex way. Thus, Baker, Loeb, and Holding (1979) found no general effect of noise on a paced, serial addition task; however, noise made women react faster, in the afternoon, and made men more accurate under fast pacing in the morning. Poulton's (1978) review suggests that the complexity of noise effects derives from the fact that noise provides distraction, in addition to masking auditory cues and to working through the arousal mechanism.

The effect of ambient heat seems to operate rather differently, tending to reduce accuracy directly, rather than indirectly by reducing the amount of activity in the way which loss of sleep appears to do. Again, it is probably significant that heat and noise do not seem to interact. Bell (1978) recently used both of these stresses in an experiment with the secondary task technique, with rotary pursuit as the primary task and the comparison of auditory digits as the subsidiary task. More errors were made on the secondary task as the temperature was raised from 22 °C to 35 °C and also when background noise at 95 dB was introduced, but the two effects were independent (see Figure 54).

This tends to confirm earlier suggestions that heat stress affects a different mechanism, separate from the arousal effect.

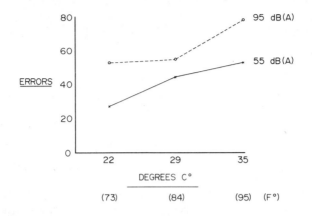

Figure 54. The effects of ambient heat and noise on pursuit rotor tracking. Both heat and noise seem to raise the error scores, but without interacting. From Bell (1978) in the journal *Human Factors*.

The effects of fatigue present a clearer picture of the breakdown of skills. Consideration must be given to two different aspects of fatigue, deterioration of performance on a prolonged task, and the more elusive results of earlier fatigue on subsequent tasks. Protracted performance of a skilled task has a number of consequences, first outlined by Bartlett (1943) in describing experiments with an aircraft simulator. Progressively larger deviations of the instrument readings were tolerated, with a general deterioration in the operator's standards of performance. Lapses of attention occurred with increasing frequency, central aspects of the task were emphasized while peripheral elements were neglected, and operators became more easily distracted. Responses became much more variable, particularly in their timing, so that many correct actions were executed at the wrong time. Responding appeared to lose coherence, such that the overall pattern of action disintegrated into separated components. This kind of disintegration has also been observed in athletic movements, as when Bates, Osternig, and James (1977) analysed film records of the running cycle during fatigue. The times for components like foot strike and foot descent increased, while forward swing decreased and other measures remained constant, thus suggesting that the central control of timing had deteriorated.

On the other hand, generalized fatigue effects have always been difficult to measure on an interpolated or subsequent test, partly because people can usually compensate for any impairment on changing to a different task. Very often there is no direct carryover from a fatiguing task, although people's attitudes towards undertaking further effort are usually changed. Tired subjects will take chances, and 'cut corners' in order to avoid effort. This may be seen in drivers' judgements of when to overtake (Brown, Tickner, and Simmonds, 1970) and, with appropriate techniques (Holding, 1974), may be quantified in the laboratory. Thus it has been shown that subjects given the choice will elect to test fewer electrical components, at the risk of a lowered probability of finding a faulty item, after fatigue on a complex monitoring task (Shingledecker and Holding, 1974). Similarly, they will choose to crank an arm ergometer for shorter periods, at the risk of lowered success in the task, after a tiring run on the treadmill (Barth, Holding, and Stamford, 1976).

Ageing

As people grow older they tend to become slower to decide and react, more hesitant and forgetful, and less inclined or able to change their ways. Sanford (in press) examines these developments, which take place throughout adult life, in detail. The deterioration of sensory functions is well known, with steady drops in visual acuity and accommodation, and progressive changes in auditory thresholds and in the apparent loudness of the higher sound frequencies. There is some decrement in muscular output from the twenties onwards, although this is only of real significance when prolonged exertion is required. More important than these peripheral changes are the limitations on central mechanisms, which increasingly constrain the quality of performance when fast or complex processing is demanded.

Slowness of reaction is evidenced in many tasks, particularly those which pose difficult choices. Some early work by Szafran (1951), for example, required subjects to reach for a choice of visual targets. The movement times were approximately constant across different ages, but the 'preparation times', involving decisions before moving, rose steadily from 0.86 second for subjects in their twenties to 1.37 seconds for fifty-year-olds. The same series of experiments also showed that older subjects were much more seriously handicapped by having to wear dark goggles than were the younger subjects. Other lines of evidence may be adduced (Welford, 1958) which suggest that this finding is actually a partial example of three different generalizations concerning the effects of ageing. Thus, it illustrates a return to a dependence upon vision, which is normally a characteristic of the early stages of skill. Next, it serves to demonstrate that older subjects typically need more information in order to act, despite the fact that they can handle incoming information less well, with the result that they tend to hesitate. Finally, it shows an effect which has been replicated in a wide variety of tasks, such that any increase in complexity tends to widen the performance gap between older and younger subjects (see Figure 55).

The effect of task complexity may also be seen in the context of short-term

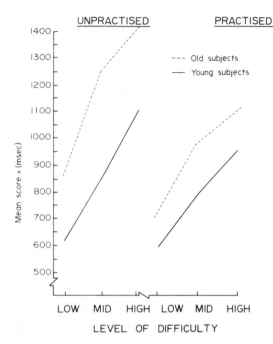

Figure 55. Relation between increasing difficulty (of transitions between choice responses) and the time taken to respond, before and after practice. The curves for older and younger subjects diverge significantly as the level of difficulty mounts. From Jordan and Rabbitt (1977). Reproduced by permission of the authors and the British Psychological Society.

memory load. A straightforward test of digit span shows little effect of age, but asking for the digits in reverse order increases the age differences. Having the subjects bear information in mind while carrying out some other manipulation such that, for instance, he has to respond by pressing a key which corresponds to a light which has appeared two or three items back in a series of lights at different positions, becomes an almost insuperable task for many of the older subjects. The same effect may be seen in tracking tasks (Griew, 1958), where masking off a preview of the target course imposes a load upon working memory for advance cues in a way which tends to defeat the older subjects. Long-term memory deficits are more difficult to demonstrate, except in cases of real senility. Thus, Franklin and Holding (1977) found that people aged up to the seventies all seemed to add steadily to their store of remembered events. However, the long-term effects of prior practice do tend to produce difficulties for transfer of training, so that veteran drivers of horse-drawn vehicles make poor students at bus driving (Entwisle, 1959). Accumulated experience is an asset, when it is relevant, but is a burden when irrelevant.

PROBABLE TRENDS

Studies of the breakdown or deterioration of skills, such as those reviewed above, will obviously continue to provide useful information at many levels. The features of performance displayed under the influence of drugs, during stress or fatigue, or as ageing proceeds, often mirror the earlier, clumsier stages of skill acquisition. Before any real breakdown has occurred, the effects of stress will tend to throw into prominence any discontinuities in the smooth performance of a skill. A steady stream of contributions to the skills area can be expected from these sources, much of it bearing on the cognitive problems of attention and arousal.

Applied work of various kinds will continue to provide the stimulus to investigate new problems, or to reconsider old problems in a new light. Theoretical research soon becomes sterile in the absence of the reinvigoration provoked by practical issues. A case in point is provided by the topics or preview and anticipation, which re-emerge alongside newer issues in the study of blind mobility. Similarly, vigilance studies were developed in response to the practical problem of submarine spotting, later received a theoretical overhaul with the advent of signal detection theory, and are now promising a resurgence in order to answer the questions posed by the problems of industrial inspection. Industrial problems in general, as represented by Holding (1969), are likely to concentrate towards the perceptual end of the skills continuum. Physical production processes have become far less important with the development of methods of automation, to be replaced by increasing concern for the inspection problems of quality control, the monitoring and selection problems of process control, and the strategy and decision problems of 'trouble-shooting' and maintenance.

In the mainstream of skills research, the emphasis will probably continue to move towards the motor end of the skills continuum, towards the elaboration of existing links with neurophysiology, and towards the further analysis of the covert processes underlying movement skills. The presence of a growing number of physical education specialists who are familiar with the methods of experimental psychology, and of psychologists with some knowledge of kinaesiology and exercise physiology, should ensure a steadily developing corpus of research concerning sports and physical skills. As with the industrial problems, facing the issues raised by physical education will stimulate further developments in pure research.

On the physiological side, necessarily under-represented in this volume, one may expect a greatly enhanced understanding of the laterality relations between the cortical hemispheres to result in a richer description of the development and transfer of skills. More technically, one may hope for a better understanding of the part played by the extrapyramidal pathways in muscle control and of the way in which the cerebellum integrates and regulates movement information. One may also hope for a much more detailed account of the way in which kinaesthesis functions, particularly with respect to the part it may play in the feedback control of ongoing movements. Techniques like the electromyographic recording of electrical activity at muscle sites, and the more dubious nerve compression block techniques, will continue to provide information. Most important, however, is the idea that an increasingly available background knowledge of physiological mechanisms will set clear limits to the kinds of theoretical speculation which are admissible.

At a theoretical level, explanations of skilled behaviour of the kind put forward by Adams (1971) and Schmidt (1975a) or, for that matter, by Laszlo and Manning (1970), will continue to attract research attention. These theories represent movement selection as a form of retrieval process, in which the appropriate movement features are extracted from long- or short-term storage for incorporation in an output program. Ongoing or completed movements are evaluated against an internal standard of some kind, which forms one step in an information flow sequence. Whether one refers to standards and programs, to perceptual traces, or to developing schemata, the general outlines are broadly similar.

Clearly, these types of theory have all the elements of a contemporary cognitive model, and are cast in a form which is compatible with such models from other areas of research. The many parallels with verbal behaviour are becoming more apparent, in a number of ways. Hence, it seems safe to predict one further development. After following a separate course for several decades, skills research should now be ready for renewed integration with the remainder of experimental psychology. The new relationship promises to be of mutual benefit, to the parent discipline and to the field of sensorimotor skills.

SUMMARY

The chapter briefly reviews the theoretical issues concerning feedback, motor programs, single-channel limitations, and motor memory, draws attention to some of the major features of discrete, sequential, and tracking skills, and surveys some aspects of motor learning and handicap research. The breakdown of skill is illustrated by outlining the effects of stimulant and depressant drugs, the effects of loss of sleep, noise, heat stress, and fatigue, and the effects of ageing. An attempt is made to forecast the directions to be taken by future research into human skills.

References
and Author Index

(The numbers in parentheses at the end of each reference indicate the pages where the references are cited.)

Adams, J. A. (1954) Psychomotor response acquisition and transfer as a function of control-indicator relationships. *Journal of Experimental Psychology*, **48**, 10–18. (224)

Adams, J. A. (1961) Human tracking behavior. *Psychological Bulletin*, **58**, 55–79. (177)

Adams, J. A. (1971) A closed-loop theory of motor learning. *Journal of Motor Behavior*, **3**, 111–150. (41, 45, 52, 141, 142, 143, 149, 203, 212, 216, 268)

Adams, J. A. (1976) Issues for a closed-loop theory of motor learning. In G. E. Stelmach (Ed.), *Motor Control: Issues and Trends*. New York: Academic Press. (41, 45, 141, 149)

Adams, J. A., and Dijkstra, S. (1966) Short-term memory for motor responses. *Journal of Experimental Psychology*, **71**, 314–318 (111, 148)

Adams, J. A., and Goetz, E. T. (1973) Feedback and practice as variables in error detection and correction. *Journal of Motor Behavior*, **5**, 217–224. (138, 141)

Adams, J. A., Goetz, E. T., and Marshall, P. H. (1972) Response feedback and motor learning. *Journal of Experimental Psychology*, **92**, 391–397. (138, 142)

Adams, J. A., Gopher, D., and Lintern, G. (1977) Effects of visual and proprioceptive feedback on motor learning. *Journal of Motor Behavior*, **9**, 11–12. (138)

Airaisian, P. W. (1972) *Evaluation of the Binaural Sensory Aid*. Washington, DC: National Academy of Sciences. (255)

Alcorn, S. (1945) Development of the Tadoma method for the deaf–blind. *Journal of Exceptional Children*, **11**, 117–119. (243)

Alles, D. S. (1970) Information transfer by phantom sensations. *IEEE Transactions on Man-Machine Systems*, **MMS-11** (1), 85–91. (234)

Allport, D. A., Antonis, B., and Reynolds, P. (1972) On the division of attention: A disproof of the single channel hypothesis. *Quarterly Journal of Experimental Psychology*, **24**, 225–235. (12, 67, 70, 71)

Annett, J. (1969) *Feedback and Human Behaviour*. Baltimore, Md.: Penguin Books. (15, 30, 204)

Annett, J. *Training for Performance*. Chichester: Wiley, in preparation. (2)

Anzola, G. P., Bertolini, G., Buchter, H. A., and Rizzolatti, G. (1977) Spatial compatibility and anatomical factors in simple and choice reaction time. *Neuropsychologia*, **15**, 295–302. (86)

Armstrong, J. D. (1972) *An Independent Evaluation of the Kay Binaural Sensor*. Blind Mobility Research Unit, University of Nottingham. (255)

Armstrong, J. D. (1975) Evaluation of man–machine systems in the mobility of the visually handicapped. In R. M. Pickett and T. J. Trigg (Eds.), *Human Factors in Health Care*. Lexington, Mass.: Lexington Books. (251, 253)

Armstrong, J. D., and Heyes, A. D. (1975) The work of the Blind Mobility Research Unit. In E. Kwatny and R. Zuckerman (Eds.), *Devices and Systems for the Disabled*. Philadelphia, Pa.: Temple University Health Sciences Center, pp.161–165. (250)

Armstrong, T. R. (1970a) Feeback and perceptual-motor skill learning: A review of information feedback and manual guidance training techniques. *Technical Report No. 25*, Human Performance Center, University of Michigan. (210)

Armstrong, T. R. (1970b) Training for the production of memorized movement patterns. *Technical Report No. 26*, Human Performance Center, University of Michigan. (54)

Ascoli, K. M., and Schmidt, R. A. (1969) Proactive interference in short-term motor retention. *Journal of Motor Behavior*, **1**, 29–36. (148)

Ashby, W. R. (1957) *Design for a Brain*. London: Chapman and Hall. (28)

Atkinson, R. C., and Shiffrin, R. M. (1971) The control of short-term memory. *Scientific American*, **224**, 82–90. (87)

Attneave, F. (1959) *Applications of Information Theory to Psychology*. New York: Holt. (66)

Audley, R. J. (1960) A stochastic model for individual choice behaviour. *Psychological Review*, **67**, 1–15. (154)

Audley, R. J. (1973) Some observations on theories of choice reaction time. In S. Kornblum (Ed.), *Attention and Performance IV*. New York: Academic Press. (154)

Audley, R. J., Caudrey, D. J., Howell, P., and Powell, D. J. (1975) Reaction time exchange functions in choice tasks. In P. M. A. Rabbitt and S. Dornic (Eds.), *Attention and Performance V*. London: Academic Press. (154)

Auerbach, C., and Sperling, P. (1974) A common auditory–visual space: Evidence for its reality. *Perception and Psychophysics*, **16**, 129–135. (112)

Axelrod, S. (1959) Effects of early blindness: Performance of blind and sighted children on tactile and auditory tasks. American Foundation for the Blind, *Research Monograph No. 7*. (238)

Bach-y-Rita, P. (1967) Sensory plasticity: Applications to a visual substitution system. *Acta Neurologica Scandinavia*, **43**, 417–426. (243)

Bach-y-Rita, P. (1972) *Brain Mechanisms in Sensory Substitution*. New York: Academic Press. (254)

Baddeley, A. D., Grant, S., Wight, E., and Thompson, N. (1975) Imagery and visual working memory. In P. M. A. Rabbitt and S. Dornic (Eds.), *Attention and Performance, V*. London: Academic Press. (71)

Baddeley, A. D., and Hitch, G. (1974) Working memory. In G. H. Bower (Ed.), *The Psychology of Learning and Motivation*, Vol. 8. New York: Academic Press. (150)

Baddeley, A. D., and Longman, D. J. A. (1978) The influence of length and frequency of training session on the rate of learning to type. *Ergonomics*, **21**, 627–635. (217, 260)

Bahrick, H. P., Noble, M., and Fitts, P. M. (1954) Extra-task performance as a measure of learning a primary task, *Journal of Experimental Psychology*, **48**, 298–302. (68)

Bahrick, H. P., and Shelly, C. (1958) Time sharing as an index of automization, *Journal of Experimental Psychology*, **56**, 288–293. (68)

Baker, M. A., Loeb, M., and Holding, D. H. (1979) Noise, time of day, and unpaced arithmetic. Paper to Psychonomic Society 20th Annual Meeting. Phoenix, Arizona. (263)

Bandura, A. (1969) Modeling theory: Some traditions, trends and disputes. In R. D. Parke (Ed.), *Recent Trends in Social Learning*. New York: Academic Press. (207)

Baron, S., Kleinman, D., and Levison, W. (1970) An optimal control model of human response. *Automatica*, **6**, 357–369. (170)

Barth, J. L., Holding, D. H., and Stamford, B. A. (1976) Risk versus effort in the assessment of motor fatigue. *Journal of Motor Behavior*, **8**, 189–194. (265)

Bartlett, F. C. (1932) *Remembering: A Study in Experimental and Social Psychology*. London: Cambridge University Press. (222)

Bartlett, F. C. (1943) Fatigue following highly skilled work. *Proceedings of the Royal Society*, **Series B**, **131**, 247–257. (264)

Bartlett, F. C. (1958) *Thinking: An Experimental and Social Study*. London: Allen and Unwin. (1)

Bates, B. T., Osternig, L. R., and James, S. L. (1977) Fatigue effects in running. *Journal of Motor Behavior*, **9**, 203–207. (264)

Begbie, G. H. (1959) Accuracy of aiming in linear hand movements. *Quarterly Journal of Experimental Psychology*, **11**, 65–75. (94)

Beggs, W. D. A. (1971) Movement Control. Unpublished Ph.D. Thesis, University of Nottingham. (105, 108, 110, 111, 112)

Beggs, W. D. A., Baker, J. A., Dove, S. R., Fairclough, I., and Howarth, C. I. (1972) The accuracy of non-visual aiming. *Quarterly Journal of Experimental Psychology*, **24**, 515–523. (104, 105)

Beggs, W. D. A., Graham, J. C., Monk, T. H., Shaw, M. R. H., and Howarth, C. I. (1972) Can Hick's law and Fitts' law be combined? *Acta Psychologica*, **36**, 348–357. (110)

Beggs, W. D. A., and Howarth, C. I. (1970) Movement control in a repetitive motor task. *Nature*, 225, 752–753. (105)

Beggs, W. D. A., and Howarth, C. I. (1972a) The accuracy of aiming at a target. *Acta Psychologica*, **36**, 171–177. (95, 102, 108)

Beggs, W. D. A., and Howarth, C. I. (1972b) The movement of the hand towards a target. *Quarterly Journal of Experimental Psychology*, **24**, 448–453. (102, 107)

Beggs, W. D. A., Sakstein, R., and Howarth, C. I. (1974) The generality of a theory of intermittent control of accurate movement. *Ergonomics*, **17**, 757–768. (109)

Behar, I., and Bevan, W. (1961) The perceived duration of auditory and visual intervals: Crossmodal comparison and interaction. *American Journal of Psychology*, **74**, 17–26. (128)

Bekesy, G. von. (1959) Similarities between hearing and skin sensations. *Psychological Review*, **66**, 1–22. (242)

Bell, P. A. (1978) Effects of noise and heat stress on primary and subsidiary task performance. *Human Factors*, **20**, 749–752. (263)

Benjamin, J. M. (1970) The bionics instruments C-4 laser cane. Paper to the National Academy of Engineering, Committee on the Interplay of Engineering with Biology and Medicine, Subcommittee on Sensory Aids, Warrenton, Va. (250)

Bernstein, N. (1967) *The Coordination and Regulation of Movements*. Oxford: Pergamon Press. (61)

Bertelson, P. (1965) Serial choice reaction time as a function of response versus signal-and-response repetition. *Nature*, **206**, 217–218. (154)

Bertelson, P. (1966) Central intermittency twenty years later, *Quarterly Journal of Experimental Psychology*, **18**, 153–163. (69)

Beurle, R. L. (1956) Properties of a mass of cells capable of regenerating pulses.

Royal Society of London, Philosophical Transactions, Series B, **240**, 55–94. (79)

Bilodeau, E. A. (Ed.) (1966) *Acquisition of Skill*. New York: Academic Press. (15, 204)

Bilodeau, E. A., and Bilodeau, I. McD. (Eds.) (1969) *Principles of Skill Acquisition*. New York: Academic Press. (2, 15)

Birmingham, H. P. and Taylor, F. V. (1954) A design philosophy for man–machine systems. *Proceedings of the I.R.E.*, **42**, 1748–1758. (193)

Birren, J. (1977) Introduction to J. Birren and J. W. Schaie (Eds.), *Handbook of Aging and the Individual*. US Public Health Service. (165)

Bizzi, E. (1974) Common problems confronting eye movement physiologists and investigators of somatic motor functions. *Brain Research*, **71**, 191–194. (55)

Bizzi, E., Deu, P., Morasso, P., and Polit, A. (1978) Effect of load disturbances during centrally initiated movements. *Journal of Neurophysiology*, **41**, 542–556. (55)

Bizzi, E., and Polit, A. (1979). Processes controlling visually evoked movements. *Neuropsychologia*, **17**, 203–213. (55)

Bizzi, E., Polit, A., and Morasso, P. (1976) Mechanisms underlying achievement of final head position. *Journal of Neurophysiology*, 39, 435–444. (55)

Bliss, J. D., Katcher, M. H., Rogers, C. H., and Shepard, R. P. (1970) Optical-to-tactile image conversion for the blind. *IEEE Transactions on Man–Machine Systems*, **11**, 58–65. (246)

Bliss, J. D., and Linvill, J. G. (1967) A direct translation reading aid. In R. Dufton (Ed.), *Proceedings of the International Conference on Sensory Devices for the Blind*. London: St. Dunstan's. (243, 246)

Bossom, J. (1974) Movement without proprioception. *Brain Research*, **71**, 285–296. (43)

Bossom, J., and Ommaya, A. K. (1968) Visuo-motor adaptation (to prismatic transformation of the retinal image) in monkeys with bilateral dorsal rhizotomy, *Brain*, **91**, 161–172. (43)

Bowditch, H. P., and Southard, W. F. (1880) A comparison of sight and touch. *Journal of Physiology*, 3, 232–245. (12)

Bowers, D., Heilman, K. M., Satz, P., and Altman, A. (1975) Intra-hemispheric competition. Simultaneous performance on motor, verbal, and nonverbal tasks by right-handed adults. Paper to the International Neuropsychology Society Annual Meeting, Toronto, Canada. (84)

Brainard, R. W., Irby, T. S., Fitts, P. M., and Alluisi, E. A. (1962) Some variables influencing the rate of gain of information, *Journal of Experimental Psychology*, **63**, 105–110. (86)

Briggs, G. C. (1969) Transfer of training. In E. A. and I. McD. Bilodeau (Eds.), *Principles of Skill Acquisition*. New York: Academic Press. (220)

Briggs, G. C. (1975) A comparison of attentional and control shift models of the performance of concurrent tasks. *Acta Psychologica*, **39**, 183–191. (84)

Briggs, G. C., and Swanson, J. M. (1970) Encoding, decoding and central functions in human information processing. *Journal of Experimental Psychology*, **86**, 296–308. (155)

Broadbent, D. E. (1958) *Perception and Communication*. London: Pergamon. (2, 67, 147, 198)

Broadbent, D. E. (1972) *Decision and Stress*. London: Academic Press. (165)

Brooks,. L. R. (1968) Spatial and verbal components of the act of recall. *Canadian Journal of Psychology*, **22**, 349–368. (71)

Brooks, V. B. (1978). Motor programs revisited. In *Posture and Movement: Perspective for Integrating Sensory and Motor Research on the Mammalian Nervous System*. New York: Raven Press. (58, 61)

Brown, G., and Campbell, D. (1948) *Principles of Servomechanisms.* London: Chapman and Hall. (192)

Brown, I. D., Tickner, A. H., and Simmons, D. C. (1970) Effect of prolonged driving on overtaking criteria. *Ergonomics,* **13,** 239–242. (265)

Brown, I. D. (1968) Criticisms of time-sharing techniques for the measurement of perceptual-motor difficulty. *Proceedings of the XVI International Congress of Applied Psychology.* Amsterdam: Swets and Zeitlinger. (71)

Brown, J. (1958) Some tests of the decay theory of immediate memory. *Quarterly Journal of Experimental Psychology,* **10,** 12–21. (147)

Brown, J. S., and Slater-Hammel, A. T. (1949) Discrete movements in a horizontal plane as a function of their length and direction. *Journal of Experimental Psychology,* **39,** 84–95. (94)

Brumbach, W. B. (1969) Do films help students learn motor skills? *National College of Physical Education for Men, 72nd Annual Proceedings,* pp.36–40. (214)

Bryan, W. L., and Harter, N. (1897) Studies in the physiology and psychology of the telegraphic language. *Psychological Review,* **4,** 27–53. (1)

Burns, J. T. (1965) The Effect of Errors on Reaction Time in a Serial Reaction Task. Unpublished Ph.D. thesis, University of Michigan. (162)

Burwitz, L. (1974a) Short-term memory as a function of feedback and interpolated activity. *Journal of Experimental Psychology,* **102,** 338–340. (124, 129, 139)

Burwitz, L. (1974b) Proactive interference and directed forgetting in short-term motor memory. *Journal of Experimental Psychology,* **102,** 799–805. (124, 151)

Callan, J., Klisz, D., and Parsons, O. A. (1974) Strength of auditory stimulus–response capability as a function of task complexity. *Journal of Experimental Psychology.* **102,** 1039–1045. (86)

Carlson, L. E. (1970) Below-elbow control of an externally powered hand. *Bulletin of Prosthetics Research,* **10–14,** 43–61. (230)

Carlton, L. G. (1978) Retention characteristics of movement rate information. *Journal of Motor Behavior,* **10,** 105–112. (137)

Caro, P. W., Isley, R. N., and Jolley, O. B. (1975) Mission suitability testing of an aircraft simulator. *HumRRO Technical Report, 75–12.* (197)

Carr, H. A. (1910) The autokinetic sensation. *Psychological Review,* **17,** 42–75. (113)

Case, R. (1978) Intellectual development from birth to adulthood: A neo-Piagetian interpretation. In R. Siegler (Ed.), *Children's Thinking: What Develops?.* Hillsdale, NJ: Erlbaum Associates. (78)

Chernikoff, R., Duey, J. W., and Taylor, F. V. (1960) Two-dimensional tracking with identical and different control dynamics in each coordinate. *Journal of Experimental Psychology,* **60,** 318–322. (186)

Chi, M. T. H. (1978) Knowledge structures and memory development. In R. S. Siegler (Ed.), *Children's Thinking: What Develops?.* Hillsdale, NJ: Erlbaum. (205)

Chistovich, L. A. (1960) Vospriyatie zvukovoi posledovatel' nosti. *Biofizika,* **5,** 671–676. (158)

Chistovich, L. A., and Klauss, Lu. A. (1962) Kamalizy skritovo perioda 'proizvol' noi reakstii na zvukovor signal. *Fiziologicheskii Zhurnal SSSR,* **48,** 899–906. (158)

Christman, R. J. (1954) Shifts in pitch as a function of prolonged stimulation with pure tones. *American Journal of Psychology,* **67,** 484–491. (128)

Clarkson, J., and Deutsch, J. A. (1978) Pitch control in the human voice: A reply to Rostron. *Quarterly Journal of Experimental Psychology,* **30,** 167–169. (30)

Clippinger, F. W., Avery, R., and Titus, B. R. (1974) A sensory feedback system for upper-limb amputation prosthesis. *Bulletin of Prosthetics Research,* **10–22,** 247–258. (234)

Coffey, J. L. (1963) The development and evaluation of the Batelle aural reading device. In L. L. Clark (Ed.), *Proceedings of the International Congress on Technology and Blindness*. New York: American Foundation for the Blind. (245)

Connolly, K. J. (1970) Response speed, temporal sequencing and information processing in children. In K. J. Connolly (Ed.), *Mechanisms of Motor Skill Development*. London: Academic Press. (205)

Connolly, K. J., and Jones, B. (1970) A developmental study of afferent–reafferent integration. *British Journal of Psychology*, **61**, 259–266. (139)

Conrad, B., and Brooks, V. B. (1974) Effects of dentate cooling on rapid alternating arm movements. *Journal of Neurophysiology*, **37**, 792–804. (57)

Cook, T. W. (1934) Studies in cross-education. III. Kinesthetic learning of an irregular pattern. *Journal of Experimental Psychology*, **17**, 749–762. (224)

Corcoran, D. W. J. (1965) Personality and the inverted-U relation. *British Journal of Psychology*, **56**, 267–273. (263)

Corrigan, R. E., and Brogden, W. J. (1948) The effect of angle upon precision of linear pursuit movements. *American Journal of Psychology*, **61**, 502–510. (94)

Corrigan, R. E., and Brogden, W. J. (1949) The trigonometric relationship of precision and angle of pursuit movements. *American Journal of Psychology*, **62**, 90–98. (94)

Cotzin, M., and Dallenbach, K. M. (1950) 'Facial vision': The role of pitch and loudness in the perception of obstacles by the blind. *American Journal of Psychology*, **63**, 485–515. (251)

Craft, J. L. (1973) A two-process theory for the short-term retention of motor responses. *Journal of Experimental Psychology*, **98**, 196–202. (125, 126)

Craft, J. L., and Hinrichs, J. V. (1971) Short-term retention of simple motor responses: Similarity of prior and succeeding response. *Journal of Experimental Psychology*, **87**, 297–302. (125, 126)

Craik, F. I. M. (1977) Age differences in human memory. In *Handbook of the Psychology of Aging*. New York: Van Nostrand, Reinhold. (78)

Craik, F. I. M., and Lockhart, R. S. (1972) Levels of processing: A framework for memory research. *Journal of Verbal Learning and Verbal Behavior*, **11**, 671–684. (86, 150)

Craik, K. J. W. (1943) *The Nature of Explanation*. London: Cambridge University Press. (101)

Craik, K. J. W. (1947) Theory of the human operator in control systems. I. The operator as an engineering system. *British Journal of Psychology*, 38, 56–61. (2, 28, 68, 101, 178)

Craik, K. J. W. (1948) Theory of the human operator in control systems. II. Man as an element in a control system. *British Journal of Psychology*, **38**, 142–148. (101, 178)

Craske, B., and Crawshaw, M. (1974) Differential errors of kinesthesis produced by previous limb positions. *Journal of Motor Behavior*, **6**, 273–278. (127)

Cratty, B. J. (1971) *Movement and Spatial Awareness in Blind Children and Youth*. Springfield, Ill.: Charles C. Thomas. (251)

Crossman, E. R. F. W. (1956) The Measurement of Perceptual Load in Manual Operations. Unpublished Ph.D. Thesis, University of Birmingham. (154)

Crossman, E. R. F. W. (1959) A theory of the acquisition of speed skill. *Ergonomics*, **2**, 153–166. (159, 160, 161, 219)

Crossman, E. R. F. W., and Goodeve, P. T. (1963) Feedback control of hand movement and Fitts' law. Paper to Experimental Psychology Society, Oxford. (102)

Davis, R. (1957) The human operator as a single channel information system. *Quarterly Journal of Experimental Psychology*, **9**, 119–129. (158, 168)

Denes, P. B., and Pinson, E. N. (1963) *The Speech Chain*. Murray Hill, NJ: Bell Telephones. (239)

Denny, M. R., Allard, M., Hall, E., and Rokeach, M. (1960) Supplementary report:

Delay of knowledge of results, knowledge of task, and the intertrial interval. *Journal of Experimental Psychology*, **60**, 327. (212)

Deutsch, J. A., and Clarkson, J. (1959) Nature of the vibrato and the control loop in singing. *Nature*, **183**, 167–168. (30)

Deutsch, J. A. and Deutsch, D. (1963) Attention: Some theoretical considerations. *Psychological Review*, **70**, 80–90. (67)

Dickinson, J. (1975) Directed forgetting in motor short-term memory. *Journal of Human Movement Studies*, **1**, 49–50. (151)

Dickinson, J. (1977) Incidental motor learning. *Journal of Motor Behavior*, **9**, 135–138. (151)

Dickinson, J. (1978) Retention of intentional and incidental motor learning. *Research Quarterly*, **49**, 437–441. (151)

Dickinson, J., and Higgins, N. (1977) Release from proactive and retroactive interference in motor short-term memory. *Journal of Motor Behavior*, **9**, 61–66. (135, 151)

Diewert, G. L. (1975) Retention and coding in motor short-term memory: A comparison of storage codes for distance and location information. *Journal of Motor Behavior*, **7**, 183–190. (124, 129, 132, 133, 139)

Diewert, G. L. (1976) The role of vision and kinesthesis in coding of two-dimensional movement information. *Journal of Human Movement Studies*, **3**, 191–198. (132, 133, 135, 139)

Diewert, G. L., and Roy, E. A. (1978) Coding strategy for memory of movement extent information. *Journal of Experimental Psychology: Human Learning and Memory*, **4**, 666–675. (135)

Diewert, G. L., and Stelmach, G. E. (1977) Intramodal transfer of movement information. *Acta Psychologia*, **41**, 119–128. (139)

Dimond, S. J., and Beaumont, J. G. (1971) The use of two cerebral hemispheres to increase brain capacity. *Nature*, **232**, 270–271. (85)

Donders, F. C. (1868) Die Schnelligkeit psychischer Processe. *Archiv Anatomie u. Physiologie*, Leipzig, 657–681. (154)

Drew, G. C., Colquhoun, W. P., and Long, H. A. (1958) Effect of small doses of alcohol on a skill resembling driving. *British Medical Journal*, **5103**, 993–999. (262)

Drury, G. C. (1971) Movements with lateral constraints. *Ergonomics*, 14, 293–343. (109)

Dudley, H. W. (1939) The vocoder. *Bell Laboratories Record*, **18**, 122–126. (242)

Duffy, T. M., Montague, W. E., Laabs, G. J., and Hillix, W. A. (1975) The effect of overt rehearsal on motor short-term memory. *Journal of Motor Behaviour*, **7**, 59–63. (124)

Duncan, J. (1977) Response selection rules in spatial choice reaction tasks. In S. Dornic (Ed.), *Attention and Performance VI*. Hillsdale, NJ: Erlbaum Associates. (86)

Duncan, J. (1979) Divided attention: the whole is more than the sum of its parts. *Journal of Experimental Psychology: Human Perception and Performance*, **5**, 216–228. (70, 76)

Easterbrook, J. A. (1959) The effect of emotion on cue utilization and the organization of behavior. *Psychological Review*, **66**, 183–201. (72)

Easton, T. A. (1972) On the normal use of reflexes. *American Scientist*, **60**, 591–599. (47, 48)

Easton, T. A. (1978) Coordinative structures — The basis for a motor program. In D. M. Landers and R. W. Christina (Eds.), *Psychology of Motor Behavior and Sport*. Champaign, Ill.: Human Kinetics. (47, 48, 59)

Ebeling, W. H. (1950) The guide dog movement. In P. A. Zahl (Ed.), *Blindness*. Princeton: Princeton University Press. (247)

Ellis, W., Burrows, A. A., and Jackson, K. F. (1953) Presentation of air speed while deck-landing. *Flying Personnel Research Committee, Report No. 841.* (189)

Entwisle, D. G. (1959) Aging: Effects of previous skill on training. *Occupational Psychology*, 33, 238–243. (266)

Erdelyi, M. H. (1974) A new look at the New Look: Perceptual defense and vigilance. *Psychological Review*, 81, 1–25. (87)

Eshkol, N., and Wachmann, A. (1958) *Movement Notation.* London: Weidenfeld and Nicolson. (209)

Estes, W. K. (1976) Introduction to Volume 3. In W. K. Estes (Ed.), *Handbook of Learning and Cognitive Processes.* Hillsdale, NJ: Erlbaum Associates. (203)

Evarts, E. V. (1968) Relation of pyramidal tract activity to force exerted during voluntary movement. *Journal of Neurophysiology*, 31, 14–27. (61)

Evarts, E. V., and Tanji, J. (1974) Gating of motor cortex reflexes by prior instruction. *Brain Research*, 71, 479–494. (45)

Falmagne, J. C. (1965) Stochastic models for choice reaction times with application to experimental results. *Journal of Mathematical Psychology*, 2, 77–124. (154)

Faust-Adams, A. S. (1972) Interference in short-term retention of discrete movements. *Journal of Experimental Psychology*, **96**, 400–406. (123, 124, 129, 131, 133)

Faust-Adams, A. S. (1975) The role of visual feedback in short-term motor memory. *Journal of Motor Behavior*, 7, 275–280. (139)

Fentress, J. C. (1973) Development of grooming in mice with amputated forelimbs. *Science*, 179, 704–705. (43)

Festinger, L., and Canon, L. K. (1976) Information about spatial location based on knowledge about efference. *Psychological Review*, 72, 373–384. (45)

Findlay, J. M. (1974) Direction, perception and human fixation eye movements. *Vision Research*, 14, 703–711. (111)

Fisher, G. H. (1960) Intersensory elements of phenomenal space. *Proceedings of the 16th International Congress of Psychology*, p.840. (111)

Fisher, G. H. (1961) Autokinesis in the spatial senses. *Bulletin of the British Psychological Society*, 44, 16–17. (111)

Fisher, G. H. (1962) Intersensory Localisation. Unpublished Ph.D. Thesis, University of Hull. (111, 116)

Fitts, P. M. (1947) A study of location discrimination ability. In P. M. Fitts (Ed.), *Psychological Research on Equipment Design.* Washington DC: US Government Printing Office. (124)

Fitts, P. M. (1951) Engineering psychology and equipment design. In S. S. Stevens (Ed.), *Handbook of Experimental Psychology.* New York: Wiley. (2)

Fitts, P. M. (1954) The information capacity of the human motor system in controlling the amplitude of movement. *Journal of Experimental Psychology*, 47, 381–391. (94, 99, 108, 259)

Fitts, P. M. (1966) Cognitive aspects of information processing: III. Set for speed versus accuracy. *Journal of Experimental Psychology*, 71, 849–857. (9)

Fitts, P. M., and Posner, M. I. (1967) *Human Performance.* Belmont, Calif.: Brooks/Cole. (231, 232)

Fleishman, E. A. (1958) Dimensional analysis of movement reactions. *Journal of Experimental Psychology*, 55, 438–453. (3)

Fleishman, E. A. (1962) The description and prediction of perceptual-motor skill learning. In R. Glaser (Ed.), *Training Research and Education.* University of Pittsburgh Press. (221)

Fleishman, E. A. (1966) Human abilities and the acquisition of skill. In E. A. Bilodeau (Ed.), *Acquisition of Skill.* New York: Academic Press. (4)

Fleishman, E. A., and Rich, S. (1963) Role of kinesthetic and spatial–visual abilities in perceptual-motor learning. *Journal of Experimental Psychology*, **66**, 6–11. (233)

Fletcher, C. (Ben), and Rabbitt, P. M. A. (1978) The changing pattern of perceptual analytic strategies and response selection with practice in a two-choice reaction time task. *Quarterly Journal of Experimental Psychology*, **30**, 417–427. (160)

Flexman, R. E., Matheny, W. G., and Brown, E. L. (1950) Evaluation of the Link and special methods of instruction etc. University of Illinois, *Aeronautics Bulletin No. 8*. (196)

Foulke, E. (1969) Non-visual communication: IV. Reading by listening. *Education of the Visually Handicapped*, **1**, 79–81. (247)

Foulke, E. (1970) The perceptual basis for mobility. *American Foundation for the Blind, Research Bulletin*, **23**, 1–8. (247)

Fowler, S. C., and Notterman, J. M. (1975) An observed short-term memory effect for isometric force emission. *Perception and Psychophysics*, **17**, 393–397. (134)

Fox, P. W., and Levy, C. M. (1969) Acquisition of a simple motor response as influenced by the presence or absence of action visual feedback. *Journal of Motor Behavior*, **1**, 169–180. (210)

Franklin, H. C., and Holding, D. H. (1977) Personal memories at different ages. *Quarterly Journal of Experimental Psychology*, **29**, 527–533. (266)

Freedy, A., Hull, F., and Lyman, J. (1971) Adaptive aiding for artificial limb control. *Bulletin of Prosthetics Research*, **10–16**, 3–15. (236)

Freedy, A., Lucaccini, L. F., and Lyman, J. (1967) Information and control analysis of externally powered artificial arm systems. *Bulletin of Prosthetics Research*, **10–8**, 112–131. (231)

Fuchs, A. H. (1962) The progression–regression hypothesis in perceptual-motor skill learning. *Journal of Experimental Psychology*, **63**, 177–182. (208)

Fukuda, T. (1961) Studies on human dynamics postures from the viewpoint of postural reflexes. *Acta Oto-Laryngologica*, Supplement 161. (48)

Garvey, W. D. (1960) A comparison of the effects of training and secondary tasks on tracking. *Journal of Applied Psychology*, **44**, 370–375. (193)

Gelb, A. (1974) *Applied Optimal Estimation*. Cambridge, Mass.: MIT Press. (35)

Geldard, F. A. (1961) Cutaneous channels of communication. In W. A. Rosenblith (Ed.), *Sensory Communication*. New York: Wiley. (234)

Geldard, F. A. (1972) *The Human Senses*. New York: Wiley. (236)

Gengel, R. W. (1977) Research with Upton's visual speech reading aid. Paper to Research Conference on Speech-Processing Aids for the Deaf, Gallaudet College, Washington, DC. (241)

Gentile, A. M. (1972) A working model of skill acquisition with application to teaching. *Quest*, **17**, 3–23. (204, 213)

Gentile, A. M. (1974) Research in short-term motor memory: Methodological mire. In M. G. Wade and R. Martens (Eds.), *Psychology of Motor Behavior and Sport*. Urbana, Ill.: Human Kinetics. (122)

Gescheider, G. A. (1970) Some comparisons between touch and hearing. *IEEE Transactions on Man–Machine Systems*, **MMS-11**, 28–35. (242)

Gibbs, C. B. (1970) Servo-control systems in organisms and the transfer of skill. In D. Legge (Ed.), *Skills*. London: Penguin Books. (50)

Glanzer, M. (1972) Storage mechanisms in recall. In G. H. Bower and J. T. Spence (Eds.), *The Psychology of Learning and Motivation*, Vol. 5. New York: Academic Press. (149)

Glencross, D. J. (1973) Temporal organization in a repetitive speed skill. *Ergonomics*, **16**, 765–776. (44)

Glencross, D. J. (1974) Pauses in a repetitive speed skill. *Perceptual and Motor Skills*, **38**, 246. (44)

Glencross, D. J. (1975) The effects of changes in task conditions on the temporal organization of a repetitive speed skill. *Ergonomics*, **18**, 17–28. (44, 54)

Glencross, D. J. (1977) Control of skilled movements. *Psychological Bulletin*, **84**, 14–29. (44, 48)

Glencross, D. J. and Oldfield, S. R. (1975) The use of ischemic nerve block procedures in the investigation of the sensory control of movements. *Biological Psychology*, **2**, 165–174. (44)

Goff, G. D. (1967) Differential discrimination of frequency of cutaneous mechanical vibration. *Journal of Experimental Psychology*, **74**, 294–299. (242)

Gottsdanker, R. M. (1956) The ability of human operators to detect acceleration of target motion. *Psychological Bulletin*, **53**, 367–375. (186)

Gottsdanker, R. (1979) A psychological refractory period or an unprepared period? *Journal of Experimental Psychology: Human Perception and Performance*, **5**, 208–215. (69)

Gottsdanker, R. M. and Kent, K. (1978) Reaction time and probability on isolated trials. *Journal of Motor Behavior*, **10**, 233–238. (8)

Granit, R. (1975) The functional role of the muscle spindles — Facts and hypotheses. *Brain*, **98**, 531–556. (50)

Gregory, R. L., and Zangwill, O. L. (1963) The origin of the autokinetic effect. *Quarterly Journal of Experimental Psychology*, **15**, 252–261. (113)

Griew, S. (1958) Age changes and information loss in performance of a pursuit tracking task involving interrupted preview. *Journal of Experimental Psychology*, **55**, 486–489. (266)

Griffin, D. (1958) *Listening in the Dark*. New Haven, Conn: Yale University Press. (28)

Grillner, S. (1975) Locomotion in vertebrates: General mechanisms and reflex interaction. *Physiological Reviews*, **55**, 247–304. (48)

Groth, H., and Lyman, J. (1961) Control problems in externally powered arm prostheses. *Orthopedic and Prosthetic Appliance Journal*, **15**, 174–177. (230)

Hagman, J. D. (1978) Specific-cue effects of interpolated movements on distance and location retention in short-term motor memory. *Memory and Cognition*, **6**, 432–437. (124, 132, 133)

Hagman, J. D., and Francis, E. W. (1975) The instructional variable and kinesthetic cue recall. *Journal of Motor Behavior*, **7**, 141–146. (132)

Hall, C. R., and Leavitt, J. L. (1977) Encoding and retention characteristics of duration and distance. *Journal of Human Movement Studies*, **3**, 88–89. (135)

Hall, C. R., and Wilberg, R. B. (1977) Distance reproduction, velocity, and the range effect. *Journal of Human Movement Studies*, **3**, 60–65. (124)

Hall, C. R., and Wilberg, R. B. (1978) Distance reproduction, velocity, response strategy, and criterion movement end-point. *Journal of Human Movement Studies*, **4**, 144–154. (124, 133)

Hamilton, C. R. (1964) Intermanual transfer of adaptation to prisms. *American Journal of Psychology*, **77**, 457–462. (115)

Hammerton, M. (1963) The components of acquisition time. *Ergonomics*, **7**, 91–93. (186)

Hammerton, M. (1967) Visual factors affecting transfer of training from a simulated to a real control situation. *Journal of Applied Psychology*, **51**, 46–49. (195, 197)

Hammerton, M., and Tickner, A. H. (1966) An investigation into the comparative suitability of forearm, hand and thumb controls in an acquisition task. *Ergonomics*, **9**, 125–130. (187)

Hammerton, M., and Tickner, A. H. (1970) Structured and blank backgrounds in a pursuit tracking task. *Ergonomics*, **13**, 719–722. (194)

Hancock, R. P. (1970) Interfacial couplings for man-machine systems. *Bulletin of Prosthetics Research*, **10–14**, 78–101. (229)

Hanson, C., and Lofthus, G. K. (1978) Effects of fatigue and laterality on fractionated reaction time. *Journal of Motor Behavior*, **10**, 177–184. (8)

Hardt, M. E., Held, R., and Steinback, M. J. (1971) Adaptation to displaced vision: A change in the central control of sensorimotor coordination. *Journal of Experimental Psychology*, **89**, 229–239. (115)

Harris, C. S. (1963) Adaptation to displaced vision: Visual motor or proprioceptive change? *Science*, **140**, 812–813. (115)

Hasher, L. and Zacks, R. T. (1979) Automatic and effortful processes in memory. *Journal of Experimental Psychology: General*, **108**, 356–388. (67)

Hatze, H. (1976) Biomechanical aspects of a successful motion optimization. In P. V. Komi (Ed.), *Biomechanics V-B*. Baltimore, Md.: University Park Press. (214)

Hayes, K. C. (1978) Supraspinal and spinal processes involved in the initiation of fast movements. In D. M. Landers and R. W. Christina (Eds.), *Psychology of Motor Behavior and Sport*. Champaign, Ill.: Human Kinetics. (59, 60, 61)

Hayes, K. C., and Marteniuk, R. G. (1976) Dimensions of motor task complexity. In G. E. Stelmach (Ed.), *Motor Control: Issues and Trends*. New York: Academic Press. (48, 205)

Head, H. (1920) *Studies in Neurology*, Vol. 11. New York: Macmillan. (222)

Held, R., and Freedman, S. J. (1963) Plasticity in human sensorimotor control. *Science*, **142**, 455–462. (115)

Held, R., and Hein, A. (1958) Adaptation of disarranged hand–eye coordination contingent upon reafferent stimulation. *Perceptual and Motor Skills*, **8**, 87–90. (115)

Hellebrandt, F. A., Houtz, S. J., Partridge, M. J., and Walters, C. E. (1956) Tonic neck reflexes in exercises of stress in man. *American Journal of Physical Medicine*, **35**, 144–159. (48)

Hellige, J. B., Cox, P. J., and Litvac, L. (1979) Information processing in the cerebral hemispheres. Selective hemispheric activation and capacity limitations. *Journal of Experimental Psychology: General*, **108**, 251–279. (81)

Helson, H. (1964) *Adaptation Level Theory*. New York: Harper and Row. (123)

Hendrickson, G., and Schroeder, W. H. (1941). Transfer of training in learning to hit a submerged target. *Journal of Educational Psychology*, **32**, 205–213. (197, 206)

Henmon, V. A. C. (1911) The relation of time of judgment for accuracy. *Psychological Review*, **18**, 186–201. (154)

Henry, F. M. (1958) Specificity vs. generality in learning motor skills. *61st Annual Proceedings of the College of Physical Education*, Washington, DC. (221)

Henry, F. M. (1974) Constant and variable performance errors within a group of individuals. *Journal of Motor Behavior*, **6**, 149–154. (122)

Herman, L. M., and Bailey, D. R. (1970) Comparative effects of retroactive and proactive interference in motor short-term memory. *Journal of Experimental Psychology*, **86**, 407–415. (123, 125, 126, 129)

Heyes, A. D., and Gazely, D. J. (1974) The effects of training on the accuracy of auditory localisation using binaural hearing and systems. *British Journal of Audiology*, **9**, 61–70. (114)

Hick, W. E. (1952) On the rate of gain of information. *Quarterly Journal of Experimental Psychology*, **4**, 11–26. (2, 8, 98, 230)

Hick, W. E. (1953) Some features of the after contraction phenomenon. *Quarterly Journal of Experimental Psychology*, **5**, 166–170. (113)

Hick, W. E., and Bates, J. A. (1950) The human operator of control mechanisms. London: *Ministry of Supply. Permanent Records of Research and Development*, 170204. (231)

Hicks, R. E. (1975) Intrahemispheric response competition between vocal and unimanual performance in normal adult human males. *Journal of Comparative and Physiological Psychology*, **89**, 50–60. (84)

Hicks, R. E., Bradshaw, G. J., Kinsbourne, M., and Feigin, D. S. (1978) Vocal-manual trade-offs, in hemispheric sharing of human performance control. *Journal of Motor Behavior*, **10**, 1–6. (84)

Hicks, R. E., Provenzano, F. J., and Rybstein, E. D. (1975) Generalized and lateralized effects of concurrent verbal rehearsal upon performance of sequential movements of the fingers by the left and right hands. *Acta Psychologica*, **39**, 119–130. (84)

Higgins, J. R., and Spaeth, R. K. (1972) Relationship between consistency of movement and environmental condition. *Quest*, **17**, 61–69. (53)

Hill, H., Gray, F., and Ellson, D. G. (1947) Wavelength and amplitude characteristics of tracking error curves. *Wright Field: AAF-AMC Engineering Report*, TSEAA-694-2D. (231)

Hiscock, M. and Kinsbourne, M. (1978) Ontogeny of cerebral dominance: Evidence from time-sharing asymmetry in children. *Developmental Psychology*, **14**, 321–392. (75, 78)

Hiscock, M. and Kinsbourne, M. (1980) Individual differences in cerebral lateralization: Are they relevant to learning disability? In J. E. Volk and W. Cruickshank (Eds.), *Recent Research in Learning Disabilities*. (78)

Ho, L., and Shea, J. B. (1978) Levels of processing and the coding of position cues in motor short-term memory. *Journal of Motor Behavior*, **10**, 113–121. (136, 151)

Hockey, G. R. J. (in press) *Stress and Fatigue in Human Performance*. Chichester: Wiley. (263)

Holding, D. H. (1962) Transfer between difficult and easy tasks. *British Journal of Psychology*, **53**, 397–407. (195)

Holding, D. H. (1965) *Principles of Training*. London: Pergamon. (17, 63, 206, 211, 218, 219)

Holding, D. H. (1968) Accuracy of delayed aiming responses. *Psychonomic Science*, **17**, 125–126. (110, 111, 112, 139)

Holding, D. H. (Ed.) (1969) *Experimental Psychology in Industry*. London: Penguin Books. (267)

Holding, D. H. (1970) Learning without errors. In L. E. Smith (Ed.), *Psychology of Motor Learning*. Chicago: Athletic Institute. (210)

Holding, D. H. (1974) Risk, effort and fatigue. In M. G. Wade and R. Martens (Eds.), *Psychology of Motor Behavior and Sport*. Champaign, Ill.: Human Kinetics. (265)

Holding, D. H. (1975) Sensory storage reconsidered. *Memory and Cognition*, **3**, 31–41. (150)

Holding, D. H. (1976) An approximate transfer surface. *Journal of Motor Behavior*, **8**, 1–9. (225, 260)

Holding, D. H. (1977) Transfer of training. In R. A. Schmidt and E. A. Fleishman (Eds.), Section 9 — Perceptual motor learning and performance. In B. B. Wolman (Ed.), *International Encyclopedia of Neurology, Psychiatry, Psychoanalysis and Psychology*. New York: Van Nostrand. (220)

Holding, D. H., and Dennis, J. P. (1957) An unexpected effect in sound localization. *Nature*, **180**, 1471–1472. (9)

Holding, D. H., and Macrae, A. W. (1964) Guidance, restriction and knowledge of results. *Ergonomics*, **7**, 289–295. (6)

Hollingworth, H. L. (1909) The inaccuracy of movement. *Archives of Psychology*, **2**, 1–87. (124)

Holst, E. von. (1954) Relations between the central nervous system and the peripheral organs. *British Journal of Animal Behaviour*, **2**, 89–94. (49)

Hoover, R. E. (1950) The cane as a travel aid. In P. A. Zahl (Ed.), *Blindness*. Princeton: Princeton University Press. (247)

Howard, I. P., Anstis, T., and Lucia, H. C. (1974) The relative lability of mobile and stationary components in a visual motor adaptation task. *Quarterly Journal of Experimental Psychology*, **26**, 293–300. (116)

Howard, I. P., and Templeton, W. B. (1966) *Human Spatial Orientation*. London: Wiley. (116)

Howarth, C. I. (1978) Strategies in the control of movement. In G. Underwood (Ed.), *Strategies in Information Processing*. London: Academic Press. (109, 111, 112, 115, 116)

Howarth, C. I., Beggs, W. D. A., and Bowden, J. M. (1971) The relationship between speed and accuracy of movement aimed at a target. *Acta Psychologica*, **35**, 207–218. (100, 101, 102, 103, 104, 106)

Hull, C. L. (1943) *Principles of Behavior*. New York: Appleton (216)

Hyman, R. (1953) Stimulus information as a determinant of reaction time. *Journal of Experimental Psychology*, **45**, 188–197. (98)

Institute of Measurement and Control (1977) *Human Operators and Simulation*. London. (194)

Jackson, C. V. (1953) Visual factors in auditory localisation. *Quarterly Journal of Experimental Psychology*, **5**, 188–197. (111, 116)

Jackson, C. V. (1954) Influence of previous movement and posture on subsequent posture. *Quarterly Journal of Experimental Psychology*, **6**, 72–78. (113)

Jackson, M. D., and McClelland, J. L. (1979) Processing determinants of reading and speech. *Journal of Experimental Psychology: General,* **108**, 151–181. (65)

Jacobson, E. (1932) Electrophysiology of mental activities. *American Journal of Psychology*, **44**, 676–694. (219)

James, W. (1890) *Principles of Psychology*. New York: Holt. (65)

Johnston, W. A., and Heinz, S. P. (1978) Flexibility and capacity demands of attention. *Journal of Experimental Psychology: General*, **107**, 420–435. (67)

Jones, B. (1972) Outflow and inflow in movement duplication. *Perception and Psychophysics*, **12**, 95–96. (134, 136, 137)

Jones, B. (1974a) Role of central monitoring of efference in short-term memory for movements. *Journal of Experimental Psychology*, **102**, 37–43. (127, 134, 135, 136, 137)

Jones, B. (1974b) The importance of memory traces of motor efferent discharges for learning skilled movements. *Developmental Medicine and Child Neurology*, **16**, 620–628. (211)

Jones, B., and Hulme, M. R. (1976) Evidence for an outflow theory of skill. *Acta Psychologica*, **40**, 49–59. (137)

Jones, R. V. (1978) *Most Secret War*. London: Hamilton. (189)

Jordan, T. C., and Rabbitt, P. M. A. (1977) Response times of increasing complexity as a function of ageing. *British Journal of Psychology*, **68**, 189–201. (266)

Judd, C. H. (1908) The relationship of special training to general intelligence. *Educational Review*, **36**, 28–42. (206)

Juurmaa, J. (1973) Transposition in mental spatial manipulation: A theoretical analysis. American Foundation for the Blind, *Research Bulletin*, **26**, 87–134. (251)

Kahneman, D. (1973) *Attention and Effort*. Englewood Cliffs, NJ: Prentice-Hall. (12, 67, 68, 70, 72, 80, 133)

Kalikow, D. N. (1974) Information processing models and computer aids for human performance: Final report second language learning. *Technical Report No. 2841*, Bolt, Beranek and Newman, Cambridge, Mass. (63)

Kalikow, D. N., and Rollins, A. M. (1973) Information processing models and computer aids for human performance: Technical report second language learning. *Technical Report No. 2654*, Bolt, Beranek and Newman, Cambridge, Mass. (63)

Kantowitz, B. . (1972) Interference in short-term memory: Interpolated task difficulty, similarity, or activity? *Journal of Experimental Psychology*, **95**, 264–274. (129, 131, 139, 148)

Kantowitz, B. H. (1974) Modality effects in recognition short-term memory. *Journal of Experimental Psychology*, **103**, 522–529. (145, 146)

Kantowitz, B. H., and Knight, J. L. (1974) Testing tapping time-sharing. *Journal of Experimental Psychology*, **103**, 331–336. (71, 72, 75)

Kantowitz, B. H., and Knight, J. L. (1976) Testing tapping time-sharing: II. Auditory secondary task. *Acta Psychologica*, **40**, 343–362. (67, 75)

Karlin, L. (1966) Development of readiness to respond during short foreperiods. *Journal of Experimental Psychology*, **72**, 505–509. (158)

Kay, L. (1972) Evaluation of the ultrasonic binaural sensory aid for the blind. Paper to Conference on Evaluation of Sensory Aids for the Visually Handicapped, National Academy of Sciences, Washington, DC. (250)

Keele, S. W. (1968) Movement control in skilled motor performance. *Psychological Bulletin*, **70**, 387–403. (42, 48)

Keele, S. W. (1973) *Attention and Human Performance*. Pacific Palisades, Calif.: Goodyear. (48, 51, 63, 123, 142)

Keele, S. W. (1975) The representation of motor programs. In P. M. A. Rabbit and S. Dornic (Eds.), *Attention and Performance V*. New York: Academic Press. (142)

Keele, S. W. (1977) Current status of the motor program concept. In D. M. Landers and R. W. Christina (Eds.), *Psychology of Motor Behavior and Sport*. Champaign, Ill.: Human Kinetics. (63)

Keele, S. W., and Ells, J. G. (1972) Memory characteristics of kinesthetic information. *Journal of Motor Behavior*, **4**, 127–134. (56, 124, 129, 130, 131, 133, 134, 135)

Keele, S. W., and Neill, W. T. (1978) Mechanisms of attention. In E. C. Carterette and M. P. Freidman (Eds.), *Handbook of Perception, Volume 9*. New York: Academic Press. (68)

Keele, S. W., and Posner, M. I. (1968) Processing of visual feedback in rapid movements. *Journal of Experimental Psychology*, **77**, 155–158. (105, 106)

Keele, S. W., and Summers, J. J. (1976) The structure of motor programs. In G. E. Stelmach (Ed.), *Motor Control: Issues and Trends*. New York: Academic Press. (43, 48, 51, 52, 61, 142, 215)

Kelley, C. (1968) *Manual and Automatic Control*. New York: Wiley. (19, 32)

Kelly, C. (1962) Predictor instruments look into the future. *Control Engineering*, **9**, 86–90. (183)

Kelso, J. A. S. (1977a) Planning and efferent components in the coding of movement. *Journal of Motor Behavior*, **9**, 33–47. (123, 124, 127, 129, 130, 134, 136, 137, 138)

Kelso, J. A. S. (1977b) Motor control mechanisms underlying human movement reproduction. *Journal of Experimental Psychology: Human Learning and Performance*, **3**, 529–543. (49, 56, 62, 137)

Kelso, J. A. S. (1978) Recognition and recall in slow movements: Separate states? *Journal of Motor Behavior*, **10**, 69–76. (144)

Kelso, J. A. S., and Frekany, G. A. (1978) Coding processes in preselected and constrained movements: Effect of vision. *Acta Psychologica*, **42**, 145–161. (139, 140)

Kelso, J. A. S., and Stelmach, G. E. (1974) Behavioral and neurological parameters of the nerve compression block. *Journal of Motor Behavior*, **6**, 179–190. (44)

Kelso, J. A. S., and Stelmach, G. E. (1976) Central and peripheral mechanisms in motor control. In G. E. Stelmach (Ed.), *Motor Control: Issues and Trends*. New York: Academic Press. (138)

Kelso, J. A. S., and Wallace, S. A. (1978) Conscious mechanisms in movement.

In G. E. Stelmach (Ed.), *Information Processing in Motor Control and Learning*. New York: Academic Press. (211)

Kelso, J. A. S., Wallace, S. A., Stelmach, G. E., and Weitz, G. A. (1975) Sensory and motor impairment in the nerve compression block. *Quarterly Journal of Experimental Psychology*, **27**, 123–129. (44)

Keppel, G. C., and Underwood, B. J. (1962) Proactive inhibition in short-term retention of single items. *Journal of Verbal Learning and Verbal Behavior*, **1**, 153–161. (147)

Kerr, B. (1973) Processing demands during mental operations. *Memory and Cognition*, **1**, 401–412. (69, 133)

Kerr, B. (1978a) Task factors that influence selection and preparation for voluntary movements. In G. E. Stelmach (Ed.), *Information Processing in Motor Control and Learning*. New York: Academic Press. (47)

Kerr, B. (1978b). The effect of invalid task parameters on short-term memory. *Journal of Motor Behavior*, **10**, 261–273. (124, 127, 129, 133)

Kickert, W. G., Bertrand, J. W., and Praagman, J. (1978) Some comments on cybernetics and control. *IEEE Transactions on Systems, Man and Cybernetics*, **SMC-8**, 805–809. (26)

Kinchla, R. A., and Smyzer, F. (1967) A diffusion model of perceptual memory. *Perception and Psychophysics*, **2**, 219–229. (111, 112)

Kinsbourne, M. (1974) Lateral interactions in the brain. In M. Kinsbourne and W. L. Smith (Eds.), *Hemispheric Disconnection and Cerebral Function*. Springfield: Thomas. (85, 88)

Kinsbourne, M. (1977) Cognitive decline with advancing age: An interpretation. In W. L. Smith and M. Kinsbourne (Eds.), *Aging, Dementia and Cerebral Function*. New York: Spectrum Press. (78)

Kinsbourne, M. (in press) Cognitive deficit and the unity of brain organization. Goldstein's perspective updated. In R. W. Rieber (Ed.), *A Kurt Goldstein Reader: Shaping of Neuropsychology*. New York: AMS Press. (86)

Kinsbourne, M., and Cook, J. (1971) Generalized and lateralized effects of concurrent verbalization on a unimanual skill. *Quarterly Journal of Experimental Psychology*, **23**, 341–345. (84)

Kinsbourne, M. and Hicks, R. E. (1978) Functional cerebral space: A model for overflow, transfer and interference effects in human performance. In J. Requin, (Ed.). *Attention and Performance VII*. Hillsdale, NJ, Lawrence Erlbaum Associates. (75, 76, 79, 80, 83, 84)

Kintsch, W., and Buschke, H. (1969) Homophones and synonyms in short-term recognition. *Journal of Experimental Psychology*, **80**, 403–407. (149)

Kirman, J. H. (1973) Tactile communication of speech: A review and analysis. *Psychological Bulletin*, **80**, 54–74. (243)

Klapp, S. T. (1975) Feedback versus motor programming in the control of aimed movements. *Journal of Experimental Psychology: Human Perception and Performance*, **104**, 147–153. (47)

Klapp, S. T. (1976) Short-term memory as a response preparation state. *Memory and Cognition*, **4**, 721–729. (47, 62)

Klapp, S. T. (1978) Reaction time analysis of programmed control. In R. S. Hutton (Ed.), *Exercise and Sport Sciences Reviews*. Santa Barbara, Calif.: Journal Publishing Affiliates, pp.231–253. (47)

Klapp, S. T. (1979) Doing two things at once: The role of temporal compatibility. *Memory and Cognition*, **5**, 375–381. (69, 76, 82)

Klapp, S. T. and Greim, D. M. (1979) Programmed control of aimed movements revisited: The role of target visibility and symmetry. *Journal of*

Experimental Psychology: Human Perception and Performance, **5**, 509–521. (47, 58)

Klein, R., and Posner, M. I. (1974) Attention to visual and kinesthetic components of skills. *Brain Research*, **71**, 401–411. (140)

Klemmer, E. T. (1956) Time uncertainty, in simple reaction time. *Journal of Experimental Psychology*, **72**, 505–509. (158)

Koch, C. G., and Dorfman, P. W. (1979) Recall and recognition processes in motor memory: Effects of feedback and knowledge of results. *Journal of Motor Behavior*, **11**, 23–34. (143)

Kohler, I. (1962) Experiments with goggles. In R. Held and W. Richards (Eds.), *Perception, Mechanisms and Models*. San Francisco: Freeman. (31)

Kohler, I. (1964) Orientation by aural cues. American Foundation for the Blind, *Research Bulletin*, **4**, 14–53. (251)

Kolers, P. A. (1969) Clues to a letter's recognition: Implications for the design of characters. *Journal of Typographic Research*, **3**, 145–168. (245)

Kristofferson, M. W. (1977) The effects of practice with one positive set in a memory scanning task can be completely transferred to a new set. *Memory and Cognition*, **5**, 177–186. (160)

Kurland, M. (1978) Operational Efficiency, Automatization, and the Development of M-space. Ph.D. Dissertation, University of Toronto. (78)

Laabs, G. J. (1971) Cue Effects in Motor Short-term Memory. Unpublished doctoral dissertation, University of Oregon. (129, 141)

Laabs, G. J. (1973) Retention characteristics of different reproduction cues in motor short-term memory. *Journal of Experimental Psychology*, **100**, 168–177. (56, 122, 124, 127, 129, 130, 132, 135, 136, 141, 146, 149)

Laabs, G. J. (1974) The effect of interpolated motor activity on short-term retention of movement distance and end-location. *Journal of Motor Behavior*, **6**, 279–288. (126, 132, 133)

Laabs, G. J. (1975a) Comments on retention characteristics of motor short-term memory cues. *Journal of Motor Behavior*, **7**, 147–149. (122)

Laabs, G. J. (1975b) Short-term recognition memory for movement distance and end-location. Paper presented at the meeting of the Midwestern Psychological Association, Chicago. (146)

Laabs, G. J. (1976) A note concerning the effect of a kinesthetic memory load on the retention of movement end-location. *Journal of Motor Behavior*, **8**, 313–316. (132, 133)

Laabs, G. J. (1977) The effects of cue designation and size on movement reproduction. Paper presented at the meeting of the Western Psychological Association, Seattle. (124, 132, 133)

Laabs, G. J. (1978) Recognition and recall of motor movements. Paper presented at the meeting of the American Psychological Association, Toronto. (146)

Laban, R. (1956) *Principles of Dance and Movement Notation*. London: Macdonald and Evans. (209)

LaBerge, D. (1975) Acquisition of automatic processing in perceptual and associative learning. In P. M. A. Rabbitt and S. Dornic (Eds.), *Attention and Performance, V*. London: Academic Press. (88)

Labuc, S. (1978) A comparison of pursuit tracking performance using thumb movement and thumb pressure controls with high and low gains. *Army Personnel Research Establishment Report No. 17/77*. (186)

Laming, D. R. J. (1968) *An Information Theory of Choice Reaction Times*. New York: Academic Press. (154)

Lashley, K. S. (1917) The accuracy of movement in the absence of excitation from the moving organ. *American Journal of Physiology*, **43**, 169–194. (42)

Lashley, K. S. (1951) The problem of serial order in behavior. In L. A. Jeffress, (Ed.), *Cerebral Mechanisms in Behavior*. New York: Wiley. (44, 55, 75)

Laszlo, J. I. (1966) The performance of a simple motor task with kinaesthetic sense loss. *Quarterly Journal of Experimental Psychology*, **18**, 1–8. (43)

Laszlo, J. I. (1967) Training of fast tapping with reduction of kinaesthetic, tactile, visual and auditory sensations. *Quarterly Journal of Experimental Psychology*, **19**, 344–349. (43)

Laszlo, J. I., and Manning, L. C. (1970) The role of motor programming, command and standard in the central control of skilled movement. *Journal of Motor Behavior*, **2**, 111–124. (268)

Lee, B. S. (1950) Effects of delayed speech feedback. *Journal of the Acoustic Society of America*, **22**, 824–826. (29)

Lee, B. S. (1951) Artificial stutter. *Journal of Speech and Hearing Disorders*, **16**, 53–55. (29)

Legge, D. (1965) Analysis of visual and proprioceptive components of motor skill by means of a drug. *British Journal of Psychology*, **56**, 243–254. (262)

Lenneberg, E. H. (1967) *Biological Foundations of Language*. New York: Wiley. (44)

Leonard, J. A. (1953) Advance information in sensorimotor skills. *Quarterly Journal of Experimental Psychology*, **5**, 141–149. (11)

Leonard, K. A. (1972) Studies in blind mobility. *Applied Ergonomics*, **3**, 37–46. (250)

Levin, I. P., Norman, K. L., and Dolezal, J. M. (1973) Response scale effects and integration processes in the averaging of motor movements. *Journal of Motor Behavior*, **5**, 1–8. (128, 142)

Levison, W. H. (1970) A model for task interference. *Proceedings of the Sixth Annual Conference on Manual Control*, Wright-Patterson Air Force Base, Ohio. (73)

Levison, W. H. (1979) A model for mental workload in tasks requiring continuous information processing. In N. Moray (Ed.), *Mental Workload: Its Theory and Measurement*, New York: Plenum. (73)

Levitt, H., and Nye, P. W. (1971) Sensory training aids for the hearing impaired. Paper to National Academy of Engineering. Easton, Md. (238, 240, 241)

Liberman, A. M., Cooper, F. S., Shankweiler, D. P., and Studdert-Kennedy, M. (1968) Why are speech spectrograms hard to read? *American Annals of the Deaf*, **113**, 127–133. (242)

Licklider, J. C. R. (1960) Quasi-linear operator models in the study of manual tracking. In R. D. Luce (Ed.), *Developments in Mathematical Psychology*. Glencoe, Ill.: Free Press. (258)

Loeb, M. (in press) *Noise and Human Behavior*. New York: Wiley. (263)

Loess, H. (1964) Proactive inhibition in short-term memory. *Journal of Verbal Learning and Verbal Behavior*, **3**, 362–368. (147)

Lomas, J. and Kimura, D. (1976) Intrahemispheric interaction between speaking and sequential manual activity. *Neuropsychologia*, **14**, 23–33. (84)

Long, J. (1976) Visual feedback and skilled keying: Differential effects of masking the printed copy and the keyboard. *Ergonomics*, **19**, 93–110. (162)

Lordahl, D. S., and Archer, E. J. (1958) Transfer effects on a rotary pursuit task as a function of final task difficulty. *Journal of Experimental Psychology*, **56**, 421–426. (223)

Loveless, N. E., and Holding, D. H. (1959) Reaction time and tracking ability. *Perceptual and Motor Skills*, **9**, 134. (8)

Lucaccini, L. F., Freedy, A., Rey, P., and Lyman, J. (1967) Sensory motor control system for an externally powered artificial arm. *Bulletin of Prosthetics Research*, **10-8**, 92–111. (231)

McClelland, D. C. (1943). Factors influencing the time-error in judgments of visual extent. *Journal of Experimental Psychology*, **33**, 81–95. (127)

McCracken, H. D., and Stelmach, G. E. (1977). A test of the schema theory of discrete motor learning. *Journal of Motor Behavior*, **9**, 193–201. (142)

McDaniel, J. W. (1969). *Physical Disability and Human Behavior*. New York: Pergamon. (238)

McGill, W. J. (1967). Stochastic latency mechanisms. In R. D. Luce, R. R. Bush, and E. Galanter (Eds.), *Handbook of Mathematical Psychology*. New York: Wiley. (154)

McLeod, P. D. (1977). A dual task modality effect: Support for multiprocessor models of attention. *Quarterly Journal of Experimental Psychology*, **29**, 651–668. (11, 67, 71, 198)

McLeod, P. D. (1978) Does probe RT measure central processing demand? *Quarterly Journal of Experimental Psychology*, **30**, 83–89. (67, 71)

McRuer, D., Graham, D., and Krendel, E. (1967). Manual control of single-loop systems. *Journal of the Franklin Institute*, **283**, 1–29 and 145–168. (193)

McRuer, D., and Krendel, E. (1974). Mathematical models of human pilot performance. *NATO AGARDograph No. 188*. (32, 33, 35)

Magill, R. A., and Dowell, M. N. (1977) Serial-position effects in motor short-term memory. *Journal of Motor Behavior*, **9**, 319–324. (151)

Malina, R. M., and Rarick, G. L. (1968) A device for assessing the role of information feedback in speed and accuracy of throwing performance. *Research Quarterly*, **39**, 220–222. (213)

Mandler, G. (1975) *Mind and Emotion*. New York: Wiley. (87)

Mann, R. W. (1974) Technology and human rehabilitation: Prostheses for sensory rehabilitation and/or sensory substitution. *Advances in Biomedical Engineering*, **4**, 209–353. (244)

Mann, R. W., and Reimers, S. D. (1970) Kinesthetic sensing for the EMG controlled 'Boston arm'. *IEEE Transactions on Man–Machine Systems*, **MMS-11**, 110–115. (234)

Marshall, P. H. (1972) Recognition and recall in short-term motor memory. *Journal of Experimental Psychology*, **95**, 147–153. (124, 145, 146)

Marshall, P. H., Jones, M. T., and Sheehan, E. M. (1977) The spacing effect in short-term motor memory: The differential attention hypothesis. *Journal of Motor Behavior*, **9**, 119–126. (151)

Marteniuk, R. G. (1973) Retention characteristics of motor short-term memory cues. *Journal of Motor Behavior*, **5**, 249–259. (124, 127, 129, 130, 136, 141)

Marteniuk, R. G. (1974) Individual differences in motor performance and learning. In J. H. Wilmore (Ed.), *Exercise and Sport Sciences Review*. New York: Academic Press. (221)

Marteniuk, R. G. (1977) Motor short-term memory measures as a function of methodology. *Journal of Motor Behavior*, **9**, 247–250. (126, 127)

Marteniuk, R. G., and Diewert, G. L. (1975) Decay and interference effects in motor short-term memory. *Acta Psychologica*, **39**, 217–223. (141)

Marteniuk, R. G., and Mackenzie, C. L. (1978) Information processing in movement organization and execution. Paper to *Attention and Performance VIII*. Princeton, NJ. (47, 57, 58, 59)

Marteniuk, R. G., and Roy, E. A. (1972) The codability of kinesthetic location and distance information. *Acta Psychologica*, **36**, 471–479. (56, 132)

Martens, R., Burwitz, L., and Zuckerman, J. (1976) Modeling effects on motor performance. *Research Quarterly*, **47**, 277–291. (208)

Mason, C. P. (1970). Practical problems in myoelectric control of prostheses. *Bulletin of Prosthetics Research*, **10–13**, 39–45. (232)

Matin, L., and MacKinnon, G. E. (1964). Autokinetic movement: Selective manipulation of directional components by image stabilization. *Science*, **143**, 147–148. (113)

Melton, A. W. (1963). Implications of short-term memory for a general theory of behavior. *Journal of Verbal Learning and Verbal Behavior*, **2**, 1–21. (147)

Mehr, M. (1970). *Newsletters*. Measurement Systems Incorporated. (187)

Meyers, E., Ethington, D., and Ashcroft, S. (1958). Readability of Braille as a function of three spacing variables. *Journal of Applied Psychology*, **42**, 163–165. (244)

Mikkonen, V. (1969). On the retention of perceptual quantities. *Commentationes Humanarum Litterarum*, **44**, 1–93. (130)

Miller, G. A. (1956). The magical number seven plus or minus two: Some limits on our capacity for processing information. *Psychological Review*, **63**, 81–97. (149)

Miller, G. A., Galanter, E., and Pribram, K. H. (1960). *Plans and the Structure of Behavior*. New York: Henry Holt. (17, 61)

Miller, R. B. (1953). *Handbook on Training and Training Equipment Design*. Wright Air Development Center, Technical Report No. 53–136. (210)

Milner, B. (1970). Memory and the median temporal regions of the brain. In K. H. Pribram and D. E. Broadbent (Eds.), *Biology of Memory*. New York: Academic Press. (149)

Milsum, J. (1966). *Biological Control Systems Analysis*. New York: McGraw-Hill. (19)

Minas, S. C. (1978). Mental practice of a complex perceptual-motor skill. *Journal of Human Movement Studies*, **4**, 102–107. (219)

Montague, W. E., and Hillix, W. A. (1968). Intertrial interval and proactive interference in short-term motor memory. *Canadian Journal of Psychology*, **22**, 73–78. (148)

Moray, M. (1967). Where is capacity limited? — A survey and a model. *Acta Psychologica*, **27**, 84–92. (67, 69)

Moray, N. (1976). Attention, sampling and control. In G. Johanssen and T. B. Sheridan (Eds.), *Monitoring Behavior and Supervisory Control*. New York: Plenum. (28, 33)

Moray, N. (1978). The strategic control of information processing. In G. Underwood (Ed.), *Strategies of Information Processing*. London: Academic Press. (170)

Moray, N. (Ed.). (1979). *Mental Workload: Theory and Measurement*. New York: Plenum. (19, 23)

Morgan, B. B., and Repko, J. D. (1974). Evaluation of behavioral functions in workers exposed to lead. In C. Xintaras, B. L. Johnson and I. de Groot (Eds.), *Behavioral Toxicology*. Washington, DC : DHEW. (263)

Mott, F. W., and Sherrington, C. S. (1895). Experiments on the influence of sensory nerves upon movement and nutrition of limbs: Preliminary communication. *Proceedings of the Royal Society of London*, **57**, 481–483. (43)

Mowbray, G. H., and Rhoades, M. V. (1959). On the reduction of choice reaction time with practice. *Quarterly Journal of Experimental Psychology*, **11**, 16–23. (153)

Moxley, S. E. (1979). Schema: The variability of practice hypothesis. *Journal of Motor Behavior*, **11**, 65–70. (142)

Murdock, B. B. (1957). Transfer designs and formulas. *Psychological Bulletin*, **54**, 313–326. (195)

Myklebust, H. R. (1964). *The Psychology of Deafness*. New York: Grune and Stratton. (238)

Nachmias, J. (1953). Figural aftereffects in kinesthetic space. *American Journal of Psychology*, **66**, 609–612. (113)

Navon, D., and Gopher, D. (1979). On the economy of the human-processing system. *Psychological Review*, **80**, 214–255. (70, 72, 79, 81)

Needham, J. G. (1934). The time-error in comparison judgments. *Psychological Bulletin*, **31**, 229–234. (123)

Needham, J. G. (1935). Rate of presentation in the method of single stimuli. *American Journal of Psychology*, **47**, 275–284. (124)

Neisser, U. (1980). The limits of cognition. In P. W. Juszyk and R. M. Klein (Eds.) *On The Nature of Thought: Essays in Honor of D. O. Hebb*, Hillsdale, NJ: Lawrence Erlbaum Associates. (77, 78)

Neisser, U. (1967). *Cognitive Psychology*. New York: Appleton-Century-Crofts. (66)

Newell, K. M. (1974). Knowledge of results and motor learning. *Journal of Motor Behavior*, **6**, 235–244. (143, 212)

Newell, K. M. (1976a). More on absolute error, etc. *Journal of Motor Behavior*, **8**, 139–142. (122)

Newell, K. M. (1976b). Motor learning without knowledge of results through the development of a response–recognition mechanism. *Journal of Motor Behavior*, **8**, 209–217. (142, 143, 209)

Newell, K. M. (1976c). Knowledge of results and motor learning. In J. Keogh and R. S. Hutton (Eds.), *Exercise and Sport Sciences Reviews*, Vol. 4. Santa Barbara: Journal Publishing Affiliates. (204, 212)

Newell, K. M. (1977). Theories of motor learning. In R. S. Schmidt and E. A. Fleishman (Eds.), Section 9 — Perceptual motor learning and performance. In B. B. Wolman (Ed.-in-Chief), *International Encyclopedia of Neurology, Psychiatry, Psychoanalysis and Psychology*. New York: Van Nostrand. (204)

Newell, K. M. (1978). Some issues on action plans. In G. E. Stelmach, (Ed.), *Information Processing in Motor Learning and Control*. New York: Academic Press. (206, 224)

Newell, K. M., and Chew, R. A. (1974). Recall and recognition in motor learning. *Journal of Motor Behavior*, **6**, 235–244. (142, 143)

Newell, K. M., and Chew, R. A. (1975). Visual feedback and positioning movements. *Journal of Motor Behavior*, **7**, 153–158. (139)

Newell, K. M., and Shapiro, D. C. (1976). Variability of practice and transfer of training: Some evidence towards a schema view of motor learning. *Journal of Motor Behavior*, **8**, 233–243. (142, 211, 223, 224)

Nickerson, R. S. (1965). Response time for the second of two successive signals as a function of absolute and relative duration of inter signal interval. *Perceptual and Motor Skills*, **21**, 3–10. (158, 168, 170)

Nickerson, R. S., Kalikow, D. N., and Stevens, K. N. (1976). Computer-aided speech training for the deaf. *Journal of Speech and Hearing Disorders*, **41**, 120–132. (63)

Noble, C. E. (1978). Age, race and sex in the learning and performance of psychomotor skills. In R. T. Osborne, C. E. Noble, and N. Weyl (Eds.), *Human Variation*. New York: Academic Press. (5)

Noble, M. E., and Trumbo, D. (1967). The organization of skilled response. *Organizational Behavior and Human Performance*, **2**, 1–25. (11)

Noble, M., Trumbo, D. A., and Fowler, F. (1967). Further evidence of secondary task interference in tracking. *Journal of Experimental Psychology*, **73**, 146–149. (69)

Nolan, C. Y., and Kederis, C. J. (1969). Perceptual factors in Braille word recognition. American Foundation for the Blind, *Research Series No. 20*. (245)

Norman, D. A., and Bobrow, D. G. (1975). On data-limited and resource-limited processes. *Cognitive Psychology*, **7**, 44–64. (67)

Nottebohm, F. (1970). The ontogeny of bird song. *Science*, **167**, 950–956. (43, 209)

Ollman, R. T. (1966). Fast guesses in choice reaction time. *Psychonomic Science*, **6**, 155–156. (156)

Orr, D. B., Friedman, H. L., and Williams, J. C. (1965). Trainability of listening comprehension of speeded discourse. *Journal of Educational Psychology*, **56**, 148–156. (239)

Osborne, R. T., Noble, C. E., and Weyl, N. (Eds.), *Human Variation*. New York: Academic Press. (5)

Osgood, C. E. (1949). The similarity paradox in human learning: A resolution. *Psychological Review*, **56**, 132–143. (230)

Pachella, R. G., and Pew, R. W. (1968). Speed–accuracy trade-off in reaction times: Effect of discrete criterion times. *Journal of Experimental Psychology*, **76**, 19–24. (156, 161)

Pascual-Leone, J. (1970) A mathematical model for the transition role in Piaget's developmental stages. *Acta Psychologica*, **63**, 301–345. (78)

Patrick, J. (1971). The effect of interpolated motor activities in short-term motor memory. *Journal of Motor Behavior*, **3**, 39–48. (124, 126)

Pauls, M. D. (1964). Speechreading. In H. Davis and S. H. Silverman (Eds.), *Hearing and Deafness*. New York: Holt, Rinehart and Winston. (241)

Peizer, E., Wright, D. W., and Pirello, T. (1970). Perspectives on the use of external power in upper-extremity prostheses. *Bulletin of Prosthetics Research*, **10–13**, 25–38. (230)

Peizer, E., Wright, D. W., Pirello, T., and Mason, C. P. (1970). Current indications for upper-extremity powered components. *Bulletin of Prosthetics Research*, **10–14**, 22–42. (230)

Pepper, R. L., and Herman, L. M. (1970). Decay and interference effects in short-term retention of a discrete motor act. *Journal of Experimental Psychology Monograph*, **83**, 2. (111, 123, 124, 126, 129, 130, 134, 140, 141)

Peterson, L. R. (1977). Verbal learning and memory. *Annual Reviews*, **28**, 393–415. (150)

Peterson, L. R., and Gentile, A. (1965). Proactive interference as a function of time between tests. *Journal of Experimental Psychology*, **70**, 473–478. (147)

Peterson, L. R., and Peterson, M. J. (1959). Short-term retention of individual verbal items. *Journal of Experimental Psychology*, **58**, 193–198. (147)

Pew, R. W. (1966). Acquisition of hierarchical control over the temporal organization of a skill. *Journal of Experimental Psychology*, **71**, 764–771. (45, 49)

Pew, R. W. (1969). The speed–accuracy operating characteristic. *Acta Psychologica*, **30**, 16–26. (9, 155, 161)

Pew, R. W. (1974a). Human perceptual-motor performance. In B. H. Kantowitz (Ed.), *Human Information Processing: Tutorials in Performance and Cognition*. Hillsdale, NJ: Erlbaum. (19, 32, 50, 53, 61, 69, 203, 211, 222)

Pew, R. W. (1974b). Levels of analysis in motor control. *Brain Research*, **71**, 393–400. (54, 142, 206, 219)

Pew, R. W., Duffendach, J. L., and Fensch, L. K. (1967). Sine wave tracking revisited. *IEEE Transactions on Human Factors in Electronics*, **5**, 2–6. (32)

Pew, R. W., and Rupp, G. L. (1971). Two quantitative measures of skill development. *Journal of Experimental Psychology*, **90**, 1–7. (11)

Philip, B. R. (1947). The effect of interpolated and extrapolated stimuli on the time order error in the comparison of temporal intervals. *Journal of General Psychology*, **36**, 173–187. (125)

Phillips, C. G. (1969). Motor apparatus of the baboon's hand. *Proceedings of the Royal Society*, **173**, 141–174. (44)

Pick, H. L., and Hay, J. C. (1965). A passive test of the Held reafference hypothesis. *Perceptual and Motor Skills*, **20**, 1070. (115)

Pick, H. L., Warren, D. H., and Hay, J. C. (1969). Sensory conflict in the judgment of spatial direction. *Perception and Psychophysics*, **6**, 203–205. (116)

Pickett, J. M., and Pickett, B. M. (1963). Communication of speech sounds by a tactual vocoder. *Journal of Speech and Hearing Research*, **6**, 207–222. (242)

Pierce, J. R. (1962). *Symbols, Signals and Noise*. London: Hutchinson. (193)

Pike, A. R. (1973). Response latency models for signal detection. *Psychological Review*, **80**, 53–68. (154)

Platt, C. G. (1933). The time-error in psychophysical judgments. *American Journal of Psychology*, **45**, 292–297. (129)

Polanyi, M. (1958). *Personal Knowledge: Towards a Post-Critical Philosophy*. London: Routledge and Kegan Paul. (206)

Posner, M. I. (1967). Characteristics of visual and kinesthetic memory codes. *Journal of Experimental Psychology*, **75**, 103–107. (131, 133, 139)

Posner, M. I., and Boies, S. J. (1971). Components of attention. *Psychological Review*, **78**, 391–408. (67, 71)

Posner, M. I., and Keele, S. W. (1969). Attention demands of movement. *Proceedings of the XVth International Congress of Applied Psychology*. Amsterdam: Swets and Zeitlinger. (133)

Posner, M. I., and Klein, R. M. (1973). On the functions of consciousness. In S. Kornblum (Ed.), *Attention and Performance IV*. New York: Academic Press. (87)

Posner, M. I., and Konick, A. F. (1966). Short-term retention of visual and kinesthetic information. *Organizational Behavior and Human Performance*, **1**, 71–88. (131, 133, 139, 148)

Posner, M. I., and Snyder, C. R. R. (1975). Attention and cognitive control. In R. Solso (Ed.), *Information Processing and Cognition: The Loyola Symposium*. Hillsdale, NJ: Lawrence Erlbaum Associates. (87)

Possemai, C. A., Granjon, M., Reynard, G., and Requin, J. (1975). High order sequential effects and the negative gradient of the relationship between simple reaction time and foreperiod duration. *Acta Psychologica*, **39**, 263–270. (158)

Postman, L. (1975). Verbal learning and memory. *Annual Review of Psychology*, **26**, 291–335. (150)

Poulton, E. C. (1950). Perceptual anticipation and reaction time. *Quarterly Journal of Experimental Psychology*, **2**, 99–112. (69, 192)

Poulton, E. C. (1952). Perceptual anticipation in tracking with two-pointer and one-pointer displays. *British Journal of Psychology*, **43**, 222–229. (180)

Poulton, E. C. (1957a). On the stimulus and response in pursuit tracking. *Journal of Experimental Psychology*, **53**, 57–65. (3)

Poulton, E. C. (1957b). On prediction in skilled movements. *Psychological Bulletin*, **54**, 467–478. (5, 11, 50)

Poulton, E. C. (1957c). Learning the statistical properties of the input in pursuit tracking. *Journal of Experimental Psychology*, **54**, 28–32. (183)

Poulton, E. C. (1973). Unwanted range effects from using within-subject experimental designs. *Psychological Bulletin*, **80**, 113–121. (186)

Poulton, E. C. (1974). *Tracking Skill and Manual Control*. London: Academic Press. (19, 37, 178, 180, 186, 187, 189, 191, 193, 194)

Poulton, E. C. (1978). A new look at the effects of noise: A rejoinder. *Psychological Bulletin*, **85**, 1068–1079. (263)

Pribram, K. H. (1960). A review of theory in physiological psychology. In *Annual Review of Psychology*. Palo Alto: Annual Reviews, **11**, 1–40.

Prior, R. E., and Lyman, J. (1975). Electrocutaneous feedback for artificial limbs. *Bulletin of Prosthetics Research*, **10–24**, 3–37. (233)

Rabbitt, P. M. A. (1965). Response facilitation on repetition of a limb movement. *British Journal of Psychology*, **56**, 303–304. (172)

Rabbitt, P. M. A. (1966a). Errors and error-correction in choice-response tasks. *Journal of Experimental Psychology*, **71**, 264–272. (162)

Rabbitt, P. M. A. (1966b). Error correction time without external error signals. *Nature*, **212**, 438. (162)

Rabbitt, P. M. A. (1968a). Repetition effects and signal classification strategies in serial choice response tasks. *Quarterly Journal of Experimental Psychology*, **20**, 232–240. (154)

Rabbitt, P. M. A. (1968b). Three kinds of error-signalling responses in a serial choice task. *Quarterly Journal of Experimental Psychology*, **20**, 179–188. (162)

Rabbitt, P. M. A. (1969). Psychological refractory delay and response-stimulus interval in serial, choice-response tasks. In Koster, W. (Ed.), *Attention and Performance 11*, pp.195–219. Amsterdam: North-Holland. (158, 162, 168)

Rabbit, P. M. A. (1971). Times for analyzing stimuli and relating responses. *British Medical Bulletin*, **27** (3), 259–265. (155)

Rabbitt, P. M. A. (1978a). Hand dominance, attention and the choice between responses. *Quarterly Journal of Experimental Psychology*, **30**, 407–416. (172)

Rabbitt, P. M. A. (1978b). Detection of errors by skilled typists. *Ergonomics*, **21**, 945–958. (162)

Rabbitt, P. M. A. (1979a). *Quarterly Journal of Experimental Psychology*, in press. (158, 162, 169)

Rabbitt, P. M. A. (1979b). *Quarterly Journal of Experimental Psychology*, in press. (158, 169)

Rabbitt, P. M. A., Cumming, G., and Vyas, S. M. (1978). Some errors of perceptual analysis in visual search can be detected and corrected. *Quarterly Journal of Experimental Psychology*, **30**, 319–332. (162)

Rabbitt, P. M. A., Cumming, C. G., and Vyas, S. M. (1979). Improvement, learning and retention of skill at visual search. *Quarterly Journal of Experimental Psychology*, **31**, 441–460. (160)

Rabbitt, P. M. A., and Rogers, M. (1965). Age and choice between responses on a self-paced repetitive task. *Ergonomics*, **8**, 435–444. (170)

Rabbitt, P. M. A., and Vyas, S. M. (1970). An elementary preliminary taxonomy of errors in choice reaction time tasks. *Acta Psychologica*, **33**, 56–76. (156, 157, 161, 162)

Rabbitt, P. M. A., and Vyas, S. M. (1979). Can slowing in old age be compensated by more sensitive statistical prediction. *Journal of Gerontology*, in press. (162, 163, 164, 165)

Rae, J. W., and Cockrell, J. L. (1971). Applications in myoelectrical control. *Bulletin of Prosthetics Research*, **10–16**, 24–37. (230)

Rashevsky, N. (1959). Mathematical biophysics of automobile driving. *Bulletin of Mathematical Biophysics*, **21**, 375–385. (109)

Rasmussen, J. (1979). Reflection on the concept of operator workload. In N. Moray, (Ed.), *Mental Workload: Its Theory and Measurement*, New York: Plenum. (65)

Reed, C. M., Durlach, N. I., Braida, L. D., Norton, S. J., and Schultz, M. C. (1977). Experimental results on Tadoma. Paper to Research Conference on Speech-Processing Aids for the Deaf, Gallaudet College, Washington, DC. (243)

Regan, J. J. (1959). Tracking performance related to display-control configurations. *U.S. NAVTADEVCEN Technical Report No. 322-1-2.* (187)

Reiter, R. (1948). Eine neue Elektrokunsthand. *Grenzgebiete der Medizin*, **4**, 133. (229)

Requin, J., Bonnet, M., and Semjen, A. (1977). Is there a specificity in the supraspinal control of motor structures during preparation? In S. Dornic (Ed.), *Attention and Performance VI*. Hillsdale, NJ: Erlbaum. (60)

Reswick, J. B. (1972). Prosthetic and orthotic devices. In J. H. U. Brown and J. D. Dickson (Eds.), *Advances in Biomedical Engineering*, Vol. 2. London: Academic Press. (232, 236)

Rice, C. E. (1970). Early blindness, early experience and perceptual enhancement.

American Foundation for the Blind, *Research Bulletin*, **22**, 1–22. (238)

Richardson, A. (1967a). Mental practice: A review and discussion I. *Research Quarterly*, **38**, 95–107. (219)

Richardson, A. (1967b). Mental practice: A review and discussion II. *Research Quarterly*, **38**, 262–273. (219)

Rogers, C. A. (1974). Feedback precision and post feedback interval duration. *Journal of Experimental Psychology*, **102**, 604–608. (212)

Rohland, T. A. (1975). Sensory feedback for powered limb prostheses. *Medical and Biological Engineering*, **13**, 300–301. (233)

Roldan, C. E. (1979). Time-shared comparatory tracking and attention. Paper presented to the 40th meeting of the Canadian Psychological Association, Quebec City. (74)

Rosenbaum, D. A. (1977). Selective adaptation of 'command neurons' in the human motor system. *Neuropsychologia*, **15**, 81–91. (55)

Rosenbaum, D. A. (in press). Stages of human movement initiation. *Quarterly Journal of Experimental Psychology*. (47)

Rostron, A. B. (1976). Pitch control in the human voice. *Quarterly Journal of Experimental Psychology*, **28**, 305–311. (30)

Rothstein, A. L., and Arnold, R. K. (1976). Bridging the gap: Application of research on videotape feedback and bowling. *Motor Skills: Theory into Practice*, **1**, 35–62. (213)

Roy, E. A. (1976). Measuring change in motor memory. *Journal of Motor Behavior*, **8**, 283–287. (122)

Roy, E. A. (1977). Spatial cues in memory for movement. *Journal of Motor Behavior*, **9**, 151–156. (124, 129, 137)

Roy, E. A. (1978). Role of preselection in memory for movement extent. *Journal of Experimental Psychology: Human Learning and Memory*, **4**, 397–405. (127, 134, 136, 138)

Roy, E. A, and Diewert, G. L. (1975). Encoding of kinesthetic extent information. *Perception and Psychophysics*, **17**, 559–564. (138)

Roy, E. A., and Diewert, G. L. (1978). The coding of movement extent information. *Journal of Human Movement Studies*, **4**, 94–101. (127, 137, 138)

Roy, E. A., and Kelso, J. A. S. (1977). Movement cues in motor memory: Precuing versus postcuing. *Journal of Human Movement Studies*, **3**, 232–239. (133)

Roy, E. A., and Marteniuk, R. G. (1974). Mechanisms of control in motor performance: Closed-loop versus motor programming control. *Journal of Experimental Psychology*, **103**, 985–991. (45)

Rubin, W. M. (1978). Application of signal detection theory to error detection in ballistic motor skills. *Journal of Experimental Psychology: Human Perception and Performance*, **4**, 311–320. (143)

Russell, D. G. (1976). Spatial location cues and movement production. In G. E. Stelmach (Ed.), *Motor Control: Issues and Trends*. New York: Academic Press. (55, 56, 139)

Russell, L. (1971). *Evaluation of Mobility Aids for the Blind. Pathsounder Travel Aid Evaluation*. Washington, DC: National Academy of Engineering. (250)

Salmoni, A. W., and Sullivan, S. J. (1976). The intersensory integration of vision and kinesthesis for distance and location cues. *Journal of Human Movement Studies*, **2**, 225–232. (124, 139)

Sanders, A. F. (1977). Structural and functional aspects of the reaction process. In S. Dornic (Ed.), *Attention and Performance VI*. Hillsdale, NJ: Erlbaum Associates. (69)

Sanders, A. F. (1979). Some remarks on mental load. In N. Moray (Ed.),

Mental Workload: Its Theory and Measurement, New York: Plenum. (69, 72)

Sanderson, F. H., and Whiting, H. T. A. (1978). Dynamic visual acuity: A possible factor in catching performance. *Journal of Motor Behavior*, **10**, 7–14. (259)

Schmidt, R. A. (1970). Critique of Henry's paper. In L. E. Smith (Ed.), *Psychology of Motor Learning*. Chicago: Athletic Institute. (122)

Schmidt, R. A. (1972). The index of preprogramming (IP): A statistical method for evaluating the role of feedback in simple movements. *Psychonomic Science*, **27**, 83–85. (45, 46)

Schmidt, R. A. (1975a). A schema theory of discrete motor skill learning. *Psychological Review*, **82**, 225–260. (53, 54, 61, 69, 122, 142, 149, 203, 211, 222, 223, 258, 268)

Schmidt, R. A. (1975b). *Motor Skills*. New York: Harper and Row. (216)

Schmidt, R. A. (1976a). The schema as a solution to some persistent problems in motor learning theory. In G. E. Stelmach (Ed.), *Motor Control: Issues and Trends*. New York: Academic Press. (49, 53, 54, 61, 69, 142, 149)

Schmidt, R. A. (1976b). Control processes in motor skills. In J. Keogh and S. Hutton (Eds.), *Exercise and Sport Science Reviews*, Vol. 4. Santa Barbara, Calif.: Journal Publishing Affiliates. (211)

Schmidt, R. A., and Ascoli, K. M. (1970a). Intertrial intervals and motor short-term memory. *Research Quarterly*, **41**, 432–438. (148)

Schmidt, R. A., and Ascoli, K. M. (1970b). Attention demand during storage of traces in motor short-term memory. *Acta Psychologica*, **34**, 497–504. (148)

Schmidt, R. A., Christenson, R., and Rogers, P. (1975). Some evidence for the independence of recall and recognition in motor behavior. In D. M. Landers (Ed.), *Psychology of Sport and Motor Behavior*. University Park, PA: Penn State HPER Series, **10**, 510–521. (142, 143)

Schmidt, R. A. and McCabe, J. F. (1976). Motor program utilization over extended practice. *Journal of Human Movement Studies*, **2**, 239–247. (46)

Schmidt, R. A., and Russell, D. G. (1972). Movement velocity and movement time as determiners of degree of preprogramming in simple movements. *Journal of Experimental Psychology*, **96**, 315–320. (44)

Schmidt, R. A., and Stelmach, G. E. (1968). Postural set as a factor in short-term motor memory. *Psychonomic Science*, **13**, 223–224. (148)

Schmidt, R. A., and White, J. L. (1972). Evidence for an error detection mechanism in motor skills: A test of Adams' closed-loop theory. *Journal of Motor Behavior*, **4**, 143–153. (143)

Schmidt, R. A., and Wrisberg, C. A. (1973). Further tests of the Adams' closed-loop theory: Response-produced feedback and the error-detection mechanism. *Journal of Motor Behavior*, **3**, 155–164. (143)

Schmidt, R. A., Zelaznik, H. W., and Frank, J. S. (1977). Motor output variability: An alternative interpretation of Fitts' Law. Paper to *Big 10 Symposium on Information Processing in Motor Learning and Control*, Madison, Wis. (100)

Schouten, J. F., and Bekker, J. A. M. (1967). Reaction time and accuracy. *Acta Psychologica*, **27**, 143–153. (156)

Schutz, R. W., and Roy, E. A. (1973). Absolute error: The devil in disguise. *Journal of Motor Behavior*, **5**, 141–153. (122)

Seibel, R. (1963). Discrimination reaction time for a 1,023 alternative task. *Journal of Experimental Psychology*, **66**, 215–226. (219)

Selling, L. A. (1930). An experimental investigation of the phenomenon of postural persistence. *Archives of Psychology*, 118. (113)

Senders, J. W. (1964). The human operator as a monitor and controller of multi-degree-of-freedom system. *IEEE Transactions on Human Factors in Electronics*, **5**, 2–6. (28)

Senders, J. W. (1979). Axiomatic models of workload. In N. Moray (Ed.), *Mental Workload: Its Theory and Measurement*, New York: Plenum. (66)

Shaffer, L. H. (1971). Attention in transcription skill. *Quarterly Journal of Experimental Psychology*, **23**, 107–112. (71)

Shaffer, L. H. (1973). Latency mechanisms in transcription. In S. Kornblum (Ed.), *Attention and Performance IV*. New York: Academic Press. (159, 161)

Shaffer, L. H. (1975). Multiple attention in continuous verbal tasks. In P. M. A. Rabbitt and S. Dornic (Eds.), *Attention and Performance V*. London: Academic Press. (159)

Shaffer, L. H. (1976). Intention and performance. *Psychological Review*, **83**, 375–393. (44)

Shaffer, L. H. (1978). Timing in the motor programming of typing. *Quarterly Journal of Experimental Psychology*, **30**, 333–345. (44)

Shaffer, L. H., and Hardwick, J. (1970). The basis of transcription skill. *Journal of Experimental Psychology*, **84**, 424–440. (159)

Shallice, T. (1978). The dominant action system: An information-processing approach to consciousness. In K. S. Pope and J. L. Singer (Eds.), *The Stream of Consciousness*. New York: Plenum. (82, 87, 88)

Shannon, C. E., and Weaver, W. (1949). *The Mathematical Theory of Communication*. University of Illinois Press. (66, 98)

Shapiro, D. C. (1977). A preliminary attempt to determine the duration of a motor program. In D. M. Landers and R. W. Christina (Eds.), *Psychology of Motor Behavior and Sport*. Champaign, Ill.: Human Kinetics.(57)

Shea, J. B. (1977). Effects of labeling on motor short-term memory. *Journal of Experimental Psychology: Human Learning and Memory*, **3**, 92–99. (127, 136)

Sheffield, F. D. (1961). Theoretical considerations in the learning of complex sequential tasks from demonstration and practice. In A. A. Lumsdaine (Ed.), *Student Response in Programmed Instruction*. Washington, DC.: National Academy of Science-National Research Council. (206)

Sheffield, F. D., and Maccoby, N. (1961). Summary and interpretation on research on organizational principles in constructing filmed demonstrations. In A. A. Lumsdaine (Ed.), *Student Response in Programmed Instruction*. Washington, DC: National Academy of Science-National Research Council. (206)

Sheridan, T. B. (1970). On how often the supervisor should sample. *IEEE Transactions on Systems Science and Cybernetics*, **6**, 140–145. (28)

Sheridan, T. B., and Ferrell, R. W. (1974). *Man–Machine Systems*. Cambridge, Mass.: MIT Press. (38)

Sherrick, D. E., and Cholewiak, R. W. (1977). Matching speech to vision and touch. Paper to Research Conference on Speech-Processing Aids for the Deaf, Gallaudet College, Washington, DC. (241)

Sherrington, C. S. (1906). *The Integrative Function of the Nervous System*. New Haven: Yale University Press. (79, 86, 88)

Sherrington, C. S. (1937–38). *Man on His Nature. The Gifford Lectures, Edinburgh*. Cambridge: Cambridge University Press. (88)

Shik, M. L., and Orlovski, G. N. (1976). Neurophysiology of locomotor automatism. *Physiological Reviews*, **56**, 465–501. (48)

Shingledecker, C. A. (1978). The effects of anticipation on performance and processing load in blind mobility. *Ergonomics*, **21**, 355–371. (252, 254)

Shingledecker, C. A., and Foulke, E. (1978). A human factors approach to the assessment of the mobility of blind pedestrians. *Human Factors*, **20**, 273–286. (250)

Shingledecker, C. A., and Holding, D. H. (1974). Risk and effort measures of fatigue. *Journal of Motor Behavior*, **6**, 17–25. (265)

Shwartz, S. P. (1976). Capacity limitations in human information processing. *Memory and Cognition*, **4**, 763–768. (71)

Siddall, G. J., Holding, D. H. and Draper, J. (1957). Errors of aim and extent in manual point to point movement. *Occupational Psychology*, **31**, 185–195. (9, 94, 108)

Simon, H. A. (1969). *The Sciences of the Artificial*. Cambridge, Mass.: MIT Press. (65)

Singer, R. N. (1977). To err or not to err: A question for the instructor of psychomotor skills. *Review of Educational Research*, **47**, 479–498. (210)

Smith, G. A. (1977). Studies in compatibility and a new model of choice reaction times. In S. Dornic (Ed.), *Attention and Performance VI*. Hillsdale, NJ: Erlbaum. (9)

Smith, K. U. (1962). *Delayed Sensory Feedback and Behavior*. Philadelphia, Pa.: Saunders. (29, 30)

Smith, K. U. (1966). Cybernetic theory and the analysis of learning. In E. A. Bilodeau (Ed.), *Acquisition of Skill*. New York: Academic Press. (29, 30)

Smith, W. M., McCrary, J. R., and Smith, K. U. (1963). Delayed and space-displaced sensory feedback and learning. *Perceptual and Motor Skills*, **16**, 781–796. (233)

Smyth, M. M. (1978). Attention to visual feedback in motor learning. *Journal of Motor Behavior*, **10**, 185–190. (6, 39, 140)

Snodgrass, J. A., Luce, R. D., and Galanter, E. H. (1967). Some experiments on simple and choice reaction time. *Journal of Experimental Psychology*, **75**, 1–17. (154)

Spelke, E ., Hirst, W., and Neisser, U. (1976). Skills of divided attention. *Cognition*, **4**, 215–230. (77)

Sperling, G. (1960). The information available in brief visual presentations. *Psychological Monographs*, **74**, No. 11. (147)

Staros, A., and Peizer, E. (1972). Veterans Administration Prosthetics Center Research Report. *Bulletin of Prosthetics Research*, 10–17, 202–233. (231)

Steger, J. A., and O'Reilly, E. (1970). Simultaneously contrasting anchors. *Perception and Psychophysics*, **7**, 281–283. (128)

Stelmach, G. E. (1968). The accuracy of reproducing target positions under various tensions. *Psychonomic Science*, **13**, 287–288. (135)

Stelmach, G. E. (1969). Prior positioning responses as a factor in short-term retention of a simple motor task. *Journal of Experimental Psychology*, **81**, 523–526. (124, 148)

Stelmach, G. E. (1970). Kinesthetic recall and information reduction activity. *Journal of Motor Behavior*, **2**, 183–194. (124, 129, 130, 131, 133, 148)

Stelmach, G. E. (1973). Feedback — a determiner of forgetting in short-term motor memory. *Acta Psychologica*, **37**, 333–339. (142)

Stelmach, G. E. (1974a). Short-term motor memory — Have we made any progress? In M. G. Wade and R. Martens (Eds.), *Psychology of Motor Behavior and Sport*. Urbana, Ill.: Human Kinetics. (122)

Stelmach, G. E. (1974b). Retention of motor skills. In J. Wilmore (Ed.), *Exercise and Sport Sciences Review*, Vol. 2. New York: Academic Press. (204)

Stelmach, G. E. (1977). Prior organization in motor control. *Journal of Human Movement Studies*, **3**, 157–168. (56)

Stelmach, G. E., and Bruce, J. R. (1970). Recall load in STM. *Psychonomic Science*, **21**, 205–207. (131, 148)

Stelmach, G. E., and Kelso, J. A. S. (1973). Distance and location cues in short-term motor memory. *Perceptual and Motor Skills*, **37**, 403–406. (129)

Stelmach, G. E., and Kelso, J. A. S. (1975). Memory trace strength and response biasing in short-term motor memory. *Memory and Cognition*, **3**, 58–62. (126, 140)

Stelmach, G. E., and Kelso, J. A. S. (1977). Memory processes in motor control. In S. Dornic (Ed.). *Attention and Performance, VI*. New York: Halstead Press. (127, 136, 137)

Stelmach, G. E., Kelso, J. A. S., and McCullagh, P. D. (1976). Preselection and response biasing short-term motor memory. *Memory and Cognition*, **4**, 62–66. (127, 137)

Stelmach, G . E., Kelso, J. A. S., and Wallace, S. A. (1975). Preselection in short-term motor memory. *Journal of Experimental Psychology: Human Learning and Memory*, **1**, 745–755. (56, 127, 134, 136, 137, 138, 149)

Stelmach, G. E., and Walsh, M. F. (1972). Response biasing as a function of duration and extent of positioning acts. *Journal of Experimental Psychology*, **92**, 354–359. (124, 126, 129, 131, 140)

Stelmach, G. E., and Walsh, M. F. (1973). The temporal placement of interpolated movements in short-term motor memory. *Journal of Motor Behavior*, **5**, 165–173. (124, 126, 129, 131, 140)

Stelmach, G. E, and Wilson, M. (1970). Kinesthetic retention, movement extent, and information processing. *Journal of Experimental Psychology*, **85**, 425–430. (124, 133)

Sternberg, S. (1969). The discovery of processing stages: Extensions of Donders' method. *Acta Psychologica*, **30**, 276–315. (67, 155)

Sternberg, S. (1975). Memory scanning: New findings and current controversies. *Quarterly Journal of Experimental Psychology*, **27**, 1–32. (155)

Sternberg, S ., Monsell, S., Knoll, R. L. and Wright, C. E. (1978). The latency and duration of rapid movement sequences: Comparisons of speech and typewriting. In G. E. Stelmach (Ed.), *Information Processing in Motor Control and Learning*. New York: Academic Press. (47, 62)

Stone, M. (1960). Models for choice reaction time. *Psychometrika*, **25**, 251–260. (154)

Stull, G. A., and Kearney, J. T. (1978). Effects of variable fatigue levels on reaction-time components. *Journal of Motor Behavior*, **10**, 223–232. (8)

Summers, J. J. (1975). The role of timing in motor program representation. *Journal of Motor Behavior*, **7**, 229–241. (57, 142, 224)

Summers, J. J. (1977a). The relationship between the sequencing and timing components of a skill. *Journal of Motor Behavior*, **9**, 49–59. (57, 142)

Summers, J. J. (1977b). Adjustments to redundancy in reaction time: A comparison of three learning methods. *Acta Psychologica*, **41**, 205–223. (63)

Supa, M., Cotzin, M., and Dallenbach, K. M. (1944). 'Facial vision': The perception of obstacles by the blind. *American Journal of Psychology*, **57**, 133–183. (251)

Suzuki, S. (1969). *Nurtured by Love: A New Approach to Education*. New York: Exposition Press. (209)

Swonger, A. K., and Rech, R. H. (1972). Serotonergic and cholinergic involvement in habituation of activity and spontaneous alternation of rats in a Y maze. *Journal of Comparative and Physiological Psychology*, **81**, 509–522. (73)

Szafran, J. (1951). Changes with age and exclusion of vision in performance at an aiming task. *Quarterly Journal of Experimental Psychology*, **3**, 111–118. (265)

Taenzer, J. C. (1970). Visual word reading. *IEEE Transactions on Man–Machine Systems*, **11**, 44–53. (245)

Tamir, L. (1979). Language development: New directions. *Human Development*, **22**, 263–269. (86)

Taub, E., and Berman, A. J. (1968). Movement and learning in the absence of sensory feedback. In S. J. Freedman (Ed.), *The Neuropsychology of Spatially Oriented Behavior*. Homewood, Ill.: Dorsey. (43)

Taub, E., Heitmann, R. D., and Barro, G. (1977). Alertness, level of activity and purposive movement following somatosensory deafferentation in monkeys. *Annals of the New York Academy*, **290**, 348–365. (43)

Taub, E., Perrella, P. and Barro, G. (1973). Behavioral development following forelimb deafferentation on day of birth in monkeys with and without blinding. *Science*, **181**, 959–960. (43)

Teasdale, A., and Reynolds, J. (1955). Two ways to get frequency response from transient data. *Control Engineering*, **10**, 55–63. (192)

Templeton, W. B., Howard, I. P., and Lowman, A. E. (1966). Passively generated adaptation to prismatic distortion. *Perceptual and Motor Skills*, **22**, 140–142. (115)

Theios, J., Smith, P. G., Haviland, S. E., Traupmann, J., and McCoy, M. C. (1973). Memory scanning as a serial, self-terminating process. *Journal of Experimental Psychology*, **97**, 323–336. (154)

Thorndike, E. L. (1903). *Educational Psychology*. New York: Lemcke and Buechner. (197)

Thorndike, E. L. (1927). The law of effect. *American Journal of Psychology*, **39**, 212–222. (1)

Thorndike, E. L., and Woodworth, R. S. (1901). The influence of improvement in one mental function upon the efficiency of other functions. *Psychological Review*, **8**, 247–261. (220)

Toates, F. (1975). *Control Theory in Biology and Psychology*. London: Hutchinson. (19, 22, 28)

Trehub, A. (1977). Neuronal models for cognitive processes: Networks for learning, perception, and imagination. *Journal of Theoretical Biology*, **65**, 141–169. (79)

Treisman, A. M. (1969). Strategies and models of selective attention. *Psychological Review*, **76**, 282–299. (70, 87)

Treisman, A. M., and Davies, A. (1973). Divided attention to ear and eye. In S. Kornblum (Ed.), *Attention and Performance IV*. New York: Academic Press. (71)

Treisman, A., and Geffen, G. (1968). Selective attention and cerebral dominance in perceiving and responding to speech messages. *Quarterly Journal of Experimental Psychology*, **20**, 139–150. (75, 76)

Trumbo, D., Milone, F., and Noble, M. (1972). Interpolated activity and response mechanisms in motor short-term memory. *Journal of Experimental Psychology*, **93**, 205–212. (126)

Trumbo, D. A., and Noble, M. E. (1970). Secondary task effects on serial verbal learning. *Journal of Experimental Psychology*, **85**, 418–424. (69)

Trumbo, D., and Noble, M. (1973). Motor skill. In B. B. Wolman (Ed.), *Handbook of General Psychology*. Englewood Cliffs, NJ: Prentice-Hall. (233)

Trumbo, D. A., Noble, M. E., and Swink, J. (1967). Secondary task interference in the performance of tracking tasks. *Journal of Experimental Psychology*, **73**, 232–240. (69)

Tulving, E., and Thomson, D. M. (1973). Encoding specificity and retrieval processes in episodic memory. *Psychological Review*, **80**, 352–373. (86)

Turner, E. D., and Bevan, W. (1962). Simultaneous induction of multiple anchor effects in the judgment of form. *Journal of Experimental Psychology*, **64**, 589–592. (128)

Turner, W. D. (1931). Intraserial effect with lifted weights. *American Journal of Psychology*, **43**, 1–25. (125)

Turvey, M. T. (1977). Preliminaries to a theory of action with reference to vision. In R. Shaw and J. Bransford (Eds.), *Perceiving, Acting, and Knowing: Towards an Ecological Psychology*. Hillsdale, NJ: Erlbaum. (59, 223, 224)

Turvey, M. T., Shaw, R. E., and Mace, W. (1978). Issues in the theory of action. In J. Requin (Ed.), *Attention and Performance VII*. Hillsdale, NJ: Erlbaum. (224)

Tustin, A. (1944). An investigation of the operator response in manual control of a power-driven gun. Metro-Vickers Electric, *C.S. Memo. 169.* (177, 192)

Twitchell, T. E. (1954). Sensory factors in purposive movement. *Journal of Neurophysiology,* 17, 239–252. (43)

Upton, H. W. (1968). Wearable eyeglasses speechreading aid. *American Annals of the Deaf,* 113, 222–229. (241)

Ursin, H, and Ursin, R. (1979). Physiological indicators of mental workload. In N. Moray (Ed.), *Mental Workload: Its Theory and Measurement,* New York: Plenum. (66)

Veldhuyzen, W., and Stassen, J. (1976). The internal model — What does it mean in human control? In G. Johanssen and T. B. Sheridan (Eds.), *Monitoring Behavior and Supervisory Control.* New York: Plenum. (36)

Vickers, D. (1970). Evidence for an accumulator model of psychophysical discrimination. *Ergonomics,* 13, 37–58. (154)

Vince, M. A. (1948a). The intermittency of control of movements and the psychological refractory period. *British Journal of Psychology,* 38, 149–157. (69)

Vince, M. A. (1948b). Corrective movements in a pursuit task. *Quarterly Journal of Experimental Psychology,* 1, 85–103. (105)

Wallace, S. A. (1977). The coding of location: A test of the target hypothesis. *Journal of Motor Behavior,* 9, 157–159. (124, 127, 135, 149)

Wallace, S. A., and Stelmach, G. E. (1975). Proprioceptive encoding in preselected and constrained movement. *Mouvement,* 7, 147–152. (136, 137)

Walley, R. E., and Weiden, T. B. (1973). Lateral inhibition and cognitive masking: a neuropsychological theory of attention. *Psychological Review,* 80, 284–302. (88)

Warburton, D. M. (in press). *Drugs and Human Performance.* Chichester: Wiley. (261)

Warm, J. S. (Ed.). (in press.) *Sustained Attention and Human Performance.* Chichester: Wiley. (5)

Waugh, N. C., and Norman, D. A. (1965). Primary memory. *Psychological Review,* 72, 89–104. (149)

Welford, A. T. (1952). The 'psychological refractory period' and the timing of high speed performance: A review and a theory. *British Journal of Psychology,* 43, 2–19. (67)

Welford, A. T. (1958). *Aging and Human Skill.* London: Oxford University Press. (265)

Welford, A. T. (1959). Evidence of a single-channel decision mechanism limiting performance in a serial reaction task. *Quarterly Journal of Experimental Psychology,* 11, 193–210. (67, 69)

Welford, A. T. (1961). Age changes in the times taken by choice: Discrimination and the control of movement. *Gerontologia,* 5, 119–145. (205)

Welford, A. T . (1968). *Fundamentals of Skill.* London: Methuen. (8, 11, 101, 154, 216, 231)

Welford, A. T., Norris, A. H., and Shock, N. W. (1969). Speed and accuracy of movement and their changes with age. *Acta Psychologica,* 30, 3–15. (108)

Whitaker, L. A., and Trumbo, D. (1976). Scaling estimates of amplitude for movements without visual guidance. *Journal of Motor Behavior,* 8, 75–82. (134, 135)

White, N., and Kinsbourne, M. (1980). Does speech output control lateralize over time? Evidence from verbal and spatial time-sharing tasks. *Brain and Language,* 10, 215–223. (78, 84)

Whiting, H. T. A., and Cockerill, I. M. (1974). Eyes on hand — eyes on target? *Journal of Motor Behavior,* 6, 27–32. (139)

Wickelgren, W. A. (1977). Speed–accuracy tradeoff and information processing dynamics. *Acta Psychologica,* 41, 67–85. (9)

Wickens, C. D. (1979). Measures of workload, stress and secondary tasks. In N. Moray (Ed.), *Mental Workload: Its Theory and Measurement*, New York: Plenum. (71, 72)

Wiener, N. (1948). *Cybernetics*. New York: Wiley. (28, 38, 101)

Wilke, J. T., and Vaughn, S. C. (1976). Temporal distribution of attention during a throwing motion. *Journal of Motor Behavior*, **8**, 83–88. (258)

Wilkinson, R. T. (1959). Rest pauses in a task affected by loss of sleep. *Ergonomics*, **2**, 373–380. (165)

Williams, H. L., Beaver, W. S., Spence, M. T. and Rundell, O. H. (1969). Digital and kinesthetic memory with interpolated information processing. *Journal of Experimental Psychology*, **80**, 530–536. (124, 129, 148)

Williams, I. D. (1971). The effects of practice and prior learning on motor memory. *Journal of Motor Behavior*, **3**, 205–212. (124)

Williams, I. D. (1978). Evidence for recognition and recall schemata. *Journal of Motor Behavior*, **10**, 45–52. (142)

Williams, I. D. and Rodney, M. (1978). Intrinsic feedback, interpolation, and the closed-loop theory. *Journal of Motor Behavior*, **10**, 25–36. (142, 211, 223)

Wilson, A. B. (1965). Control of external power in upper-extremity rehabilitation. *Bulletin of Prosthetics Research*, **10–3**, 57–59. (235)

Wilson, D. M. (1961). The central nervous control of flight in a locust. *Journal of Experimental Biology*, **38**, 471–490. (43)

Winneke, G. (1974). Behavioral effects of methylene chloride and carbon monoxide as assessed by sensory and psychomotor performance. In C. Xintaras, B. J. Johnson and I. de Groot (Eds.), *Behavioral Toxicology*. Washington, DC: DHEW. (263)

Woodrow, J. (1933). Weight discrimination with a varying standard. *American Journal of Psychology*, **45**, 381–416. (124)

Woodworth, R. S. (1899). The accuracy of voluntary movement. *Psychological Review*, **3**, *Monograph Supplement No. 2*. (1, 92, 119)

Wright, J. M. von, (1957). A note on the role of guidance in learning. *British Journal of Psychology*, **48**, 133–137. (211)

Wright, J. M. von, Anderson, K., and Stenman, V. (1975). Generalization of conditioned GSRs in dichotic listening. In P. M. A. Rabbitt and S. Dornic (Eds.), *Attention and Performance V*. London: Academic Press. (70)

Wrisberg, C. A. (1975). The serial-position effect in short-term motor retention. *Journal of Motor Behavior*, **7**, 289–295. (151)

Yellott, J. T. (1967). Correction for fast guessing in choice reaction time. *Psychonomic Science*, **8**, 321–322. (156)

Young, L. R. (1969). On adaptive manual control. *Ergonomics*, **12**, 635–675. (31, 34)

Zahorik, D. M. (1972). Subject strategies and interference in a discrete motor task. *Psychonomic Science*, **28**, 349–351. (132)

Zaichkowsky, L. D. (1974). The development of perceptual motor sequencing ability. *Journal of Motor Behavior*, **6**, 255–261. (151)

Zelaznik, H. N., Shapiro, D. C., and Newell, K. M. (1978). On the structure of motor recognition memory. *Journal of Motor Behavior*, **10**, 313–323. (143)

Zelaznik, H. N., and Spring, J. (1976). Feedback in response recognition and production. *Journal of Motor Behavior*, **8**, 302–312. (143)

Ziegler, P. N., Reilly, R., and Chernikoff, R. (1966). The use of displacement, flash and depth-of-flash coded displays. US Navy Research Laboratory, *Report No. 6412*. (189)

Subject Index

acceleration control, 181
accuracy, 91–117, 153, 155–157
action plans, 206
age effects, 77–79, 86, 154, 164–168, 265
aids, sensorimotor, 245–250
alternative displays, 188
amplitude, tracking, 179
anticipation, 7–11, 170, 253
arousal, 72, 263
assimilation, 125–128
attention, 12, 49, 61, 65, 68, 72, 75, 78, 80, 119, 172, 264
augmented displays, 182
augmented feedback, 210
autokinesis, 111, 113

ballistic movements, 28, 44, 93, 143, 171
bandwidth, 20
bats, 28
blindness, 244–255
Braille, 244–247

channel capacity, 11, 65–89, 198, 200, 236, 253
closed-loop control, 2, 16, 20–27, 41, 45, 52, 54, 58, 64, 69, 141, 191, 231, 257
compatibility, 85, 153, 187, 232, 234
compensatory tracking, 19, 180, 183, 189, 200
conditions of practice, 216–220, 260
consciousness, 87
control characteristics, 181–188, 200
control theory, 15, 18, 21, 101–109, 178, 199
controlled element, 22, 35
coordinative structures, 48
corollary discharge, 49

cybernetics, 101

deafferentation, 42–44, 56
deafness, 238–243
delayed feedback, 29
demonstration, 205–209
discrete movements, 3, 6, 91–117, 119–147
display/control ratio, 184–187
displays, 180–200
distribution of practice, 216
disturbance, 16, 26, 59, 61
drugs, 86, 154, 165, 261

efference copy, 49, 137
effort, 66, 71–73, 251
encoding strategies, 119, 135
end-location, movement, 55, 131–133, 137, 139
equilibrium point, 56
error measures, 37, 91, 101, 112, 120–122, 190
error signal, 16, 25, 27
expected sensory consequences, 49, 51, 53, 59
external feedback, 163
eye movements, 45

facial vision, 251
factor analysis, 3
fatigue, 164, 264
feedback, 6, 15–39, 41–46, 48–51, 54, 59, 61, 63, 101, 122, 139, 141, 143, 163, 210–216, 232–234, 237, 257
feedforward, 58
forcing function, 16, 38
frequency, tracking, 179
functional cerebral space, 79–86, 259

gain, 25, 35, 185
generalization, 220–225
goals, 17, 27, 207
guidance techniques, 6, 139, 211

handicaps, 227–256, 261
hierarchical organization, motor programs, 58
homeostasis, 28

index of preprogramming, 45
individual differences, 5, 164–168, 220
information processing, 11, 119, 123, 147, 171, 203–216, 228, 230, 253, 255
information theory, 2, 8, 95–101, 110, 231
instability, closed-loop systems, 27
interference, 73–77, 82–86
internal models, 32–37
intersensory judgements, 113
intersensory localization, 111–113

judgements, psychophysical, 113–116, 124, 128

Kalman filters, 35
kinaesthesis, 4, 6, 30, 41–45, 48–51, 55, 112, 139, 233
kinematics, 208, 213
knowledge of results, 1, 6, 17, 25, 204, 208, 212–216

Laplace transforms, 21–26
learning, 32–37, 51, 76, 203–226
learning theory, 220
limited-capacity channel, 2, 11, 65–89, 253
long-term memory, 12, 173, 259, 266

measurement, performance, 37, 91, 101, 112, 120–122, 141, 155–161, 190
memory, 11, 55–58, 119–151, 170, 173, 259, 266
mental practice, 63, 218
mobility, 247–255
models, 32–37, 51, 61, 66–76, 81–86, 140, 154–168, 191–194, 228, 232
motor memory, 12, 55–58, 62, 119–151, 259
motor programs, 6, 41–64, 141, 224, 235, 258
movement cues, 55–58, 131–133, 137
movement notation, 209

movement reproduction, 120–130
movement strategies, 114–116
multiprocessing, 11, 67, 70–72, 199

negative feedback, 15–39
noise, 16, 165, 263
notation, movement, 209

open–closed skills, 3, 50, 62, 205, 213
open-loop control, 3, 17, 24, 30, 32, 41–48, 52, 54, 58, 69, 142, 258
optimal control theory, 35
order of control, 181
outflow model, 49, 137, 232

passive movements, 50, 115, 134, 144, 211
perceptual skills, 3
peripheral vision, 189
phase shifts, 27, 29
power spectrum, 28
practice effects, 93, 153, 159–164, 171, 210–212, 216–220
prediction, 19, 23, 26, 32–37, 183
preparatory set, 9, 59, 158, 168
preplanning, 136
preprogramming, 45–47, 49, 80
preselected movements, 62, 131, 136–138
preview, 6, 10, 162, 183, 252
prey–predator behaviour, 28
processing models, 65–89
progression–regression hypothesis, 208
psychophysics, 113–116, 124, 128
pursuit tracking, 5, 180, 189

reaction times, 2, 7–11, 18, 44, 47, 50, 98, 102, 106, 109, 153–175, 252
recall memory, 130–142, 144–147
recognition memory, 130, 142–147
reference of correctness, 53
reflexes, 47, 50, 59, 79
response selection, 50
response specifications, 54, 58

sampling behaviour, 28
schema theory, 52–55, 57, 62–64, 142, 211, 222–225, 258
secondary task technique, 12, 65–89, 252, 258
sensory compensation, 238
sequential reactions, 153–175
servo-mechanisms, 2, 7, 16, 27, 191, 258

short-term memory, 12, 147, 173, 240, 252, 259, 265
simulators, 196
sine-wave courses, 179
single-channel theory, 11, 65–89, 259
speech perception, 239–243
speechreading, 241
speed/accuracy, 9, 10, 74, 92–117, 156, 161–168
spinal tuning, 49, 56, 59–61
stimulus–response theory, 16, 32, 220
strategies, 9, 32–37, 114–116, 138–140, 219, 257
stress, 154, 164–168, 263

task classification, 3–5
task difficulty, 81, 195
template, for feedback, 51, 53, 62
time-sharing, 74, 76, 170–172

timing, 5, 10, 46, 57, 153, 164, 168–172, 224
tracking, 2, 6, 19–27, 31, 37, 85, 177–201, 260
trade-offs, speed–accuracy, 9, 74, 156, 161–168
transfer of training, 73–77, 195–198, 220–225, 260
transfer function, 24–27, 35, 192
transmission delay, 27, 32

ventriloquism, 116
verbal memory, 147–151, 173
videotape feedback, 213
vigilance, 4, 199, 267
vocoder, 242

whole–part practice, 218
working memory, 150
workload, 66, 70, 227